Towards a Renewed Biblical Understanding of Health & Healing

Biblical Hermeneutics Rediscovered

The Series as the name suggests will focus on Biblical Hermeneutics, i.e., literary works concerned with methods of interpreting the Old and New Testaments of Bible via different stream of topics like Literature & Poetry, Indigenous Philosophizing, Ethical response towards Ecology, Health & Healing, Science & Technology, Feminist Theology, Sociological approach towards Human Rights, Law & Politics, Arts, History of Ideas, Ancient Civilizations, Cultural Contiguity, Religious Cosmologies & Mysticism, Appraisal of various Theologians, World Peace & Harmony, Global Capitalism, Network Marketing, Cybertheology, Population & Demographics, Epigraphic Studies, Contextualized Education, and many others. We welcome a Mss. on any topic/s mentioned, whether they are original works, scholarly monographs, collections of conference papers, revised dissertations, or translations of historical documents. Through the Series we, the Publishers, are striving to put forward published works that may help Institutions, Academic Bodies, Researchers, Scholars and the World at large in furthering their respective knowledge and understanding on the concerned subject. We welcome your comments on our efforts and further suggestions on how we can enshrine new ray of analysing & explaining the written Texts through our upcoming books.

Biblical Hermeneutics Rediscovered - 8

Towards a Renewed Biblical Understanding of Health & Healing

A Prophetic Response

Atula Ao

CWI
Christian World Imprints™

First Published in 2017 by

Christian World Imprints™
Christian Publishing & Books from India
H-12 Bali Nagar, **New Delhi-110015**
info@christianworldimprints.com
www.ChristianWorldImprints.com
Phone: +91 11 25465925

ISBN: 978-93-5148-227-7 (HB)　　ISBN: 978-93-5148-228-4 (PB)

Cataloging in Publication Data--DK
Courtesy: D.K. Agencies (P) Ltd. <docinfo@dkagencies.com>

Ao, Atula, 1972- **author**.
Towards a renewed biblical understanding of health & healing : a prophetic response / Atula Ao.
pages cm. -- (Biblical hermeneutics rediscovered ; 8)
ISBN 9789351482277 (HB)
ISBN 9789351482284 (PB)

1. Health--Religious aspects--Christianity. 2. Healing--Religious aspects--Christianity. 3. Bible. Old Testament--Criticism, interpretation, etc. I. Title. II. Series: Biblical hermeneutics rediscovered ; 8.

BT732.A5 2017　　DDC 261.8321　23

Printed in India

Dedicated to my loving brothers:

Mr. Imtimar Tzudir

&

Mr. Lanuyanger Tzudir

Contents

Foreword

When we analyse the health care system being practiced in the contemporary India and in the world, there are few consequential factors that have led into a crisis of health care today. They are namely:

1. The predominance of the medical model with its reductionism and depersonization.
2. The rise of corporate based medical care system that has been on economies and not on the care of the patient as a physio-psychic and spiritual being who is one of God's creation.
3. There is a lack of understanding of the holistic health care system. The medical model of health care system looks at human being merely on the biological and mental parameters. An individual who is a spiritual being along with his/her emotional quality is neglected completely.

In such a context, Dr. Atula Ao has made an erudite attempt to draw insights for a clear understanding of health and health care from the perspective of God, especially how the prophets as God's chosen instruments have propounded to eradicate the wrong understanding of health and healing. This book is a revised edition of Dr. Atula's doctoral dissertation which she had submitted to the Senate of Serampore College (University) under my supervision. Dr. Ao has pursued her research on the holistic perspective of health with special reference to the prophets of the Isaianic, Hoseanic and Jeremianic traditions which were permeated during the eighth to sixth centuries of B.C.E. in Israel. In this monograph, Dr. Ao has identified four significant terms such as *Rapha*, *Arukah*, *Shalom*, and *Marpe* that portray the restoration of the societal health that was lost due to the socio-political sickness of the respective societies. She has elucidated how the ancient West Asians had understood health in their respective nations. The seven chapters of the book have important resources for highlighting the metaphorical and tangible portrayals pertaining to health and healing. I am certain that this monograph is a well-researched presentation that will clarify several problems that afflict the human communities due to the wrong approaches in our health care mechanism.

I am sure that this work would immensely contribute towards the Old Testament studies.

Prof. Dr. Daniel Jones Muthunayagom
Chairperson, Department of Biblical Studies
The United Theological College
Bengaluru

Acknowledgment

The original work of this book: "Towards a Renewed Understanding of Health in Light of the Concept of Rapha, Arukah, Shalom and Marpe with Reference to Select Passages in the Prophetic Oracles of Hosea, Isaiah, and Jeremiah," was submitted to the Senate of Serampore (University), India as a Doctor of Theology (Old Testament) dissertation. The university has kindly granted the necessary permission to publish the same in a book form (email dated September 23, 2016).

I would like to thank all who contributed in some way to the work described in this research. My deepest gratitude:

To my guide and mentor, Rev. Dr. **Daniel Jones Muthunayagom**, for his excellent guidance, caring, patience, and providing me with an outstanding atmosphere for doing research, by giving me intellectual freedom in my work, supporting my attendance at various conferences, engaging me in new ideas, and demanding a high quality of work in all my endeavours.

To my external examiners, Rev. Dr. **Eliya Mohol** and Dr. **Monica Jyotsna Melanchthon** for having the patience to go through my research and for their valuable comments and suggestions.

No research is possible without the support of Libraries, the centres of learning resources. I take this opportunity to express my gratitude to all the library staffs of the United Theological College, Bangalore, for their services. Every result described in this research was accomplished with the help of libraries and collaborators, therefore, gratitude to the following libraries: **Lutheran Theological Seminary, Philadelphia**; **Princeton Theological Seminary, New Jersey**; **SAIACS, Bangalore**; **St. Peter's Pontifical Seminary, Bangalore** and **Dharmaram Vidya Kshetram, Bangalore** and all other mediums who helped me in my research by providing the resources needed for this research.

I also thank **Kumlong Baptist Church** and **Mangmetong Baptist Church**, Mokokchung, Nagaland for standing with me throughout my theological journey.

Words cannot express how grateful I am to my family for all of the sacrifices that they have made to make this dream realized.

To my **Mom** and **Dad** for all their sacrifices and for believing in me. All that I am is because of them.

To my sister Ms. **Arenla Tzudir** who has been my greatest source of encouragement and strength.

My elder brother Mr. **Imtimar Tzudir,** who is currently battling with cancer, has been the best brother that I would ever want by being a careful listener and an encourager.

To my youngest brother Mr. **Lanuyanger Tzudir** who has the biggest of heart for selflessly coming forward and donating one of his kidnies for me. The reason I am alive today is all because of his unselfish love and I owe it to him and to God. I dedicate this Book to my brothers, **Imtimar Tzudir** and **Lanuyanger Tzudir**. May you experience the grace of God and may this grace take you a step closer to God every day.

To my brothers-in-law: Mr. **Along Longchar**, Rev. **Lephen** and Mr. **Jayan** for their unwavering love and encouragement to me.

To my sisters-in-law: Ms. **Bendangla Ozukum**, Ms. **Sentiyala Jamir**, Ms. **Lydia**, Ms. **Sheba** for being there always for me, for their support and care.

To my **father-in-law** and **mother-in-law** who stood by me through my ups and downs by being a prayer warrior.

To all my nieces and nephews, **Moamongla**, **Anungba**, **Watienla**, **Yimtenrenla**, **Sentimongla**, **Imkongsenla**, **Rusemdong**, **Sambhav** and **Saakshiyah** for all the joy and happiness they brought into my life. I deeply love them.

To my husband, Dr. **Samuel George**, whose unconditional love, patience, and continual support of my academic endeavours over the past several years enabled me to complete this work. A true and great supporter and has unconditionally loved me during my good and bad times and instrumental in instilling confidence. Life was not an easy ride for me last year both academically, physically and personally but I truly thank him for sticking by my side, even in my toughest times.

I also thank all my friends (too many to list here but you know who you are) for providing support and friendship that I needed. It would be unfair for me if I don't mention you all my friends, well-wishers and prayer partners who untiringly stood with me and for me when I went through my Kidney failure last year, i.e., 2016. Thank you friends for your love and support that came to me through your constant reminder that you are there for me, through your monetary help that gave me back my life and through your prayers that reached the ears of God to have healed me and gave me this new life. This book is also a part of my experience that, health and healing does not mean only physical but it is wholistic where we need psychological, mental, physical, and spiritual healing. Your presence and encouragement to me has evolved in me a new being which I dedicate it to God my healer.

It would be incomplete if I do not thank Rev. Dr. **Wati Longchar** for being my teacher and an encourager, for initiating crowd funding among the theological community to help me in my kidney transplant process.

Through all of you, I have learned a lot about life that strengthened my commitment and determination to God and to live life to the fullest.

Finally, I thank **God** from whom all healing comes, for sailing me through all the difficulties. I have experienced your guidance, your grace and your healing day by day. I wholeheartedly keep on trusting you for my future. Thank you, Lord.

Abbreviations

BDB	Brown- Driver- Briggs Hebrew and English Lexicon
BHS	Biblica-Hebraica-Stuttgartensia
BTESSC	Board of Theological Education of the Senate of Serampore College
CCA	Christian Conference of Asia
CSI	Church of South India
CTQ	Concordia Theological Quarterly
G	The Greek Version of LXX
HAT	Handbuch zum Alten Testament
Heb.	Hebrew
ISPCK	Indian Society for the Promotion of Christian Knowledge
IQH	Hadayot
JL	Jeremiah Lament
JSOT	Journal for the Study of the Old Testament
LXX	Septuagint
MT	Masoretic Text
MSS	Manuscripts
NAB	New American Bible
NEB	New English Bible
NIV	New International Version
NRSV	New Revised Standard Version
OT	Old Testament
Q	The Qere
RSV	Revised Standard Version
SATHRI	The South Asia Theological Research Institute
SCM	Student Christian Movement

Targ.	Targum
TDNT	Theological Dictionary of the New Testament
TDOT	Theological Dictionary of the Old Testament
WBC	Word Biblical Commentary
WCC	World Council of Churches
WHO	World Health Organization
ZAW	Zeitschrift für die alttestamentliche wissenschaft

Introduction

1. Statement of the Problem

This work examines the different interpretations of the understanding of illness, health and healing by the prophets in order to address the issue/issues related to this concept in our contemporary context.

In today's context of war and globalization, health is often [misunderstood] as individualistic. Community well-being or corporate wellness is not an option now a days. Biblical understanding of health more specifically the prophetic oracles of the Old Testament gives prominence to health as a corporate aspect.

Even though infrequently used, health is one of the vital indications reflecting the quality of life in the Old Testament. The concept of healing and health in the Bible especially, that of in the Old Testament has not adequately been dealt with by the scholarly world, especially the issues pertaining to our society. The problem lies in the faulty understanding of health and healing and skewed interpretation of the scripture.[1]

---

[1] The formative period of Christianity and Judaism until 5th century C. E. is crucially significant in its role of interpretation of scripture. The writings of scriptures, the process of canonization and formulation of fundamental doctrinal creeds of the church were completed during the period. The dominant philosophical movement that antagonistically assaulted and influenced Christianity to a vast extent in these centuries of Palestine was Hellenism - a teaching, which stressed that matter, is temporal, transitory and therefore inherently evil, whereas the soul is eternal and intrinsically good. The body - flesh/carnal - being matter was considered essentially evil. Hence the dictum of the Epicureans, Stoics, Hedonists (Acts 17: 18), was "Eat drink and be merry for tomorrow you die" (I Cor. 15:32). To these erroneous teachings of immoral living, Paul says, "Your body is the temple of the living God" (I Cor. 6:19; II Cor. 6:16). Christianity sees the body as quintessentially good. God terms his material/physical creation as "good." God, who is the Word/*Logos* in his wisdom, chooses to incarnate himself into a body (John 1:1, 14).

Asceticism and monasticism emerged in history as an offshoot of the Aristotelian influence and preference of the soul to the body. The body is seen as the prison of the soul that needs to be weakened and broken. In the same ideological milieu, the early church Christians fearlessly and heroically welcomed physical torture and martyrdom in the coliseums and amphitheatres of the Romans with joy, possibly because they derived their strength from the belief that the body is evil and death is the only way to escape imprisonment. In due course of time, the Catholic Church

Each culture has its own attitude toward illness and health.[2] In the Old Testament, it was specifically believed that if one is sick and suffering was because of sin.[3] The sickness metaphor to designate ill health from physical aspect was always considered, according to the classical Israelite idea, as a direct result of sin. Very often the disruption of health is interpreted as a consequence of disobedience, idolatry, sin. Such ill-founded and prejudicial attitude toward illness led to the ambiguous definition of health.[4] The Bible insists often on a connection between

---

came to recognize and enshrined the act of inflicting physical punishment and injury on the body as a legitimate spiritual act of disciplining the body for liberation. Such influences have created a dichotomy between what is good and bad, that the soul is good and the body is bad. This artificial dichotomy has dealt a severe blow to a clear understanding and interpretation of the scripture in the given context. Over the centuries, the Bible is interpreted from this fault line creating a dichotomy between the body and the soul. Such understanding has also blurred the interpreters to define their understanding of health without seeing human in his/her integrity and in the wholeness of ones being and the nexus of his/her total relationship. Hence, the concept of health was also interpreted in terms of its individualistic and physical aspect. According to K. M. George, "In biblical theology, the gift of God's image is often interpreted on an individualistic basis." K. M. George, "The Threat of HIV/AIDS: Some Theological Considerations," in *HIV/AIDS: A Challenge to Theological Education*, ed. Samson Prabhakar and George Mathew Nalunnakkal (Bangalore: BTESSC/SATHRI, 2004), 9. (B. A. Supit, "Health, Healing and Wholeness," in *Towards Health-Care for All: CCA's Concern in Community Health, 1973-1983* (Singapore: Christian Conference of Asia, 1986), 85.

[2] In the *Mishnah*, and also later in the *Talmud*, we find the conviction that sin is the root cause of illness. Rabbi Jonathan, quotes "plague comes for seven sins, for bloodshed, perjury, unchastity, pride, embezzlement, pitilessness, and slander (Babylonian Talmud, 'Arakin' 16a).

[3] For e.g., Job's three friends who came to comfort him in his affliction wind up preaching to him (Job 11:1-6). Health and wealth are the rewards of God, and sickness and misfortune his punishments. From the beginning the law went into details about the kind of disease Yahweh would send upon those who did not live by His covenant. Morton T. Kelsey, *Healing and Christianity in Ancient Thought and Modern Times* (London: Harper & Row Publishers, 1973), 35.

[4] God, being good and just, would not allow a righteous person to suffer. Thus to be healthy and wealthy was a mark of favour from God, and conversely, poverty and illness were the just deserts of sin. This attitude lingered for a long time in the sin culture of the Biblical world. In some quarters, the Old Testament attitude that illness is a result of sin appears in a subtle way. Consequently, sin and healing was understood to be interconnected in the Old Testament. A common theme in the scriptures, especially in the Old Testament, and mostly in pre-exilic texts was to interpret the disruption of health as a consequence of disobedience, idolatry and sin, therefore, connecting between sin and sickness. Such connections were borne out by the history. Beginning in Genesis, Pharaoh's whole household was struck down by severe plagues because Sarah was taken into his place (Gen. 12:17). When Abimelech unwittingly planned to take Sarah, Yahweh made all the women of his household barren. Because Onan wasted his ability to procreate when it was needed, Yahweh caused him to die as *Er* because of his offence. Miriam was stricken with leprosy for her slander of Moses (Num. 12:10). There is certainly no question how sickness was looked upon in the major strand of the Old Testament; it was sent by Yahweh to punish humans for breaking the ritualistic or moral law. One of the unpleasant consequences of sin is physical illness. This is used as a warning for those who might contemplate flouting God's will. It also becomes a way of interpreting illnesses, which afflict individuals and groups. Therefore, a common biblical understanding of sickness is that it is the result of sin.

sickness and sin in particular instances but no doubt rightly. In the biblical record, illness might be the direct result of sinful action—that is, as divine punishment—but that need not be the case. "Illness has special significance for the OT in that it is either experienced as distress that leads to lament... or is understood as the effect of God's curse."[5] The either/or is essential. Not everyone in the Bible sees a direct connection between their illness and their sin.[6] But sometimes sickness and diseases are the ways to their liberative and wholistic aspect of their life. Gerhard von Rad concurs: "[T]here was a very close connection between sin and physical disease. But he indicates how all the disturbances in our natural life have their roots in a disturbed relationship to God."[7]

There is a lack of consensus among the scholars concerning the precise definition of health. The following lines will be dealt with the different facets of understanding the term health.

2. Elaboration of the Problem

2.1. Health: Debate

The diverse and manifold debates on the concept of health led to many conclusions about the way we perceive illness, health and healing.

According to Walter Brueggemann, "Health refers to stability enough to share in the costs and joys, the blessings and burdens of the community. To be healthy means to be functional fully in terms of the norms, values, and expectations of the community."[8] Brueggemann continues to stress that,

> Healing refers to restoration and rehabilitation of persons to their full power and vitality in the life of the community. Sickness then does not refer primarily to physical pain as much as it refers to the inability to be fully, honourably and seriously engaged in the community in all its decisions and celebrations.[9]

Alastair Campbell is of the opinion that,

> . . . Health is best understood as an aspect of freedom.... I view the essence of good health care as liberation, a setting free; and I see the fundamental injustices in the delivery of health care in modern society

[5] Fritz Stolz, "*Hala* (Chalah)," in *Theological Lexicon of the Old Testament*, ed. Ernst Jenni et al. (Massachusetts: Hendrickson, 1997), 427.

[6] Mueller, *Sickness and Healing*, trans. Douglas W. Stott (Nashville: Abingdon Press, 1981), 148.

[7] Von Rad, *Old Testament Theology*, trans. D. M. G. Stalker, vol. 1 (London: SCM Press Ltd., 1975), 275.

[8] Walter Brueggemann, *Living Toward a Vision: Biblical Reflections on Shalom* (New York: United Church, 1978), 181.

[9] Ibid.

> as being forms of oppression, the taking away of the freedom of weaker members of society by those who hold power.[10]

Christopher Boorse defines health as,

> A functional normality that can be biologically assessed according to what is typical for a particular species. All cells, organs, and organ systems function within an organism with specific purposes typical of those functions in other members of the species, and diseases are those biological phenomena that interfere with those functions.[11]

Health is also understood as multi-dimensional and interrelated experience of well-being. It includes their experience of physical well-being as reflected in actual wellness of body and/or in the caring attention by self/others to bodily health.[12] Health is relational and material well-being, that includes people's positive connectedness with their past, with other people, and with the environment, a psychological well-being, or wellness of the emotional self as reflected in persons' self-affirmation and capacity to deal with the changes and losses comprising life circumstances, a spiritual well-being, or persons' affirmation of life through connectedness with an affirming, life-giving, meaning-generating force beyond the self.[13]

The World Health Organization defines health, as "a state of complete physical, mental and social well-being and not merely the absence of disease or infirmity."[14]

A similar definition was put forward by the Office of Research and Analysis of the former American Lutheran Church, following two years of study by its Task Force on Ethical Issues in Human Medicine,

> Health is the total well-being of persons; it is more than the absence of disease. Health encompasses the integration of each person's spiritual, psychological, and physical dimensions. It includes the harmonious

---

[10] Alastair Campbell, *Health as Liberation: Medicine, Theology and the Quest for Justice* (Cleveland: Pilgrim Press, 1995), 44.

[11] Christopher Boorse, "The Distinction between Disease and Illness," in *Concepts of Health and Disease: Interdisciplinary Perspectives*, ed. Arthur L. Caplan and H. Tristram (Massachusetts: Addison Wesley, 1981), 551.

[12] William Rakowski, "Health Beliefs," in *The Encyclopedia of Aging*, ed. George L. Maddox (New York: Springer Publishing Company, 1987), 306.

[13] Mary Grace Kovar, "Health Assessment," in *The Encyclopedia of Aging*, ed. George L. Maddox (New York: Springer Publishing Company, 1983), 302.

[14] *World Health Organization: Basic Documents* (Geneva: WHO, 1948), 1.

interrelationship of environmental, nutritional, social, cultural, and all other aspects of life.[15]

Such definitions recognize the breadth of the concept of health by defining it as total well-being.[16] The concept of health could be construed as primarily physical in nature although this is pursued in the broader context of human well-being. The biblical texts value good health because it is the essence of life itself.

For the writers of the Jewish scriptures especially (for whom concepts of "life after death" were rather vague), "life here and now" was of paramount importance. For example, the Jewish scriptures show how life started, while Ecclesiastes 9:4 emphasises the value of- life and survival. Throughout, the premium is on good health, survival and the continuation of the species. In brief then, the Old Testament's understanding of good health comprises the physical and mental ability to fulfil the normal social and physical roles as determined by society. This physical and functional comprehension is further supported by the metaphors used to portray health and illness. For example, the Hebrew word for "bones" ("*esteem*", "*gerem*") signifies the body, life strength and substance. As the solid framework of the body, the bones are the scat of health and strength, whilst "breaking", "rottenness" and "dryness" of bones are frequent metaphors to indicate sickness. Anderson points out; in the Old Testament, the term flesh was used to highlight human weakness.[17] Thus, health is associated with the purely physical facets of humankind and indeed a number of texts (e.g. Ps. 31:10 and 38:3) appear to link health/ill health with physical strength. Therefore, the physical agenda for health put forward in the Old Testament is continued in the present context where physical well-being of eating the right food and doing the right exercise is all it means to health. No doubt such understanding is viable as long as one is concerned with the figurative aspect, but will such perception address to today's society that is crippled with fear and terror, injustice and oppression and which is in need of solidarity and relationship with one another? In such a context, what does the Bible say about the concept of health?

According to Wilkinson, given the importance of health in our post-modern world, it seems strange that at first sight the Bible appears to say little about it. This apparent lack of interest in health, however, is not the case; the concern

---

[15] *Office of Research and Analysis of the American Lutheran Church, 'Health, Life, and Death: A Christian Perspective'*, (Minneapolis: The American Lutheran Church, 1977). Quoted in Mark J. Hanson, "Defining Health and Health Related Concepts: Conceptual and Theological Considerations," *Word & World* 21, no. 1 (Winter 2001): 26.

[16] A holistic approach to health involves the following characteristics: it focuses on self-healing/ ascertain the root causes of the problem/treats the mind and body as tightly interconnected systems with each affecting the other. Cf. "The Meaning of 'holistic'", http://encyclopedia.thefreedictionary.com/holistic (accessed 01 October, 2008).

[17] A. Anderson, *Psalms (1-150)*, The New Bible Commentary, vol. 1-2 (London: Marshall, Morgan & Scott, 1972), 303.

for human well-being lies at the very heart of the Jewish scriptures.[18] No doubt, the *Torah* has been a source of drawing strength in understanding health laws in the Bible. There are some interesting discoveries concerning physical health in the Mosaic Law, especially in the books of Exodus, Leviticus, and Deuteronomy. These ancient laws are interesting because they are built upon a sound common-sense attitude toward the integrity of the person. Therefore, the laws deal with the religious life of the people, their worship, their priesthood, and their tabernacle, as well as with their personal hygiene, their behaviour in the community, and their inter-personal relationship. We find instructions concerning the Sabbath not so much designated as a time of worship, but originally as a time of rest and recreation, a time for persons to be restored physically and emotionally, because on this restoration depends a person's well-being. The Sabbath has a therapeutic as well as a prophylactic purpose and effect. The same is true for other laws. Prophylactic measures such as the rules of sanitation, isolation of disease, and personal hygiene, occupy an enormous amount of space in the Mosaic Law. They are, according to R. K. Harrison, "the special contribution of the Hebrews to medical theory, and the principles enshrined in the Pentateuch are in harmony with the basic concepts of contemporary preventive medicine."[19] No doubt, the *Torah* provides fundamental principles to guide our personal choices in ways that promote health and prevent disease. However, all these attempts to explain the Old Testament concept of health are inadequate.

The above definitions indicate the difficulties in understanding health and its related concepts. Nevertheless, the terms health and healthy may be used variously. We may speak of a healthy body, but also healthy minds and spirits in the same way we talk about physical, mental, spiritual, and social health. One might also question relationships among forms of health. Whether physical health can be achieved without spiritual health or vice versa, or achieving healthy life without relationships being healthy?

Despite all the progress achieved, there is a quest for the well-being of everyone.[20] In such a context our understanding of health and healthy life has come to mean comfort and individualistic. Wholistic well-being is not an option now a day. This perspective of health is often neglected or sidelined in our approach to health.

[18] John Wilkinson, *Health and Healing: Studies in New Testament Principles and Practice* (Edinburgh: The Handel Press, 1980), 1.

[19] R. K. Harrison, "Healing," in *The Interpreter's Dictionary of the Bible*, ed. George R. Buttrick and Keith R. Crim (Nashville: Abingdon Press, 1976), 543-546.

[20] Thoraya Ahmed Obaid, "Religion and Reproductive Health and Rights," *Journal of the American Academy of Religion* 73, no. 4 (December 2005): 1157.

In a context like today, the power and possibility of health is missed because the focus is seemingly only on individuals' physical well-being. [21]

There is also the tendency to sideline the prophetic literature as not being concerned with health. Such tendencies with regard to health as referring only to individual's physical well-being have led many scholars (Leon R. Kass, Leroy Walters, William Rakowski), to view the concept of *Rapha, Arukah, Shalom* and *Marpe* in the prophetic texts as exclusive *sans* wholistic approach. Therefore, the present study seeks to throw new light in the difficulties of interpreting the concept of illness, health and healing.

3. Previous Research

It is striking to note, however, that while some of these themes have been treated individually and others touched on in a piecemeal fashion, to date no full-scale synthesis of the relevant material has been undertaken.

The important Studies of U. B. Mueller focused primarily on sickness and healing.[22] Articles in Biblical Dictionaries and Encyclopaedias have generally focused on technical descriptions of diseases and/or *materia medica* attested in the Scriptures. While entries in Biblical Hebrew Wordbooks and Theological Dictionaries have for the most part treated the Old Testament, material only as it indicates with the specific roots in question. Among the Old Testament theologies, G. Von Rad's treatment of Yahweh as *rope*, barely covering two pages, actually stands out for its completeness.[23] Major Old Testament anthropologists like L. Kohler deals briefly and almost exclusively with the human dimension of sickness and healing.[24] Hans Walter Wolff's, seminal work treats the full scope of humanity and personhood in the Old Testament canon. Several sections treat issues of health, illness, and healing.[25] The influential works on Israelite religion of such scholars as W. F. Albright, G. Fohrer, H. Ringgren and W. H. Schmidt give surprisingly little attention to the subject at hand.[26] The most recent writing

[21] There is evidence of a functional view of health in the Bible. Avalos, for example, has found that in the Ancient West Asia "illness" was having visible symptoms which rendered individuals as being physically and/or mentally unable to fulfil the normal social and/or physical role ascribed to them by society. H. Avalos, *Illness and Health Care in Ancient Near East* (Atlanta: Scholars, 1995), 246-250. Health is also understood as multi-dimensional and interrelated experience of well-being. It includes their experience of *physical well-being* as reflected in actual wellness of body and/or in the caring attention by self/others to bodily health

[22] U. B. Mueller, *Sickness and Healing*, trans. D. W. Stott (Nashville: Abingdon Press, 1981), 9-96.

[23] G. von Rad, *Old Testament Theology*, trans. D. M. G. Stalker, vol. 1 (New York: Harper & Row, 1962), 274-276.

[24] Ludwig Kohler, *The Hebrew Man* (London: 1956); Hans Walter Wolff, *Anthropology of the Old Testament* (Philadelphia: Fortress, 1974).

[25] Wolff, *Anthropology of the Old Testament.*

[26] Cf. W. F. Albright, *Archaeology and the Religion of Israel*, 5th ed. (Baltimore: John's Hopkins University Press, 1968); W. F. Albright, *Yahweh and the Gods of Canaan* (London: Althone Press,

on this topic is by Seong-Hyuk Hong. His work on "The Metaphor of Illness and Healing in Hosea and its Socio-Economic Context of the Eight Century Israel and Judah"[27] is commendable. Yet there is a need to probe deeper the issue in relation to holistic health. Also other scholars deal with the understanding of health in a different light.

Scholars like Walter Brueggemann,[28] and Paul Hanson,[29] treat health as community of solidarity. Brueggemann, in Isaiah *40-66*, highlights the themes of neighbourliness and community as integral to understanding health and asserts that the well-being of the community is dependent on a community of neighbours who care for each other. This theme is quite commendable and needs further investigation especially in the context of the prophets. Freeman in an anthology of Jewish writings on health, illness, and recovery reflects on the experience of being ill from a Jewish spiritual perspective. The selections are Jewish because they come from Jewish religious texts, or they take a Jewish religious perspective on the subject, or they describe an experience that is viewed through the context of Jewish culture.[30]

E. John Hamlin,[31] further adds when war, destruction, and sin is turned into wholeness (*Shalom*) and healing (*Rapha)* then the new revelation will take place. He further adds in certain prophetic contexts *Rapha* is used for the healing of sin and apostasy, presupposing the figure of sin as a serious illness. Thus, Israel's unfaithfulness, waywardness, backsliding is a dangerous condition that only God can cure. In our investigation we have to enquire whether the different facets of sickness and suffering is referring to people's sinful condition or the people and nation pictured as ill that are in need of *Rapha* and *Shalom*.

In addition, other scholars have looked into the concept of *Shalom* in its totality. These include Hugh C. White, *Shalom in the Old Testament* (1973), Edward A. Powers, *Signs of Shalom* (1973).

White affirms cogently that the biblical concept of *Shalom* cannot be limited to "the conventional notion of peace as the absence of war". The fundamental meaning of *Shalom* is "totality," that is, "those conditions which would permit

1968); G. Fohrer, *A History of Israelite Religion*, trans. David E. Green (Nashville: Abingdon Press, 1972); H. Ringgren, *Israelite Religion*, trans. John Sturdy (Philadelphia: Fortress, 1966).

[27] Seong-Hyuk Hong, *The Metaphor of Illness and Healing in Hosea and its Significance in the Socio-Economic Context of Eight-Century Israel and Judah* (New York: Peter Lang, 2006).

[28] Cf. Brueggemann, *Isaiah 40-66.*

[29] Cf. Paul D. Hanson, *Isaiah 40-66, Interpretation: A Bible Commentary for Teaching and Preaching* (Louisville: Westminster John Knox Press, 1995). Hanson, in the process of his discussion on Isaiah 58 highlights the significance of community solidarity demonstrated through compassionate justice and suggests that healing will result from such community building.

[30] Cf. David L. Freeman and Judith Z. Abrams, eds., *Illness and Health in the Jewish Tradition: Writings from the Bible to Today* (Philadelphia: The Jewish Publication Society, 1999).

[31] Cf. E. John Hamlin, *A Guide to Isaiah 40-66* (London: ISPCK, 1979).

the free growth of the soul' to its wholeness or totality." Pedersen recognized that the wholeness of an individual can never be realized apart from wholeness in community, thus linking individual and communal wholeness. In short, even as sick persons and sick society would be interrelated, so also would personal health/ wholeness be related to societal *Shalom*.

James Ward suggests that the concept of *Rapha* is attributed to God only because everything Hosea utters is about God. The richness of the metaphors and similes he employed in referring to God's being and activity is unsurpassed in other biblical writings. Hence, the metaphor of God as *Rapha* is best expressed in the words of Hosea to a nation that is in need of restoration.[32] To this understanding, there is a need to see whether there is a tendency to relate the metaphors used by the prophets for health and healing in the same social-historical circumstances.

No doubt, the Biblical concept of health and healing has been formulated according to its own context and social location. The texts selected for this study is from diverse socio-historical background. Therefore, it will be interesting to study the diverse metaphors used by the prophets in different times and in different situations in order to understand the concept of health and healing in today's context. These observations suggest that the systematic study of illness, health and healing in Hosea, Isaiah and Jeremiah has been unduly neglected. A fresh study on these metaphors on health and healing will pave the way to 'new' 'renewed' 'wholistic' approach towards health and healthy life. It will also help shed light on the study of Israelite religion in its broader ancient West Asia context.

4. Terms Pertaining to *Rapha* in the Old Testament

The Old Testament employs many metaphors for Yahweh because no single metaphor can describe everything about Israel's God: Yahweh as judge, king, warrior, father, artist, gardener-vinedresser, mother, shepherd, et cetera. Yahweh as healer is not a major metaphor in the Old Testament, but it plays a significant role in the prophetic books.[33] In most instances the healer metaphor is conveyed by the Hebrew root ב רָפָא with Yahweh as subject; however, there are several other verbs and nouns that form the semantic domain of the healer metaphor.[34] According to Wilkinson, most of them contain the idea of restoration of something to its

[32] James M. Ward, "The Message of the Prophet Hosea," *Interpretation* 23, no. 4 (1969): 387-407.

[33] Walter Brueggemann, *Theology of the Old Testament: Testimony, Dispute, Aadvocacy* (Minneapolis: Fortress, 1997), 230-261.

[34] The following Hebrew roots refer to health and healing: גהה (heal) אסף (to gather or remove); עלה together with ארוכה (health restored or repair); חבש (to bind up, bandage a wound); חיה (live, put to life, revive, heal), חלם (to be or become healthy and strong; restore to health); מתם (soundness); שׁוב, especially with the noun נפשׁ (return to health, restore, refresh, keep alive); שׁלם (peace, health, well-being or wholeness) (Seybold, 1980:401; Brown, 1995:28-36; Chan, Song & Brown, 1997:1162-1173; Wilkinson, 1998:11, 53). See also Hasel, (1983:191-202).

previous normal state, or the removal of something, which is causing ill health or an abnormal condition.[35]

The meaning of Heb. רָפָא means to restore or to mend (eg., "you have shaken the land and torn it open; mend its fractures, for it is quaking" Ps. 60:2 [4]). This is also most commonly used, in terms of physical disease or wounds, e.g., Miriam's צָרַעַת (Num. 12:10) the Philistines' tumors עֳפָלִים 1 Sam. 5:6), Hezekiah's boil (שְׁחִין), (2 Kgs. 20:8) Jehoram's wounds, (2 Kgs. 8:29), (2 Chro. 22:6) and diseases (תַּחֲלֻאִים'), (Ps. 103:3). In Leviticus 13-14, the *niphal* of (וְנִרְפָּא) רָפָא is used 4 times with נגע-הצרַעת as the subject, 3 times with reference to humans (13:18, 37; 14:3) and once with reference to houses (14:48), suggesting that remit may serve as a more appropriate and uniform rendering here than heal, cure.

In Genesis 20:17; cf. also 12:17, God heals Abimelech and his household, all of whom had been smitten with infertility. This usage, however, does not indicate that רָפָא includes the nuance of "re-fertilizing," as some scholars have argued, rather, barrenness, impotency, and infertility were perceived as maladies that needed to be healed (or as defective conditions that needed to be made whole). This is in keeping with the covenantal understanding that equated health and fertility with divine blessing (Exod. 15:26; 23:25-26; Deut. 7:12-15) and sickness and infertility with divine curses (Deut. 28:27, 35), which threaten incurable diseases as a consequence of covenantal breach, since God, Israel's Healer, was rejected, a theme which was common in the Ancient West Asia.

Rapha is also used for human physicians (e.g., 2 Chro. 16:12; Gen. 50:2). It is used for the Egyptian physicians who embalmed Jacob) as well as for the Lord as Israel's Healer (Exod. 15:26; Ps. 103:3; 147:3).

The book of Proverbs, in keeping with Wisdom literature in general—not to mention the Old Testament as a whole—sees godliness as the very real path to life and well-being, while godlessness is the sure road to death and destruction. In this light, and with physical referents such as flesh (שְׁאֵר; the precise meaning of the Heb. is uncertain) and bones (עֲצָמוֹת) in 3:8 and body (בָּשָׂר, flesh) in 4:22. The force of the verses is clear: Godly living is a key to healing and health. Elsewhere in Proverbs, in keeping with the general imagery of the OT, אין מרפא speaks of the disastrous state of those whose defiant sinfulness takes them beyond the brink of possible recovery: They "will suddenly be destroyed—without remedy" (Pro. 6:15 and 29:1). In positive contexts, Proverbs 12:18 states that "the tongue of the wise brings healing" to the sword-like wounds inflicted by a chatterbox; according to 13:17, in contrast to the wicked messenger who always falls into trouble, "a trustworthy envoy brings healing" (ציר אמונים מרפא—i.e., by faithfully delivering his message), while 16:24 notes that "pleasant words are a honeycomb, sweet to the soul and healing to the bones" (cf. also 15:4a). "The tongue that brings healing is a tree of life," underscoring the healing power of the words of the wise,

[35] J. Wilkinson, *The Bible and Healing: A Medical and Theological Commentary* (Grand Rapids: William B. Eerdmans Publishing Company, 1998), 53.

first seen in 4:20-22, where מרפא occurred in close proximity to חַיִּים. Hence, "The heart at rest is the life of the body," in spite of the presence again of חיים רָפא, however, that the LXX relates מרפא here to רפא. Thus, in Proverbs, מרפא (or, רפאות) is the concrete remedy for physical or emotional wounding and collapse. Thus, we can see the diverse definitions of illness, health and healing in the Old Testament which needs further study.

5. Metaphors and Terms Pertaining to Health and Healing in Hosea, Isaiah and Jeremiah

The Prophets use metaphors in order to express about them and or on behalf of God. The prophetic usage of the metaphorical images and languages are of diverse nature, depending on the context of their time. The understanding of health in the prophetic literature is equally important as in the *Torah*. The reason, because the contexts in which the prophets lived, especially, the 8th century and 7th century and the Post-Exilic period was important and critical. This was a time when the prophets addressed to a society that was sick and wounded within a particular socio-economic, political and cultural context. The prophets like Hosea, Isaiah and Jeremiah use *Rapha, Arukah, Shalom* and *Marpe* to refer to health and healing. They characteristically insisted that the healing, intervening power of God cannot be controlled for private interest. They univocally raised their voices for the well-being of the people in different times and at different situations using different metaphors.

It is common to classify the usage of *Rapha, Arukah, Shalom* and *Marpe* in contexts that do not specifically deal with bodily ailments as "figurative," but this needs to be qualified and, at times, corrected. This is due to the fact that, in the prophetic understanding, the usage of *Rapha, Arukah, Shalom* and *Marpe* includes a wide range of meanings as deliverance from sickness, demons, death, and sin.[36] Therefore, there is a need to see whether *Rapha, Arukah, Shalom* and *Marpe* are more than figurative. There was a wide range of conditions that were candidates for healing, and one must ask if, to the biblical mind, the restoration of an individual's health would be seen as literal while the restoration of a nation's health would be understood to be figurative. At times, the problem is one of reading prophetic concepts in terms of our compartmentalized canons of thinking as opposed to adjusting our thinking to their more holistic outlook. Moreover, it is inappropriate to presuppose that every occurrence of *Rapha, Arukah, Marpe and Shalom* in the prophetic texts means to heal physical disease,[37] which we need to unearth further.

---

[36] Alan Kam-Yau Chan, Thomas B. Song, and Michael L. Brown, "*Rapha*," in *New International Dictionary of Old Testament Theology and Exegesis*, ed. Willem A. VanGemeren (Carlisle, Cambria: Paternoster Press, 1996), 1162-1173.

[37] Brueggemann, *Living Toward a Vision: Biblical Reflections on Shalom*, 178-179.

The fundamental meaning of Heb. רפא is to restore, make whole. Specific nuances include: (a) repair or fix; (b) make fresh, wholesome, pertaining to deadly salt water (c) mend (but never sew, stitch), (d) most commonly, heal, in terms of physical disease or wounds. In the *Torah*,[38] the historical books,[39] and the wisdom literature,[40] the concept of *Rapha* is mainly used as healing from sickness.

The centrality of the metaphors in Hosea can be seen both in the explicit references to the term "illness" and "healing" (E.g., Hos. 5:13; 6:1; 7:1, 5; 11:3; 14:4) and in the allusions to their aspects in the text (e.g., Hos. 6:2; 7:9-14; 9:4, 11-12, 14, 16; 13:16; 14:5-7). The metaphor of Yahweh as healer is employed in various ways by Hosea in order to describe Yahweh as the healer. (Hos. 6:1-2; 7:1; 14:4). Strikingly interesting in Hosea's metaphors is his description of socio-political and economic deviation of Israel in terms of illness (5:13; 6:1; 7:1, 5).

In Isaiah 38:16 *Rapha* is sometimes found in proximity to or parallel with *Shalom* (Isa. 57:18-19, Jer. 6:14; 8:11; 14:19; 33:6).

According to the prophets, Yahweh's healing was more than a medically verifiable physical process. The prophetic books focus more on the spiritual healing of Israel and Judah than on the physical healing of an individual (cf. Isa. 57:18-19; Jer. 3:22; 30:17; Hos. 14:5 [4]). In some instances Yahweh offered comprehensive deliverance or concrete promises for a "sick" nation.

James Muilenburg is of the opinion that, in certain prophetic contexts, *Rapha,* is used for the healing of sin and apostasy, presupposing the figure of sin as a serious illness (Jer. 3:22; Hos. 14:3).[41] Thus, in this case, the translation of "to heal" is retained as opposed "to forgive", although it is acceptable to speak of figurative usage here, since the specific object of *Rapha, Arukah, Marpe* and *Shalom* is abstract, that is, the people's sinful condition is pictured as an illness, rather than the people and nation pictured in illness. *Rapha*, is also referred in Jeremiah to a clay jar, "smashed-repaired" (Jer. 19:11), with reference to a bone, "fractured–treated" (Jer. 6:14; 8:11), with reference to a body "injured-healed" (Jer. 30:12-14).[42] The healing activity of the prophets mentioned in 6:14 refers to their mediatory role in securing a *Shalom* oracle. The mention of a "wound" in this context presupposes a "break" in the existing order of creation, that is, a violation of that order on the part of the community resulting in their collective injury. For Schmid, the contents of the text reveal a discrepancy between the Shalom of the order of creation and the well-being of the individual within that order, who is often described as suffering with illness, economic distress, or the

[38] Gen. 20:17; cf. also 12:17 (Exo.15:26; 23:25-26; Deut. 7:12-15), Deut. 28:27, 35.

[39] 2 Chro. 36:16.

[40] Ps. 103:3; 147:3; Pro. 29:1.

[41] James Muilenburg, "The Terminology of Adversity in Jeremiah," in *Translating and Understanding the Old Testament,* ed. Harry Thomas Frank and William L. Reed (Nashville: Abingdon Press, 1970), 60-61.

[42] Chan, Song, and Brown, "*Rapha,*" 1164.

animosity of personal enemies.[43] Thus, health, which is related to Shalom, needs to be looked extensively.

Jeremiah's concept of *Rapha* is to heal, restore. Mend is also used in *niphal* form as "be healed," "be cured" or "be made wholesome." Specific nuances include repair or fix (Jer. 19:11), make fresh, wholesome, to mend or heal in terms of disease or wounds. ארוכה (*Arukah*) which means "lengthening" is never used to refer to the individuals but to the health of the nation by the prophet (Jer. 8:22). The word *Marpe*, מרפא, not only implies healing or curing in Jeremiah 8:15, but also restoration to spiritual soundness, general well-being or wholeness.

Jeremiah also uses poignant metaphors and images around which the theme is carefully designed to play upon the imagination of the community. Muilenburg offers one of the clearest examples of such a function. According to him, "Jeremiah delights in the language of wound and healing to re-characterize Israel's political situation. Remarkably, in a single poem he is able to speak about an "incurable wound" (30:12), yet a "wound to be healed" (30:17)."[44] The lexical data for wounding and healing here are ample and diverse. Such diverse understanding demands a look into the whole development of the concept of *Rapha* in Jeremiah as to whether restoration to health and well-being has been attached to the psycho-physical character of Israel's mentality.

With the aftermath of exile, Trito-Isaiah speaks on restoration as well being in lieu of the salvation that is to come. Healing in Trito-Isaiah is the restoration of health. The word for healing is *Arukah,* which refers to the repairing of a wound. What is being restored here is the covenant relationship with God. The use of this word for healing indicates that those being addressed have been wounded by their own self-righteousness, which has allowed them to ignore the poor and oppressed. In addition to the explicit promise of the restoration of health, well-being is further described in images of light, having strong bones, abundant water, and the care of God, which are all characteristics of health.

The prophets used *Rapha, Arukah, Marpe and Shalom* in terms of divine restoration for the nation after a time of judgment and chastisement. Alan Kam is of the opinion that healing of physical diseases was certainly not excluded from the wider metaphor of national healing and restoration. The analysis made by Chan is that, the metaphorical imagery, powerfully expressed through vivid figures such as Israel's "new skin" arising (e.g., Jer. 30:17; 33:6, or a physician applying healing balm (8:22; 46:11; 51:8; cf. also Isa 1:6), must therefore be seen as inclusive and not as exclusive.[45] However, many in today's context often misunderstand such understanding of health. For example, Lennart Nordenfelt, defines health as follows: "A person is in a state of complete health, if and only if this person is in

[43] H. H. Schmid, *Shalom im Alten Testamentum* (Stuttgart: Katholisches Bibelwerk, 1971), 55.

[44] Muilenburg, "The Terminology of Adversity in Jeremiah," 42-63.

[45] Chan, Song, and Brown, "*Rapha*," 1162-1173.

a physical and mental state such that he or she is able to realize all his or her vital goals given a set of accepted circumstances."[46]

The understanding of health as "soundness of body"[47] is misconceived by many even today. Such a definition clearly imports particular social values, which are shaped by the standard that what is good for an individual becomes the standard social norms in the society, which led to the definition of Health as individual goals. Such concepts suffer from shortcomings by conceptualizing the understanding of health narrowly so that not all of life's experiences are reducible to matters of health. Health does seem to be more than merely the opposite of disease. We are reminded often that the opposite to health is sickness, illness, disease, ailment, weakness, debility, infirmity, and frailty as part of the human condition along with the antonyms to healing as wounding, hurting, injuring, harming, breaking, making worse, getting worse. However, can the concept of health go beyond such bias understanding?

The understanding health as the absence of disease focuses only on the absence of a negative state. Therefore, it is incomplete, because though it is true that healthy people are free of disease, health involves much more than this. That is, as Kass suggests, health is more like concepts of pleasure, strength, or justice, and less like being pregnant or being dead.[48] Health is not limited to our personal well-being only.

The prophetic usage of *Rapha, Arukah, Shalom and Marpe* provides the conceptual background to the larger prophetic picture of health and healing, which takes in national, covenantal issues and focuses for the most part on corporate restoration, often in the context of corporate repentance. It is important to see how the prophets have understood these concepts in understanding health and healing. Questions like the following will be probed in our research to find its implication for our context: Do the prophets address health as well being of the physical being, or of the nation? Do the prophetic oracles of health give us an opportunity for creating a healthy global community? Does the Old Testament language of healing reflect a decidedly holistic mentality? Do the prophetic metaphors on illness, health and healing echoes for a holistic health? To what extent was the hope of a national (and even universal) profusion of divine healing eschatological? This is just a sampling of some of the issues that must be addressed to. As noted earlier, these concepts have been an integral part of the prophetic oracles in speaking to the audience of their time especially in terms of the healing

---

[46] Lennart Nordenfelt, "On Medicine and Other Means of Health Enhancement: Towards a Conceptual Framework," in *Goals of Medicine: The Forgotten Issues in Health Care Reform*, ed. Mark J. Hanson and Daniel Callahan (Washington DC: Georgetown University Press, 1999), 72.

[47] Richard O. Straub, *Health Psychology* (Michigan: Word Publishers, 2002), 6.

[48] Leon Kass, "The End of Medicine and the Pursuit of Health," in *Concepts of Health and Disease: Interdisciplinary Perspectives*, ed. Arthur L. Caplan, Jr. H. Tristram Engelhard, and James J. McCartney (Massachusetts: Addison Wesley, 1981), 11.

of the society. We feel these prophetic oracles have a lot to offer to our present society also.

Against the backdrop of the extreme sociological problems of Israel and Judah, lies the historical context. The socio-historical setting plays an important role in their prophetic understanding of health. Therefore, there is a need to identify the inter-connectedness of *Rapha, Arukah, Shalom* and *Marpe* in their socio-historical setting. How do the prophets understand human life and health within a particular social, economic and political aspect? The prophets use *Rapha* in relation to wounds, ulcers, and injuries as images for the critical status of the people.[49] The prophets express sickness, which is generally accepted as physical ailments, as "wound" that are not pictures of corruption but of disaster, which resulted from corruption deserves a clearer enquiry in understanding health and healing.

There was a "sick role" in Israel as surely as there is a "sick role" today. Today "the sick" are largely exempted from normal social responsibilities, largely exempted from understanding the health of others. A sick Community as in the time of the prophets is alive in today's context. Sickness which is not only in its physicality but also in all spheres of human life is seen. The concept of violence and war, inequality, injustice, corruption and poverty makes us to search for a renewed understanding of health. The time of the prophets and ours may have a gap of distance in its time but an obvious similarity is seen in its understanding of health. Health which is one of the prerequisite of God is understood as a selfish means by human beings to gain one's end. The concept of health has been a focus for the people for learning about themselves, their lifestyle, and their priorities. Today, as in the time of the prophets, an analogical similarity between the people of prophetic times as well as today is found, where individualism is celebrated as the ultimate goal, and where poverty, religious intolerance, social and moral disruption and individualistic understanding to life becomes the topmost agenda.

In such a context, it is important to interrogate and dialogue with the prophets in their understanding of health and well-being. Such enquiry will help us in our approach to health towards an inclusive approach to life, that is, human beings are not divided but a single totality, that is, health is total.[50]

Hence, this research aims to identify the dimensions of health and explore the relationship of these dimensions to wholeness and its relevance for our context. Hence, the aim is to unearth the nexus between the different concepts that the prophets used for health and to pave way in the quest for the well-being of the society in general by proposing a theology of health, healing and wholeness.

---

[49] H. J. Stoebe, "Rapha", in *Theological Lexicon of the Old Testament*, ed. Ernst Jenni et al. (Massachusetts: Hendrickson, 1997), 1257.

[50] Walter Brueggemann, *Isaiah 40-66* (Louisville: Westminster John Knox Press, 1998), 190.

6. Scope and Method of Research

6.1. Scope of the Research

The focus of our study is to attempt to understand health in light of *Rapha, Arukah, Marpe* and *Shalom* in the oracles of Hosea, Isaiah and Jeremiah. Since the metaphors in these three Books arose out of different contexts, to unearth the interconnectedness of the terms is important. Only passages relevant to our theme are chosen for an exegetical analysis. The aim of this study is to bring forth all the important metaphors that are used by the prophets to address the health and well-being of the community. Apart from looking into the prophetic oracles of health, we shall also attempt to discover whether the prophetic books are also associated with the concept of illness and health that refers to both physical and wholistic aspect. The scope of the research is also to present parallels of thought in individual and communitarian aspects of health, to find out the interconnectedness of *Rapha, Arukah, Shalom and Marpe* and its development, to understand the prophetic understanding of *Rapha, Arukah, Shalom and Marpe* in relation to health, and to respond biblically to the issues related to health in the context of a sick and a marginalised society.

6.2. Method of the Research

In order to understand the fuller meaning of health in the light of *Rapha, Arukah, Marpe* and *Shalom* in the prophetic oracles, what is required is a detailed exegetical study of the relevant texts with all the methodological tools available. In the process of expounding the texts, all available critical tools and synchronic and diachronic approaches are taken into account. A survey of the understanding of the concept of Health and sickness in Ancient West Asia and in the Israelite society is also given its due importance. The research shall further attempt to find out whether the concept of health and healing was developed in ancient Israelite society in the respective context of their own social and religious context, and how it was transformed and transmitted to later generations through its metaphors of *Rapha, Arukah, Marpe* and *Shalom.*

This approach will be used to probe deeper into the understanding of illness and healing in ancient times and biblical thinking. Such an approach will also highlight various other biblical perspectives of understanding health, healing and wholeness. Moreover, all available methodological means will be utilised in order to identify the socio-historical factors that were behind the shaping of the theology of the prophets.

For this research, selected texts from the passages of pre-exilic prophetic literature in the books of Hosea and Isaiah, exilic prophecy of Jeremiah and Deutero-Isaiah, the post-exilic strata of the book of Isaiah will be taken into account.

The research will also be investigated by employing an integrated approach of synchronic and diachronic methods. Diachronic and synchronic exegesis must not be opposed as rivals but coordinated as complements. This new theoretical understanding therefore necessitates a diachronically reflected synchronic reading of the text. Barr states as follows: "... the diachronic consideration explains the synchronic ... fact;"[51] that is to say, they are inextricably linked to one another. Therefore, it can be deduced that synchronic analysis without diachronic input only touches the textual surface.

In modern biblical studies, synchronic exegesis is an approach, which focuses attention both on texts as totalities and also on the interaction of interpreters with the texts they are studying.[52]

- Synchronic exegesis evinces a primary exegetical respect for the final literary work itself and a productive concentration upon interpreting that work in its own terms. It gives the full expression to the hermeneutical principle that the part is to be related to the whole and the whole to the part. It resists the atomizing of the text, and respects its genre.[53]
- It focuses on the interaction of reader and text. Synchronic exegesis is often sharply distinguished from diachronic and dogmatic approaches, yet synchronic and diachronic approaches are not incompatible. The synchronic approach relies on sound textual scholarship.[54]
- Synchronic approach is the final form of the text from two angles, namely canonical criticism, new literary criticism with its variants such as narrative criticism, rhetoric criticism, the application of reader response theory to exegesis, and deconstruction. Since the holistic approach assists the interaction of the text and the socio-political realities of the interpreter's context, synchronic exegesis is also evident in modern liberation and political theology.[55]
- The synchronic methods complete the historical-critical methods by making the observations of textual phenomena an explicit step in analyzing the text as it is found in its present final form.
- Synchronic analysis opens the way to the meaning of the text by showing the structures present in the text itself.

---

[51] J. Barr, "The synchronic, the diachronic and the historical: A triangular relationship?" in *Synchronic or Diachronic?: A Debate on Method in Old Testament Exegesis*, edited by J. C. De Moor (Leiden: Brill, 1995), 7.

[52] J. I. H. McDonald, "Synchronic Exegesis," in *The SCM Dictionary Of Biblical Interpretation*, ed. R. J. Coggins and J. L. Houlden (London: SCM Press Ltd., 1990), 657.

[53] Ibid.

[54] Ibid.

[55] Ibid., 658.

- The diachronic approach takes the critically reconstructed history of Biblical text as the basis, and using methods such as form, source, traditions, literary and history with an intention of finding what is behind the text.[56]
- This method explores not only one definite point in time but also a series of different points of time during which the biblical text was being formed from its first origin until its final editing or reduction.
- The task of the diachronic method is to explore the origin and changes of the biblical test with its sources.
- Diachronic analysis opens an access to the text by shedding light on its inner textual prehistory.
- Diachronic analysis comprises of the broad field of reconstructing individual texts and their literary connections within the text-corpus of the Old Testament. Diachronic analysis compares a text with other texts both within and outside of the Old Testament corpus in terms of linguistic characteristics, literary form, and content. Relationships between texts, shifts or inconsistencies in language and style are reasons for positing a hypothesis regarding earlier phases of the text, later redactions, and their religious background.

The synchronic approach is undertaken on three levels. Firstly, a fresh translation of the Hebrew original is made with critical notes. Secondly, detailed exegetical analysis of every verse with particular attention to the semantic aspect of important terms and phrases is attempted. Thirdly, the results of the exegetical analysis are brought into a theological synthesis, in which the major theological motives of Hosea, Isaiah and Jeremiah are studied against the contexts of these three books. Using the synchronic approach, will help us to see how the author outlined the *Rapha, Arukah, Shalom* and *Marpe* in the three different periods to emphasize on health and healing. In the synchronic approach, one takes the given final text as a unit despite the fact that the materials may have been brought together by the final author. The diachronic reading is mainly intended to understand the various processes of redaction, which might have taken place before the text reached its final form.

After having considered the major theories of redaction of the Book of Hosea, Isaiah and Jeremiah with special focus on *Rapha, Arukah, Shalom* and *Marpe*, an attempt is made to propose a plausible account of the genesis of the text. The diachronic approach will help us to speculate of various hypotheses and theories regarding the source behind the text.

---

[56] K. T. K. Lim, "Toward a Final Form Approach to Biblical Interpretation," *Stulos Theological Journal* 7, no. 1-2 (1999): 6.

Since the aim of the research is to unearth the different usages of the Hebrew word *Rapha, Arukah, Shalom* and *Marpe*, the exegetical study will be limited to select texts from Hosea, Isaiah and Jeremiah. Consequently, the following texts will be taken into consideration:

Hosea 5:12-13; Hosea 6:3; Hosea 11:3; Isaiah 1:5-6; Isaiah 6:10; Isaiah 19:22; Isaiah 26:3; Isaiah 33:24; Isaiah 53:4-5; Isaiah 57:18-19; Isaiah 58:2-8; Jeremiah 3:22; Jeremiah 6:7,14; Jeremiah 8:11, 15, 18, 22; Jeremiah 14:18, 19; Jeremiah 15:18; Jeremiah 17:14; Jeremiah 30:13-18; and **Jeremiah 33:6.**

The method of the research will be as follows:

The **first** chapter will deal with the concept of Illness in the Old Testament. In this chapter, we will deal with its definitions and meanings to help us to understand the background before studying further the concept of health and healing in the Old Testament.

In chapter **two**, we will deal with the background study of Health in Old Testament with special reference to *Rapha, Arukah, Shalom and Marpe* (exclusive of prophetic literature): Its meanings and Definitions

In chapter **three**, we will investigate further the concept of illness, health and healing in Ancient West Asia in order to help us probe further the relatedness of illness, health and healing in the Old Testament.

The Exegetical study will be divided into three chapters according to three different contexts.

In chapter **four**, we will deal with the understanding of Health and Healing in select passages of Pre-Exilic Prophetic Literature in the Books of Hosea and Isaiah.

Chapter **five** deals with the study of the concept of Health and Healing in Exilic Prophecy of Jeremiah and Deutero-Isaiah.

Chapter **six** deals with Health and Healing in the Post-Exilic Strata of the Book of Isaiah.

In Chapter **seven** we will analyze the concept of health and healing in the Light of the Prophetic understanding of *Rapha, Arukah, Shalom* and *Marpe* and draw out some findings. In the concluding chapter, Challenges of Prophetic Understanding of Health to the Contemporary World will be proposed in the light of our deliberations. The concluding chapter will focus on health and healing in the context of India.

6.3. The Format of the Investigation

After surveying the understanding of sickness and health in the Ancient West Asia and in the Israelite society a methodical exegetical study of the texts, concerning to health and healing in the prophetic oracles will be done. Text critical notes and form critical notes will also accompany the exegetical study. Since the texts selected are from different sections, the structure and the genre of the books will also be taken into account not isolating the socio-historical context of the text treated. This will be followed by a section of comments on the passage with special reference to illness, health and healing in the light of *Rapha, Arukah, Shalom* and *Marpe* in Isaiah, Hosea and Jeremiah. Each passage will be treated in its totality and a brief summary of the investigation will be made at the end.

Chapter 1

Illness in the Old Testament Its Definitions and Meanings

Introduction

In this chapter, we will deal with illness in Israel during the Old Testament period. Since our main concern is on health and healing, the material discussed here will explore pertaining to the nature of illness and the cause of illness. It will also explore on how any form of illness or sickness in ancient Israel is related to the societal norms of 'normal' and 'abnormal' behaviour. The chapter will also give importance to study on how keeping a healthy and covenantal relationship with Yahweh amounts to health and well-being.

1.1. Illness and Its Cause

The understanding of illness in Israel involved social as well as physical factors. Avalos defines illness as "any condition that, regardless of physical danger as defined by modern western medicine, renders a person physically or mentally unfit to execute a social role defined as 'normal' by the society at issue, here ancient Israel."[1] What he means by the term 'normal' points to the state that the permitted one is to participate in the temple to display the harmony between God and his people.[2] In short, he suggests that at the bottom of the notion of illness lies a disturbed relationship with God. The general view of illness is in terms of disturbed relationship with God, which prevented the person in illness, from performing his/her normal social role in society. In ancient Israel, the understanding of illness in terms of the disturbed relationship with God is confirmed easily by the study of the causes of illness.

---

[1] H. Avalos, *Illness and Health Care in Ancient Near East* (Atlanta: Scholars, 1995), 250.

[2] Ibid., 248.

In the past, medical science has dealt primarily with diagnosing physical symptoms, seeking physical causes of illness, and administering physiological treatments. Most of the definitions of 'health' from scientists emphasize two things: our ability to react adaptively to those forces causing us stress, and our ability to function to our satisfaction in the society of which we are a part.[3] Social and cultural patterns affect how a person perceives symptoms, if medical care treatment is sought, and the response to pain. Culture also influences beliefs concerning causes of illness and alternative treatment. This concept of illness behaviour is relevant with respect to cultural-religious differences contributing to norms and values in health and illness.

Kleinman, among other medical anthropologists, has advanced a useful distinction between illness and disease. He states, "Disease refers to malfunctioning of biological and/or psychological processes, while the term illness refers to the psycho-social experience and meaning of perceived disease."[4] Hence, disease refers to modern biomedical classifications of physical and mental abnormalities and illness refers to those conditions that an ancient society saw as abnormal.[5]

The Bible had various general terms for illness as well as some relatively more specific ones. K. Seybold,[6] among other scholars, has provided extensive study of this terminology, and, except, insofar as we relate the terminology to larger-socio-religious issues, including the concept of illness itself.

One of the principal words to describe illness in the Hebrew Bible is חלה. However, the original Semitic root is unclear, and so is the original meaning.[7] The various nouns and verbal forms of the word are applied in a wide variety of situations that depict conditions ranging from one that does not appear to be serious (e.g., 1 Sam. 19:14), to that of potentially deadly (e.g., 2 Kgs. 1:2ff, 2 Kgs. 8:7f, Isa. 38:9). The word may be applied to conditions where the patient seems to be more depressed than physically ill (e.g., Neh. 2:22). In Jeremiah 12:13, it is applied to someone who is exhausted from labour, though not necessarily suffering from 'disease' in the modern sense. The word can also be applied to physical defects in animals that render them unfit for sacrifice (e.g., Mal. 1:8). Another word דוה, is applied to a woman during their menstruation (e.g., Lev. 12:12 and 15:23), as well as conditions involving psychological distress (Lam. 1:22).

---

[3] Just as physicians seek to make conditions for healing to take place in those who are ill, they should make conditions ideal for the proportion of health of everyone in their communities.

[4] A. Kleinman, *Patients and Healers in the Context of Culture* (Berkeley: University of California, 1980), 69.

[5] Hector Avalos, *Illness and Health Care in the Ancient Near East: The Role of the Temple in Greece, Mesopotamia, and Israel* (Atlanta, Georgia: Scholars Press, 1995), 246.

[6] Cf. Klaus Seybold and Ulrich B. Mueller, *Sickness and Healing* (Nashville: Abingdon Press, 1978).

[7] Avalos, *Illness and Health Care in Ancient Near East*, 247.

In addition to terms that are general descriptions of illness as it affects the whole person, there is a common term that often refers to the localization of pain. For instance, one finds the term באב applied to those suffering pains from circumcision in Genesis 34:25 or from extraneous concrete causes such as a thorn (Ezek. 28:24). However, the term can also be applied to the general state of physical or mental pain (e.g., Ezek. 13:22). Illnesses such as צרעת could also be localized, and yet the whole person was regarded as ill.

The definition of illness in Israel is a complex one, and it involved social as well as physical factors. The terminology and references to illness in the Old Testament allow one to characterize an illness as a condition with visible symptoms that render a human being physically and/or mentally unable to fulfil the normal social and/or physical role assigned by the society. A normal state, in particular, was one that allowed the person to participate in the temple cult. A normal healthy state was one, which valued the harmony (שלום) between Yahweh and his people.

The Israelite idea of health is complicated by the fact that the idea interacted with notions of purity and impurity. There could be some sick conditions, for example, that might not pose much of a physical danger to the patient, or that would not render them physically unfit to most tasks. However, Israelite ideology would view them as sick because there was a visible abnormality, which, even if not regarded as physically dangerous by a modern physician, was dangerous in other ways. For example, a hierocracy might propose that the presence of physically defective persons in the temple might bring the wrath of Yahweh upon the nation.

The dividing line between someone who is simply impure and someone who is defined as ill in Israelite society is not always easy to discern. One may say that to be categorized as ill, one had to show visible signs that were regarded as indicative of a condition that rendered the person unable to execute the roles assigned to them. For instance, lack of children, a sad countenance, and a headache may all qualify as symptoms of an illness in ancient Israel.

Illness is any condition that, regardless of physical danger as defined by modern medicine, renders a person physically or mentally unfit to execute a social role defined as normal by the society in ancient Israel. Such definitions allow historical changes because the definition of a normal role underwent changes, as did the types of conditions that were regarded as sufficiently abnormal to exclude one from participation in the cult.[8] It should be noted that any non-human entity that could not execute the role assigned to it, was also deemed to be sick.

1.1.1. Illness as a Result of Sin and Disobedience

A number of Old Testament texts suggest that obedience to God's commands - the means by which the people maintained a right relationship with Him and

[8] That is the reason why the land in 2 Chronicles 7:14, or a nation could be described as ill.

therefore with others – was conducive to health, if not a determining factor in good health. Indeed there are many texts which indicate that obedience to God's law means freedom from disease, whilst disobedience means the opposite.[9] Obedience to God's righteousness leads to health and well-being for all. This theme is repeated throughout the Old Testament. When the people of Israel follow God's word and law, they experience health, and when their behavior defies God's word and law, they experience illness (Exod. 15:26).[10] On the whole, the Bible suggests that one's health largely depends on the nature of one's relationship with God, which necessarily influences relationships with others. In order to maintain a right relationship with God and thus maintain one's health then, a person needs to be focused on God and this requires loving Him before anything else. Indeed, it involves keeping His commandments which involves loving others and looking after their needs and well-being. Obedience to God then, was a responsibility that both the individual and society shared this sense of responsibility expressed itself in Israelite law. Indeed, Elazah and Cohen show how the *Torah* emphasized social relationships, commitment, obligation and preferential action. Thus, in Jewish thought two concepts were endorsed, "humans are partners with the sovereign universe in the development and governance of the world," (and) "every citizen is linked to his neighbour by covenant obligation."[11] According to Walter Brueggemann,

> . . . the imperatives speak against individualism in order to assert that we are 'members one of another.' My own judgment is that the imperatives challenge our current passion for 'privatization,' a social ideology and strategy that denies our mutual obligation to all members of the community.[12]

---

[9] Exod. 15:26, 20:12, 23:25-26, Lev. 26:14-16, 23-26, Num. 5:20-23, 27-28, Deut. 7:12-15, 28:27-29, 58-62, Pro.3:7-8, cf. Ps. 32:3-5, 38:1-8. There are many indications that maintaining righteousness - (a right relationship with God) was understood to be conducive to good physical health. For example, we find that a right relationship with God produces *shalom* (Isaiah 32:17) while righteousness and *shalom* flourish together (Ps. 72:7, 85:10, Isa. 48:18, Mal. 2:6) We also find that the pursuit of righteousness is the pursuit of life (Pro. 11:4, 19, 28 and 30) Further there is the indication that those who are obedient to the law survive and live to a good age. For example, obedience and the maintaining of righteousness is illustrated in the lives of Noah, whose family alone survived the flood (Gen. 6:9ff); Joseph, who lived to see his great great-grandchildren (Gen. 39:2, 21, 23; 50:22-23) and Abraham who lived to an old age and became a father of many (Gen. 12:4, 15:6,15, 25:8). Other biblical characters who maintained righteousness and were seen to live to a good age were Isaac (Gen. 35:29) and Jacob (Gen. 49:33).

[10] John Wilkinson, *The Bible and Healing: A Medical and Theological Commentary* (Edinburgh: The Handsel Press Ltd, 1998), 14.

[11] Daniel J. Elazar and Stuart A. Cohen, *The Jewish Polity* (Indiana: Indiana University Press, 1985), 4, 7.

[12] Walter Brueggemann, *Isaiah 40-66* (Louisville: Westminster John Knox Press, 1998), 186.

Recognizing the mutual obligation of humanity, our beliefs shape the kinds of communities and opportunities for health, we allow ourselves to exist for ourselves and for others.

It was, therefore the responsibility of the community as a whole to maintain the relationship with God, whilst individuals would enjoy the relationship through the tribe. Therefore, owing to the interrelatedness of all life, it was essential that the community maintained a right relationship with God in order to have well-being as a whole.[13] Anderson suggests that the supplication is a metaphor of a greater misfortune, which like any disaster, brought weakness and a general lack of vitality and perhaps illness. The Psalmist prays for deliverance because the disaster was understood to be (like any disaster in Hebrew thought) linked with sin and disobedience.[14] In this case the suffering occurs not so much because of the Psalmist's own negative spiritual condition (i.e. disobedience to God) but due to society's disobedience.[15] Holiness and obedience to God are the means by which we can have a relationship with Him, obeying the command to love Him necessarily involves loving others. It is therefore, our relationship with God and accordingly with others that indicate the nature of one's spiritual condition which may determine health.

The most debatable issue is about the general emphasis on the link between disobedience[16] (sin) and disease.[17] The Old Testament insists often on a

[13] M. Maddocks, *Journey to Wholeness* (New Delhi: ISPCK, 1995), 4-5.

[14] A. Anderson, *Psalms (1-150)*, The New Bible Commentary, vol. 1-2 (London: Marshall, Morgan & Scott, 1972), 86-89. Again, in Psalm 102:5 (given the context in which this lament was written, being the destruction of Jerusalem) the afflictions of the individual may be related to the condition of the Jewish society at that time. That is to say, the illness of the individual is the result of the disease in society, which was brought about by sin and disobedience.

[15] Conversely, failing to love God will often result in neglecting the well-being of others. The Book of Isaiah provides numerous examples of how the well-being and needs of the weaker members of society were neglected, because the more powerful failed to love God and keep His commandments, which by nature ensure justice and equity. The implication is that as we are instructed to keep the commandments (and love one another (a sign that we love God), we have a responsibility for the well-being of each other. In this vein, we recognize that our relationship with God -our spiritual condition-may affect not only our own personal health, but also the nature of our relationships with others, and accordingly their health.

[16] The most obvious passage which associates disobedience with disease is to be found in Deuteronomy where God tells His people that if they disobey His commands then they would be cursed with physical problems (disease, famine, blight, drought etc) (Deut. 28:15ff). Nevertheless, this does not justify the argument that all diseases are the result of sin.

[17] For example, the ten discontented spies died of a plague before the Lord (Num. 14:36-37) the Lord sent venomous snakes to bite and kill many Israelites when the people spoke against Him and Moses (Num. 21:4-9); Miriam contracted an unclean skin disease because she spoke against Moses (Num. 12:1-15); a plague ("*negeph*") killed 14,700 Israelites following the rebellion of Korah (Num. 16:41-50); again a plague killed 24,000 Israelites following the people's worship of the Baal of Peor (Num. 25:1-9); the baby born to Bathsheba was ill and died as a result of King David's sin (2 Sam. 12:13-23); Jehoram contracted a fatal intestinal disease because of his unfaithfulness to God

connection between sickness and sin in particular instances but no doubt rightly. In the biblical record, illness might be the direct result of sinful action, that is, as divine punishment, but that need not be the case. According to Fritz Stolz, "Illness has special significance for the Old Testament in that it is either experienced as distress that leads to lament... or is understood as the effect of God's curse."[18] Mueller opines that, "The either/or is essential. Not everyone in the Bible sees a direct connection between their illness and their sin."[19] However, sometimes sickness and diseases are the ways to their liberative and wholistic aspect of their life. Gerhard Von Rad concurs: "[T]here was a very close connection between sin and physical disease. But he indicates how all the disturbances in our natural life have their roots in a disturbed relationship to God."[20] Nonetheless, the view that disease is sent by God must be put into its proper context, otherwise the danger is that God is perceived as one who punishes immediately those who disobey Him.

Although, the presence of disease is believed to have been caused by demons,[21] the Israelites believed that everything, both good and evil, sickness and health, ultimately proceeded from the almighty God. However, much of the attempt was to bring the people of Israel to a worship of Yahweh alone, who was seen as the sole source of both good and evil, of sickness as well as health. Sickness therefore, was based on spiritual causes; this made it unnecessary for the Israelites to revert to magic or to incantations; rather, sickness confronted them directly with Yahweh and with the condition of their relationship to their God. This did not mean that the righteous people always enjoyed perfect health, while the evil ones were condemned to perpetual sickness; it did emphasize, however, the Israelites strong belief that affliction of the body was not primarily a physical, an organic matter, but instead depended largely on the moral and spiritual state of the person.[22] Therefore, sicknesses and diseases are to be understood as God's way of restoring not only the physical aspect but also even the spiritual aspect of

---

(2 Chro. 2 1:11 19) and Gehazi contracted an unclean skin disease because of his greed and deceit - which the Lord decreed was then to be forever inherited by Gehazi's descendants (2 Kgs. 5:26-27).

[18] Fritz Stolz, "*Hala* (*chalah*) " in *Theological Lexicon of the Old Testament*, ed. Ernst Jenni et al. (Mass: Hendrickson, 1997), 427.

[19] Mueller, *Sickness and Healing*, trans. Douglas W. Stott (Nashville: Abingdon Press, 1981), 148.

[20] Von Rad, *Old Testament Theology*, trans. D. M. G. Stalker, vol. 1 (London: SCM Press Ltd., 1975), 275.

[21] The belief was common among most peoples at the time of the early Hebrews. Both the Egyptians and the Babylonians held that sickness resulted from demonic ill will of various good or evil spirits. The Persians with their well-developed dualism looked on disease or to the demon who caused it, so closely are the two related. Morton T. Kelsey, *Healing and Christianity in Ancient Thought and Modern Times* (London: Harper & Row Publishers, 1973), 38.

[22] Karen S. Carter, "A Biblical Vision of Wholeness," *Brethern Life and Thought* 33, no. 1 (Winter 1988): 61.

life i.e., wholistic life. Outward purity and inward righteousness were united in the laws of purity and holiness.[23]

God is described as the source of illness. God's involvement in the origin of illness may be seen in at least two different perspectives. First, illness results in from divine punishment for sins. Yahweh used illness as consequential punishment for the violation of covenantal stipulations that are fully disclosed to the members of Israelite society.[24] The typical example of this notion is found in Deuteronomy 28,[25] where the series of threatening curses against disobedience to Yahweh's stipulations appears,

> But if you will not obey the Lord your God by diligently observing all his commandments and decrees, which I am commanding you today, then all these curses shall come upon you and overtake you…The Lord will send upon you disaster, panic, and frustration in everything you attempt to do, until you are destroyed and perish quickly, on account of the evil of your deeds, because you have forsaken me. The Lord will make the pestilence cling to you until it has consumed you off the land that you are entering to possess. The Lord will afflict you with the boils of Egypt, with ulcers, scurvy, and itch, of which you cannot be healed. The Lord will afflict with madness, blindness, and confusion of mind… (Deut. 28:15f).

The passage stresses that if Israel disobeys the laws, there will be no avenue of escape from Yahweh's curses, in particular, illnesses. Herein is the emphasis that sin is closely linked to illness. In other words, illness mirrors the moral inadequacy of the patient.

Although, Leviticus 13-14 on צרעת does not overtly associate this disease with sin, it at times displays a strong connection with sin in the rest of the Old Testament; thereby it was often considered to be a divine punishment and disgrace.[26] At this point, it seems appropriate to point out that the idea of illness in

[23] Allen P. Ross, *Holiness to the Lord: A Guide to the Exposition of the Book of Leviticus* (Grand Rapids: Baker Academic, 2002), 56.

[24] Avalos, *Illness and Health Care in Ancient Near East*, 34.

[25] There is a difference between Mesopotamia and Deuteronomy 28 regarding divine instrumentality of illness: "Whereas in Mesopotamia the god may use illness for a variety of reasons, which may be entirely arbitrary from a human standpoint, Deuteronomy 28 limits the use of illness to the enforcement of covenants. Deuteronomy 28 affirms that illness is not caused by any arbitrary reason that the deity may hide from the patient. Yahweh restricts his use of illness to the enforcement of stipulations that have been fully disclosed to the patient." Ibid., 243.

[26] Seybold and Klaus and Muller, *Sickness and Healing* (Nashville: Abingdon Press, 1981), 71. For instance, Miriam (Num. 12:10-15; Deut. 24:8-9) was smitten with leprosy as a divine punishment for her rebellion against Moses. Other people stricken with leprosy as Yahweh's punishment for their sins are Gehazi and his descendants (2 Kgs. 5:27) and Uzziah (2 Kgs. 15:5; 2 Chro. 26:16-21).

ancient Israel was also connected with that of impurity,[27] which is a little different perspective from the idea of illness, and it implied an interrupted relationship with Yahweh. The disturbed relationship with Yahweh is characterized by the forbidding of the patient's presence in the cult.[28] Milgrom views 'life' and 'death' as the fundamental criteria for separating purity and impurity. According to his criteria, צרעת is closer to 'death' than 'life,'[29] and therefore the person smitten with צרעת is considered impure. This impurity renders the patient unacceptable to participate in the cult and to maintain the presence of Yahweh (e.g., Lev. 13:45-46; cf. 12:4; 15:31).[30] Therefore, illness in the Old Testament can be viewed in terms of the concept of impurity as well as God's punishment for sins,[31] in certain cases,

---

[27] Impurity as the condition of a person that rendered him/her unfit to participate in the temple cult, while overlapping with conditions regarded as illness. Avalos, *Illness and Health Care in Ancient Near East*, 249.

[28] As seen in the account of Miriam's leprosy above, for example, a person afflicted with צרעת was reckoned as one dead (Num. 12:12). This account will be meaningful if we relate it to Milgrom's proposals with respect to the criteria for impurity in Leviticus.

[29] Indeed צרעת shows decaying flesh as its symptoms, which is indicative of nearly corpses (cf. Num. 12:12; Avalos, *Illness and Health Care in the Ancient Near East: The Role of the Temple in Greece, Mesopotamia, and Israel*, 306. Not simply physically, but socially she is counted as dead. In Num. 12:14, Yahweh's afflicting with leprosy is likened to a father spitting on his daughter's face, which is a sign of contempt and rejection from the community. Similarly, the leprous king Uzziah who was smitten by burning incense in the temple lives in isolation in "a separate house" and is "excluded from the house of the Lord" (2 Chro. 26:16-21). In this regard, the view of van der Toorn (K. Van Der Toorn, *Sin and Sanction in Israel and Mesopotamia: A Comparative Study* (Assen/Maastricht: Van Gorcum, 1985), 72-75.) deserves our attention. He holds that in ancient Mesopotamia leprosy was understood as the manifestation of divine punishment and thus ostracism from the community followed. Even king had to suffer from the disastrous consequences of the illness. "Leprosy will rob him of his crown and throne; he will end his reign in sights and tears and his life will become 'similar to death'. The outbreak of leprosy was equal to a social death certified for the party concerned.

[30] Avalos, *Illness and Health Care in the Ancient Near East: The Role of the Temple in Greece, Mesopotamia, and Israel*, 302.

[31] There are many other instances where it is indisputable that Yahweh employed illnesses to punish evildoers, whether the whole people or individuals. On the one hand, God smote the philistines with tumours because they captured the ark (1 Sam. 5:6-12). Israel, seduced by the Moabite women into bowing down to their idols, was smitten by Yahweh with the plague, which took 24,000 lives (Num. 25:1-9). The judgment nature of plague appears more vividly in the account of David's unwise order to take a census, finally leading to an outpouring of divine wrath (2 Sam. 24:1-17; 1 Chro. 21: 1-17). After David committed sin, three options of punishment-famine, devastation by enemies, or plague- are offered, so that he may choose one of them. Thus, David says, instead of direct choice, "…let us fall into the hand of the Lord" (2 Sam. 24: 15; 1 Chro. 21:14), although an accompanying 'angel of Yahweh' acts in accordance with Yahweh's commands. This suggests that a devastating plague more directly implied the involvement of Yahweh himself in punishing the people as a whole. On the other hand, sometimes individuals are singled out to be struck by illness as a consequential punishment for sins. Miriam was afflicted with leprosy for challenging Moses' authority (Num. 12: 9-16). Yahweh afflicted Uzziah, the king with leprosy for

but this does not indicate that sickness is the result of sin. Illness whether it is of physical or spiritual is never attributed in positive terms by the prophets and even in the Old Testament.

Brown explains,

> Destructive maladies are a curse! Painful, wasting diseases are terrible afflictions, not divine blessings. Health is good; illness is bad. Debilitating sickness and devastating plague are signs of God's anger, not his pleasure. In fact, nowhere in the Bible does the Lord ever promise sickness, disease, or calamity as blessings for his obedient children. Nowhere in the Bible is sickness, in and of itself, described as a good thing.[32]

To sum up, illness is an indicator of the condition of the relationship with God. That is, illness is not just a physical problem, but rather, in a comprehensive sense, an indication of the interrupted relationship.

1.1.2. Illness from Yahweh's Mysterious Motive

According to Seybold and Muller, the so-called "iron-clad law of behaviour consequence" governs the general understanding of illness in ancient Israel.[33] However, it must be noted that one must be careful not to make the sweeping assumption that in the Old Testament illness was always conceived as the consequence of personal sin; there are few cases where illness is not linked to personal sin. Several Psalms (especially Ps. 73), along with Job and Ecclesiastes, question the concept that manifestations of illness are always the outcome of sins.

Job is portrayed as an ideally righteous and thus richly blessed man. However, the disasters that overwhelm him from all directions come as total surprises. Such things are expected for the righteous. According to the traditional view of the Old

---

burning incense in the temple, which was the priests' prerogative (2 Kgs. 15:5; 2 Chro. 26:16-21). He afflicted the child born of the adulterous union of David and Bathsheba, causing the infant's sickness and death, despite the king's pleas (2 Sam. 12:13-18). Although, David's confession of sin resulted in Yahweh's sparing his own life, the very wording of the pardon presupposes that sin inevitably leads to death. The close link of personal transgression of illness can also be seen in Psalm 38. Psalm 38:8 says, "There is no soundness in my flesh because of your indignation; there is no health in my bones because of my sin." The Psalmist attributes divine anger to his own sin (Ps. 4). Many scholars think that these demonstrate that illness is an indication of divine wrath for sin. However, this does not always imply that illness is a divine instrument to punish sin. It could be attributed to a test, a reprimand, a punishment, or a pedagogical measure, but subjectively and generally, one cannot say whether it is indeed one of these things in each concrete case.

[32] M. L. Brown, *Israel's Divine Healer* (Grand Rapids: Zondervan Publishing House, 1995), 79-80.

[33] Seybold and Muller, *Sickness and Healing*, 95.

Testament, the suffering of the wicked is no mystery; it is their lot. In contrast, the suffering of the righteous could be mysterious.[34] In other words, inexplicable things sometimes occur to the truly righteous. However, Job's friends, Eliphaz, Bildad and Elihu too, stick to "the only 'orthodox' options available. Either 'righteous' Job strayed from the path-after all no human is perfect-and God is chastening him, or else job is positively weak, in which case God has judged him."[35] By applying to Job's case the traditional view that illness is punishment for guilt, they pretend to know all the divine motives associated with illness. They speak wrongly about both Job and Yahweh's dealing with him. His illness does not mean that he is under divine judgment, but rather his suffering is a divine mystery. This implies that illness is not always a divine instrument to punish sin. It could be attributed to "a test, a reprimand, a punishment, or a pedagogical measure, but subjectively and generally one cannot say whether it is indeed one of these things in each concrete case."[36] Hence, we can speculate that illness does not have "an aetiology that is always understandable by a patient."[37]

The problem of the suffering of the righteous person referring to a divine mystery is also found in Psalm 73 - a Wisdom Psalm. Though righteous and godly, the Psalmist has been smitten by some disaster, perhaps illness. What made the distress so bitter is to see the wicked prosper, while he himself has been plagued all day long and punished every morning (Ps. 73:14). Even if the problem of God's righteousness is resolved for him later, the Psalmist questions whether his illness is unconnected with his personal sin. While he does not question whether illness is a punishment for the wicked, he questions why it is that he, a righteous man, should be afflicted. The Psalmist intends to show that a patient might not understand all the causes of illness, which is associated with mysterious divine purposes.

There is a certain cynicism or scepticism in Ecclesiastes that occasionally questions whether the wicked or righteous are, in fact, paid back in this life.[38] This is only a suggestive mention of a mysterious life phenomenon, rather than a direct mention of illness. If we look at Ecclesiastes 15:13-6:2, Qoheleth speaks about the fundamental nature of illness in a figurative sense. While he attributes illness to God's own action, he remarks that illness is a disturbance in life, which is difficult to comprehend. This suggests that illness could be an instrument to disclose unknown divine purpose and God does not necessarily work on the basis of the principle of behaviour consequence like a mathematical formula.

[34] Brown, *Israel's Divine Healer*, 166.

[35] Ibid.

[36] Seybold and Muller, *Sickness and Healing*, 60.

[37] Avalos, *Illness and Health Care in Ancient Near East*, 374.

[38] Cf. Ecclesiastes 7:15, "In my vain life I have seen everything; there are righteous people who perish in their righteousness, and there are wicked people who prolong their life in their evil doing."

1.1.3. Supernatural Beings as Source of Illness

There are other explanations of illness. It probably caused by supernatural beings such as evil spirits, angels, the Satan or demons. In the Old Testament, they for the most part seem to cause illness at the command of Yahweh. However, in rare cases they act on their own volition, although there is no doubt that they are ultimately under Yahweh's mastery.

In the account of King Saul in 1 Samuel 16:14-18 an evil spirit sent by Yahweh afflicted Saul from time to time. Saul probably suffered "from depression or melancholy, or any case, from some spiritual illness."[39] His illness is obviously connected with disobedience to the command of Yahweh, which resulted in his being rejected as king of Israel (1 Sam. 15-16). While the evil spirit is responsible for Saul's illness, which stems from his sin, the evil spirit appears to be under God's control.

An angel, another supernatural being in the Old Testament, is also involved in causing illness, though this creature certainly acts in accordance with Yahweh's commands. In the account of the census and pestilence in 2 Samuel 24, David orders a census to be taken and it finally leads to causing divine anger and the death of large numbers of people. An 'angel of Yahweh' (מלאד יהוה)[40] takes orders from Yahweh and performs his task of slaughtering all the people by sending a plague (2 Sam. 24:16; 1 Chro. 21:16, 30). This account shows that an 'angel of Yahweh', as a divine assistant, executes judgment against David's sin by means of illness. On the other hand, there appears in the same story such expressions as 'the angel who was bringing destruction' (ה מלאד ה משחית [2 Sam. 24:16]), and 'the angel of the Lord destroying' (מלאד יהוה משחית [1 Chro. 21:12]), which are indicative of מלאד יהוה. These expressions refer to the angel's engaging in mass slaughter, just as the 'destroyer' performed, "the task of destroying large numbers of people, typically by means of plague."[41] Given this notion, it is very likely that

---

[39] Seybold and Muller, *Sickness and Healing*, 74.

[40] מלאדיהוה in Hebrew. The NRSV translates it as "the angel of the Lord." S. A. Meier points out a problem that comes out when this translation is employed: "Is this figure a unique envoy who is always sent by God, or can a number of different supernatural beings be dispatched as 'the angel of Yahweh'?" Bringing out several reasons, he suggests that the term be translated as indefinite, "an angel of the Lord", when it first appears in a narrative. Of the reasons he mentions, what is most appealing is that parallel passages within the MT simply signify an angel: 2 Chro. 32:21 rephrases the "angel of Yahweh" of 2 Kings 19:35 to read simply "an angel" (cf. 1 Kgs. 19:5-7; 1 Chro. 21:15-16). In addition, there are a few other reasons: (1) The Septuagint generally translates the phrase in the Old Testament as "an angel of the Lord", although there are a few exceptional cases (Num. 22:23; 2 Sam. 245:16). (2) Not all construct phrases with a proper name are to be constructed as definite. (3) Extra-biblical Jewish literature presents the "angel of Yahweh" as a designation applicable to any number of different angels. S. A. Meier, "Angels and Demons," in *Dictionary of Deities and Demons in the Bible*, ed. K. van der Toorn, B. Becking, and P. W. van der Horst (Leiden: Brill, 1995), 54-55.

[41] Ibid., 240.

the means by which the destroyer killed the Egyptian first-born was a plague, even if no obvious mention of the means is made. From the foregoing, one may speculate that the destroyer also uses illness in order to punish sins, although he acts at the specific command of Yahweh.

The image of another supernatural being (Satan) causing illness at the command of Yahweh is observed in Job 2. The Satan was seeking to move Yahweh to afflict Job with illness. He urged Yahweh, "But stretch out your hand now and touch his bone and his flesh..." (v. 5). There is no reason to doubt that the Satan here proposes the physical affliction of illness. Then Yahweh answered: "very well, he is in your power; only spare his life" (v.6). The Satan is allowed to smite Job with illness, short of killing. This shows that the Satan is subject to Yahweh's power, although the Satan challenges Yahweh at the very profound level.[42] Like the supernatural beings, Satan cannot act without Yahweh's authorization.

In Psalm 91, illness is attributed to demons. Although 'there are certain ambiguities that make it especially difficult to ascertain the background to this psalm,"[43] there appear various expressions that might be suggestive to demonic activities, which are often associated with illness. For instance, after 'the terror of the night' (פחד לילה v.5) 'the narrow that flies by day' (v.5) and 'the pestilence that stalks in darkness' (v.6) are enumerated. The 'terror of the night' in consideration of its traits is alluded to the Mesopotamian night-demon Lilû and Ardatlilî, more likely in its occurrence in Song of Solomon 3:8. These demons are known as harmful to the newly weds, whom they attack on their wedding night to prevent the consummation of the marriage.[44] M. Dahood holds that the 'arrow' in v.5 could be related to *resheph*[45] on the condition that it is read anticipating the 'pestilence' in v.6a.[46] The Babylon pest-demon, Namtar, has been suggested for the 'pestilence' in v.6a.[47] Moreover, noteworthy are the verbs 'to stalk' (v.6), 'to waste' (v.6), 'to draw' (v.7) and 'approach' (v.10), all of which are commonly perceived as associated with activities of demons.[48]

---

[42] Day L. Peggy and C. Breytenbach, "Satan," in *Dictionary of Deities and Demons in the Bible*, ed. K. Van der Toorn, B. Becking, and P. W. Van der Horst (Grand Rapids, Michigan: William B. Eerdmans Publishing Company, 1995), 728.

[43] Brown, *Israel's Divine Healer*, 152.

[44] M. Malul, *The Comparative Method in Ancient near Eastern and Biblical Legal Studies* (Kevelaer: Butzon & Bercker, 1990), 852-854.

[45] *Reseph* occurs as *ršp* in Ugaritic, Phoenician, and Aramaic, and is conceived of as one of the most popular West-Semitic gods. In the Old Testament *Reseph* is demonized and generally considered as bringing pestilence at the service of Yahweh (Deut. 32:24; Ps. 78:48).

[46] Mitchell Dahood, *Psalms II: 51-100* (Garden City, NY: Doubleday & Company, 1968), 852-854.

[47] A. A. Anderson, *The Book of Psalms (73-150)*, vol. 2 (Grand Rapids: William B. Eerdmans Publishing Company, 1972), 657.

[48] M. Malul, "Terror of the Night," in *Dictionary of Deities and Demons in the Bible*, ed. van der Toorn, B. Becking, and P. W. van der Horst (Leiden: Brill, 1999), 852.

No specific command from Yahweh is given to demons with respect to illness. This suggests that an understanding of demons as causing illness of their own accord began to develop, even if it is not disputed that they are ultimately under Yahweh's control. Indeed, such a demonological view of illness is hardly prominent in the Old Testament.[49] The demonological view of illness increasingly appears later in the Inter-Testamental literature (Jubilees 10:1-2; Tobit 3:8). In the Testament of Solomon 18, which may have been composed as early as the first century B.C.E., the view goes so far as to become systematized, assigning specific demons to the individual illness of which they are thought to be the cause.[50]

It is worthy to note that Psalm 91 has no connection with sin and illness. The psalmist presupposes that even the faithful one who trusts Yahweh is vulnerable to demonic attack, which brings about life-threatening or debilitating illnesses. This indicates that even one who has done no wrong might be afflicted with illness.

1.1.4. Illness as Natural

A few illnesses in the Old Testament might be described, which ascribes their origin to neutral and naturalistic causes. A couple of factors supports this observation. Firstly, certain Old Testament references to illness do not give any indication of the origin of illness in question. Secondly, they make no explicit mention of sin.[51] The account of the healing of Naaman (2 Kgs. 5) also refers to neither the origin of Naaman's leprosy nor sin. Thus, it would be reasonable to say that illness may be called neutral or natural in terms of origin.[52] Yet we should also note that the mention of the natural cause of illness meant absolute exclusion of a supernatural origin. It is highly probable that natural and supernatural causes are intertwined in the mind-set of the average patient in the ancient society. While illness could arise from sin or a divine mysterious motive, it was suggestive of a broken relationship

---

[49] Seybold and Muller, *Sickness and Healing*, 112.

[50] Seong-Hyuk Hong, *The Metaphor of Illness and Healing in Hosea and its Significance in the Socio-Economic Context of Eight-Century Israel and Judah* (Bern Frankfurt am Main: Peter Lang, 2006), 68.

[51] For instance, in the story about Elisha and the Shunamite woman (2 Kgs. 4:8-37), her son, who was bestowed on her in appreciation for the hospitality shown to Elisha, grows up, becomes sick, and eventually dies on her lap without any particular reason noted. There is no explicit statement as to whether the illness came from either Yahweh or supernatural beings. Besides, there is no mention of sin.

[52] Whether natural or supernatural, illness in ancient Israel occurred due to attacks from Yahweh as well as supernatural agents such as angels, evil spirits, demons and the Satan, which were at the service of Yahweh. However, the reasons may be for the cause of illness, in its broadest terms, it refers to the condition of a relationship with Yahweh. If illness stems from sin, it represents a disturbed relationship with Yahweh. If it is rooted in a certain divine plan, it serves as an instrument or message to strengthen the healthy relationship with Yahweh. Although illness may have brought to the mind of the patient a certain problem in the relationship with God, i.e., sin, it may lead to severing the relationship with even his fellow beings.

with Yahweh. Therefore, the patient in ancient Israel was aware of the relationship with Yahweh as a factor crucial to his health and life.

1.2. The Social Situation of the Patient

Whether illness was caused by sin, by divine mysterious motive or naturally, in its broadest terms, it refers to the condition of a relationship with Yahweh. If illness stems from sin, it represents a disturbed relationship with Yahweh. If it is rooted in a certain divine plan, it serves as an instrument or message to strengthen the healthy relationship with Yahweh. Although, illness may have brought to the mind of the patient a certain problem in the relationship with God, i.e., sin, it may lead to severing the relationship with even his/her fellow beings.

Illness in Israel was not just physical problem, but an indication of a disturbed relationship with God, reminding the patient and his/her neighbours of his/her sin. Accordingly, the attitude of the community toward the patient was so negative that a person was excluded from the community life in general. Job 19:13-19 depicts vividly the deplorable social situation in which the patient found himself,

> He has put my family far from me, and my acquaintances are wholly estranged from me. My relatives and my close friends have failed me; the guests in my house have forgotten me; my serving girls count me as stranger; I have become an alien in their eyes. I call to my servant, but he gives me no answer; I must myself plead with him. My breath is repulsive to my wife; I am loathsome to my own family. Even young children despise me; when I rise, they talk against me. All my intimate friends abhor me, and those whom I loved have turned against me (Job 19:13-19).

The text shows vividly the social consequences that illness has brought on the sick person (cf. Ps. 38:11; Num. 12:9-15). Illness has resulted in the patient's isolation from his/her family as well as friends, beyond that from the community. Even more, illness has incurred the patient's exclusion from the temple cult (Lev. 12:4; 13:45-46; 15:31; cf. 2 Chro. 26:21), which has represented the disturbed relationship with God. However, we must not conclude too quickly that all illnesses might lead a patient to being excluded from the temple cult; except for someone suffering with unclean, infectious diseases, there is no obvious indication that a patient was precluded from participation in the temple cult.[53]

Infectious illnesses like leprosy rendered the patient unfit to participate in the temple cult; the person was regarded as impure. This notion raises a question. Why those with infectious illnesses were not allowed to participate in the temple cult? It may be that its punitive nature or fear of contagion caused lepers to be

---

[53] Brown, *Israel's Divine Healer*, 132.

labelled as impure. However, divine punishment or fear of contagion alone does not explain why these illnesses were deemed unacceptable to the temple. Though the blind and the lame were not usually perceived as having contagious illnesses, they were excluded from the temple.[54] Why? Because, it was simply felt that they had, been punished by God? Avalos thinks that there might be some other reason involved. As it is indicated in Leviticus 13-15, priestly groups are supposed to determine purity or impurity based on diagnostic examination of suspected leprosy. However, the focus of their decision was not on therapy, but on expulsion of the patient from the temple.[55]

There seems to be a strong socio-political and socio-economic motive for the exclusion of the person with illness by the priestly group from the temple.[56] The socio-political intention is associated with expressing status difference according to gradations in access to the temple, in particular in the wake of the exile. In addition, the degree of access to the temple was directly linked to the degree of purity. Social status was the principal determination in the degree of access to the temple and the degree of purity as well.[57] On the other hand, the socio-economic motives were involved in the exclusion of the patient from the temple. The priestly class evaluated persons by their economic worth (Lev. 27:1-8) and their productivity, particularly when they assigned a degree of purity to them. Since the ill people were less productive in the society, they were assigned the lowest status and thus impurity, leading to excluding them from the temple and further from the community. Avalos writes, "The idea that they could contaminate others and the temple itself simply added to the notion that they were a burden, and danger."[58] In other words, the patients were excluded from the temple and community, since they were nothing but a burden in a socio-economic sense.

Taken as a whole, the social situation of the patient in the Old Testament times was lamentable. People must have experienced considerable human distress deriving from exclusion from the temple cult and isolation from the community as well as the physical suffering itself. The traditional thought of illness as God's punishment for past sins most likely induced one into condemning the patients without considering divine purpose in their suffering. The attitude of the community toward the patient was certainly influenced, for the most part, by the

[54] Avalos, *Illness and Health Care in the Ancient Near East: The Role of the Temple in Greece, Mesopotamia, and Israel*, 319-320.

[55] Ibid., 365.

[56] Ibid., 377-391.

[57] In the post-Exilic Israelite society, Aaronite (or Zadokite) priests, who controlled the temple and assigned the degree of purity, were allowed themselves access to the inside of the temple building and next in status came the Levites, who in the wake of the Exile, became temple servants who were not allowed to enter into the temple building itself. Below the Levites in status were healthy Israelites who were allowed only to enter the courtyard. Ibid., 383-384.

[58] Ibid., 388.

dominant religious ideology with its law of behaviour. Consequently, throughout the entire history of ancient Israel, and furthermore by the interests of the priestly class who controlled the assignment of the degrees of purity in Israelite society in the post-exilic period, the people with illness were looked down with social domain.

Although the presence of disease is believed to have been caused by demons,[59] the Israelites believed that everything, both good and evil, sickness and health, ultimately proceeded from the almighty God. However, much of the attempt was to bring the people of Israel to a worship of Yahweh alone, who was seen as the sole source of both good and evil, of sickness as well as health. Sickness, therefore, was based on spiritual causes; this made it unnecessary for the Israelites to revert to magic or to incantations; rather, sickness confronted them directly with Yahweh and with the condition of their relationship to their God. This did not mean that the righteous people always enjoyed perfect health, while the evil ones were condemned to perpetual sickness; it did emphasize, however, the ancient Hebrews' strong belief that affliction of the body was not primarily a physical, or an organic matter, but instead depended largely on the moral and spiritual state of the person.[60] Therefore, sicknesses and diseases are to be understood as God's way of restoring not only the physical aspect but also even the spiritual aspect of life i.e., wholistic life. Outward purity and inward righteousness were united in the laws of purity and holiness.[61] To retain the connection between sickness and sin, will avoid a therapeutic solution to the problems of the world.

In view of the link between health and disobedience, disease or ill health is not so much a question of punishment from God, but more the case of unavoidable consequences, which humans may bring upon themselves through disobedience - which signifies a disrupted relationship with God. In this vein, it may be more appropriate to suggest that health is not equated with holiness as, but rather that physical wholeness, is a result of holiness.

Summary

Illness in the Old Testament thus connotes both the social and physical factors. When one is ill then it affects the whole social life of the person who is ill. The essence of life in the Old Testament is looked from the way an individual keeps his/her relationship with God. The understanding of illness in terms of personalistic etiology had a negative impact on the social situation of the patients. At the

[59] The belief was common among most peoples at the time of the early Hebrews. Both the Egyptians and the Babylonians held that sickness resulted from demonic ill will of various goods or evil spirits. The Persians with their well-developed dualism looked on disease or to the demon who caused it, so closely are the two related. Kelsey, *Healing and Christianity in Ancient Thought and Modern Times*, 38.

[60] Carter, "A Biblical Vision of Wholeness," 61.

[61] Ross, *Holiness to the Lord: A Guide to the Exposition of the Book of Leviticus*, 56.

outbreak of illness, the patients were deemed as receiving divine punishment for their sin, although the cause of illness is not always the case. This view added socio-religious stigma to their suffering and gave them as isolated position in society. The patients were excluded from their family and friends, the temple and further the community. Sicknesses and diseases are to be understood in the Old Testament as God's way of restoring not only the physical aspect but also even the spiritual aspect of life i.e., wholistic life.

Chapter 2

Health in Old Testament with Special Reference to *Rapha, Arukah, Shalom and Marpe* Its Meanings and Definitions

Introduction

The present study will deal with the understanding of *Rapha, Arukah, Shalom and Marpe* in the Old Testament. The study will also help us to see and understand how these concepts are intertwined with each other and how the concepts have different faced of interpretations in the light of health and healing in the Old Testament.

The Old Testament puts great emphasis on health, and does not rely on divine intervention for medical cures. The effects of Jewish culture on illness and health have developed a unique ethnically distinct 'illness behaviour.'[1] John Wilkinson rightly states,

> The Old Testament sets out that perfect pattern and high quality of life which is health, and which was God's intention that human beings should enjoy. They were created in the image of God and, therefore, were healthy as He was healthy. They were intended to continue to live in health, which would be maintained by their constant enjoyment of his presence and their obedience of his will as revealed in his laws and commandments. This is why we are constantly reminded in the Old Testament of God's presence with, and concern for, his people.[2]

---

[1] Dale Dobin Oller, "Jewish Genetic Diseases and Jewish Illness Behavior: A Review of Selected Sociocultural Literature," *Jewish Social Studies* 6, no. 2 (1984): 77.

[2] John Wilkinson, *The Bible and Healing: A Medical and Theological Commentary* (Edinburgh: The Handsel Press Ltd., 1998), 7.

This means that in general the Old Testament has more to say about health. However, the people of Israel found their relationship to God was a demanding one, if they were to continue enjoying good health. Such a relationship demanded obedience. On the contrary, disobedience produced disease and disturbed their relationship with God and with one another. The means of healing or restoration of these relationships was provided by institution of sacrifices and the occasional direct healing of disease, but something more generally effective and more permanent was required.[3]

Wilkinson therefore opines,

> The nature of well being is implied in the characteristics of human beings and derives its identity from the human constitution and the human relationship with God. This well-being is holistic for it affects the whole of human being. If the desire of well-being is confined to the body then the result is likely to be not health, but ill health resulting from a 'healthism' in which the health of the body is regarded as a desirable end in itself. On the other hand if the desire is confined to the soul or spirit this too will lead to ill-health from neglect of the body. Thus, the nature of well being is that wholeness of being and uprightness of character which are related to Old Testament calls 'holiness.'[4]

In order to understand the prophetic concept of health and healing, it is imperative for us first to unearth the understanding of *Rapha, Arukah, Shalom and Marpe* in the Old Testament.

2.1. *Rapha*: Lexical and Etymological Discussions in the Old Testament

A number of different words are translated as 'healing' in the Old Testament. Most of them contain the idea of the restoration of something to its previously normal state, or the removal of something, which is causing ill-health or an abnormal condition. When we come to examine the concept of healing, we find that there is one root word רפא that is which M. L. Brown describes as 'central to the Old Testament language of healing.'[5]

This root is 'central' to the Old Testament language of healing רָפָא occurring 67 times in verbal conjugation (38 Qal, 17 niphal. 9 piel, 3 hitpael) and 19 times in derived nominal forms (*marpe* 14). The total occurrences by individual books are as follows:

---

[3] Ibid., 8.

[4] Wilkinson, *The Bible and Healing: A Medical and Theological Commentary*, 17.

[5] M. L. Brown, *I am the Lord Your Healer: A Philological Study of the Root rapha in the Hebrew Bible and the Ancient Near East* (New York: New York University, 1985), 25.

13 times in Jeremiah; 7 times each in Psalm and Isaiah; 6 times in 2 Kings; 5 times in Hosea; 4 times each in 2 Chronicles, Leviticus, Ezekiel; 3 times each in Exodus, Genesis, Deuteronomy; 2 times in Job; once each in Ecclesiastes, Lamentations, 1 Samuel, Zechariah, 1 Kings. In nominal forms, מַרְפֵּא (or, sometimes מַרְפֵּא) occurs 16 times: 8 times in Proverbs; 4 times in Jeremiah; 2 times in 2 Chronicles; once each in Ecclesiastes and Malachi. רְפֻאָה (always רפאות) occurs 3 times: 2 times in Jeremiah; once in Ezekiel; תְּרוּפָה] occurs once (Ezek. 47:12; and cf. Ben Sira 38:4); רִפְאוּת occurs once (Pro. 3:8).

Outside of the Old Testament, *rapha* is attested in Amorite, El Amarna Akkadian, Aramaic. Ugaritic, Phoenician-Punic, Old South Arabian, Arabic and Ethiopic, although in some of these languages, the evidence is meager.[6] Scholars have generally posited: (1) a root meaning for *rapha* in Proto-Semitic of "to bring together, draw near" and (2) a fundamental meaning for *rapha* in Hebrew of "to heal" (i.e., physical illness and disease). However, according to Brown, the suggested root meaning for both Proto-Semitic and Hebrew are questionable and have themselves led to questionable renderings.[7]

The standard lexicon of Brown, Driver, and Briggs begins its entry on *rapha* with the Qal meaning of "heal:" Firstly, literally citing instances of physical healings in the Bible. The second meaning of "be healed of national hurts"[8] follows.

The fundamental meaning of Heb. רפא is to restore, to make whole. Specific nuances include: (a) repair or fix; (cf. Jer. 19:11 cf. also 1 Kgs. 18:30): (b) make fresh, wholesome, pertaining to deadly salt water (c) mend (but never sew, stitch) (cf. Ps 60:2 [4], (d) most commonly, heal, in terms of physical disease or wounds. In the *Torah*,[9] the historical books,[10] and the wisdom literature,[11] the concept of *rapha* is used most commonly, in terms of physical disease or wounds from sickness.

A survey of the references in Old Testament where the term *rapha* appears indicates two or perhaps three semantic ranges for its meaning. Physical healing is explicitly meant in at least a dozen texts as in its first appearance in Genesis 20:17

---

6 Ibid., 97-160.

7 Michael L. Brown, *Israel's Divine Healer* (Grand Rapids, Michigan: Zondervan, 1995), 25.

8 K. Beach, *Preaching from the Types and Metaphors of the Bible* (Grand Rapids, Michigan: Kregel, 1981), 161.

9 Gen. 20:17; cf. also 12:17; Exo. 15:26; 23:25-26; Deut. 7:12-15, Deut. 28:27, 35. Miriam's צָרַעַת, Num. 12:10.

10 2 Chro. 36:16, Hezekiah's boil (שחין) , 2 Kgs. 20:8; Jehoram's wounds, 2 Kgs. 8:29 [2 Chro. 22:6]; In Lev. 13-14, the niphal of (וְנִרְפָּא) רָפָא is used 4 times with נֶגַע־הַצָּרַעַת as the subject, 3 times with reference to humans (13:18, 37; 14:3) and once with reference to houses (14:48), suggesting that remit may serve as a more appropriate and uniform rendering here than heal, cure.

11 Ps. 103:3; 147:3); Prov. 29:1,

where God healed Abimelech.[12] It is also used metaphorically to mean restoration to wholeness or wellness. This may refer to water becoming not salty or poisonous as in 2 Kings 2:21-22 and Ezekiel 47:8-11. This meaning could however be viewed as merely a subset of that indicated by the metaphorical understanding of restoration to wholeness.

A careful analysis of the biblical material indicates that in every instance *rapha* is used with reference to restoring a wrong, sick, broken, or deficient condition to its original and proper state.[13] Consequently, 'restore,' 'make whole,' not 'heal,' should be recognized as the common semantic denominator of Biblical Hebrew *rapha*, and should list 'heal' as the first subheading, beginning their entries with the general definition of "restore, make whole."[14] All the semantic streams is attested in one or flow freely from this one source: the word repair is used as 'healing' of a sick body (2 Kgs. 20:5), the 'repairing' of a broken down altar (1 Kgs. 18:30), the 'restoration' of a drought-stricken and locust eaten land (2 Chro. 7:14), the 'making wholesome' of undrinkable waters (2 Kgs. 2:21-22), the 'mending' of the earth's fissures (Ps. 60:4), the 'fixing' of a mildew infected house (Lev. 14:48).[15] While it is possible that 2 Chronicles 7:14 pictures the drought-stricken and locust-ravaged land as sickly (cf. Deut. 29:22) and hence in need of healing. The broader meaning of 'restore' is correct here (accordingly render: "then will I hear from heaven and forgive their sin and restore their land)."

Accordingly, the general term for healing, רפא describes the act of restoring someone or something to a normal or physical state in the society. The root is common in West Semitic languages, but not in Akkadian, which principally uses as *bullutu* as an equivalent. The term is applied to those healed from infertility (e.g., Gen. 20:17), to someone who recuperates from physical assault (e.g., Exod. 21:19). All these acts call for healing of either the individual or the community

---

[12] God heals Abimelech and his household, all of whom had been smitten with infertility (Gen. 20:17; cf. also 12:17). This usage, however, does not indicate that רָפָא includes the nuance of "re-fertilizing," as some scholars have argued; rather, barrenness, impotency, and infertility were perceived as maladies that needed to be healed (or as defective conditions that needed to be made whole). This is in keeping with the covenantal understanding that equated health and fertility with divine blessing (Exod. 15:26; 23:25-26; Deut. 7:12-15) and sickness and infertility with divine curses (see especially Deut. 28:27, 35, which threaten incurable diseases as a consequence of covenantal breach, since God, Israel's Healer, was rejected, a theme common in the Ancient West Asia; cf. also לְאֵי מַרְפֵּא ו אֵי מַרְפֵּא, without remedy, with reference to the nation [2 Chron. 36:16] or individuals [e.g., Pro. 29:1] whose recalcitrance has resulted in a condition of judgment that is beyond cure).

[13] W. E. Vine, M. F. Unger, and W. White Jr., *An Expository Dictionary of the Biblical Words* (New York: Thomas Nelson, 1985), 175.

[14] Brown, *Israel's Divine Healer*, 29.

[15] M. C. A. Kropel, *A Rift in the Clouds: Ugaritic and Hebrew Descriptions of the Divine* (Munster: Ugarit-Verlag, 1990), 334.

at large. The call for healing is not merely for physical disease. The condition is primarily moral.[16]

Healing of the moral violation, the rebellion represented by the murmuring is the pre-requisite for the healing of the physical violation. Restoration of intimacy, return to peace that effects relationships between a person and God, nature, and fellow persons cannot be established automatically or by rituals but all these characteristics calls for obedience. Violations of the integrity of the community undercut the operation of intimacy in the ritual. However, the ritual of intimacy brings strength, health, indeed, life that provides for the integrity of the individual within the community.

One would ask the question whether every exercise of searching for a root's original or fundamental meaning is the real cause of both linguistic and interpretative errors. The writings of J. Barr and others on semantics have exposed what is called the 'root fallacy,'[17] which means that the pseudo-linguistic practice of imposing an alleged fundamental meaning of a root on all its varied conjugations and derivations.

In the case of *rapha* in the Old Testament, this has produced infelicitous renderings such as 'stitchers of lies' in Job 13:4b. It should also be pointed out that the South Semitic evidence itself can be utilized to argue against the likelihood that a *Rophe* was so called because he 'mended' and 'stitched together' the human body, since *Rophe* was never used with regard to physical healing in classical Arabic, nor did it become the primary root for 'heal,' 'healer.'[18]

Scholars are virtually unanimous in their understanding that Hebrew *rapha* fundamentally means 'to heal,' tracing virtually all other semantic derivations back to this common Old Testament sense. According to Brown,

> This has produced: (1) forced translations (e.g. 2 Ch. 7:14: "I will heal their land;" "I have healed these waters);" (2) an exaggerated dichotomy between 'literal' healing (i.e., of physical illness) and 'figurative' healing (i.e., "the hurts of a nation" as if individual healing were "literal and national healing 'figurative'); contributing to (3) a tendency to read the prophetic, often metaphorical usage, of *rapha* in overly spiritualized terms.[19]

---

[16] In the wilderness, the people rebel against God. That violation brings on the attack by fiery serpents. Healing with the bronze serpent brings not only recovery from physical agony that can lead to death but also recovery from the moral violation represented by the murmuring of the people.

[17] James Barr, *The Semantics of Biblical Language* (Oxford: Oxford University Press, 1961), 100-106, 114-116.

[18] Brown, *Israel's Divine Healer*, 27.

[19] Ibid., 65.

Robert Gordis points out that this provides for several basic insights, also improving on the traditional etymological understanding.[20] Such an understanding proceeds from a meaning that can easily be posited as the common denominator of all other attested meanings.

Several texts that casually allude to medical practices and treatments indicate that the healings were normal and, from a religious standpoint, neutral during the time of the Old Testament. In Ezekiel 30:21, we see that binding up a broken bone would promote healing. Thus, healing was viewed as a natural process. In Ezekiel 34:4; Zechariah 11:16 the literal imagery behind these prophetic metaphors, which is that of a shepherd calling for his sheep can be seen. Here, as a rule, shepherds were expected to take care of the basic medical needs of the flock: strengthening the weak, treating the sick, binding up the injured.

Much of the healing, which occurred in Israel must have come about by the operation of the natural and defensive processes of the body and mind, and the practices of folk-medicine based on these processes. In addition, however, there are references in the Old Testament to healing mediated, by God, through the physicians and by the prophets.

2.1.1. Yahweh as *Rophe*

God is consistently referred to in the Old Testament as *Jehovah Rapha*, "the God who heals." The Hebrew word *rapha* and its derivatives occur 86 times in the Old Testament. It means to restore a wrong, sick, broken or deficient condition to its original and proper state. The verse, which is the foundation of the Old Testament theology of healing, begins in Exodus 15:26. Karl Barth called 'the divine Magna Carta in all matters of health and all related questions.'[21]

The recognition that *rapha* fundamentally means 'restore,' 'make whole,' provides insight into ancient Israel's understanding of the Lord as *Rophe*, as well as into their concepts of 'wholeness,' since one and the same root was used for the 'healing/making whole/ restoring' of body and spirit, land and water, city and nation. The Lord as *Rophe* could be supplicated to make infertile wombs fruitful, mend earthquake-torn lands, make poisonous water wholesome, or restore an apostate people.

While it is true that regardless of a word's etymological and semantic development, it still has but one meaning in any given context. It is also true that the culminative evidence of a word's usage must be taken into consideration. In this case, the fact that God revealed himself as *Rophe* cannot be separated from the wide range of broken/sickly/deficient objects that he was expected to *rapha*. Thus, Exodus 15:26, which is best rendered as "I am the Lord your healer" fits naturally in a context that recounts that (a) the Lord is making undrinkable

[20] Robert Gordis, "Studies in Hebrew Roots of Contrasted Meanings," *Journal of Quarterly Review* 27 (1936): 55-56.

[21] Karl Barth, *Church Dogmatics*, vol. 3 (Edinburgh: T & T Clark, 1961), 369.

waters wholesome, and (b) his promise to keep obedient Israel free of all the 'sickness' he inflicted on Egypt. Clearly, Yahweh was more than Israel's 'Great Physician.' Rather, Yahweh was the Restorer, the One who made them whole. Klaus Seybold and Ulrich B. Mueller, state that, "the Lord your Healer" conveys a wider range of meanings than do the terms physician, doctor, or medicine.[22] Klaus Seybold and Ulrich B. Mueller continue to stress that; "either physical or spiritual" dichotomy often seen in comments in Old Testament verses with *rapha* is extremely faulty.[23] Consequently, Brown concludes that, "in fact, regardless of one's understanding of the etymological origin of Semitic *rapha*, Old Testament usage insists that references to the Lord as Israel's *Rophe* be taken in the broadest possible sense."[24] Thus, *Jehovah Rapha* portrays God as the one to whom appeal and prayer are made for the restoration of a wide variety of things that are broken, sick, or deficient.

2.1.2. רפיא *(Rophe)* by the Physicians

Physicians are not prominent in the Old Testament. Their existence is acknowledged or implied, and their activity and worth are not denied. This is in marked contrast to what we know of physicians and their status and practice in Egypt and Mesopotamia. In Israel, physicians are much more prominent in Post-Biblical times. The Hebrew name for a physician is *Rophe* (רפיא) which comes from the root *rapha*, 'to restore'. The Rabbis found the specific mandate for the practice of healing by physicians in the interpretation of Exodus 21:19. The texts refer to a person who has been wounded in quarrel with another and has to take to his bed until he is thoroughly healed and is able to return to work. This indicates that in Israel, as in neighboring nations, there were acceptable, customary, religiously neutral medical practices. What is important about this text is that it mandates medical treatment. The phrase "shall take care of him until he is completely healed" implies payment for the injured human's medical expenses and taking steps to ensure, he receives proper treatment. It also indicates the obligation of a person suffering from a wound or a disease to seek treatment, and the divine authority for the physician to provide treatment.

Another important text that needs special attention is 2 Chronicles 16:12. This text has often been interpreted as an indictment of human physicians and/or medical treatment. In fact, it has little of anything to do with the issue of divine healing versus human healing. Rather, it deals with the issue of trusting in God versus trusting in the flesh. Clearly, under the old covenant, obedience to God's laws ensures good health. Thus, the qal of רפא (רפיא) is used for human physicians (e.g., 2 Chro. 16:12; in Gen. 50:2). It is used for the Egyptian physicians who

[22] Klaus Seybold and Ulrich B. Mueller, *Sickness and Healing* (Nashville: Abingdon Press, 1978), 65-66.

[23] H. Hanegraaff, *Christianity in Crisis* (Eugene, Ore: Harvest House, 1993), 249-250.

[24] Brown, *Israel's Divine Healer*, 30.

embalmed Jacob as well as for the Lord as Israel's Healer (Exod. 15:26; Ps. 103:3; 147:3). In their comments on human physicians, J. M. Myers and Hasel suggest that the physicians were probably foreign priest physicians who mixed medical art with magic.[25] Given the fact that most physicians in Ancient West Asia were sponsored by a deity, it is very likely that Asa consulted physicians sponsored by Yahweh.[26] Even if Asa consulted a prophet sponsored by Yahweh, it would not be reckoned as a satisfactory option without primarily calling upon Yahweh. In short, while Yahweh is the supreme physician, human physician, in particular foreign physicians were considered to be strictly negative in the Old Testament. It is significant to note that after the collapse of the prophetic office in the early second temple period, human physicians appeared widely in Israel as legitimate consultants.

2.1.3. רפיא by the Prophets

There are some references to the involvement of prophets in healing either by way of giving advice or by carrying out healing procedures. Examples of *Rophe* רפיא, which follows prophetic advice, include Elisha's advice to Naaman in 2 Kings 5:1-14, 2 Kings 20:7. Sometimes this advice included the giving of a prognosis in a particular disease or situations (2 Sam. 12:14-23; 1 Kgs. 14:12-13; 2 Kgs. 1:1-4, 16-17). All these prognosis were given verbally, but on one occasion a prognosis was sent by letter when the prophet Elijah wrote a letter to King Jehoram of Judah foretelling the occurrence of the plague or slaughter which would come upon his people and the bowel illness which would afflict the king himself (2 Chro. 21:12-15).The knowledge that the prophets of Israel were skilled in the prognosis and treatment of disease appears to have spread beyond the borders of that land (2 Kgs. 8:7-15). In all these healing activity, the prophets insist that all healing comes from God and that they are only his agents. They look forward to a future time of restoration when none in Zion shall be able to say that they are sick and there will be none whose sins have not been forgiven.

2.2. ארכה (*Arukah*): Its Meanings and Definitions

Most of the other words used for healing in the Old Testament are used only infrequently, and do not add much to the concept of healing found there. However, there are one or two interesting words, which should be mentioned. The word *arukah* means 'to be long', usually referring to time.[27] However, it is also used for healing in the prophetic texts. Thus, ארכה, means healing, restoration, which is

[25] Gerard F. Hasel, "Health and Healing in the Old Testament," *Andrews University Seminary Studies* 21 (1983); Jacob M. Myers, *II Chronicles* (Garden City, New York: Doubleday, 1965), 95.

[26] Hector Avalos, *Illness and Health Care in the Ancient Near East: The Role of the Temple in Greece, Mesopotamia, and Israel* (Atlanta, Georgia: Scholars Press, 1995), 292.

[27] F. Brown, S. Driver, and C. Briggs, "'arûkâ," in *The Brown- Driver-Briggs Hebrew and English Lexicon* (Peabody, Massachusetts: Hendrickson Publishers, 2005), 73.

in the form of feminine passive participle of '*arak*' (in the sense of restoring to soundness); wholeness (literally or figuratively) - health, made up, perfected. It is one word, which is translated as health, which means health, wholeness, or perfect. Thus, *Arukah* is the transliteration of a Hebrew word meaning "wholeness."

According to BDB, *Arukah* means, "healing of a wound," "restoration (properly the new flesh that grows at the wounded spot)," with reference to Arabic *arika.*[28] *Arukah* is also used three times in Jeremiah 8:22; 30:17; 33:6, in the same figurative sense, which literally means, "repairing or restoring." It is used always with אעלה, and contextually coupled with *rapha* and once in Isaiah (58:8), always as a prophetic metaphor.[29] *Arukah* is also used figuratively for rebuilding of Jerusalem's walls by Nehemiah (Neh. 4:1) and the repairing of the temple (2 Chro. 24:13). Related to the concept of אעלה ארכה is "healing, or new skin," [30] which means the new skin that rises on the wound.

The connection of *arukah* with healing may be because *arukah* denotes the 'proud flesh' or granulation tissue, which covers the surface of an open wound during the process of healing.[31] The appearance of this tissue means that wound will take much longer time to heal than a narrow incised wound, and this fact may explain the application of this word to healing.

All these words presuppose a state of ill-health and may also be used figuratively for the restoration of Israel to God's favour after a period of declension. While these words are usually used to describe healing, they are also used occasionally for the health, which is the result of healing.

2.3. שׁלום (*Shalom*): Its Meanings and Definitions

The Hebrew word which expresses the fullness and well-being of life, and which comes to the nearest expression of health is the word שׁלום. This word occurs about 250 times in the Hebrew Bible. It is most frequent in the prophetical books of Jeremiah (thirty one) and Isaiah (twenty seven time), and in the Psalms (twenty seven times). The word *shalom* connotes more than one meaning:

a). In a material or secular sense שׁלום designates well-being, prosperity, or bodily health (e.g., Gen. 29:6; 43:27; Ps. 38:3; Isa. 57:18). It also expresses the state of mind or internal condition of being at ease, satisfied, or fulfilled. In such instances it is sometimes accompanied by the vbs. "go" or "come" (Gen. 26:29; Exod. 18:23); "sleep" (Ps. 4:8); "be buried" (Gen. 15:15; 2 Kgs. 22:20); "speak" (Gen. 37:4), etc. שׁלום is also used in a formulaic way when enquiry is made about someone's well-being or in the general greeting, "peace with you" (e.g., Judg. 6:23; 18:15; 1 Sam. 10:4; 25:6; 2 Kgs. 10:13). In the Wisdom literature the expectation

[28] Ibid., 74.

[29] D. J. A. Clines, *The Dictionary of Classical Hebrew* (Sheffield: Sheffield Academic Press, 1993), 372.

[30] Brown, *Israel's Divine Healer*, 32.

[31] Brown, Driver, and Briggs, "arûkâ," 74.

exists, that someone who lives in accordance with the prescriptions of wisdom will experience a long life and peace (Pro. 3:2, 17). The wicked, on the contrary, will experience no peace (Isa. 48:22; 57:21; 59:8). Therefore, שלום in such contexts designates a state of existence in accordance with Yahweh's created order.

b). The nom. שלום is also used to express the social or communal relations between friends, parties, and nations. In these contexts it gives expression to the absence of strife and war, representing, in other words, a friendly alliance (e.g., Gen. 34:21; Judg. 4:17; 1 Kgs. 4:24 [5:4], 12 [26]; Zech. 6:13). The state or condition that prevails when strife or war is ended is שלום (e.g., 1 Kgs. 2:5; Ps. 120:6-7; Isa. 59:8). In a technical sense it also means "treaty" (עשה שלום) (e.g., Isa. 27:5). In Yahweh's blessing of peace to David in 1 Chro. 22:9-10, the state of *shalom* here also is typified as a state of calmness and tranquility.

c). The expression ברית שלום, peace covenant, (ברית), occurs 4 times and needs special attention because of its theological implication. In Numbers 25:12 Phinehas demonstrates his zeal for God's honor and kills the two sinners who defiled Israel, and in so doing assuages God's anger against his people. Restitution is thus, effected, and God promises to make his "peace covenant" with the priest Phinehas. This story indicates that the "peace covenant" is a promissory covenant that expresses God's blessing and salvation for his people. In Ezekiel 34:5 it is said that the sovereign God will make a "covenant of peace" and the people will prosper and live in peace. Ezekiel 37:26 makes it evident that the "covenant of peace" means a restoration of the old idealized condition of the people in their inherited land, where they will once again become the recipients of the blessings of the Lord. The ברית שלום is, therefore, the promissory covenant of God given to his restored people as an eternal blessing and salvation.

d). As a religious concept שלום is an essential part of Yahweh's plan of salvation. All peace comes from him and he is the foundation of peace (1 Kgs. 2:33; Job 25:2; Ps. 35:27; 122:6; Mic. 4:5). If the relationship with Yahweh is corrupted, there can be no peace. From the Aaronic blessing (Num. 6:24-26) it is evident that the person to whom God gives peace (שלום) is blessed (ברך), guarded (שמר), and treated graciously (חנן). The coming of the king of peace of Zech 9:9-10 is portrayed as the beginning of a comprehensive state of peace and universal dominion.

e). This idea is also expressed in the cultic songs of Israel. In the prayer for the restoration of Israel in Psalm 85, the path of Yahweh's salvation is prepared by righteousness (v. צדק 13 [14]). Yahweh promises peace (שלום) to his people (v. 8 [9]), and righteousness צדק and שלום will kiss each other. This metaphor gives expression to the dimension of life that will be experienced when the Lord's salvation is granted to his people. From these instances it is evident that the שלום prediction of the future dispensation of salvation is closely linked with righteousness as the ideal category of existence in accordance with God's will. Such an existence is blessed with divine peace as fulfillment of the ultimate purpose of being.[32]

The diverse definitions of *shalom* invites us for a further probe in this meaning and its connotations, especially in terms of health and prosperity in the Old Testament.

The English translates שׁלם as peace but its essential meaning is not of peace that is understood simply as the absence of war. According to Briggs,[33] it means completeness, soundness, welfare, peace. Von Rad gives its root meaning as 'well-being' and quotes a number of scriptures such as Judges 19:20 and 1 Samuel 16:5 with a strong emphasis on the material side.[34] In the poetic books we read of the שׁלם of the wicked (e.g., Job 21:7-13, Ps. 73:3-5). *Shalom* (שׁלם) here is certainly not their spiritual well-being. Although, these particular texts have a strong reference for שׁלם, it may indicate the peace of mind that results from (apparent) guilt-free enjoyment of prosperity as much as the comfort and security that such prosperity brings.[35]

F. DuToit is of the opinion that, *Shalom* (שׁלם), is 'the advent of the justice of God', communicates the sense of "human welfare, health, and well-being, in both spiritual and material aspects."[36] Bradshaw rightly states, "it is a way of life that characterizes the covenant relationship between God and his people."[37] It is the best description of what the reign of God will be like: a place of safety, justice, and truth; a place of trust, inclusion, and love; a place of joy, happiness, and well-being.[38] Long adds the exercise of dominion as central to the covenants of שׁלם.[39] Atkinson too rightly argues that שׁלם means "wholeness, well-being, vigour and vitality in all dimensions of human life."[40]

---

[32] Philip J. Nel, "Shalom," in *Dictionary of Old Testament Theology and Exegesis*, ed. Willem A. Van Gemeren (Grand Rapids, Michigan: Zondervan Publishing House, 1997), 130-135.

[33] Francis Brown, S. R. Driver, and C. A. Briggs, "Shalom," in *A Hebrew and English Lexicon of the Old Testament* (Oxford: Clarendon, 1951), 1022.

[34] G. Von Rad, "Eirene," in *Theological Dictionary of the New Testament*, ed. G. Kittel (Grand Rapids: William B. Eerdmans Publication Company, 1964), 402.

[35] F. Brown, S. Driver, and C. Briggs, "Shalom," in *The Brown- Driver-Briggs Hebrew and English Lexicon* (Peabody, Massachusetts: Hendrickson Publishers, 2005), 402.

[36] F. DuToit, "Seeking to Establish Democratic values South Africa: Can truth help us?," *Journal of Theology for Southern Africa* 103 (1999): 1.

[37] B. Bradshaw, *Bridging the Gap: Evangelism, Development and Shalom* (Monrovia: MARC, 1993), 16.

[38] R. J. Schreiter, *The Ministry of Reconciliation* (Maryknoll, New York: Orbis Books, 1998), 53.

[39] W. M. Long, *Health, Healing and God's Kingdom: New Pathways to Christian Health Ministry in Africa* (Oxford: Regnum, 2000), 40.

[40] D. Atkinson, "Towards a Theology of Health," in *Health: The Strength to be Human*, ed. A. Fergusson (London: InterVarsity Press, 1993), 25.

Indeed, Wilkinson also understands that health is synonymous with right relationships and concedes that the Old Testament concept of health is comprised of wholeness and holiness.[41] He summarizes the biblical concept of health thus,

> It is only when man's [*sic*] being is whole and his [*sic*] relationships right that he [*sic*] can be truly be described as healthy. The basic relationship of all is man's [*sic*] relationship to God and when this is disturbed all human relationships are disturbed whether they are of man [*sic*] to himself [*sic*], to his [*sic*] fellows, or to his [*sic*] environment.[42]

However, Atkinson rightly understands that the biblical view of health also takes into account the state of a fallen world riddled with the consequences of sin (disease, suffering, etc) and accordingly, health is limited and never fully attainable in this world.[43] It is because the world and all creation is sinful and therefore alienated from God, that humans are in need of a renewed humanity - in fact all of creation is in need of renewal and restoration.

In essence then, Atkinson understands the biblical view of health as,

> A holistic one in which all aspects of life are involved, a dynamic one which acknowledges that we are part of a salvation-history process in God's dealings with the world, yet a limited one which acknowledges that perfect *shalom*, perfect health, is not possible this side of heaven.[44]

Hence, if the Old Testament understanding of שׁלם is correct, then, there is no doubt to translate the term that we usually translate our modern ideas of health. This concept is much more comprehensive and inclusive than our modern idea of health and is not primarily related to the body alone but to our whole being.

We have seen that the underlying reason for the commonly held belief that the Bible has a holistic view of health revolves around the concept of *shalom* which appears to be the nearest word to health. Scholars such as Wilkinson use this in turn to confirm that the Old Testament concept of health is holistic and indeed "not related to the state of the body."[45] In essence, however, it is arguable that all they are doing is no more than equating a more holistic word (*shalom*) with health and coming to the conclusion that the biblical concept of health is holistic. This understanding can also overlook the strong physical and material aspects of

---

[41] John Wilkinson, *Health and Healing: Studies in New Testament Principles and Practice* (Edinburgh: The Handel Press, 1980), vii.

[42] Ibid., 1.

[43] Atkinson, "Towards a Theology of Health," 26, 29.

[44] Ibid., 1.

[45] Wilkinson, *Health and Healing: Studies in New Testament Principles and Practice*, 5.

shalom. With regard to *shalom* and physical health, we see that von Rad gives the root meaning of *shalom* as simply 'well-being' and quotes a number of scriptures such as Judges 19:20 and 1 Samuel 16:5 to show that it has a strong emphasis on the material side. There is evidence of a functional view of health in the Bible. Avalos, for example, has found that in the Ancient West Asia 'illness' was having visible symptoms which rendered individuals as being physically and/or mentally unable to fulfill the normal social and/ or mentally unable to fulfill the normal social and/or physical role ascribed to them by society.[46]

The words 'health' and 'life' in biblical thought were interchangeable and synonymous and indicated survival and well-being. Thus, the biblical view of health could be construed as primarily physical in nature, although this is pursued in the broader context of human well-being. This understanding of health is associated with material concepts such as life, fertility, plenty, prosperity, rain and the possession of cattle.[47] Here then, we see a similarity with Deuteronomy 28 in which the health of the people was associated with the physical aspects of life although set within the context of a broader vision for human well-being.

The physical agenda for health is put forward in the Old Testament.[48] In essence then, it can be seen that the Bible as a whole understands health in primarily physical terms. Although, this view is pursued in the context of a broader vision for human well-being, the fundamental concern stressed throughout the Bible is of physical well being.

2.4. מרפא *(Marpe)*: Its Meanings and Definitions

Another term that is used for health in the Old Testament is *marpe*. The term can also mean healing of the body, but is used in a figurative sense as of promoting soundness of mind and moral character in Proverbs 4:22; 12:18; 13:17; 16:24, as also in Jeremiah 8:15, where the Revised Version renders it as "healing." The word is used only once in Jeremiah and is often associated with *rapha*. Therefore, since the term *marpe* appears only once in Jeremiah, this term will be studied in relationship with *rapha* and *shalom* in the exegetical sections.

[46] H. Avalos, *Illness and Health Care in Ancient Near East* (Atlanta: Scholars, 1995), 246-250.

[47] J. Mbiti, *Concepts of God in Africa* (New Delhi: ISPCK, 1975), 60.

[48] J. Wilkinson, *Health and Healing. Studies in New Testament Principles and Practice* (Edinburgh: The Handel Press, 1980), vii. This view is continued in the New Testament. However, the New Testament texts contain no dynamic equivalent to the word health but content themselves with terms for healing. As such, these texts limit instances of healing to three areas which are definitely tangible: physical healing, the casting out of demons and the raising of the dead. In the light of this, it could be argued that the New Testament understanding of health comprises physical and mental well-being - the absence of illness, physical disability and the expulsion of demons or evil spirits which could have an effect upon the physical and mental health of persons. (Luke 8:26(ff) Mark 9:14(ff)).

Summary

Different meanings and terms are being discussed in relation to *Rapha, Arukah, Shalom and Marpe* in the Old Testament understanding of health and healing.

Rapha is used in terms of *healing* a sick body, *repairing* a broken down altar, r*estoring* a dry, locust-eaten land, *making wholesome,* and the otherwise undrinkable water. Most of the healing factor in the Old Testament is on physical healing of a person who is inflicted with physical ailments. However, this does not specifically deal with bodily ailments as "figurative," which needs to be qualified and, at times, corrected.

The word *arukah* is used only in few references in the Old Testament. It is used in terms of wholeness and in terms of repairing of a wound that is inflicted; the healing of the body and mind cannot be separated from the concept of *marpe* in the Old Testament.

Shalom has several nuances in the Old Testament. It certainly does not emphasize only their spiritual well-being but also to their wholistic life. This concept is so much more comprehensive than our modern idea of health and is not related primarily to the body but to our whole being. It also explains why *shalom* and its relative words are among the most important theological words in the Old Testament. Here, it is described as God's gracious gift to his people and the result of that gift is their health and healing. Reduced to its simplest terms, *shalom* in the Old Testament means health and well-being.

One cannot study about health and healing without understanding the context of their time. In the same manner it is imperative to know how in the Ancient West Asia have understood the concept of illness, health and healing. Therefore, in the next chapter we will deal with the understanding of illness, health and healing in Ancient West Asia.

Chapter 3

The Concept of Illness, Health and Healing in Ancient West Asia

Introduction

In the earlier chapters, we have studied how the terms pertaining to *Rapha, Arukah, Shalom and Marpe* is associated with health and healing. This chapter will be devoted to exploring the concepts of illness, health and healing in Ancient West Asia as a background study. In order to probe fully, the features of illness, health and healing in ancient Israel, especially in the prophetic texts it is worthwhile to compare them with the understanding of illness and health in different societies, especially in the Ancient West Asia. It can not only serve as an effective check on accepted explanations and models for the concepts of illness, health and healing but also provide new theoretical insights for thinking about them in ancient Israel.

In Ancient West Asia, specifically in Mesopotamian and Egyptian Art, healthcare, illness, and the beliefs surrounding illness have been depicted in various ways.

Illness has been one of the most constant features of human experience among all and this is seen in the earliest written language of Ancient West Asia that persistently writes about illness and health care. The earliest civilizations (Mesopotamia, Egypt and Greece) all produced an extensive corpus of medical literature. The literature of Israel, particularly the Bible, also produced a variety of ideas about illness and health care.

3.1. Illness, Health and Healing in Egypt

The Egyptian medicinal knowledge comes from early collections of medical practices, in particular the Egyptian medical papyri. Though most of these are likely to have been derived from, or to be direct copies of, texts of much earlier date, the extant medical papyri date to the second millennium B.C.E. Among them, the Edwin Smith papyrus and the Ebers papyrus are well known.[1]

3.1.1. Illness and Its Cause

Ancient Egyptian ideas of the cause of illness can be divided into two groups; naturalistic causes and personalistic causes. The naturalistic causes may furthermore be separated into those from outside and those from within the body. The exogenous illnesses were frequently attributed to overeating or improper eating and drinking,[2] famine, winds,[3] and worms. According to Ghalioungui, the view that illness is caused by the presence of worms may be divided into two. The first view is concerned with the factual observation of worms wriggling in the stools, in wounds, eyes, nose or skin. The second view draws our attention to the fact that worms decay all organic matter, living or dead. In the Egyptian mind, decay by worms was a real illness that led to final death. They believed that the mummy is the continuation of the body in after life.[4]

Ghalioungui continues to argue that, while gods could send the great scourges or epidemics, it was foreign to the Egyptian view that deities inflicted illness upon individuals in punishment for sin. However, Peet opines there is a case in which a man was stricken with blindness because he committed the sin of swearing falsely by Ptah, Lord of Truth: "I am a man [*sic*] who swore falsely by Ptah, Lord of Truth; and he caused me to behold darkness by day."[5] Obviously, illness could be attributed to moral or ethical lapses that bring about divine punishment.

---

[1] The Edwin Smith papyrus is far the most important Egyptian medical document. The book, which was compiled about 17th century B.C.E., for the most part deals with forty-eight different wounds in a systematic way. It not only provides the case histories, but also discusses the diagnosis and treatment in an elaborated pattern. Along with this, there is also Ebers papyrus, which was compiled about the 16th century B.C.E., and comprises about 800 prescriptions arranged in sections in accordance with organs and illnesses. Many of the therapeutic measures adopted in the Ebers papyrus are in the nature of spells and incantations. While the Ebers papyrus deals primarily with internal illnesses, the Edwin Smith papyrus is a manual of surgery. Henry E. Sigerist, *A History of Medicine: Primitive and Archaic Medicine,* vol. 1 (New York: Oxford University Press, 1951), 303-315.

[2] Paul Ghalioungui, *The House of Life; Magic and Medical Science in Ancient Egypt* (Amsterdam: B. M. Israel, 1973), 52.

[3] The word "wind" occurs as a pathogen in more than one meaning: It may mean just air in movement, and it may refer to weather, e.g., 'the wind of the year of the plague' (the Edwin papyrus XVII, 1, 8). Other phrases suggest wind conveyed pathogens, e.g., "the flesh has caught some air" (the Edwin Smith papyrus XXXI), as one would say today that a sick person has caught wind or a cold, or that food has become unwholesome because it was left uncovered and "caught air." Ibid., 53.

[4] Ibid., 54-55.

[5] T. Eric. Pitt, *A Comparative Study of the Literature of Egypt, Palestine, and Mesopotamia* (London: Pedersen, 1931), 89.

There is also another possible resource of metal or physical problems, which is the malignant activity of spirits or demons. They entered the body from the outside 'in an unguarded moment through the eyes, ears, mouth, or nose and then made a vicious attack, breaking bones, sucking the marrow, drinking the blood, gnawing the intestines, heart, or lungs, and devouring the vital substance.[6] While the Babylonian demons had names and their characteristics were depicted in numerous texts,[7] the Egyptian spirits and demons that caused illness were "anonymous ghosts or demons who sometimes 'arrived in darkness, gliding in, the nose backwards and the face turned' so that they might not be recognized what they were.[8] Of special interests are the expressions of illness in which demons striking the body are described. Demons shot arrows at the victim (cf. Ps. 91:5) or took possession of him/her or of parts of his/her body, of a bone or some other organ.[9] Illness could occur as the result of curses or attack from an enemy and a person with an evil eye, too.[10] In such instances, no wrongdoings on the patient's part may be found. Strangely enough, in the Egyptian view gods were also subjected to illness; this view is contrasted with the Israelite view of Yahweh as one who shows no hint of illness and weakness. The Egyptian gods suffered from illness in the same manner as a human being. When they were ill, they asked their fellow deities for help.[11] Jayne notes,

> Re had sudden disease of the eye (assumed to have been symbolic of eclipses), together with other ailments, and came near death when a scorpion stung his heel. Isis was afflicted with an abscess of the breast following the birth of Horus; and Horus suffered from headache and internal pains, and not only had dysentery and an anal weakness, but would have lost his life from a scorpion's sting had it not been for the prompt help of Isis and Thoth.[12]

In short, in Egyptian thought illness could be caused supernaturally or naturally. In the broadest sense, the supernatural source of illness refers to the patient's disharmony with supernatural beings, whether either sin or a spirit's

---

[6] John F. Nunn, *Ancient Egyptian Medicine* (No Place: University of Oklahoma Press, 1996), 103.

[7] The Babylonian demons with different names attacked the different parts of the body, causing different illness: *utukku* (throat); *alu* (chest); *gallu* (hand); rabisu (skin); *lamastu* (nightmare and ills of women); *labasu* (epilepsy); *lilu* and *lilitu* (infirmities of the night); *asakku* (fever and consumption); etc. Walter Addison Jayne, *The Healing Gods of Ancient Civilization* (New York: University Books, 1962), 104.

[8] Sigerist, *A History of Medicine: Primitive and Archaic Medicine*, 274.

[9] Ibid.

[10] Jayne, *The Healing Gods of Ancient Civilization*, 39.

[11] Ibid., 41.

[12] Ibid.

disfavour is involved. The natural view of illness in ancient Egypt indicates that the Egyptians not only recognized such exogenous illnesses as overeating, winds and worms, but also began to take a somewhat rational approach to the cause of illness, as seen in the notion that putrefaction in the bowel could spread to other parts of the body.[13] Another important aspect that needs our attention is the social situation of the person with illness. Although, the Egyptians began to take a rational view of illness, yet they were always a religious people and thereby their relationship with supernatural beings was crucial for their life.[14] If an individual fell sick, he/she was dropped out of society, since the fellow humans could interpret illness as a sign of divine disfavour.[15] This notion may be grasped in the prayer of a person who was stricken with blindness owing to the sin of swearing falsely by *Ptah*, Lord of Truth.

3.1.2. Health and Healing

As discussed above, that the natural and supernatural forces alike are responsible for illness. These forces commonly enter the body from the outside. Hence, it is essential for therapy to remove external elements, either personal agents (e.g., demons, spirits, or gods) or impersonal but harmful materials (e.g., food and worm). In the former case, however, the successful therapy rested on identifying which of many possible invasive agents have been involved in illness. The therapy is also successful on contacting, appeasing or expelling them through rituals, incantations, and prayers.[16] The key to therapy is to identify the correct invasive agents. Demons or spirits must be driven out from the body. When sin was the reason for this attack, the patients had to pray to the appropriate God with accompanying confession. This was the logical way to restore the lost harmony with the transcendental world and to regain health.[17] On the other hand, when illnesses are attributed to impersonal materials, there is the need simply to get rid of them. For example, the removal of material, which originated from a putrid process in the bowels, might prevent the occurrence and spread of illness. This is strongly supported by the Egyptian's reliance on purgatives and enemas.[18] However, it should be noted that removing excessive or harmful material from the body is different from expelling alien agents from the body. While the focus

[13] Seong-Hyuk Hong, *The Metaphor of Illness and Healing in Hosea and its Significance in the Socio-Economic Context of Eight-Century Israel and Judah* (Bern Frankfurt am Main: Peter Lang, 2006), 36.

[14] Sigerist, *A History of Medicine: Primitive and Archaic Medicine*, 268.

[15] Pitt, *A Comparative Study of the Literature of Egypt, Palestine, and Mesopotamia*, 89.

[16] Hector Avalos, *Illness and Health Care in the Ancient Near East: The Role of the Temple in Greece, Mesopotamia, and Israel* (Atlanta, Georgia: Scholars Press, 1995), 160.

[17] Hong, *The Metaphor of Illness and Healing in Hosea and its Significance in the Socio-Economic Context of Eight-Century Israel and Judah*, 37.

[18] Nunn, *Ancient Egyptian Medicine*, 62.

of the former healing is on restoring the equilibrium of the body, that of the latter healing is on restoring harmony with the appropriate supernatural beings.

Though the involvement of the many deities is seen in ancient Egypt in causing illness, yet they are also engaged in therapy. While there was perhaps no specific deity that was known primarily as a healer,[19] almost all deities in the Egyptian pantheon were praised for their healing deeds; when provoked, they sent illness and when placated or invoked in the correct way, they recalled it. Among the gods most frequently invoked in the healing process were Thoth, Isis, Horus, Sekhmet, and Ptah.[20] Thoth, the Egyptian moon-god, was the inventor of letters, language, and numbers, and of the arts and sciences.[21] Especially he was a protector against all illness, delivering human from the evil demons.[22] He was the physician's patron to whom they prayed for guidance. In the introduction to the Ebers papyrus, Re, the sun God, said,

> I will save him from his enemies, and Thoth shall be his guide, he who lets writing speak and has composed the books; he gives to the skilful, to the physicians who accompany him, skill to cure. The one whom the god loves, him he shall keep alive.[23]

Thoth was also a physician to gods. He restored the eye of Horus, which Seth pulled out in their fighting for the throne of Egypt.[24] Isis, a healing deity of the first rank was distinguished in the treatment of children.[25] She is also known as "the great magician whose counsel is the breath of life, whose saving acts drive out illness, and whose word gives life to him/her [those] whose breath is failing."[26] Ptah, 'the God of the propitious face," was the chief of the Memphite triad, together with his wife Sekhmet and his son Nerfertem.[27] Ptah was famous for his therapeutic activities. His Memphis shrine was renowned for its marvellous healing. The patients at his shrine prayed to Ptah and, as his epithet *Ptah-Sotmu* (Ptah who hears) indicates, expected him to respond to their prayer during a

---

[19] M. L. Brown, *Israel's Divine Healer* (Grand Rapids: Zondervan Publishing House, 1995), 54.

[20] There are many other deities praised for their healing deeds: Anuqet, Apis, Bes, Epet, Hathor, Heqet, Imhotep, Khnosu, Meskhenet, Neith, Nekhbet, Nephthys, Renenutet,Serapis, ubaster, Uzoit. Ibid; Jayne, *The Healing Gods of Ancient Civilization*, 52.

[21] Jayne, *The Healing Gods of Ancient Civilization*, 79-80.

[22] Ibid., 81.

[23] Sigerist, *A History of Medicine: Primitive and Archaic Medicine*, 287.

[24] Jayne, *The Healing Gods of Ancient Civilization*, 81.

[25] Ibid., 66.

[26] Sigerist, *A History of Medicine: Primitive and Archaic Medicine*, 288. Horus, the child of Isis and Osiris, was bitten by a deadly scorpion in escaping from Seth. Isis called upon Re to save him and Re sent Thoth, who with his magical power saved him. This experience of illness enabled Horus to acquire himself special faculties to heal people bitten by venomous animals.

[27] Jayne, *The Healing Gods of Ancient Civilization*, 75.

period of incubation. As noted above, the gods of Egypt, like humans suffered from illness and recovering from illness, made the gods of Egypt function as a healer.

According to J. V. K. Wilson,[28] there were two kinds of doctors in ancient Egypt: the *heri-ha ab* and the *seynu*. He argued that while the one accorded with the Akkadian *asipu*, the "exorcist" or "incantation priest", the other matched with the Akkadian *asu*, the practical physician or surgeon.[29] P. Ghalioungui supports this, "Many physicians bore 'double qualifications' and practiced both kinds simultaneously."[30] He himself divides the healing consultants into three types: the priest-physician, the lay physician, the magician. On the highest rank in the scale of healers; priest-physician, the lay physician, the magician. While as far as his extreme heirarchization is concerned, more study is necessary, there can be little doubt that priests, physicians and magicians, all were engaged in healing. The Ebers papyrus (8542) makes this point clear,

> There are vessels in him to all his limbs. As to these: If any doctor, any (*wab*) priest of (Sekhmet) or any magician (*sau*) places his two hands or his fingers on the head, on the back of the head, on the hands, on the place of the heart, on the two arms or on each of the two legs, he measures the heart because of its vessels to all his limbs. It speaks from the vessels of all the limbs.[31]

The text distinguishes three categories of medical consultants, but as such, there is no hint of distinction in their work.

The chief means of healing in ancient Egypt may be divided broadly into two kinds; magic and medicine. Whereas Sigerist assigned the worship of the gods, primarily to the realm of religion, he defined magic as the "means to force an event that seemed desirable to man [*sic*], or to avert threatening evil."[32] W. Farber defines magic as the "whole area of religious behaviour which tries to influence man's [*sic*] success, well-being, health, and wealth by using methods based neither on rational experience nor solely on private or public worship of a deity."[33] While Sigerist assumes a boundary between religion and magic, Farber's definition takes into consideration the probable existence of common ground between religion and magic. In fact, there were no sharp distinction between magic and worship of the gods or supernatural beings in the ancient Egyptian mind. Thus, Farber

---

[28] J. V. K. Wilson, "Medicine in the Land and Times of the Old Testament," in *Studies in the Period of David and Solomon and Other Essays*, ed. T. Ishida (Winona Lake: Eisenbrauns, 1982), 338.

[29] Ibid.

[30] Ghalioungui, *The House of Life; Magic and Medical Science in Ancient Egypt*, 105.

[31] Nunn, *Ancient Egyptian Medicine*, 113.

[32] Sigerist, *A History of Medicine: Primitive and Archaic Medicine*, 272.

[33] Walter Farber, "Witchcraft, Magic, and Divination in Ancient Mesopotamia," in *Civilizations of the Ancient Near East*, ed. J. Sasson (New York: Charles Scribner's Sons, 1995), 1895.

states that magic was homogeneously integrated into the mainstream concept of religion.[34] Jayne goes so far as to name it "so-called religion" or "applied religion."[35] In any case, magic was an essential part of the Egyptian healing system.

3.2. Illness, Health and Healing in Mesopotamia

In Mesopotamia, there is an ample amount of evidence with regard to medical practices and understandings of illness and healing. Textual evidence comes in the form of letters, administrative documents, prayers, rituals, incantations, diagnostic medical omens and wisdom texts from the second millennium to the fourth century B.C.E.[36]

We have no treatises on medicine as such from ancient Mesopotamia to make explicit their understanding of sickness, health, and the treatment of illnesses. Whatever information we are acquainted with, is from the so-called medical texts, from letters, and from literary sources. The major source is obviously the "medical" texts themselves. The earliest medical prescriptions we have date from the Third Dynasty of Ur (about 2000 B.C.E) and are written in Sumerian. The largest proportions of the medical texts, however, are Neo-Assyrian in date, coming mainly from Assurbanipal's library in Nineveh and from the Assyrian site of Asshur (modern Qalat Sharqat). Smaller numbers come from other sites such as Nippur (Nuffar), Sippar (Abu Habba), Nimrud (Kalkhu), and Sultantepe. Relatively few medical texts are known from Mesopotamia itself from the second millennium, but they obviously once existed, as is evidenced by the numerous Babylonian medical texts from the Hittite capital of Khattusha, near the modern village of Boğazköy in central Turkey. In a number of cases, there are word-for-word parallels in later texts, suggesting the corpus of texts as we have it from Neo-Assyrian times, may well reflect the medical practices of nearly a millennium earlier. Thus, these texts can hardly provide evidence for any innovations that may have occurred in the treatment of illnesses or any specific changes in attitudes or beliefs that might have affected the treatment of illness. It has been rightly argued by A. Leo Oppenheim that the very fact that there was a written tradition, had a stultifying effect and made medical practice hidebound. It seems likely, however, that, there were changes in attitudes, evolution of skills, and innovations of various kinds, some perhaps are due to the result of differing traditions among various ethnic groups, which our texts do not reflect. Our descriptions are thus not necessarily applicable to the whole time span or area of ancient Mesopotamia.[37]

---

[34] Ibid.

[35] Jayne, *The Healing Gods of Ancient Civilization*, 25.

[36] Hong, *The Metaphor of Illness and Healing in Hosea and its Significance in the Socio-Economic Context of Eight-Century Israel and Judah*, 42.

[37] Robert D. Biggs, "Medicine, Surgery, and Public Health in Ancient Mesopotamia," *Journal of Assyrian Academic Studies* 19, no. 1 (2005): 2.

An ideal in Babylonia was to enjoy good health and to have contentment, to be viewed favourably by the gods and fellow humans, and to enjoy a long life with one's descendants. A full life included, having children who would provide funerary offerings after one's death. A statement attributed to Adad-guppi, the mother of the Babylonian king Nabonidus, telling of her long and contented life (which she attributed in part to her piety and zealous worship of the moon-god) illustrates the point,

> He (the moon-god) added many days and years of happiness (to my life) and kept me alive . . . one hundred and four happy years. . . . My eyesight was good (to the end), my hearing excellent, my hands and feet were sound, my words well chosen, food and drink agreed with me, my health was fine and my mind happy. I saw my great-great grandchildren, up to the fourth generation, in good health and (thus) had my fill of old age.[38]

This quotation gives an indication of what approximated an ideal. In real life, however, there were many deviations from this ideal, and prayers seeking deliverance from troubles often enumerate some of them: crying spells, insomnia, nightmares, and fears, inability to enjoy food or drink, sexual inadequacies, and so on. One can assume from the medical texts that generally a person who considered himself ill was considered so by those around him. The symptoms described usually include those perceived by the patient, such as localized pain or itching, nausea, or the inability to get up and walk. In other cases, it is those around the person in illness who perceive him/her to be ill, as when his/her behaviour is irrational, he/she keeps forgetting what he/she has said, or he/she does not recognize people whom he/she knows. It is probable that home remedies were administered in many cases, and these were most likely fairly simple traditional treatments, utilizing medications that did not carry any unusual risks. The medical texts, however, reflect only the measures taken by professional healers. The various apothecaries' inventories that have been preserved may indicate, however, that a good many of the most commonly utilized ingredients were readily available to whoever sought them, whether or not a professional healer had prescribed them for a particular illness.

3.2.1. Perceived Origin of Illness

Healing is a theological theme, which runs throughout the Bible. The Hebrew Bible contains sporadic references to healing especially in the Book of Psalms and in accounts of the prophets. In the West Asia, during the time that the Bible was written, "health" was not seen as purely physical, but rather as a more holistic term encompassing complete well-being. The most important quality in health was

[38] *Ancient Near Eastern Texts Relating to the Old Testament*, ed. James B. Pritchard, trans. A. Leo Oppenheim (New Jersey: Princeton University Press, 1969), 561.

maintaining a good relationship with God. Thus, healing was expected through prayer, petition, and supplication to God. God would either heal directly, or in some cases he would heal through the prophets, such as when Elisha cures Naaman (2 Kgs. 5:1-14) or Isaiah cures Hezekiah (Isa. 38).

Illness had a variety of explanations, which often blurred distinction between naturalistic causes and personalistic ones. Illness might occur owing to naturalistic causes such as heat, cold, food, exposure to a sick person, or the bite of animals. Over exposure to heat or cold, over eating or eating spoiled food might bring about illness. As was said in Egypt, nevertheless, this view does not exclude those supernatural beings that were most likely involved in the occurrence of illness. In Mesopotamian, thought magico-religious beliefs and empirico-rational thoughts were intimately combined.[39] According to Marvin A. Powell, "The attitudes and ideas about disease and health in ancient Mesopotamia differ profoundly from ours in almost every point except one: health is desirable and disease is not. In order to understand ancient Mesopotamian medicine, we need to try to translate ourselves into a cultural world that is profoundly different from ours. These differences begin with the material environment, especially technology, and run through the whole spectrum of cultural concepts about the nature and about human life itself."[40]

Robert D. Biggs opines that in Mesopotamian mind, illness was viewed as a divine punishment due to sins committed by the sick person.[41] However, K. Van Der Toorn holds that illness was not always associated with divine punishment.[42] H. Avalos also asserts that not all illnesses could be attributed to divine punishment for the patient's wrong doing.[43] Nevertheless, he acknowledges that "most illnesses were divine instruments or messages of which punishment was one, though not only, sub-category or motive."[44]

Illnesses and diseases in Mesopotamia were attributed to spiritual forces, such as demons or the spirits of the dead. According to Van Der Toorn,

> Demons can be divided into two groups: illegitimate demons and subordinate demons. The former group could wilfully threaten women and new-borns during childbirth, and they could steal suckling infants

---

[39] Ibid., 409-410.

[40] Marvin A. Powell, "Drugs and Pharmaceuticals in Ancient Mesopotamia," in *The Healing Part: Pharmaceuticals in the Biblical and Rabbinic World*, ed. Irene and Walter Jacob (Leiden. E. J. Brill, 1993), 51-52.

[41] Robert D. Biggs, "Medicine, Surgery, and Public Health in Ancient Mesopotamia," *Journal of Assyrian Academic Studies* 19, no. 1 (2005): 1912.

[42] K. Van Der Toorn, *Sin and Sanction in Israel and Mesopotamia: A Comparative Study* (Assen/ Maastricht: Van Gorcum, 1985), 67-72.

[43] Avalos, *Illness and Health Care in the Ancient Near East: The Role of the Temple in Greece, Mesopotamia, and Israel*, 128-139.

[44] Ibid., 134.

as well. The latter group could also afflict one with illness of their own volition, but were often sent by the gods for the execution of their judgments."[45]

To this latter group belongs the spirits of the dead, who could inflict illness on the living to remind them of their duties towards the gods. Another possible source of illness was sorcery. The malignant influence of sorcerers could inflict illness with "devious and, to modern eyes, supernatural skill.[46] While the disgruntled gods might deliberately allow the sorcerers a freedom of action, the gods' mood could also be influenced by the sorcerers.[47] This notion suggests that mutual interaction between the gods and the sorcerers is possible, but nevertheless, the latter seemed to be under the control of the former.[48] As for the source of illness, it is also noteworthy that different supernatural beings attacked different parts of the body. W. A. Jayne writes,

> If the person was struck in the neck, it was the hand of Adad; if in the neck and breast, it was the hand of Ishtar; and if in the temples, a ghost had seized him. Evil spirits of all kinds-fiends, devils, and demons- had special powers and caused particular diseases. The utukku were extremely vicious, and with several attendant fever-demons they assailed the throat; alu attacked the chest, gallu, the hand, the skin....[49]

Here illness is understood in terms of the invasion of alien agents from the outside. Indeed, it was believed that the supernatural agents caused illness by entering through "some natural, but unguarded, opening of the body,"[50] such as the mouth, nose, ears, or eyes. As a whole, in the Mesopotamian mind the source of illness was various: gods, demons, spirits, and sorcerers. Whereas illness could be sent because of the violation of stipulations that have already been disclosed to the patient, i.e., sin, it could also be caused by supernatural beings for a variety of hidden reasons other than sin, which might have been arbitrary from their standpoint. Namely, disharmony with supernatural beings was a vital reason for illness. Even the naturalistic causes of illness were recognized as deeply relevant to divine will.

The social situation of the person in illness is looked as the patient has a broken relationship with supernatural beings, whether or not illness was associated with sin. Such a broken relationship could be interpreted by other people as divine

---

[45] Toorn, *Sin and Sanction in Israel and Mesopotamia: A Comparative Study*, 70.

[46] Ibid., 71.

[47] Ibid.

[48] Hong, *The Metaphor of Illness and Healing in Hosea and its Significance in the Socio-Economic Context of Eight-Century Israel and Judah*, 44.

[49] Jayne, *The Healing Gods of Ancient Civilization*, 103-104.

[50] Ibid., 104.

disfavour.[51] It was a predominant presupposition in Mesopotamian society that sin was the reason for illness. Thus at the initial stage of his/her illness any patient would, though he was not aware of having done anything wrong, have tried to find out which sin was responsible for his illness.[52] The public view of illness as sin branded the patient with the disgrace of sinfulness.[53] Furthermore, illness frequently brought the person "slander, curses, false accusations and various signs of disrespect."[54] There can be no doubt that this social view of illness gave the person in illness an isolated position in society. The following passage concerning a sick person depicts well the patient's isolated situation

Translation

> To my many relations I am like a recluse.
> If I walk the street, ears are pricked;
> If I enter the place, eyes blink.
> My city frowns on me as an enemy;
> Indeed my land is savage and hostile.
> My friend has become foe,
> My companion has become a wretch and a devil.[55]

The patient's fear of exposure to public scorn or ridicule most likely discouraged him from venturing to a public place.

3.2.2. Health and Healing

Whether illness was caused by sin, or whether it was a message requiring fulfilment of a supernatural being's wish, it signified that the equilibrium with the supernatural beings was disrupted. In this light, health refers to the harmonious relationship with them and healing to the restoration of the harmonious relationship with them. Hence, in such a polytheistic society as Mesopotamia, the key to healing consisted in discovering which of many possible supernatural beings had sent illness, and in contacting, appeasing or expelling those supernatural beings.[56] The most imperative thing in the process of healing, the patient was to identify the correct deity of a *qāt*, that is to identify the specific supernatural causes or motives for illness, and the next step was to perform rituals and prayers to the appropriate gods.

---

[51] Brown, *Israel's Divine Healer*, 53.

[52] Avalos, *Illness and Health Care in the Ancient Near East: The Role of the Temple in Greece, Mesopotamia, and Israel*, 133.

[53] Sigerist, *A History of Medicine: Primitive and Archaic Medicine*, 426.

[54] Toorn, *Sin and Sanction in Israel and Mesopotamia: A Comparative Study*, 88.

[55] W. G. Lambert, *Babylonian Wisdom Literature* (Oxford: The Clarendon Press, 1960), 34-35.

[56] Avalos, *Illness and Health Care in the Ancient Near East: The Role of the Temple in Greece, Mesopotamia, and Israel*, 160.

However, the following prayer shows that it was not an easy task to figure out the motives of the specific supernatural beings for inflicting illness on the patient,

> 'Why have you inflicted upon me worry and distress' let them show to me in a dream and tell me! Let them reveal my [s]in, premeditated or unintentional, and I shall resign myself to my punishment! Šamaš, speak to the ghost of my family, that they may show me and explain to me the meaning of the ominous incidents which befall mankind, which I have been made to suffer. I shall proclaim your greatness, I shall sing your praises![57]

Avalos postulates that the patient likely relied on two strategies for therapy. On the one hand, the patient might have prayed to all the possible gods or supernatural beings that could be responsible for the illness.[58] Moreover, the patient could have entreated a divine intermediary who could locate the correct supernatural beings responsible for the illness.[59] These strategies on the part of the patient were intended to restore his/her memory with the appropriate gods or beings, ultimately leading to healing.

In Mesopotamia, there were a variety of healing deities. Out of the many healing gods in Mesopotamia,[60] Ea, Gula and Marduk appear to be most prominent. Ea ("House of Water"), one of the chief gods of the Babylonian pantheon, was known as the supreme god of healing and the last resort of the sick person.[61] His healing qualities were depended particularly on the use of waters. The body of the patient was sprinkled or bathed with the waters of the Euphrates or of the Tigris, or with those of some sacred stream or spring, with accompanying incantations for purification (cf. 2 Kgs. 5).[62] He knew the potent magic, which averted evil, thwarted the designs of evil spirits, demons, and witches, and exorcised the demons of disease.[63] He was also acclaimed the raiser of the dead. Gula, and early goddess of the Assyrians, was a divinity of fertility, the "mother of man [*sic*] kind," and the consort of Ninib at Nippur and at Calah. In portrayals of her, the dog appears as her emblem.[64] The epithets of Gula provide

---

[57] Toorn, *Sin and Sanction in Israel and Mesopotamia: A Comparative Study*, 153.

[58] Avalos, *Illness and Health Care in the Ancient Near East: The Role of the Temple in Greece, Mesopotamia, and Israel*, 139-141.

[59] Ibid., 141.

[60] Although they are not known as strictly healing gods, those who appear most prominently in the incantation texts are: Allatu or Ereshkigal, Ea, Gibil or Girru, Gula, Bau, or Nin-karrak, Ishtar, Marduk, nabû, Ninib, Nusku, Sarpântîtum, Shamash, Sin.

[61] Jayne, *The Healing Gods of Ancient Civilization*, 119.

[62] Ibid., 120.

[63] Ibid., 119.

[64] Ibid., 121.

adequate evidence of her role as a healer.[65] She was praised as *azugallatu* 'the great healer', *azugal kalam-ma,* 'healer of the country and *azu gal kalam-ma,* the great healer of the land. She even speaks of herself as a physician,

> I am a physician, I can heal, I carry around all (healing) herbs, I drive away disease. I gird myself with the leather bag containing health-giving incantations, I carry around texts which bring recovery, I give cures to man [sic] kind. My pure dressing alleviates the wound, my soft bandage relieves disease. At the raising of my eyes the dead comes back to life,[66] at the opening of my mouth palsy disappears.[67]

As the passage suggests, Gula was a great physician who brings back to life one who is at death's door. Gula appears to rely on such magical methods as the use of charms and the pronunciation of incantation in order to expel illness.

As regards to Marduk, although he was not primarily a healer, he was often extolled for his healing powers. If Gula was the "lady of life," then Marduk was the "lord of life," who gave life and health to the gods.[68] He was well known as an expert healer to be praised as a life-giver and saviour from death; 'The Lord took hold of me, the Lord set me on my feet, the Lord gave me life, he rescued me, he summoned me [from] destruction, [...] he pulled me from the *Hubur* river, [...] he took my hand. [he who] smote me, Marduk, he restored me."[69]

There were two types of priests in Mesopotamia who functioned as healing consultants: *asû* and *āšipu*. The *āšipu* often dealt with illness of a supernatural origin and read omens[70] skilfully. E. Ritter refers to the *āšipu* as follows,

> The *āšipu qua* healer views disease as a particular expression of the wider beliefs that he holds, namely that a chain of events, initiated under the influence of 'supernatural' powers or forces, proceeds on

[65] Avalos, *Illness and Health Care in the Ancient Near East: The Role of the Temple in Greece, Mesopotamia, and Israel,* 105.

[66] Illness was commonly reckoned by the Babylonians as "a state of falling near death." As the context suggests, it seems unwarranted to link the expression "the dead comes back to life" with a belief in the resurrection of the dead. Brown, *Israel's Divine Healer*, 56-57; H. Ringgren, *Israelite Religion*, trans. D. E. Green (Philadelphia: Fortress Press, 1966), 245.

[67] Lambert, *Babylonian Wisdom Literature*, 121.

[68] Brown, *Israel's Divine Healer*, 56.

[69] Lambert, *Babylonian Wisdom Literature*, 58-59.

[70] According to Biggs, an omen is a 'divine sign given to a person as a warning about a specific danger foreshadowed by an observable fact or as an alert of a propitious development in the future." The god through omens showed people their will, intentions, or fateful decision to people. Biggs, "Medicine, Surgery, and Public Health in Ancient Mesopotamia," 1899.

> a predetermined course to an outcome that can be predicted by the skilful reading of 'signs.'[71]

Here Ritter assumes that the *āšipu's* view of illness relies mainly on its supernatural causation and treatment.[72] The other consultant *asû*[73] was regarded as a specialist in the *materia medica* and surgery. Thus, the *asû* is usually called the physician in a strict sense of the word. Ritter does not seem too far from this view: "The *asû*, without reference to a more general system of notions, views disease as a complex of presenting symptoms and findings; by his 'practical grasp' (intuition plus accumulated experience) of the immediate situation he proceeds with treatment."[74] Ritter also states that the *asû* proceeds with treatment on the basis of his empirical findings, i.e., the physical symptoms of the patient. She claims that whereas the *asû* specializes in empirical causation and treatment on the basis of the symptoms of the patient, the *āšipu* primarily relies on the supernatural and magic causation and treatment. Avalos also argues that the *āšipu* likewise is engaged himself in treatment based on the empirical findings.[75] In this light, there appears to be no sharp distinction between the function of the *āšipu* and that of the *asû*.

Hence, the best possible conclusion we can draw concerning their function is that while the *āšipu,* as a specialist, in diagnosing the supernatural causes of an illness and treating it, primarily identifies the sender of the illness, provides a prognosis, and effects a reconciliation with, or expulsion of the sender,[76] he may also deal within *materia medica*, especially when the *asû* is not available. Conversely, when the *asû* primarily treats illnesses with the *materia medica* or performs surgery, he may also treat illnesses caused by supernatural agents by means of exorcism.

---

[71] Edith K. Ritter, "Magical-expert and Physician: Notes on Two Complimentary Profession in Babylonian Medicine," in *Studies in Honour of Benno Landsberger on His Seventy-fifth Birthday*, ed. Hans. G. Guterbock and Thorkild Jacobson (Chicago: The University of Chicago, 1965), 301.

[72] Ritter proposes four corollaries that were concomitant with the understanding of the *āšipu*. Firstly, the patient's symptoms indicate that he is the victim of malignant influence be it for obscure reasons, known and unknown sins or natural causes. Secondly, on the basis of his knowledge of the signs, the *āšipu* specifies a cause responsible for the symptoms. Thirdly, he makes a prognosis. When it is hopeless, he gives up. When it is hopeful, he provides a necessary treatment to free the patient from the hostile forces. Fourthly, The *āšipu* concerns with the course and pattern of events, conditions, his interests in temporal aspects of disease. Ibid., 301-302.

[73] The *asû* is depicted in several texts as one who manipulates and sets broken bones, lances boils, and treats battle wounds, and treats internal and external illnesses with herbal medicine. Biggs, "Medicine, Surgery, and Public Health in Ancient Mesopotamia," 1918.

[74] Ritter, "Magical-expert and Physician: Notes on Two Complimentary Profession in Babylonian Medicine," 302.

[75] Avalos, *Illness and Health Care in the Ancient Near East: The Role of the Temple in Greece, Mesopotamia, and Israel*, 149.

[76] Ibid., 166.

Summary

The understanding of illness, health and healing in Ancient West Asia was mostly in terms of their physical calamities. Thus, in the ancient Egyptian mind therapy consisted of restoration of balance by means of removing or expelling. On the other hand, illnesses that were ascribed to personal agents (i.e., gods or spirits) were treated by appeasing or expelling the appropriate supernatural beings through rituals and prayers. Thus healing signified the restoration of harmony with the transcendental world. Illness in Ancient West Asia fundamentally implies disharmony with the transcendental realm, while on the surface level it indicates physical and /or mental malfunction. In the theology of Mesopotamia, illness is caused due to host of causes, sometimes contradictory, that were not understood by the patient. Some causes were regular (e.g., breach of covenants) but the myriads of gods were metaphors for the inexplicability of illness. The response to this inexplicability in Mesopotamia is a therapeutic strategy that can be quite a maximalist approach that seeks to address all the possible causes of illness.

In the Old Testament, such disharmony meant the disrupted relationship with Yahweh, including the possibility of illness that arises from a divine mysterious motive. In ancient Israel, illness and diseases were not attributed to demons, as in Mesopotamia, but to the wrath of Yahweh. Some texts (e.g., Ps. 38:3, 41:4) clearly state that the sick person provoked the divine wrath by his/her own sins. Although, the cause of disease seems to differ in Mesopotamia and Israel, one may conclude that In Israel as well as in Mesopotamia, illness and diseases were viewed primarily as a spiritual state and needing spiritual intervention. In Israel and Mesopotamian gods, are entreated to heal the sick. In Mesopotamia, many different gods are called upon, but in Israel, the sick only trusted Yahweh to bring healing.

As understood both in ancient Israel and in Ancient West Asia illness and diseases were viewed as a spiritual state that is in need of healing. Such understanding will help us to probe further in the next chapter how in the prophetic texts especially in Hosea, Isaiah and Jeremiah, health and healing is perceived.

Chapter 4

Health and Healing in Select Passages of Pre-Exilic Prophetic Literature in the Books of Hosea and Isaiah

Introduction

In order to study the concept of health and healing in the Pre-exilic prophetic literature, it is imperative for us to first study the socio-historical context that prompted the prophets to speak. The following three chapters will be investigated through the exegetical study taking into account the text critical note, the form critical note, the setting of the text and the comments on the text.

4.1. The Socio-Historical Background of the Pre-Exilic Prophets

4.1.1. Pre-Exilic Time: A Time of Prosperity

The heart of the issue in the eighth-century socio economic reality was the concentration of vast amounts of land in the hands of a small minority, which accumulated a large quantity of land at the expense of the common peasants.

Two aspects stand out about eighth-century B.C.E. Israel (and Judah). First, Israel and Judah experienced unprecedented economic growth and political stability under Jeroboam II and Uzziah. Second, in light of the above, it is anomalous and quite striking that the prophetic materials that relate to this period do not give the impression that all was well. In fact, ironically, this period gives rise to the greatest number and the most intense of the prophetic oracles of judgment.

That the first part of the eighth century was a period of prosperity and growth can be substantiated by looking at some specific indicators: colonization, regional specialization, demographics, and trade and commerce.

Colonization refers to the expansion on the part of Israel and Judah towards the east, the west, and the south (2 Chro. 26:6-8 which witnesses to the colonizing activities of Uzziah). Not only was Uzziah (Jeroboam II as well) successful in forging a strong state locally, but he was powerful enough to extend his control beyond his borders. Territorial expansion and political subjugation were often motivated by and as a result of economic gains. Regional specialization refers to specialized economic activities such as viticulture, olive orcharding, mining and metallurgy, dyeing and weaving, and farming and herding. Changes in demographics often reflect the changes in the socioeconomic realities. One such avenue of information is the growth of cities.[1]

Trade and commerce flourished in the eighth century B.C.E. The available information indicates that interregional and international trade was initiated, maintained, and monopolized by the crown. It is precisely at those times when there was a strong centralized power that there was also thriving trade. The geopolitical advantage enjoyed by Israel and Judah in the eighth century enabled them to control trade and commerce through the control of trade routes. This had two very favourable outcomes for the wealthy. First, the entire trade enterprise was geared towards procuring items of interest and demand for the elites. This included military items such as horses and chariots, and luxury items such as fine linen, jewellery, perfume, and spices. Second, since the elites controlled trade, they were also the beneficiaries of such lucrative enterprises. The profitable nature of interregional and international trade prompted the production of commodities or articles that had good exchange value. Commodities such as wine and oil were worth more in terms of their exchange value per unit of volume or weight than grain. Hence, wine and olive oil, the agricultural specialties of Palestine, were prominent items in export/import exchanges.[2] There seemed to be no end to the prosperity of Israel during this time.

---

[1] D. N. Premnath, "Amos and Hosea: Socio-historical Background and Prophetic Critique," *Word & World* 28, no. 2 (Spring 2008): 126.

[2] In discussions concerning eighth-century Israel and Judah, one question is often neglected: Who were the beneficiaries of the growth and prosperity, or at whose expense were such prosperity and growth achieved? It would be erroneous to assume that the growth and prosperity benefited everyone in the society. Further, the anomaly one needs to explain is this: Why did the largest number and the most intense of prophetic oracles come from a period that enjoyed significant prosperity and growth? One explanation is that the growth and prosperity witnessed especially in the first part of the eighth century benefited only a small minority of the population—the members of the ruling class. Through an organized system of taxation, they were able to extract the economic surplus. The surplus went to support a life of leisure and luxury, which is marked by palatial private residences, conspicuous consumption, use of luxury items such as fine linen, expensive ornaments, and perfume, and non-productive recreational activity. Considerable surplus was also invested in providing for military means in order to gain political control. Stronger political control resulted in greater socio-economic benefit. This in turn enabled the elite to invest even more in the military. The cumulative effect of this vicious cycle was the impoverishment of the peasantry, who constituted the majority of the population.

It was the best of times. Materialism was reigning. Those who were rich and powerful abused the poor by legal manipulation and got richer while the poor got poorer.

However, it was also the worst of times for Israel. The religion of the Israelites became void of any truth and sincerity. The best of times, therefore, was the worst of times. It was a period when people lived a good life materially, but this materialism produced a false sense of security and independence. The people forgot about God and his covenant during the forty years-793 through 753-when they enjoyed the greatest material prosperity. It was during this time of hopelessness and national insecurity that Hosea brought the message of healing to the people.

4.2. Health and Healing in Hosea

4.2.1. Historical and Textual Background of Hosea

Despite the literary genius of the book of Hosea, historical details regarding its author and its historical referents are sketchy. What is gleaned of the prophet himself and of his own historical epoch is found principally in the superscription of the work and in various geographical and political references. The superscription reveals him as Hosea *ben*-Beeri, living in the eighth century B.C.E. His own references about Gilgal, Bethel, and Samaria indicate that his prophetic ministry was situated in the Northern Kingdom between the years of 760 - 723 B.C.E. before its fall to Assyria.[3] While recorded prophetic callings often involve direct address to the prophet, Yahweh's initiatory revelation to Hosea is transmitted in third person language by an "unknown voice."

This unnamed speaker is obviously aware of the event "When the Lord first spoke through Hosea" and "to Hosea" (1:2) as well as of the enigmatic and troubling command to "take to yourself a wife of harlotry." The marriage to Gomer assumes the character of prophecy in itself and begins the course of judgment, which is brought to implicit fulfilment toward the conclusion of the work.[4] Although attempts to historicize specific events in the book have yielded a variety of plausible conjectures,[5] the available evidence seems, in one commentator's estimation, to be "masterfully obscure." While anonymous allusions, references to Assyria and Egypt, and cross texting of biblical and extra biblical sources provide some parameters for speculation, pinpointing specific historical occasions is a "frustrating task."[6]

Whether this ambiguity is the result of a stylistic choice of the prophet, a function of damaged texts, or the linguistic peculiarities of Northern Kingdom dialects, historical accuracy is deliberately elusive. It has been suggested in fact

---

[3] Elizabeth Achtemeier, "Minor Prophets 1," in *New International Bible Commentary* (Peabody: Ma: Hendrickson Publishers, 1996), 4.

[4] Ibid., 5-6.

[5] P. Kruger, "Prophetic Imagery: On Metaphors and Similies in the Book of Hosea," *Journal of Northwest Semitic Languages* 14, no. 1988 (1988): 147.

[6] Francis I. Andersen and David Noel Freedman, *Hosea, The Anchor Bible* (New York: Doubleday, 1998), 35.

that such attempts at historicizing may be a violation of the intent of the prophet himself. Therefore, the historical value of this prophetic book may lie more in its religious and metaphorical perspectives on political and cultural entanglements than its capacity to yield any information about actual historical events.

The prophetic text may be divided into two broad sections. Chapters 1 through 3, introduce the spousal metaphor between Yahweh/Hosea and Israel/ Gomer and combine narrative and poetic elements. Chapters 4 through 14, conversely, contain fewer prose elements and constructions that are more poetic. This difference is consistent with the function of this portion of Hosea as prophetic utterance or oracular discourse, which, though recognizable from its content, lacks typical (e.g. "Thus says...") prophetic introductions and conclusions.[7] These textual peculiarities convey the sense that Hosea and, by extension, his audience are privy to the "actual deliberations of Yahweh in divine council" through the mode of "direct divine discourse."[8]

The predominant use of the first person pronoun for Yahweh and of shifting pronouns for Israel/Ephraim accentuates the theological dimension of the oracles. This theological revelation, furthermore, is distinguished by "turbulent vacillations"[9] of divine pathos reflected in Yahweh's impassioned utterances. The circumstances which provoke such torment in Yahweh and which are voiced in Hosea's unparalleled literary style are both cultic and political in nature. The chosen people of Yahweh have turned away to idolatry and apostasy, both in the worship of the false gods of Baalic cults (11:2) and graven images (4:12-13). They also have aligned themselves in the security of military might and political alliances (12:1). In contrast, Yahweh passionately challenges them to devote themselves to steadfast love and knowledge of God (6:6).

Hosea's northern roots are evident in the book through the frequent use of specific place-names from the north—more references to "Ephraim" than "Judah," coupled with the absence of references to Jerusalem and the Davidic line (with the exception of Hos. 3:5, often seen as a later addition).[10]

Further, the prophet addresses the socio-political and economic realities, but they are envisioned and articulated in very different literary constructs.

While scholars disagree widely on their view of the book's smaller structural units, there is general agreement among scholars that the book is divided into two unequal sections, 1-3 and 4-14. Paying close to the thematic pattern that begins with words of judgment (4;1; 12;2) and ends with material concerning

---

[7] Ibid., 44,61.

[8] Ibid., 44.

[9] James Mays, *"Hosea": The Old Testament Library* (Philadelphia: Westminster John Knox Press, 1969), 9.

[10] Cf. G. I. Davies, "Hosea," ed. R. W. Whybray (Sheffield: JSOT, 1993).

restoration (11:1-14:1-8), however, J. L. Mays[11] and H. W. Wolff,[12] further break the second and larger section into two parts, 4-11 and 12-14.

4.2.2. Metaphorical Images in Hosea

Hosea relentlessly announces both desolation and consolation to a people who seem to be manifestly unable or unwilling to hear, and he does so by means of an ever-shifting multiplicity of viewpoints, catchwords, assonance, alliterations, hyperbole, wordplay, parallelism, chiasm, and – pre-eminently - metaphors and similes.[13]

In its simplest definition, a "metaphor is that figure of speech whereby we speak about one thing in terms of another."[14] Numbering in the dozens in this prophetic work, these metaphors and similes explicitly or implicitly cast Yahweh variously as husband (1:2f), parent (11:1f), shepherd (4:16), carnivore (5:14, 13:7f), hunter (7:12), wound and infection (5:12) and Israel /Ephraim as harlot (1:2f), son (11:1-4), herd (13:5-6), heifer (10:11), vine (10:1), bird (7:11), and cow (4:16), to name but a few. Some are developed in fine detail, as those of husband and wife or parent and son, while others are strung together "as if beads," one image after another (cf. 5:12- 6:1).[15]

Although, developed in various ways, metaphor theory fundamentally explores aspects of the interaction between the two thoughts in a metaphorical expression. That thought which is the underlying idea of the text has been most simply termed as the tenor or topic, while the thought expressed in figurative speech has been termed as the vehicle. In addition, each of these thoughts is part of a semantic field, which is generally understood as that area of life, experience, or thought from which the topic (tenor) and vehicle are drawn. In the composition of this prophetic book, Hosea and/or his redactors, employ vehicles like those noted above from a range of semantic fields including the anthropomorphic, anthropopathic, theriomorphic, and physiomorphic.[16]

Therefore, metaphors play an important part in conveying the message of God. According to Gottwald, all religious language is metaphorical. He states,

> I choose to locate Biblical theology in its metaphorical range of reference to Israelite socio, economic, political, and cultural life by

---

[11] James Luther Mays, *Hosea: A Commentary* (London: SCM Press Ltd., 1969), 15-16.

[12] Cf. H.W. Wolff, *A Commentary on the Book of Hosea,* trans. G. Stansell Hermenia (Philadelphia: Fortress Press, 1974).

[13] P. A. Kruger, "Prophetic Imagery: On Metaphors and Similies in the Book of Hosea," *Journal of Northwest Semitic Languages* 14 (1988): 144.

[14] Janet Soskice, *Metaphor and Religious Language* (Oxford: Clarendon, 1985), 15.

[15] Kruger, "Prophetic Imagery: On Metaphors and Similies in the Book of Hosea," 143-144.

[16] Eva Kittay, *Metaphor: Its Cognitive Force and Linguistic Structure* (Oxford: Clarendon, 1987), 25-44.

> showing how the basic assertions of that theology correspond to socio-economic, political, and cultural interests and desiderata in ancient Israel. I claim that anything experience or claim with respect to human life in the concrete Israelite community.[17]

However, Izaak J. De Hulster opines that, this however, would deny that there are phrases without metaphors to express experience with the transcendent, the divine and to convey information about such. Even then, people may choose phrases, which are not figurative; admitted human beings can only speak within a human framework of experience and not express the being of God in God's own understanding.[18] There are not many references to divine healing of the body in the prophetic literature. Some have argued that there is none, and insist that the terminology for 'healing' is simply a metaphor for religious conversion. Certainly, there are a number of texts that use the imagery of physical affliction and disease to portray the desperate spiritual condition of Israel. See, for example, Isaiah 1:5-6; Jeremiah 8:22; 14:19; 30:12-13, 17; 33:6; Hosea 5:12-13; 6:1. Michael Brown rightly makes the following observation,

> It would be thoroughly unbiblical to translate these graphic terms – larvae, decay, sickness, sores; tear, smite, heal, bind up, and cure – into mere poetic figures, as if they did not entail real suffering, hardship, deprivation, starvation, war, disease, and exile, to be followed by real relief, resettlement, and healing. While it is true that the prophetic usage of these terms is, to a great extent, metaphorical, it should be stressed again that it is extremely misleading to reduce them to non tangible, poetic figures.[19]

Thus, such terminology is probably inclusive of both spiritual degeneration and physical affliction and healing looks to restoration of both soul and body.

One of the central metaphors in the Book of Hosea is the metaphor of illness and healing, which is explicitly or implicitly mentioned with frequency throughout the text. The centrality of the metaphors can be seen both in the explicit references to the term "illness" and "healing" (E.g., Hos. 5:13; 6:1; 7:1, 5; 11:3; 14:4) and in the allusions to their aspects in the text (e.g., Hos. 6:2; 7:9' 14; 9:4, 11-12, 14, 16; 13:16; 14:5-7). It incorporates a theoretical analysis of metaphor into a sociological discussion about the social reality of eighth-century Israel and Judah as well as a comparative study of the concept of illness and healing in the Ancient West Asia. The metaphor of Yahweh as healer is employed to describe the restoration of Israel (Hos. 6:1-2; 7:1; 14:4). Strikingly interesting

---

[17] N. K. Gottwald, "Social Matrix and Canonical Shape," *Theology Today* 42 (1985): 318.

[18] Izaak J. de Hulster, *Illuminating Images: An Iconographic Method of Old Testament Exegesis with Three Case Studies from Third Isaiah* (Utrecht: The British Museum, 2007), 261.

[19] Michael L. Brown, *Israel's Divine Healer* (Grand Rapids, Michigan: Zondervan, 1995), 187.

in Hosea's metaphors is his description of socio-political and economic deviation of Israel in terms of illness (5:13; 6:1; 7:1, 5).

In addition, it is readily discerned in commentators' frequent references to illness and healing in an effort to play up despair and hope in the life of Israel.[20] For all the various attempts to interpret the image of illness and healing in Hosea, scholars' discussion about this image has often remained broad and oversimplified. They view illness as associated merely with sin and military devastation by an enemy, and healing with forgiveness and national restoration. Walker provides the most recent, detailed exploration on the subject by bringing into focus mainly Israel's inability to repent its sin and the role of Yahweh's grace in forgiving its sin with respect to Israel's illness and healing.[21]

While the understanding might be true, it does not show the full significance of the metaphor in Hosea. Scholarship is largely agreed that, as in the other eight-century prophets, Hosea criticizes the various socio-economic dynamics of Israel, which breach the norms of social justice and unity. The pervasive metaphor should be expected to be a part of the critique, representing the painful reality and wishful agrarian Israel. In this wider endeavour, metaphor as a strategy of discourse is employed to create and communicate meaning.

The primary concern of this chapter will be to explore the social meaning of the metaphor of illness and healing and the etiology of illness as key background assumption for interpreting the metaphor. The common root for "healing" in the Old Testament is רפא. while it conveys a wide range of meanings such as "repair," "mend," "make wholesome," "heal" and "restore," its fundamental meaning can be characterized as "restore." Thus healing means a restoration to a state of health or well being defined as "normal" by the society, for which שלום provided the broadest term. For this understanding, several texts will be taken into consideration in order to draw out the concept of illness, health and healing in the Book of Hosea.

4.2.3. Exegetical Study

4.2.3.1. Hosea 5:12-13

Verse 12: Therefore I am like *pus*[a22] to Ephraim,
And like *rottenness* to the house of Judah
Verse 13: When saw his *sickness*,

---

[20] Mays, Wolff, Andersen and Freedman, Stuart, Davies, and others.

[21] Cf. T. W. Walker, "The Metaphor of Healing and the Theology of the Book of Hosea" (Ph. D. dissertation, Princeton Theological Seminary, 1997).

[22] עש, which is derived from the root עשש, "to putrefy" should be read as "pus" rather than "moth" or "maggot." The imagery in verse 13 makes the above suggestion more convincing in comparison with the customary translation "moth." Moreover, the moth not only destroys people's clothing (Is 50:9; 51:8), but also represents transience rather than destructiveness (Job 4:19).Davies, "Hosea," 157.

And Judah his *wound,*
Then Ephraim went to Assyria,
And sent to the great king.[a23]
But he is not able to cure you
Or heal your wound.

Form Critical Notes

Wolf argues that while a new beginning, comparable to 5:8 does not occur until 8:1, the whole of 5:8-7:16 are syntactically, stylistically, and thematically interrelated. He finds that the series of prophetic sayings in 5:8-7:16 is a kerygmatic unity that is addressed at a single historical moment.[24] Wolf dates the entire section after the Assyrian invasion into Israel in 733 B.C.E. This suggests that Wolff regards the historical event as the most probable point of reference for the entire unit. However, his reliance on the literary features such as metrical continuity, even when there is definite shift of mood weakens his argument for the unity of the whole section.[25]

There are some scholars who take the view that 5:8-6:6 belongs together in a group. The reason being relating to the so-called Syro-Ephraimite war and its aftermath (735-732 B. C. E.). For A. Alt, the historical setting serves as a lever to form the unity in the series.[26] However, this attempt was challenged by Andersen and Freedman. They hold that it is hardly possible to force the different parts of the text into a specific historical situation during the war, since Hosea has made literary use of some archaic motifs, which refer to the old tribal league. Mays also considers the whole piece of 5:8-6:6 as a unit on the basis of literary and thematic interrelation as well as common setting: 91) 5:8-9: a prophetic saying in which Hosea appears as a watchman; (2) 5:10-12: a divine saying about Israel and Judah and their guilt in the war; (3) 5:13-14: the divine announcement of judgment; (4) 5;15: Yahweh who awaits Israel's penitence; (5) 6:1-3: a liturgical expression of the demanded penitence; (6) 6:4-6: the divine saying answering the song.[27]

Against these view Davies argues that a break should be made between 6:1-3 and 6:4-6; he believes that 6:4-6 does not constitute Yahweh's direct response to

---

[23] LXX ßασιλεα ίαριμ corresponds to the MT מלך ירב, which is to be understood as the proper name "King Yareb". However, it is unusual for the anarthrous מלך to precede the proper name of a king in this fashion. This most likely arose from incorrect separation of the original expression מלכי רב, "great king." The expression serves as the Hebrew dialectal rendering of the Akkadian *Šarru rabû,* it seems to relate to the Assyrian King.

[24] Ibid., 108-112.

[25] G. I. Davies, *Hosea* (Grand Rapids, Michigan: William B. Eerdmans Publishing Company, 1992), 147.

[26] As quoted by, Zeev Herzog, "Settlement and Fortification Planning in the Iron Age," in *The Architecture of Ancient Israel: From the Prehistoric to Persian Periods*, ed. A. Kempinski and R. Reich (Jerusalem: Ahva Press, 1992), 250.

[27] Mays, *Hosea: A Commentary*, 87.

6;1-3.[28] In other words, vv 4-6 are not tightly linked to vv 1-3; the genre of vv 1-3 is not "a song of repentance" but "an exhortation" designed to call one forth.[29] The prophet, in an exhortation, encouraged his contemporaries to join him in turning back to Yahweh. In addition, 6:4, with its opening rhetorical questions, has all the appearance of being the beginning of a new section. Accordingly, it has to be admitted that 6:3 marks the end of the unit, which begins with 5:8.

Setting

The section 5:8-6:3 is composed of several subsections that, taken together shows Hosea's growing alarm over "foreigners" in the socio-economic and political system of Israel and Judah and the consequences of such system. It is frequently accepted that the historical setting of this section alludes to Judah's counter attack against Israel during the Syro-Ephraimite war. However, two difficulties arise from this scenario. First, there is no evidence that Judah ever invaded Israel during the war. Neither Assyrian nor Biblical sources provide any trustworthy evidence that Judah attacked Israel. Secondly, Hosea 5:13 envisages a situation in which Israel turned to Assyria for protection. This stands in conflict with the goals of the Syro-Ephraimite coalition to rebel against Assyria.[30] With respect to the first point, moreover, Hosea presents Judah as the aggressor (5:10). However, in the Syro-Ephraimite war Judah was on the defence. It may be that the passage contains incidents before or after the war.[31]

It is conceivable that the passage contains allusions to more than one historical situation. In this light, Garrett's comments are persuasive: "It is more likely that this passage refers in general to political events of the latter half of the eight century, but not especially to the events of this particular war."[32] However, it is quite common to associate Hosea 8-6:6, or at the very least 5:8-14, either as a compositional or redaction unit, with circumstances of the Syro-Ephraimite War.[33] Thus, for instance, Alt and others have suggested the events during the Syro-Ephraimite War for 5:8-6:6. Hence, the following interpretation is built basing on this understanding of historical background.

---

[28] Davies, *Hosea*, 149-151.

[29] Seong Hyuk Hong, *The Metaphor of Illness and Healing in Hosea and its Significance in the Socio-Economic Context of Eight-Century Israel and Judah* (New York: Peter Lang, 2006), 143.

[30] Marvin. A. Sweeney, *The Twelve Prophets*, vol. 1 (Brit Olam: Collegeville: Glazier/Liturgical Press, 2000), 60-61.

[31] Mays and Hubbard place the context of this section in events after the Syro-Ephraimite War. (D. A. Hubbard, *Hosea: An Introduction and Commentary* (Downers Grove: InterVarsity Press, 1969); Mays, *"Hosea": The Old Testament Library*, 86-91.

[32] Garrett, *The New American Commentary: Hosea, Joel*, 149.

[33] Albrecht. Alt, *Hosea 5:8-6:6* (Munchen: Chr. Beck, 1964), 85-98; Mays, *Hosea: A Commentary*. 85-98, Andersen and Freedman, *Hosea*, 399-431.

Resuming the analysis of the intellectual setting of the primary readership of the book, the image of the king of Assyria is for them not only a distant memory, but also a paradigmatic figure. The king of Assyria is referred to as מל ירב in 5:13, and the same expression is used in Hosea 10:6; there is no reason to doubt or assume that it is the result of textual corruption. Israel's decision to accept the Assyrian king as a protecting or patron king is absolutely folly from the viewpoint of the discourse of the literary intelligentsia within whom and for whom the book of Hosea was written.[34] Therefore, for this perspective, Israel's patron king, the only one who is able to protect and heal Israel, is Yahweh. The contrast between Yahweh and the Assyrian king is explicitly conveyed by the double use of verbal forms from רפא "heal" in 5:15; 6:1 and 7:1.The Assyrian king cannot heal, but when Israel shows wisdom (6:1), it recognizes that Yahweh is the only one who can heal, as well as punish those who accepted other kings over Yahweh. Hosea 7:1 reaffirms the basic characterization of Yahweh as Israel's healer. In other words, Yahweh is the only champion of Israel. No human king, not even the most powerful, can fulfil that role. This theme is explicitly brought back to the attention of the readers of the book in Hosea 14:4-5; moreover the explicit reference to Yahweh's healing (רפא) serves as a signpost that reminds the readers that this reading and that in chapter 14 inform each other.

The structural basis for the interpretation of the passage might look like this:

5:8 summons to alarm
5:9 reason for summons to alarm
5:10-11 accusation of sin
5:12-14 Yahweh as the cause of illness and source of healing
5:15 need for repentance
6:1-3 exhortation to return to Yahweh.

4.2.3.1.1. Comments on Hosea 5:13 in relation to Illness, Health and Healing

The central passage in which Hosea perceived the answer to this question is found in 5:12 to 6:3. The expressions *rākāb* at 5:12 and *mazor* in 5:13 are used by the prophet. The antonym of the term "disease" is the verb *rapha* (healing), which the prophets always have used in a metaphorical sense. Hosea has mentioned the terms, which express primarily the sickly state of the people as a community.

Assyria is understood as the subject of רפא but one can assume that 5:13 refers indirectly to Yahweh as the healer of Judah and Ephraim. Assyria or the great king of Assyria is not able to heal; therefore, Yahweh, the only King of Israel is the healer. Hosea uses two different words to describe the sickness and healing

---

[34] Ehud Ben Zvi, *Hosea* (Grand Rapids, Michigan: William B. Eerdmans Publishing Company, 2005), 143.

of foe people. This may emphasize the great extent of Israel's sickness and the fact that Assyria is not able to do anything. Yahweh alone is healer because He alone is the initiator of the covenant with Israel. When Israel and God are turned away from one another, the covenant is violated.

Hence, in 5:13, Hosea is speaking realistically and metaphorically all kinds of misdeeds and atrocities of the people that lead into question the viability of the country. The usage of the metaphorical language *"rapha"* "mended" "improved" "heal" signifies the use of metaphors in a figurative sense. The subject of these metaphors is the image of God as a physician, as the one who saves and restores (cf. Exod. 15:26; Deut. 32:39; 1 Sam. 2:6). Specifically, the disease in the Old Testament is psycho-physical reality, but is often used as a metaphor for social, economic, political and religious realties in the book of Hosea. Hammer's idea of salvation of Israel from political bondage involves salvation to be a light of persuasive justice to the nations. God's concern for the health of all peoples and nations, also for Israel's ancient enemies, calls Israel to that prophetic task.[35]

The foreigners of the socio-economic system are highlighted by the metaphor of illness and healing presented in vv.12-14. The metaphor will draw our special attention to such categories as the source of illness and healing as well as the pattern of illness and healing.

4.2.3.1.1.1. Metaphor of 'Pus' and 'Rottenness'

Hosea 5:12-14 presents the situation of the Israelite society of Hosea's time as a state of sickness. In verse 12, Yahweh is described as "pus" and "rottenness" in the body of Israel and Judah. This means that Yahweh is the source of illness that is afflicting Israel and Judah. Though Israel perceived the symptoms of her disease, she did not search for its cause and did not approach the doctor, who is able to cure her.

What is the sickness that is afflicting Ephraim and Judah? Various scholars speak of this sickness in terms of "pus" and "rot". The usages of "pus" and "rot," need not necessarily refer to Israel and Judah suffering tangibly from pus and rot but they are symbols or metaphors of another kind of sickness. The pus symbolizes what happens on the outside of human being, to his/her physical existence. The rot symbolizes what happens to the inside of human being, to his/her spiritual being. The context of the text exposes the religious apostasy that Israel loved to worship.[36]

[35] Paul L. Hammer, "God's Health for the World: Some Biblical Understandings of Salvation," *Ex Auditu* 5 (1989): 85.

[36] They brought sacrifices and offerings to the Lord by the thousands. The land was filled with the smoke of incense and offering. On the surface everything looked so good. But the Lord could see the truth. He could see the holes that were forming, that were already there. He knew it was all show and pretence and sham. He knew that moths were busy at work. It isn't only Israel's worship that is being exposed. In earlier verses God announced what would happen to the land, to the people, to the cattle, to the outward existence.

The metaphor of "rot" that Hosea speaks of means that the decay will affect not only the outside but also the inside; not only Israel's clothes but also her body; not only outward appearances but also the inner existence. Ephraim was suffering from some such horrible disease. She seemed to know she had this disease. Therefore, she sought medical help from the great king of Assyria. The moth and the rot are only symbolic, a metaphor, of another illness. The rot, like the pus, symbolizes Israel's broken communion with God. Ephraim's communion with God was broken, but she didn't want to admit it, and she liked to think she was on the best of terms with God. She liked to think the relationship was healthy, that all was well with her soul. However, things were not well at all. In fact, doom and destruction were on the way.

4.2.3.1.1.2. Image of 'Sickness' and 'Wounds'

The "sickness" and "wounds" are understood as the precipitous loss of power and wealth that Israel and Judah experienced in the later part of the 8th century. The prophet looks upon Israel's seeking the aid of a foreign power to survive the political upheaval without turning to Yahweh, as a mistake and apostasy.

D. K. Stuart rightly notes: "The figure of the sick person continues to describe Israel and Judah metaphorically. Both 'illnesses and its parallel 'sores' represent covenant plagues and can connote miseries afflicted by an enemy, rather than merely human illnesses."[37] In their situation of sickness, they failed to look up to Yahweh, their healer because they had not realized the historical fact that Yahweh brought Israel from the situation of malady to that of well-being. Added to this fact was that they did not perceive the true healer. They even went to other human and divine agents expecting cure (Hosea 5:13, 11:12). The direct address of Verse 13 seems to include both Israel and Judah. Neither Samaria nor Judah will be helped by appeal to Assyria. Assyria's ultimate policy toward Israel, either north or south, was unpredictable, and trusting it to help was folly.

Assyria is understood as the subject of רפא but one can assume that Hosea 5:13 refers indirectly to Yahweh as the healer of Judah and Ephraim. Assyria or the great king of Assyria is not able to heal; therefore, Yahweh, the only King of Israel, is the healer. This fact is emphasised if you read Hosea 5:13 together with Hosea 6:1. It is interesting to note that Hosea 5:13 uses two different word to describe the sickness (מזור ̱הלי) and the healing of the people (גהה רָפא). This may emphasise the great extent of Israel's sickness and the fact that Assyria is not able to do anything. Yahweh alone is healer because He alone is the initiator of the covenant with Israel. When Israel and Yahweh are turned away from one another, the covenant is violated

The prophet promptly declares that Assyria is no adequate physician, for the real enemy is the Lord who will not be frustrated in his intent to punish. The

[37] Douglas Stuart, "Hosea," in *Word Biblical Commentary*, ed. David A Hubbard and Glenn W. Barker (Waco, Texas: Word Books Publishers, 1987), 105.

people describe their problem in disease terms (Hos. 6:1). Yet one must not lose sight of the fact that conditions brought about by siege and war (some of the miseries afflicted by an enemy) lead to an increased bodily illnesses as well, along with a large number of casualties. Thus, the prophets often threatened Israel with the sword, famine, and plague especially if the warfare was accompanied by siege. Adding to this the fact that the covenant curses speak of further judgement of plagues and the metaphors of sickness and sores become more graphic still.[38]

Yahweh as a punishment for their sin caused the illness of both kingdoms. This is in agreement with the cause of illness in ancient Israelite society. It is said that in the ancient west Asia illness was caused by attacks of foreign agents, either personal agents (gods or evil spirits) or impersonal harmful materials, on the body from the outside. Hence, it should be understood that "pus" and "rottenness" were caused by Yahweh's attack on the body. In addition, the illness is associated with divine punishment for the sins of the ruling elite of Israel and Judah, which most probably refer to the establishment of the oppressive and unjust socio economic system and its destructive effects on ordinary subjects.[39] Based on the notion of illness discussed above the following three elements can be drawn out that:

1. The cause of illness is because of the invasion of a foreign agent or nation
2. The destructive effects of illness
3. Illness is cause because of a broken relationship with Yahweh

These elements come from the syntactic relations between lexemes in the vehicle field of illness such as illness, invasion, foreigners, agent, destruction, Yahweh, relationship, break, etc. Based on socio-economic factors the elements in the field is divided as follows:

1. The oppressive socio-economic system as a foreign form
2. The destructive effects of the oppressive socio-economic system
3. The oppressive socio-economic system as the disrupted relationship with Yahweh.[40]

Here the socio-economic system is identified with the monarchy, which is foreign in Hosea's perspective. The systematic study of socio-economic dynamics in eighth-century Israel and Judah and the foreign nature of monarchy in Hosea's eyes is characterized by commercialization through foreign alliances. This means that centralization of political and economic power was to maximise the leader's profits at the cost of ordinary subject. The oppressive structure of the society is

---

[38] Brown, *Israel's Divine Healer*, 187.

[39] Hong, *The Metaphor of Illness and Healing in Hosea and its Significance in the Socio-Economic Context of Eight-Century Israel and Judah*, 148.

[40] Ibid.

also associated with land consolidation in the hands of the ruling elite, failure of political leadership, political treachery, regicide, increasing social cleavage, etc. All these drove the whole Israelite society into chaos, i.e., illness. However, the ruling elite did not realize that these are related to the influence of Yahweh. In sum, the metaphor of illness highlights the foreignness of the monarchy, its destructive effects, and the broken relationship with Yahweh.

In v. 13, Hosea points out that Israel and Judah do not perceive the ultimate source of their illness and healing. Instead of recognising Yahweh as the only source of their illness and healing, they wrongly appealed to Assyria and its great king. The focus of this verse with regard to the metaphor of illness is on Israel's alliances with foreign powers, which is the cause of suffering or punishment by Yahweh. Here the topical domain of the oppressive-socio-economic system is structured in the perspective offered by the cause of illness as the invasion of foreign alliances that are the focus of v.13. Foreign involvement represented by tribute and trade, brought the dire consequences to the general populace. This is the destructive effect of illness, i.e., the foreign socio-economic system. The alien system devoured the identity and communal solidarity of Israel (Hos. 7:9). The following statement from Keefe is pertinent,

> Dabbling in cosmopolitan value, binding itself in foreign alliances, and increasingly dependent upon interregional market economy-all these have effect, says Hosea, of cultural homogenization with 'the nations'. Such homogenization leads to the dissolution of Israel's own identity, and ultimately, warns the prophet, to literal destruction.[41]

Taken as a whole, Hosea expresses his hostility toward foreign alliances with Assyria with the imagery of illness. At the same time, Hosea employs the imagery to suggest that the present suffering of Israel and Judah from illness is derived from Yahweh.[42]

Healing for Hosea means removing the foreign system and restoring the system of the old tribal society based on the covenantal relationship with Yahweh and communal solidarity. The socio-economic structures characterised by commercialization, land-grapping, taxation, debt servitude, and court corruption to support the ruling elite including the crown are in Hosea's eyes foreign to a

---

[41] Alice A. Keefe, *Woman's Body and the Social Body in Hosea* (London: Sheffield Academic Press, 2001), 208.

[42] Taken together, while they recognise that it is Yahweh who brought about illness, and he alone who can heal, Israel and Judah need to acknowledge and confess their sins in prayer for healing or restoration. This implies that the harmonious or right relationship with Yahweh is fundamental to the restoration of one's health. The recovery of the harmony with Yahweh leads to revoking, his influence of afflicting or making other foreign agents withdraw from the patient's body. In other words, the concept of healing does not confine itself merely to restoration of the physical condition, but that of the sound relationship with Yahweh.

traditional tribal society based on communal solidarity and reciprocity. All this reflects a disturbed relationship with Yahweh. Hosea identifies these oppressive structures with illness.

4.2.3.1.1.3. Image of 'Health' and 'Healing' as Removing and Restoring the Oppressive System

For Hosea "healing" consists in removing the oppressive and foreign system and restoring the system of the old tribal society, which is rooted in mutuality and reciprocity on the basis of covenantal relationship with Yahweh and community solidarity. Pre-monarchic decentralised society was normative at least in Hosea's perspective in that for all the existence of social inequalities in practice, the communitarian values were upheld free from state intervention in the social, economic, and political spheres of life and hence, the metaphor of healing highlights the expulsion of foreignness from Israelite society and restoration of communal solidarity based on the intimate relationship with Yahweh.

The image of the Healing is applied metaphorically in Hosea to the nation, which was ravaged by misfortunes, which is capable of full restoration of health. The vocabulary and the particular expressions of this usage are from an examination of the context, properly interpreted of sickness and healing.[43] Hosea's metaphorical images of illness and sores also connote the miseries afflicted by an enemy, along with merely human illnesses.[44] That is to say, the metaphorical prophetic usage of *healing* must be seen as inclusive and not exclusive. While it may not focus on literal healing of corporeal ailments, it certainly does not exclude that.

4.2.3.2. Hosea 6:1-3

V. 1. Let us return to Yahweh;
For he has torn, and he will *heal* us;
He has struck down,[a] and he will bind us up.
V. 2.He will revive us after two days,
On the third day he will raise us up,
That we may live in his presence.
V. 3. Let us know, let us strive to know the Lord.
His going forth is certain as the dawn.
He will come to us like rain, like the spring rain that water the land.

---

[43] Ulrich Duchrow and Gerhard Liedke, *Shalom: Biblical Perspectives on Creation, Justice, and Peace* (Geneva: WCC, 1989), 48-49.

[44] Brown, *Israel's Divine Healer*, 188.

4.2.3.2.1. Comment on Hosea 6:1-3 in relation to Illness, Health and Healing

4.2.3.2.1.1. Return (שׁוּב) as the Pre-requisite for Healing

In some prophetic texts repentance or return (שׁוּב) are seen as a prerequisite for Yahweh's healing (Isa. 6:10; 19:22; Jer. 19:22; Hos. 6:1). However, this cannot be true for all the 'healing' passages. Repentance is not always seen as a pre-condition for healing.

There is no doubt in this text that the prophet is more concerned about the people. They express a desire to return (שׁוּב) to Yahweh. In this regard, Mays rightly argues that for Hosea the word שׁוּב means forsaking the "Baalized practices current in religion" and returning to the "original relation to Yahweh of the wilderness period."[45] Baalism signifies the socio-economic system that is based on the commercialization of agriculture and the centralization of land ownership and economic power in urban centers. To the contrary, the harmonious relationship with Yahweh in the wilderness period is suggestive of the segmentary tribal society based on the covenantal relationship with Yahweh, mutual help and communal solidarity. Hosea again presents the communitarian style of society as the norm to which the people should return. Moreover, he reaffirms Yahweh as the ultimate source of illness and healing by means of the employment of parallelism: "he has torn, and he will heal us, he has struck down,[46] and he will bind us up."

The healing continues in verse 2 where it expresses the presumptuous confidence of the people in Yahweh's quick response to bring therapy to those who return to him in penitence. The statement "He will revive us after two days, on the third day he will raise us up" has been the source of much scholarly debate. Commentators like E. K. Holt, find here the connection between the cult of a dying and rising god.[47] However, the people are the subject of rising and not deity, since they do not seem to be dead but ill.[48] Moreover, in view of the imagery of illness and healing, it is to be understood in terms of healing from illness. This position is corroborated by Barre's analysis of parallels in the Mesopotamian medical texts to the concepts of living (חיה) and raising up (קום) in Hosea 6:2. In the Mesopotamian texts, "three days" is a synonymous expression for a short

---

[45] Mays, *"Hosea": The Old Testament Library*, 94.

[46] The root נכה has the overtones of illness, since the terms "striking" and "smiting" or "attacking" were used to depict what occurred to the patient in the Ancient West Asia. According to van der Toorn, "such vocabulary suggests that diseases were understood by analogy with injuries received in battle, fights or accidentally at the hands of a fellow human being, with blows being administered this time by supernatural agents. Van Der Toorn, *Sin and Sanction in Israel and Mesopotamia: A Comparative Study* (Assen/ Maastricht: Van Gorcum, 1985), 68.

[47] E. K. Holt, *Prophesying the Past: The Use of Israel's History in the Book of Hosea* (Sheffield: Sheffield Academic Press, 1995); Flemming Friis Hvidberg, *Weeping and Laughter in the Old Testament* (Leiden: E. J. Brill, 1962), 126.

[48] Davies, "Hosea."; Wolff, *A Commentary of the Book of the Prophet Hosea*, 118-119.

period of time.[49] The identical configuration of terms 'healing," "binding" prior to "living" and "raising up" is associated with medical language as well.[50] Therefore, the expressions "living" "raising up" refer to healing in a short time. The phrase "living in his presence" suggests that Yahweh can give healing to Israel on the condition that the people live before Yahweh, not before a king. This demand for a renewed relationship with Yahweh from the people.

4.2.3.2.1.2. Healing as the result of 'Knowing God'

The verbal root ידע, "to know" has a sense of intimacy that often involved sexual connotation in Genesis 4:1, 17, 25; Judges 19:25 and 1 Samuel 1:19. It signifies something that must be gained by deliberate effort and laborious searching. These notions suggest that the knowledge of Yahweh refers to the intimate relationship with Yahweh and must be achieved by deliberate effort on the part of the people of Israel. Thus, the verse emphasizes the importance of deliberate effort to know Yahweh by using the expression "strive" (רדף), which displays contrast with 2:7, where the same verb is used of Israel's passionate pursuit of her lovers, i.e., the Baal's.[51] Hosea utilizes this imagery to revive the ideal life of socio-economic system based on the intimate relationship with Yahweh, which is compared with the oppressive socio-economic system based on commercialism and foreign collaborations.

The pursuit of the knowledge of Yahweh is followed by an expression of reliability of Yahweh's "going forth." The expression "as the dawn" implies the constant appearance of the sun in the morning. The daily event points to Yahweh's reliability and predictability in terms of healing power. The yearly event of the spring and fall rains also alludes to the predictability and certainty of the divine intervention in healing. As rain refreshes dry land,[52] so also healing will also make the person afresh. This implies that the restoration of intimate relationship with Yahweh will in turn give birth to the harmonious relationship with nature. Here the people of Israel have uttered many right words in order to express their desire to restore the harmonious relationship with Yahweh, but something is still missing. There is no mention of a confession of sin that is essential for restoration or healing. This means that the people of Israel have not yet initiated the expulsion of foreignness.

---

[49] M. L. Barre, "New light on the Interpretation of Hosea VI 2," *Vetus Testamentum*, no. 28 (1978); Mays, *Hosea: A Commentary*, 95.

[50] Barre, "New light on the Interpretation of Hosea VI 2," 241-245.

[51] Davies, *Hosea*, 162.

[52] Wolff, *A Commentary on the Book of Hosea,* 119.

4.2.3.3. Hosea 11:3

V. 3. "I was the one who taught Ephraim[a] to walk,
taking them by the arms;
"they have not realised (ידע)
that I[b] healed (רפא) them.

Form Critical Notes

The unit is a kind of divine and authoritative summary of the history of Israel. But unlike most histories it includes events in the future. This concept provides much hope to an Israel that considers itself as existing after a terrifying divine judgment and before the worldly manifestation of Yahweh's promises of restoration and hope (Hos. 11:10-11). The text reflects and shapes a discourse in which past and future seem to be fixed in a closely linked relationship that is expressed and communicated even at the level of word choice.[53]

The internal structural division advanced here is one of several possibilities. A complementary structure of the unit can be easily discerned involving two major units. (1) vv. 1-9- which by itself is subdivided into (A) 1-4, (B) 5-7 and (C) 8-9 or into (A) 1-7 and (B) 8-9 and (2) vv 10-11.[54] Eidewall supports that there is a sequential structure similar to the one proposed by Sweeney. He also refers to an inclusion structure (v. 1- out of Egypt; v. 2-walk away from Yahweh; v. 10-walk behind Yahweh; v. 11- out of Egypt).[55] Even if one does not fully accept all the details of Eidewall's position, yet there is a sense of similarities between vv. 2 and 10.

In addition, numerous other proposals have been advanced.[56] Wolff divides the unit into (i) vv 1-7 and (ii) vv 8-11. Andersen and Freedman,[57] between (i) vv 1-4 and (ii) vv. 5-11. According to them 'there are serious structural dislocations in the chapter" which may be "an authentic reflection of the turbulence of indecision, or the by product of varieties of textual disarray."[58] The multiplication of proposed structures is directly related to different interpretations of the text, in some cases to redactional assumptions, and to different understanding of the interplay of the different literary subunits.[59] The text of Hosea 11 implies an awareness of social memories reflected in other books and it uses language and metaphors that appear elsewhere in the repertoire of post monarchic communities.

---

[53] Zvi, *Hosea*, 226.

[54] Sweeney, *The Twelve Prophets*, 112-117.

[55] G. Eidewall, *Grapes in the Desert: Metaphors, Models, and Themes in Hosea 4 -14* (Stockholm: Almqvist & Wiksell, 1996), 166-167.

[56] Hans Walter Wolff, in *Hosea*, ed. P. D. Hanson (Philadelphia: Fortress Press, 1974), 193-196.

[57] Andersen and Freedman, *Hosea*, 574-576.

[58] Zvi, *Hosea*, 229.

[59] Ibid.

Setting

The historical retrospect closely connects this chapter with the preceding passages beginning with 9:10. The nature of chapter 11's transmission shows it to be related to all the units beginning with 4:1. However, the message concerning the end of Yahweh's wrath and judgment and of the kindling of his pity has parallels in the previous material only in chapters 2 and 3 and later in 14:2-8.[60] In 2:4-17; 3:1-5, the impending judgment is described as an approaching deed of Yahweh which serves the purposes of his love; it will return to Yahweh and thus lead to a new salvation. In chap 11 on the other hand, the anguish is brought on by judgment, which already dominates the past and the present (vv4-7), although there are no visible signs of Israel's return (vv5b:7a). Yahweh's own change in attitude, in which his holy love shines through, provides the motivation for the salvation that now approaches. In this decisive point, Yahweh's attitude which is closely related to the present historical situation. Chapter 11 stands much closer to chapter 14:5 concerning Yahweh's spontaneous love, which heals Israel's unfaithfulness and to the supplements to chapter 2:18-25.[61]

The text provides us with minimal criteria for determining its date. Verse 11 certainly presupposes more than a mere delegation of diplomats sent to Egypt and Assyria. It would appear as though at least a considerable part of the population were living in foreign lands. In addition, it is conceivable that, parallel to the Assyrian deportation, many people fled to Egypt. The earlier threats (cf. 9:3, 6) and announcements of new military struggles (10:6-8, 14f) very likely were being fulfilled as Hosea received these words from Yahweh and then proclaimed them (cf. vv5f). It should also be noted that Israel's turning to Egypt and Assyria is no longer placed parallel, as in 7:11; rather v. 5 attests to Assyria's supremacy as unshakable; Assyria is no longer spoken of as a superior power whose help Israel seeks (5:13; 8:9).[62]

Robinson dates chapter 11 to the time of Shalmaneser V's reign (727-2), when Israel's new turn toward Egypt provoked Assyria's retaliation (2 Kgs. 17:4). It hardly recommends itself to date the passage later than 724 or even 721. Chapter 11 is closely related, with chaps 9-10, which belonged to the period between 733 and 727. It is also related to 2:18-25, which must have originated soon after 733. In view of these considerations, the most likely period would be the first half of the reign of Shalmaneser V, perhaps at the beginning of his punitive measures, especially since Samaria itself is not yet expressly mentioned as a besieged or even a conquered city.

---

[60] Wolff, *A Commentary on the Book of Hosea,* 196.

[61] Ibid.

[62] Ibid., 197.

4.2.3.3.1. Comment on Hosea 11:3 in relation to Illness, Health and Healing

In the opening verses of Hosea 11, the prophet deals with Israel's infancy in Egypt (v.1),[63] her subsequent turning after idol's (v. 2) and her ultimate failure to realise that it was God who taught her to walk, taking her on his arms. Yet the people of Israel did not recognise that it was God who made them healed or made them whole.

4.2.3.3.1.1. The Healer as the 'Saviour'

The great majority of interpreters understand רפא to mean here to simply heal,[64] but there is no adequate explanation as to the specific condition from which Israel was healed. For example, David Kimchi and Keil[65] understand *rephatim* with reference to the broad promise of healing in the context of Exodus 15:22-26; others refer it to the deliverance from Egypt.[66] Robinson understands *rephatim* against the background of Yahweh's physician-like care for Israel in the desert.[67] Andersen and Freedman further comment, "Hosea's polemic against healers in rivalry with Yahweh makes us wonder if one of the unnamed gods was a god of healing."[68] However, the concept of *rapha* not only expresses the healing of a sickness, but also the restoration or repair of a defect of any kind. M. L. Brown's argument of *rapha* gave evidence of its broader semantic range, specifically, bringing Israel to a state of wholeness from its physically immature, weak, and underdeveloped condition.[69]

The Old Testament understanding of the verb רפא refers in addition to its proper meaning "to heal" "to make whole," also to ideas that are not in line to the realm of medicine. For example, it is used for the repairing of some damages in 1 Kings 18:30; Jeremiah 19, 11 or for the betterment of certain state of affairs in 2 Kings 2:21; Ezekiel 47: 8-9 and 11.the verb said of Yahweh occurs once in the sense of "repair" in Psalm 60:4. But referring to Yahweh, רפא often implies

[63] Hosea specifically mentions Israel's beginning, which is only presupposed by the other historical retrospect. Here, Yahweh elected Israel by calling him out of Egypt. Hosea expresses the election as the "ascending" (עלה qal) or the "leading up" (עלה hiphil) from Egypt. The tradition is part of Israel's initial relationship with Yahweh, he was a child (cf. 2:17). נער can also mean an infant (Ex 6:2), a child that is weaned (cf. Gen. 21:12), or a young, still dependent person. Hence, it shows the interdependent relationship between Yahweh and Israel. In this, the metaphor of parent son relationship is used with the word "love" (אהב) as an interpretation of the election of God's people.

[64] Andersen and Freedman, *Hosea*, 575.

[65] As quoted by Brown in, Brown, *Israel's Divine Healer*, 189.

[66] Wolff, *A Commentary of the Book of the Prophet Hosea*, 199.

[67] Th. Robinson, *Die Zwolf Klienen Phopheten* (Tubingen: HAT, 1964), 26.

[68] Andersen and Freedman, *Hosea*, 581.

[69] M. L. Brown, *I am the Lord Your Healer: A Philological Study of the Root rapha in the Hebrew Bible and the Ancient Near East* (New York: New York University, 1985), 66-68.

salvation from misfortune or the forgiveness of sins-either of the individuals or of the people, (Exod. 15:26; Isa. 30:26; Jer. 30:17; Hos. 7:1; 14:5; Ps. 147:3; Job 5:18). Therefore, if healing is understood as leading to death, Yahweh's healing is understood as life-bringing.

Lohfink argues that in the later prophets the concept of disease and healing have been transferred from the family and individual sphere to communitarian aspect on two levels. First, the subject who is sick, and is in need of healing from Yahweh is Israel, Judah and Jerusalem. Second, the very idea of illness is expanded to the various physical diseases of individuals. Other elements are added: societal and economic disturbances, and privations of every sort. All these together are Israel's sickness. The core of the sickness is the broken relationship with God.[70] It may be possible that Hosea is here pointing to Yahweh's bringing out Israel from Egypt and the subsequent dealing with them as a healing process. The metaphor of Yahweh as healer reflects the notion that a healer is also the saviour of the one healed.[71]

At the same time Hosea may be alluding to the actual salvation of the contemporary Israelite society as a situation of political and socio and religious that is in need of healing. For Hosea, only Yahweh can heal the sickness of Israel. It is to be noted that Hosea employs this root elsewhere to indicate the ruins of his contemporary Israelite society.

4.2.3.3.1.2. Yahweh's Love as Healing from 'Oppressive Structures' and 'Politics'

Hosea does not hesitate to depict God as being affected by his unfaithful human lovers. Like other prophets, he typically expresses the divine "hurt" as lying in the rejection of his loving care. A motif that runs through his prophecy is the cry from the heart of God that "they did not understand." Israel has taken God's good gifts and rejected the giver. In the area of agricultural life, "she did not know that it was I who gave her the grain, the wine and the oil," and she attributed these love-gifts to Baal (2:8). In political life, she did not realise that it was Yahweh who was disciplining her through her circumstances, and instead resorted to diplomatic alliances with the super-powers of Assyria and Egypt (5:13).[72] In her history of growth as a nation, pictured as the development of a young child, she did not know that it was Yahweh who was nurturing her and helping her to grow towards maturity.

---

[70] Lohfink, "Ich bin Jawheh Dein Arzt," *Ich Will Euer Gott Werden, Biespiele Biblischen Redens Von Gott* 100 (1982): 601.

[71] Brown, "Rapha," in *Theological Dictionary of the Old Testament*, ed. G. Johannes Botterweck, Helmer Ringgren, and Heinz-Josef Fabrey (Grand Rapids, Michigan: William B. Eerdmans Publishing Company, 2004).

[72] Paul S. Fideles, "The Cross of Hosea Revisited: The Meaning of Suffering in the Book of Hosea," *Review and Expositor* 90 (1993): 179.

Yahweh's complaint that "they do not realise that I healed them" focuses on the sin of the people. They failed to perceive that it was Yahweh who delivered them from Egypt, the land of oppression and ailment. This verse echoes Jeremiah 2:13, "for my people have committed two evils: they have forsaken me, the fountain of living waters and hewed out cisterns for themselves, the broken cisterns, that can hold no water." In the following lines of Hosea 14:5, Hosea envisages the sickness as the nation's apostasy and Yahweh's healing as an act of forgiving. Thus, רפא in Hosea 11:3 may be considered as referring figuratively to Yahweh's historical interventions in favour of Israel as healing from oppressive structures and politics.

Israel as a deadly tired and exhausted child is carried by Yahweh through the desert, taken care of them and treated them to recover and prosper. Yahweh fulfilled the role of the parent who cares for children's health as well as who teaches them to walk, especially because children are prone to injury and not immune to the disease. In this context, the verb רפא certainly contributes to the intense image of God as a parent. The exodus from Egypt to Israel has meant liberation from slavery and this exempts any kind of oppressive possibilities-social, political, economic and religious. Therefore, healing here refers to salvation, which most scholars agree to as political salvation. This view is also rightly supported by Hans Walter Wolff. According to him,

> If verse 3a is to be understood in the pluperfect, then like verse 1, it would further describe the divine deliverance from Egypt in the metaphor of the father and son relationship and v3 would not refer to Yahweh's guidance through the wilderness. "To heal" (רפא) is better understood in connection with the liberation from Egypt than as Yahweh's care of Israel in the wilderness. Hosea uses the word for deliverance from "political" disaster. Yahweh, not the Baals, was the physician who saved Israel from the deadly peril in Egypt.[73]

In Hosea 11 healing and forgiveness is granted despite the fact that Israel kept sacrificing to the Baals and offering incense to idols. The child Israel disrespected the love of God her father (cf. 11:1-3).This readings coveys a strong message of hope in terms of a divine self-disclosure in which Yahweh characterizes himself not only as a deity unable to completely destroy Israel, no matter the gravity of its deeds, but also the one who will bring back to Yahweh and to the land at some point in the future. Such metaphorical image of Yahweh as a parent alludes us to the understanding of Yahweh who heals and restores Israel from their sickness and oppressive status to healing and restoration.

---

[73] Wolff, *A Commentary on the Book of Hosea,* 199.

4.2.3.4. Hosea 14:5

V. 5. I will *heal* their disloyalty,[a]
I will love them freely,
for my anger has turned from them.

Form Critical Notes

The general structure of Hosea 14:1-9 is threefold: an opening summons to return (1-3), a divine utterance of resolution and restoration (4-8), and a concluding admonition in the wisdom tradition (9). At the outset, two questions may be asked. The first question involves whether this passage is part of the original prophecy of Hosea or whether a later redactor added it.

Hosea 14 fits the pattern of renunciation and relents within Yahweh, which is exemplified from the outset of the text. The elements of this passage are finely crafted and they reflect the recurrent themes of the prophecy as a whole. Furthermore, the retrieval and reversal in this conclusion of many of the metaphors, which have been used from the beginning of the text renders it most plausible to ascribe this passage to Hosea himself.

The second question involves the issue of whose voice is being heard throughout the threefold structure of this passage. As it has been earlier noted, the shifting of pronouns and perspectives here, as throughout the book, presupposes different suppositions about speakers and referents.

Moreover, a comparison between this passage and Hosea 6: 1-6 supports these different possibilities. Perhaps the most logical conjecture concerning the opening voice in this passage is to attribute this summons and the supplication it contains to the prophet Hosea himself.

Confronted with both the assurance of the people's destruction (13: 3-16) and the assurance of Yahweh's unconditional love and acceptance (14: 4-8), Hosea entreats Israel to return to Yahweh with an implicit assurance that this turning will not be rejected (cf. 6:5 - 7:16). This certainty is grounded in the divine utterance, which follows the opening sequence, placed here as if to answer his hearers' implicit questions, "How can you assure us that we shall be received? Why should this turning be different?" Not only does the divine utterance provide this unequivocal assurance. (14:4), but it also offers multiple rich and sensual metaphors of the envisioned future restoration of the remnant which returns (14:5-7).

There seems to be little doubt that the speaker of verses 4-8 is Yahweh's own self, either in the mode of direct divine discourse or through the prophet, despite the characteristic absence of "Thus says..." here as elsewhere. The origin of the final verse of this passage and of the book as a whole is another issue. The majority of commentators ascribe this verse to a later redactor.[74]

[74] Brevard Childs, *Introduction to the Old Testament as Scripture* (Philadelphia: Fortress Press, 1979), 472; Page E. Kelley, "The Holy One in the Midst of Israel: Redeeming Love (Hosea 11-14)," *Review and Expositor* 72 no. 4 (1975): 472.

However, the influence of the wisdom tradition on other prophetic books and connections with that tradition in the text itself,[75] leaves open the possibility, in the final analysis, of attributing this verse to Hosea himself.

This study proposes, therefore, that, against the backdrop of overwhelming Divine anger and condemnation, Chapter 14: 1-9 may be characterized as the final of three specific movements of "relent" in the heart of Yahweh. It represents the decisive moment, when the relentless barrage of threats and denunciations, gives way to the possibility of healing and hope, through the unconditional love of God.

Setting

This oracle of salvation is difficult to date but it is probably best understood at the time when the end of the Northern Kingdom was in view. The fall is as good as complete, since it has now become apparent that neither Assyria nor the Canaanite cult can help Israel. The expression in v.9a: "What has Ephraim any more to do with idols," especially indicates with the word that a turning point has been reached, which puts the entire past into question. Therefore, it is conceivably the time of Shalmaneser V, when Samaria's end was near.[76]

The theme of 14:2-9 is closely related to that of chapter 11. It is noted that the same important catchwords occur in both passages: "to return" (שׁוב vv 2f, 8; cf. 11:5); "apostasy" (משׁובה v 5; cf. 11:7); "to heal" (רפא v5; cf. 11:3); "to dwell" (ישׁב v. 8; cf. 11:11). In chapter 14, the final hour for Egypt is nearer has disappeared from view and words of accusation have fallen completely silent. God's inner struggle, which the audience witnessed in 11:8f, has given way to a straightforward proclamation of salvation.

According to Wolff, "Hosea spoke these words (14: 2-9) before the inner circle of the opposition group,"[77] and he dates the event to probably when the end of the Northern Kingdom was in view, even though he concedes that there is no clear criteria on which to base its date.[78] According to Bright,

> If Hosea ever entertained such a hope [that Israel would repent and God avert judgment], it appears that God has abandoned it as the years went by. Hosea saw, or came to see, his people incapable of repentance....So it was that in the farther future, beyond the judgment. Hosea looked for the restoration of Israel in the mercy of God.[79]

---

[81] Wolff, *A Commentary on the Book of Hosea,* 231.

[75] Ibid.

[76] Wolff, *A Commentary of the Book of the Prophet Hosea*, 234.

[77] Wolff, *A Commentary on the Book of Hosea,* 234.

[78] Ibid.

[79] John Bright, *Covenant and Promise* (London: SCM Press Ltd., 1977), 92-93.

Similarly, Wolff also claims that at first Hosea thought that "after Israel has broken the covenant (1:9), a new beginning of saving history was not to be expected from a reformation among the people in response to the prophet's warnings. Rather it was to come only as a result of the preconditions which God himself created: in his judgment he would block Israel's path to her idols..."[80] In other words, Yahweh's judgment will bring Israel back to the wilderness and to the saving history. According to Wolff, later in his career, after 733 B.C.E, Hosea changed his mind for "it...became clear that Yahweh's judgment could not bring Israel to obedience."[81] Therefore, Hosea began to understand that Israel will be saved only by Yahweh's unconditional love. Hosea 14:2-4 is presented to the readers as reflecting true repentance. Contrary to the summons to repent in Hosea 10:2, Hosea 14:2-4 is followed by an announcement of disaster, but of future deliverance.

4.2.3.4.1. Comments on Hosea 14:4 in relation to Illness, Health and Healing

This metaphor is found in the last chapter of Hosea's book. The context of the metaphor is an excerpt from 14:2 to 14:9. Chapter 14:4 highlights the proclamation of salvation, which finds the key of God's salvific action that is generous and unconditional, free love of God towards his people.

This declaration of Yahweh begins the reversal of the metaphors of devastation and denunciation, which represented the rupture between Yahweh and Israel throughout Hosea's prophecy.[82]

---

[80] Wolff, *A Commentary on the Book of Hosea,* xxix.

[81] Ibid., 237-238.

[82] In view of all the anguish and vacillation that the reader has witnessed throughout the first thirteen chapters of Hosea's revelation, this unequivocal declaration of Yahweh seems almost incredible. The anguish and vacillation are conspicuously absent; the pronouncement is serene and resolute. Were it not for the actual devastation, which this people had already suffered, this profession of Yahweh could seem like a revocation of impending doom. However, several peculiarities of this verse must be considered, especially in relation to the summons and the supplication, which precede it. The first aspect of this verse that must be noted is that it is not a response to the prayer, which precedes it. Yahweh refers to Israel in the third person "them."

This conveys the impression that Yahweh is speaking to someone about Israel, rather than to Israel. The identity of the hearer is undisclosed. It may be the prophet or the reader to whom Yahweh directs this marvellous revelation. One might even imagine that it is a response to an unrecorded question, as researchers suggested earlier in this research. In view of the dismal failure of Israel to make choices in keeping with their covenant relationship and the repeated rejection by Yahweh of their feeble attempts, why should this prayer make any difference? What hope has Israel of being received? What has Israel to offer but its brokenness and supplication as the fruit of their lips?

The answer is that Israel, in truth, has only itself to offer, only its suffering and need. It is not any power or prayer on Israel's part, which effects this declaration by Yahweh. It is the resolution and the reconciliation within Yahweh's own being which makes possible Israel's restoration, a resolution foreshadowed in the recoiling of the Divine heart and the stirring of Divine compassion in 11:8.

4.2.3.4.1.1. Apostasy (מְשׁוּבָה) versus *Rapha* (רפא)

The healing metaphor appears in Hosea 14:4 in the statement, "I will heal their apostasy." Throughout the book of Hosea, the prophet repeatedly stresses the fact that Israel is apostate in Hosea 4:15-19; 5:3; 6:10-11; 9:10-17; 10:5-8; 11:2, 7, 12. Here, Yahweh promises to "heal" their apostasy. The word "waywardness" in NIV is best translated as "apostasy", a technical theological term that describes defection from Yahweh, the covenants and the truth. It is not simply a matter of occasionally going astray but implies that apostasy is more than an act of the will, but it is also a kind of mental derangement that God himself must cure.[83] Oestreich's investigations clearly demonstrate that the prophet draws upon a well-established metaphor, but he argues that it is employed in a new way to express Yahweh's healing of apostasy. The portrayal of a broken relationship with Yahweh as a "disease" heightens the prophet's contention of the cause of Israel's political misfortunes.[84]

In Hosea 14:4, God answers his penitent people with the promise, "I will heal their backsliding, I will love them freely, for my anger has turned away from them." Here, in contrast to 5:13 (with sickness, sores, and cure), and 11:3 (with train to walk), there is no physical imagery. Yet once again, the root שׁוב plays an important role. When the people turn away from their sins and turn back to God in contrition, he turns away from his wrath and turns back to his people in mercy, thus bringing healing and restoration. This is the essence as well as the expression of forgiveness.[85] Healing of the corporate heart produces healing of the corporate body. It expresses Yahweh as healing Israel's unfaithfulness. In other words, the latter is treated as a disease that can be cured only by the Supreme Physician

---

The only choice within the power of Israel/ Ephraim is the decision to return based on Yahweh's self-assertion that "I am God not man, the Holy One in your midst,"

God refuses to execute anger or cause destruction (11:8, 9). This is Yahweh's revelation of the definitive truth of the Divine Self, whose Being is unconditional love and compassion unmitigated by the iniquity of human beings. If this proposal leaves unanswered the question of the action of God in salvation history, perhaps the reader finds her/himself in the very state of wonder and awe of their religious ancestors before the mystery of Yahweh's unbounded love in the face of their own iniquity.

[83] Garrett, *The New American Commentary: Hosea, Joel*, 273.

[84] Cf. Bernhard Oestreich, *Metaphors and Similes for Yahweh in Hosea 14:2-9 (1-8): A Study of Hoseanic Pictorial Language* (Frankfurt: Peter Lang, 1998).

[85] O' Kennedy mentions three prominent reasons why the verb רפא in Hosea 14:5 (4) may be understood as forgiveness: (1) The verb רפא is used together with the word מְשׁוּבָה expressing the forgiveness of disloyalty; (2) One finds other terms or expressions for forgiveness and mercy in the same passage: נשׂא עו/׳ ("take away/forgive all guilt"), אהב׳ נדבה ("I will love them freely"); and ממנו שׁב אפי ("my anger has turned away from them"); (3) Several metaphors appear in Hosea 14:1-10 (9) describing the restored relationship between God and Israel as a result of divine forgiveness: "I will be like the dew to Israel"; "he shall blossom like the lily", etc. D. F. O'Kennedy, "Healing as/or Forgiveness? *The use of the term* רפא *in the book of Hosea,*" *Old Testament Essays* 14, no. 3 (2001): 456

(Yahweh). Israel cannot heal itself, and without being healed of unfaithfulness, no stable idyllic future can be imagined.

The very apostasy (משׁובתם) which characterized Israel in the past (5:4; 7:2; 11:5) is what Yahweh promises to heal (רפא). The term משׁובה is used only in the book of Hosea (here and in 11:7), once in Proverbs and nine times in Jeremiah in the Old Testament. The connection of רפא "to heal" with the form of שׁוב "return" is paralleled by the use of these terms together in Isaiah 6:10. In the vocabulary of the covenant curse, רפא appears in Deuteronomy 28:27 and 35, where there are mentioned respectively the itch and the sore which cannot be healed as punishments for disloyalty. Now healing is promised for the repentant nation in the future, where as no healing was possible in the past.

4.2.3.4.1.2. 'Steadfast Love' (אהב) of God as Healing to the Nation

The promise of generous love utilises a primary covenant term אהב love, in its technical sense found in treaties expressing the notion "be loyal to, show faithfulness to," as well as in its more common connotation of emotional closeness. This indicates to a love that will not be earned but rather reflected by the sense of נדבה as "voluntary offering" or "offering made out of generosity."[86] The terms חסד "steadfast love" or אמת "loyalty" and "faithfulness" also refer to the kinship bond based on mutual obligations. N. Glueck is of the opinion that, underscoring the aspect of reciprocity implicitly in the term, goes so far as to say that, "Where חסד is used alone and not in the combination of חסד ואמת, as is frequently the case, one may still picture mentally אמת next to חסד."[87] The two words, in connection with each other, characterized the kinship tie on the basis of reciprocity.

The metaphor has royal connotations in so far as the king is responsible for the well-being of the people. Israel's political turn to the Assyrian king, of course, raises questions about its covenant with Yahweh. Israel's fornications to other nations for their political and economic support have led the nation to an upheaval sickness, which Hosea has condemned. Thus, the metaphorical image of "love" does not employ about Israel's dependency on the foreign kings but it affirmatively holds on the steadfast love of Yahweh to the people, in spite of their waywardness. The people's socio-economic, political and religious apostasy will be healed, and it will bring the nation to a state of health and well-being through the love of Yahweh.

Summary

While the eighth century B.C.E. was a time of great prosperity and luxury, only a minority of the population felt the effects. Military successes and economic prosperity masked social, moral, and religious decay throughout the land. This period does not give the impression that all was well. In fact, ironically, this period

[86] Stuart, "Hosea," 215.

[87] N. Glueck, *Hesed in the Bible* (Cincinnati: Hebrew Union College Press, 1967), 40.

gives rise to the greatest number and the most intense of the prophetic oracles of judgment. Hosea upbraided his contemporaries for their moral degradation. All around the prophet were the symptoms of moral decay. Home life was destroyed by immorality, and the foundations of society were weakened by swearing, lying, murder, stealing, greed and lust (4:2). The crown was often in sympathy with evil; judges were venal; and the royal court was drunken and profligate. To him, indifferent and corrupt religious and political leaders were a major contributing factor in the moral breakdown of the nation (4:6, 9; 5:1, 10; 7:3). Housebreaking was common and roving bands of bandits pillaged the land (6:9; 7:1). Hosea accused the priests of divorcing morality from religion; indeed, he accused them of feeding on the sin of their people (4:8).

Against this background, Hosea asked the people to return to Yahweh in order that they might be restored to their wealth and health. The prophet Hosea used *rapha* synonymously as to be free from sickness or to cure (6:1b, 5:13). This is to denote the restoration of the people's wounded body, and event which happened repeatedly in the course of Israel's history. To heal also includes the meaning to forgive (14:5), for which concept Hosea uses no other terms.

Illness for Hosea means that the whole of Israel is overcome by a state of illness. The concept of disease which is understood as psycho-physical reality is often used as a metaphor for social, economic, political and religious realties in the book of Hosea. The metaphors in passages: 5:12-13, 11:3 and 14:5 are not related to the terms used for illness, but rather, diametrical expressions such as 'to heal' and 'healer'. Consequently, for Hosea illness is not an exclusively psychophysical reality, but rather foremost a metaphor indicating difficulties and problems of a religious, social, economic and political nature. Illness is also an image of the broken covenant and the ruining of the healthy relationship between God and his People of Israel. The metaphorical manner of discourse in the book of Hosea brings to mind other associations of the state of ill people and land. An analysis of Hosea's texts also shows that the metaphors depicting Israel as an ill person are related to the usage of expressions in the semantic family of antonymous roots (*rapha*), and in the five existing cases (5:13, 6:1, 7:1, 11:3, 14:5) are not used according to their original meaning. All of this leads to a conclusion and theological reservation: Yahweh is a healer, but the people do not understand this. Consequently, the healer (Yahweh) can become the devouring lion (5:14).

Yahweh's healing attends to the sickness and woundedness of Israel/Judah/Ephraim, which could not be cured by their turning to Assyria and Egypt (5:13). Yahweh's healing is the antithesis of the dry rot (5:12), the rending (5:14), the tearing and devouring (13:8) which Yahweh envisioned inflicting upon the chosen people. Yahweh is disclosing the healing, which was hidden from Ephraim when he was a child (1:3) and affirming Israel's earlier presumption that "he has torn, that he may heal us; he has stricken, and he will bind us" (6:1). Furthermore, Yahweh promises not only to heal them of their woundedness, but also to heal their faithlessness, their backsliding, and their waywardness. Yahweh will facilitate their return and restoration by "taking away all iniquity" (14:2) and bearing the burden of their guilt.

One should not assume that the *metaphorical* usage discussed here had the same significance for the ancient Israelite society as it might be for the contemporary reader. In other words, it is probable that in the biblical mentality, societal life in general was viewed in more holistic terms than it is today, with religion, family life, political and economic stability, and general health and welfare was seen as thoroughly intertwined. Thus, concepts such as health and healing were more wide ranging in their import and the idea of Israel being sick and in need of healing might not have been perceived strictly as metaphorically by the ancient hearer. The terms could have simply conveyed the wider concepts of suffering and affliction on the one hand, and restoration and rehabilitation on the other hand, with everything those words entailed. That does not mean that healing of physical disease was absent. This idea of healing of physical diseases was certainly not excluded from the wider metaphor of national healing and restoration. The hope of the prophet was nothing less than the whole human, wholly healed, which has classically expressed in Hosea.

4.3. Health and Healing in Isaiah

4.3.1. Introduction

The Book of Isaiah has its diverse and vast interpretations regarding the unity of the Book. The several literary layers reflecting different chronological backgrounds urge us to postulate that the contents of the book have been composed and transmitted by different authors in different historical and social contexts.[88] However, despite its diversified arguments that have emerged at different times and context, it rings out a voice about God's well being to the people and their hope for healing. Therefore, the following lines will deal with the metaphorical languages that the prophet Proto-Isaiah used for health and healing.

The fact that the opening reference opens with: "The vision of Isaiah the son of Amoz" (Isa. 1:1) was taken to point out that all the prophetic oracles were proclaimed by the eight century prophet of Jerusalem. Such assertive ideology dominated the authorship of the book of Isaiah for a long time until the time of the publication of Duhm's Commentary in 1892. The literary critical analysis applied by scholars led to prove with evidences to show that the contents of Chapters 40-55 must be ascribed almost entirely to the era of the Babylonian exile in the 6th century B.C and the contents of chapters 56-66 must be later still in the post-exilic period.[89] Duhm's hypothesis has been widely accepted by scholars. In

---

[88] Daniel Jones Muthunayagom, *The Relationship Between Election and Israel's Attitude Towards the Nations in the Book of Isaiah* (Delhi: ISPCK, 2000), 15-16.

[89] O. Eissfeldt, *Old Testament: An Introduction* (Oxford: E. T. P. R. Ackroyd, 1996), 304.

other words, it has been greatly accepted that the book of Isaiah is composed of three major parts, which have only limited, direct relationship to each other.[90]

Traditionally chapters 1-39 have been associated with Isaiah of Jerusalem who lived in the eight century B.C and Isaiah 40-55 to an anonymous prophet, Deutero-Isaiah who is believed to have lived in Babylon in the second half of the sixth century and Isaiah 56-66 to another prophet who is believed to have been the disciple of Deutero-Isaiah. It is frequently assumed that Isaiah 1-39 contains several independent collections of sayings; that chapters 40-55 form a reasonable coherent and unified whole usually dated in the period of 540-538 B.C.E; Chapters 56-66 though Post-Exilic in origin, are much more difficult to be assigned to a specific date.[91] Many scholars take the above mentioned tri-partition of Isaiah as a working hypothesis, especially when dealing with an overarching theme in studies without particular redaction historical interest.

The following texts will be investigated in order to understand the concept of illness, health and healing in first Isaiah.

4.3.2. Exegetical Study

4.3.2.1. Isaiah 1:5-6

v. 5. Why do you seek further beatings?
Why do you continue to rebel?
The whole[a] head is sick
And the whole heart faint.[b]

v.6. From the sole of the foot even to the head,
[a]there is no soundness in it,
but bruises and sores
and bleeding wounds; [a]
they have not been drained, or bound up,
or softened with oil.[b]

Form Critical Notes

On thematic grounds, v. 4 seems to fit right in with vv.2f. Once again, the discussion about 'sons' and פשׁע (rebel) is further explicated by the use of the roughly synonymous verbs עזב (abandon) and נאץ (scorn). However, in actual fact the הוי (alas) introduces a new section. Yahweh himself does not speak here,

[90] Muthunayagom, *The Relationship Between Election and Israel's Attitude Towards the Nations in the Book of Isaiah*, 16.

[91] Daniel Jones Muthunayagom, "Contemporary Approaches to Old Testament Interpretation," in *Interweaving Methodology and Praxis: Exploring Disciplinary Options in Today's World*, ed. Indukuri John Mohan Razu (Bangalore: BTESSC/SATHRI, 2007), 16.

as he did previously; instead, the discussion refers to him now in the third person. There is no disagreement about the fact that v.10 starts a new section.[92]

The meter is irregular. After removing נזרו אחור (turned themselves backwards) each of the first two lines in v.4 contains a two-stress bicolon, the third a five-stress colon with an uncommon pattern of two, then three stresses (2+3), which serves to identify a breaking point. The actual lament ends at this point. In vv.5 and 6a, 4 two- stress bicola follow; in v.6b there is a three-stress bicolon, which once again points to the end of another part of the section: the image of a sick, bruised body. In the third section, vv7f, once again there are four more two-stress bicola, following which v.9 closes the section with an impressive three-stress bicolon and then a final two-stress bicolon, which concludes the description of the devastation.[93]

Setting

Isaiah chapter 1 is divided into smaller units that differ in meter, form, historical background. Usually they are so divided: vv. 2-3; 4-9; 10-17; 18-20; 21-26; 27-31. The units do not stand in a chronological sequence. The description of Zion's physical desolation (vv. 7-8) precedes the portrayal of Isaiah's opulent but empty cultic exercises (vv. 10-17) from an earlier period. Often a catchword connection is evident (vv9-10).[94]

Genre

R. J. Marshal points out that the literary background of this introductory chapter is designed after the general characteristics of a covenant lawsuit, a literary form that drew upon the vocabulary and cultural background of a trial at court.[95] H.B. Huffmon, gives the general structure of the covenant lawsuit and explains how the prophets used this structure in individual passages.[96] J. Oswalt argues that since this chapter has several derivations from the normal pattern of other covenant lawsuits (Mic. 6; Hos. 4), it seems to be more accurate to conclude that this chapter might be compared to the negotiations that take place before a trial, rather than a court trial itself.[97]

---

[92] Hans Wildberger, *Isaiah 1-12*, trans. Thomas H. Trapp (Minneapolis: Fortress Press, 1991), 20.

[93] Ibid., 20-21.

[94] Brevard S. Childs, *Isaiah* (Louisville: Westminster John Knox Press, 2001), 16.

[95] R. J. Marshal, "The Structure of Isaiah 1-12," *Biblical Review* 7 (1962): 93-94.

[96] H. B. Huffmon, "The Covenant Lawsuit in the Prophets," *Journal of Biblical Literature*, 78 (1959): 285.

[97] John Oswalt, *The Book of Isaiah 1-12*, ed. R. K. Harrison and R. D. Patterson, New International Commentary of the Old Testament (Grand Rapids, Michigan: William B. Eerdmans Publishing Company, 1986), 85.

Accusations are brought against the defendant (1:2b-9) and the defensive reasoning of the accused is refuted, similar to what one might expect at an arrangement (1:10-15). Then come unexpected exhortations on acceptable behaviour (1:16-17), and one party offers to resolve the case (1:8-20), making known the consequence of both a positive or negative response (1:21-31). By using the general literary framework of a trial arrangement to structure his theological message, the prophet communicated the seriousness of Judah's sinful rebellion in a logical way that clearly demonstrated to the reader why people of Judah proved that there was a guilty party. Therefore, the people of Judah in the audience needed to confess their sins and transform their behaviour if they wanted to avoid further punishment. The clear portrayal of what God would do if they do not change, gave Isaiah's sermonic appeal "to reason together" (1:18) strong persuasive power. They could respond positively to God and be blessed or reject God and suffer under his destructive power along with the wicked (1:19-20).[98]

Historical Setting

The historical setting of the chapter can be traced back to the time when religious apostasy was at its heights. Chapter 1:2-4 portrays the time when the people were rebellious against God and despised the Holy One of Israel. Not long before this sermon, the nation suffered a major military attack by some enemy (1:5-7), and only Jerusalem was spared (1:8-9). Some people in Judah were busy offering sacrifices (1:10-15) but many of their hearts were not right with God. Most of these people were offering detestable sacrifices, shedding innocent blood and not upholding justice (1:15-17). In the past, Jerusalem had just rulers, but now the city was characterized by murder, robbery, bribery of judges, pagan worship and injustice toward the poor (1:21-23, 28-29).[99]

The date of Isaiah chapter 1 is not stated, it needs to fit somewhere shortly after a major military event when its rulers were leading the nation away from God. Four possible dates is considered.

1. Y. Gitay believes the book of Isaiah is arranged in chronological order, so he suggested that the battle in 1:5-9 was the Syro-Ephraimite war (734-732 BC) when Israel and Syria attacked Judah to force Judah to join their coalition against Assyria (cf. Isa. 7; 2 Kgs. 16; 2 Chro. 28).[100]

The setting fits the military situation required, for the rebellious king Ahaz was ruling Judah and the nation did survive this war as a weak vassal of Assyria. It was also a time when pagan worship infiltrated Jerusalem (2 Kgs. 16:1-5, 10-18). Nevertheless, it is hard to determine who the earlier righteous king was (1:21)

---

[98] Gary V. Smith, *Isaiah 1-39* (Nashville: B & H Publishing Group, 2007), 93-94.

[99] Ibid., 94.

[100] Y. Gitay, *Isaiah and His Audience: The Structure and Meaning of Isaiah 1-12* (Assen: Van Gorcum, 1991), 23.

when the city had a faithful ruler, unless the author was referring all the way back to the time of David.[101]

2. H. Wildberger and most others suggest that the historical situation was during the 701 B.C.E attack on Judah by Sennacherib, when the whole nation of Judah was destroyed except Jerusalem (Isa. 36-37; 2 Kgs. 18-19; 2 Chro. 32).[102] This is a time of restored worship of God at the temple (2 Chro. 30: 31), but since Hezekiah was a righteous king, it is hard to fit the negative comments about the evil leaders or pagan worship in the temple into this time frame.[103]

3. C.R. Seitz suggests a date in the reign of Manasseh, a few years after 701 B.C.E attack by the Assyrians.[104] E. J. Young also suggests that Isaiah's ministry continued into the initial years of Manasseh.[105]

This view has the advantage of identifying Hezekiah's reform as the period when righteousness characterized the city and the early reign of Manasseh (2 Kgs. 21; 2 Chro. 33) as the time of wickedness described in 1:4, 21-23, 27-29. If one hypothesizes that Isaiah's message was given when Manasseh was a co-regent with his father Hezekiah, this would explain why Manasseh's name was not mentioned in 1:1. In this scenario, Isaiah was warning the nation not to reject the godly ways that were promoted by Manasseh[106]

4. Finally, E. J. Kissane concluded that this was a prophecy about the future fall of Jerusalem in 586 B.C.E.[107]

Since Jerusalem did not escape the conquest (1:8-9) and chapter 1 seems to describe a present problem, this suggestion seems to be an unlikely interpretation.[108]

Smith is of the opinion that the third view satisfies the various factors outlined in the setting of chap 1. Accepting these dates leads to several conclusions that:

(a) This was not Isaiah's first sermon. It was not composed at the beginning of his ministry but near the end.
(b) Isaiah most likely added Chapter 1 when his sermons were collected, edited and put in their present form.
(c) Chapter 1 serves as something of an introduction to the collection of prophecies attributed to Isaiah.[109]

---

[101] Smith, *Isaiah 1-39*, 95.

[102] H. Wildberger, *Isaiah 1-12: A Commentary* (Minneapolis: Fortress Press, 1991), 21.

[103] Smith, *Isaiah 1-39*, 94.

[104] C. R. Seitz, *Isaiah 1-39: Interpretation* (Louisville: Westminster John Knox Press, 1993), 34.

[105] E. J. Young, *The Book of Isaiah* (Grand Rapids, Michigan: William B. Eerdmans Publishing Company, 1965), 33.

[106] Smith, *Isaiah 1-39*, 95.

[107] E. J. Kissane, *The Book of Isaiah 1* (Dublin: Brown & Nolan, 1960), 9-10.

[108] Smith, *Isaiah 1-39*, 95.

[109] Ibid. Sweeney dates Isaiah 1:2-3, 4-9 at the time of Sennacherib's invasion in 701, and also argues that the prophetic torah in 1:10-17 comes earlier. The condemnation of cultic practices

Despite the different opinions regarding the setting of this text, the utterance of these words by Isaiah in Isaiah 1:4-9 can be determined with great accuracy. This is spoken at a time when the nation is devastated, the cities of Judah have been burned down, and Jerusalem is the only city left alone, heavily weighed down by its isolation. Such situations can only refer to a time after a siege of the city by Sennacherib in the year 701 (cf. 2 Kgs. 18:13-16). Apparently, the population of Jerusalem was happy about the fact that they were not forced into an unconditional surrender. Thus, they had not reached the point of fully assessing the magnitude of the catastrophe and this had not yet reached the point of deciding to repent. On the other hand, the prophet had a positive outlook to the future that the new beginning could still come, even after the shock of punishment, which they had managed to survive. This message could not have been spoken very long after the actual disastrous events of 701.[110] Therefore, the setting in life would have been a lamentation ceremony, at which the prophet, instead of delivering an oracle of salvation, would have called for the people to consider their own guilt. But again we do not find here the prophet talking about confession. The content of the message would seem like it was uttered in a Zion festival, where the invincibility and majesty of God is found in its celebration.

4.3.2.1.1. Comments on Isaiah 1:5-6 in relation to Illness, Health and Healing

Chapter 1:4-9 is one unit that begins with a "woe" formula. The passage begins with a woe oracle in v.4 as indicated by the introductory *hoy*.[111] The first part of this oracle is a woe address, which uses four different vocative appellations to address the party to which the oracle is directed. Each of these oracles characterizes the nature of the people. Thus in verse 4, the people are called "sinning nation," "people with heavy guilt," "wicked offspring", and "corrupt sons". The second part of the woe oracle, contains three plural perfect verbs.[112] These three accusations against the people substantiate their negative characterization in the first part of the woe oracle. Thus, the entire woe oracle is accusatory in nature.

The second part of this passage begins in v.5 with a rhetorical question addressed to the people asking them why they would be stricken again. The

mentioned in v. 13 must date from the period of Hezekiah's cultic reforms (2 Kgs. 18: 1-8). Moreover, the "routine nature of the festival observances mentioned in v. 13" does make sense for Sweeney in a time when the temple service could function normally as opposed to the chaotic time of 701. It is difficult to determine Sweeney's statement but his arguments are conceivable. M. A. Sweeney, *Isaiah 1-39 with an Introduction to Prophetic Literature, Forms and Literature* (Grand Rapids, Michigan: William B. Eerdmans Publishing Company, 1996), 74-77.

[110] Hans Wildberger, *Isaiah 1-12: A Commentary*, trans. Thomas H. Trapp (Minneapolis: Fortress Press, 1986), 20.

[111] Wildberger, *Isaiah 1-12*, 20.

[112] Marvin A. Sweeney, *Isaiah 1-4 and the Post-Exilic Understanding of The Isaianic Tradition* (Berlin, New York: Walter de Gruyter, 1988), 104.

following verses do not answer the question in 5 but they relate directly to it in that they demonstrate how much the people have suffered already. The suffering of the people in these verses suggests that the people should feel that they had enough. The description of suffering in vv. 5-9 serves as a motivation for the people to end their wrongdoing and consequently their suffering.

4.3.2.1.1.1. 'Wounds' 'Open Sores' and 'Sickness'

The explanation in vv. 5b-9 focuses on the sickness of the people. These verses constitute a figurative speech, which uses language of physical sickness to describe the present misery of the people. The unit describes the sickness itself, beginning with a general statement that both head and heart are ill (5b) followed by a description of the extent nature of the disease (6a). V.6b consists of three statements, which claim that the disease is left untreated.

The text pictured here is not of a sick person, but someone whipped within an inch of his life, yet asking for more. In verse 5, this point is made, and the symptoms of 6b are those of inflicted injuries (cf. 53:5).

In vv. 5-8 Isaiah delineates the ways in which Israel was now experiencing the results of her sin. First vv. 5-6, Isaiah uses the metaphors of health, which fits in with his appeal to the natural order. Health is the natural and normal state of the body, all other things being equal. On the other hand, if there are wounds, open soars, and sickness, then it should be understood that something is wrong. Just as naturally, as disease produces certain symptoms so also the nation, which is desolate, stripped, forsaken surely should be a sign that a cure is needed.[113]

Israel's ill health is not merely a matter of disease. She has been beaten and smitten. The words occurring in v.6 describe injuries received in battle, slash wounds, lacerations and bleeding wounds. This is the result of offending God. In verse 6, the metaphor of the nation as a beaten and untended person continues before it is explained in the following two verses. After the looser description of the immediately preceding line, the whole verse can be understood in terms of one who is suffering from a severe beating.[114]

In Isaiah 1:5, חלי, "illness", is used to describe the condition in the land following the Assyrian invasion. In Isa 1:5-6 the image of a sick person is used in a way that is distinctly reminiscent of the way in which the servant is described in Isa 53. The "we" in Isaiah 53, who are now healed and reconciled, are probably identified with the ones who continue to rebel in Isaiah 1:5. This is not the Kings and the nations, but God's sinful nation, laden with iniquity.

The people of Israel are considered as a whole under the image of a single body. The transition is natural and unforced, but important in the wider context,

[113] John N. Oswalt, *The Book of Isaiah: Chapters 1-39*, New International Commentary of the Old Testament (Grand Rapids, Michigan: William B. Eerdmans Publishing Company, 1986), 89.

[114] Hugh Godfrey Maturin Williamson, *A Critical and Exegetical Commentary on Isaiah 1-27*, vol. 1 (New York: T & T Clark, 2006), 62.

where this same duality has already occurred in v.v. 2-3 and 4 and will reappear in verse 7-8. Together with the repeated whole, the reference to head and heart is clearly intended to demonstrate that 'sickness' is both all-encompassing and deep-rooted. The body politic is rotten to the core, so that we are close to a fulfilment of the time when the chance of 'healing' following repentance referred to in 6:10 will be past.[115]

While the word used here חלי, can refer to physical wounds (e.g. 2 Kgs. 8:29; Jer. 6:7), it is unlikely in the present context that we should so limit it, as though the figure had been beaten on the head as well as the rest of the body. The parallelism "the whole heart is faint" indicates that more is at stake. The whole image in this verse may refer to, even if the wounds do not produce fever, and his circulation is likely to be severely impaired.

The text "from the sole of the foot to the head there is no soundness in it" reinforces the emphasis of the previous verse on the devastating extent of the blows that have fallen. No soundness is expanded and explained by the following three words for different types of wound. Isaiah uses several metaphorical images in order to explain about the condition of the lives of the people.

1. **Bruises**: פצע can refer either to open wounds (e.g. 1 Kgs. 20:73) or to confusions (Deut. 23:2). The latter is marginally preferable here, since the former is covered by the third term in the list, which seems to aim at being as comprehensive as possible.[116]
2. **Blow**: חבורה usually occurs in association with פצע, as here (Gen. 4:23; Exod. 21:25), so that it is difficult to arrive at a distinction. Psalm 38:6 suggests an open wound (though a number of commentators think of leprosy). Perhaps the best clue comes from the remaining occurrence, Isaiah 53:5, where it appears to be the consequence of rsym, 'physical "discipline", that is, "beating a rod', as in a number of passages in Proverbs. "Stripe" or 'weal' therefore seems to be the most appropriate equivalent.[117]
3. **Wounds**: מכה in context,[118] is the result of 'being beaten' (הכו), but distinguished here in that, they are טריה, literally 'fresh, moist, raw', hence probably still bleeding; these stripes were so severe that they cut deep into flesh.

Wound occurs in combination with wound or bruise. The word occurs in Isaiah 1:6. The nominative is used of individually of physical wounds in Genesis

---

[115] Ibid.

[116] Ibid., 63.

[117] Ibid.

[118] The word can also refer to a wide variety of wounds and diseases. The more restricted use of the word suggests that we should not directly associate it with 'covenant curse' of Lev. 26:21 or Deut. 28:61.

4:23; Exodus 21:25; Proverbs 20:30 except in Isaiah 1:6 the case is different. By using a motif of ill health, Isaiah describes the results of Israel's spiritual rebellion as a severe laceration suffered in battle (Isa. 1:6). The most crucial occurrence of the nominative appears in 53:5, where the prophet observes, "By his wounds we are healed", seen in one of the four great servant passages in Isaiah (Isa. 42:1-4; 49:1-6; 50:4-9; 52:13-53:12). The issues in the verses are the identity of the servant and the nation of his wounding and the effected healing.[119]

Granted this identification, 'wounds' is a metonymy for the violent substitutionary death that was suffered by the righteous Servant so that all may be healed (*rapha*). This means restoration to the total well being. The punishment that brought them peace (*Shalom*) was upon him. This peace indicates "a rounded wholeness comprising of personal fulfilment, harmonious society and a secure relationship with God"[120] In this vein, health is understood to be part of the concept of שלם for as Atkinson puts it,

> Health is clearly part of *Shalom*, as can be illustrated by the numerous times in the Old Testament when *Shalom* is bracketed together with a Hebrew word translated 'health' or 'healing'. Thus, the vision of peace in Isaiah 2:1-5 (which could almost stand as a definition of *Shalom*) is set in contrast to the sickness of the nation (1:5-6), its idolatry (2:6-22) and social injustice (3:13-15) which bring the judgment that the Lord will not be a healer (3:7b).[121]

With this understanding of שלם, perceiving health as a part of it, it can be alluded that health is a holistic concept.

A particularly poignant instance of the nominative is found in Isaiah1:6, where several synonymous words for wounding occur. Drawing upon a motif of ill health due to wounds referred to in battle, Isaiah laments that the nation's spiritual rebellion has earned for it only "slash wounds" and "bleeding wounds." The political and social catastrophes that they were experiencing were the natural results of living in ways contrary to those, which God designed for them.[122] Failure to live out God's standards, which have been given to human beings for their good, will lead to spiritual and moral decay for societies and peoples just as surely as physical disease debilitates the body.[123]

---

[119] R. K. Harrison and R. D. Pastterson, "Wound," in *New International Dictionary of Theology and Exegesis*, ed. Willem A. Van Gemeren (Carlisle, Cumbria: Paternoster Press, 1996), 4.

[120] J. Alec Motyer, *Isaiah: An Introduction and Commentary* (Downers Grove: InterVarsity Press, 1999), 430-431.

[121] D. Atkinson, "Towards a Theology of Health," in *Health: The Strength to be Human*, ed. A. Fergusson (London: InterVarsity Press, 1993), 25.

[122] Oswalt, *The Book of Isaiah 1-12*, 89.

[123] Ibid., 656.

The necessary treatment for such wounds, here neglected, is straight forward: pressed out, to remove dirt, which might cause infection, and any 'purulent matter', bandaged and softened with oil, both to soothe pain and perhaps also to soften scalp.[124]

However, according to the traditio-historical background this would not bring to mind someone who suffered maltreatment by being struck repeatedly, but rather someone whose body was covered, over every square inch, with running sores.

4.3.2.1.1.2. The Metaphors of Physical Impairments

Since both the head and the heart have been affected by this illness, the disease is described as terribly threatening. Since there is no healthy spot left, from head to toe, it is shown to be affecting people totally. אין מתם (no unhurt place) is also used when one describes sicknesses (Ps. 38:4, 8, where, in 4, it is parallel to שלם אין, "no health," after the text is emended, and also characterizes the disease as the consequence of God's wrath. The three substantives in v.6a, פצע (bruises) חבורה (blows) and מכה (wounds) are difficult to delineate but these expressions are heaped up to have the effect of intensifying the seriousness of the sickness.

Verse 6b helps us to discover the treatment of wounds. According to Hans Wildberger,

> One is reminded of the tender care offered by the merciful Samaritan in Luke 10:34. Even way back in Sumerian times, the doctor could be known as an *iazu*, "one who applies oil", and, in antiquity, oil is often mentioned as something which is applied in an attempt to alleviate pain. The doctor of Babylon carried a satchel with him when he went to visit the sick, in which bandages were to be found along with other implements. Diseased parts of the body could have oil trickled onto them, could be lightly sprinkled, could be rinsed, could have generous amounts of oil poured over them, could be completely washed.[125]

Although, the language in Isaiah 1:5-6 is metaphorical, the physical image on which it is based, implies that there was a standard medical procedure ("pressed out, bandaged, softened with oil") to be followed when such injuries occurred.

The passage depicts that from the sole of the foot even to the head; from the meanest peasant to the greatest peer, there is no soundness. There is no good principle, no religion, for that is the health of the soul, nothing but guilt and corruption. This passage declares the total depravity of human nature. While sin remains un-repented, nothing is done toward healing these wounds, and preventing the fatal effects. Jerusalem was exposed and unprotected, like the huts or sheds

---

[124] Williamson, *A Critical and Exegetical Commentary on Isaiah 1-27*, 63.

[125] Wildberger, *Isaiah 1-12: A Commentary*, 24-25.

built up to guard ripening fruits.[126] It is incorrect to state that in the prophetic books, sickness and pain are merely figurative expressions representing sin and alienation, as if healing is equated there only with forgiveness and reconciliation. Yet this view is commonly seen in biblical and theological studies.

In this passage, the metaphors of physical impairments serve to illustrate Yahweh's attempts to prod the people of Judah into turning again to Yahweh. However, in spite of repeated bludgeoning by Yahweh, Judah appears to be not willing to accept its badly wounded state without modifying its actions. Thus, the prophetic passage portrays God's beatings as a means to motivate the people of Judah to return to proper relationship with God.[127]

The metaphorical usage of physical healing in Isaiah is determined by the prior metaphor of apostate Israel as a disease ridden body. Hence, Isaiah 1:5 was not merely spiritualising analogy. Israel's sin-sickness had affected every area of life. The nation of the corporate body was literally reeling from the effects of a deadly disorder. Even Jerusalem has become a prostitute, the faithful city once filled with justice, where righteousness used to dwell-but now murderers. This was the condition of the dying patient. It is only God who could retrieve and revive and her. Israel's spiritual disease, with all of its physical, social and national implications, required a comprehensive healing.

4.3.2.2. Isaiah 6:10

V. 10.[a] Make the mind of this people dull
And stop their ears,
and shut their eyes[a]
So that they may not look with their eyes,
and listen with their ears,
and comprehend with their minds,[b]
and turned and be healed.[c]

Form Critical Notes

For several reasons Isaiah 6 has not been an easy passage for interpreters. The nature of the prophet's vision, the time when the vision took place in the prophet's career, various textual and literary uncertainties, and the meaning and extent of the fate-laden message itself encompass most of the difficulties. Recent studies

[126] These are still to be seen in the East, where fruits form a large part of the summer food of the people. The evil nature is in every one and it is only God who can restore us to spiritual health.

[127] Sarah J. Melcher, "With Whom Do the Disabled Associate? Metaphorical Interplay in the Later Prophets," in *This Abled Body: Rethinking Disabilities and Biblical Studies*, ed. Hector Avalos, Sarah J. Melcher, and Jeremy Schipper (Atlanta: SBL, 2007), 124.

have challenged critical orthodoxy's understanding of (First) Isaiah's eschatology and have made it possible to view Isa 6:9-13 in a new light.[128]

Chap. 6 has unity and movement. Wildberger calls it a "kerygmatic unity."[129] It is composed of five parts: (1) vv 1–4: the Hall of the Lord, Heavenly King; (2) vv 5–7: the purging of the prophet's sin; (3) vv 8–10: the task for "this people;" (4) v 11: how long?; (5) vv 12–13: if some survive and return, what of them? Each builds on what precedes and moves the thoughts along.

The combination of the parts is unique. The nearest parallel is the account of Micaiah's prophecy (1 Kgs. 22) which also involves kings of Israel and Judah and which also deals with the fate of Israel's king. That passage also deals with prophecy, which manipulates the one God intends to execute.

According to Koch, the chapter is not a call narrative,[130] because the word "send" is never used of a "call"-always of a particular task and message. The purpose is to show that the nature of God's actions towards Israel and Judah, which had emerged in Uzziah's reign would remain the same until a complete destrúction would come (i.e., Over Samaria in 721 B.C). The time clause "in the year of Uzziah's death" points backward, making this a closing scene. There is no indication that this is the prophet's first vision or first prophetic experience.

Setting

One of the first questions the interpreters must answer whether this is Isaiah's original call or important revised commissioning of the prophet for a new task due to changes in the historical setting. Since there is no prophetic call of Isaiah in the first chapters of his book, it would be natural for the reader to conclude that chapter 6 is a record of his inaugural calling.[131]

This suggests that Chapter 6 is out of chronological order and placed here for a theological and literary reason devised when Isaiah himself or a future redactor edited these messages in the written form that exists today. Those who take this approach imply that in Chapters 6-12 Isaiah was concerned that people understand his unique role and prophetic authority to harden the people's hearts during the reign of Ahaz. His prophetic call is strategically placed here to support and justify what happened during these difficult circumstances. However, if the prophetic call in chap 6 actually happened before the messages in chapter 1, one would expect that this same evidence would be found in Chapters 1-5, not just 6-12.[132]

[128] Craig A. Evans, "Isaiah 6:9-13 in the Context of Isaiah's Theology," *Journal of the Evangelical Theological Society* 29, no. 2 (June 1986): 139.

[129] Wildberger, *Isaiah 1-12*, 234.

[130] Klaus Koch, *The Prophets I* (Philadelphia: Fortress Press, 1983), 113.

[131] Young, *The Book of Isaiah*, 72.

[132] Smith, *Isaiah 1-39*, 183.

Therefore, Isaiah chapter 6 was an inaugural call and prefer to think of it as re-commissioning for a specific historical task. J. H. Hayes and S. A. Irvine, suggest that:

(a) No other original calls primarily involve giving messages to harden the hearts of listeners
(b) It is clear that Isaiah was functioning as an inspired prophet of God during the reign of Uzziah in 2-5, so this could be his initial call
(c) There is a change in Isaiah's messages after ch 6 with special emphasis on political affairs and refusal to follow God's instructions (7:1-12). Thus the new commission chronologically fits here rather than before Chap 1 and,
(d) The structure and content of this experience is more like the special re-commissioning of Micaiah ben Imlah, rather than like Jeremiah's initial call.[133]

W. Zimmerli's form critical analysis of call narratives divides them into two groups. In the first group Moses (Exod. 3), Gideon (Jud. 6) and Jeremiah (Jer. 1) have a divine vision, a divine sending, as series of excuses by the person being called, a divine sign and promise and then a divine commissioning to give the word of God. In contrast, the second group, including Micaiah ben Imlah (1 Kgs. 22) and Isaiah were prophets before they received a new message, experience some sort of theophany of the divine council, and were told about the task of hardening the listeners.[134]

This second type of commissioning does not fit into the pattern of other prophetic inaugural callings. Thus, it seems best to understand Is 6 as God's special re-commissioning for a new task because the nation would be facing a new political situation led by a new unbelieving King.[135]

Seitz rejects the view that this is a call narrative and sees it as a "specific commission to make hearts fat-or commission that is carried out in the events of 734-732 B.C.E." Blenkinsopp writes, "that it functions in a more limited way as Isaiah's commissioning for a specific political mission in connection with the threat of a Syrian-Samaritan invasion."[136]

---

[133] J. H. Hayes and S. A. Irvine, *Isaiah, the Eight Century Prophet: His Times and Preaching* (Nashville: Abingdon Press, 1987), 108-109.

[134] W. Zimmerli, *A Commentary on the Book of Isaiah* (Philadelphia: Fortress Press, 1979), 97-100.

[135] Seitz, *Isaiah 1-39: Interpretation*, 53.

[136] Joseph Blenkinsopp, *Isaiah 1-39* (New York: Doubleday, 2000), 223.

Edgar W. Conrad argues that the vision of Isaiah is a book (6-39) within the Book of Isaiah. Isaiah is portrayed as a prophet from an Assyrian past; a time when his community is blind and deaf to his message (Isa. 6:9-10).[137]

Isaiah's vision is to be understood to be another time, unlike his own time, when the blind will see and the deaf will hear (Isa. 42:18-20 and 43:8; cf. 29:18). Hence, the book of Isaiah portrays the period of Babylonian decline and Persian ascendancy as the occasion when the command is given for the vision to be read.[138]

The legal ambience of Isaiah's written vision, that it is to be a "witness," 'a testimony" and a "teaching" and that, like a legal document, it is to be "sealed" (cf. Jer. 32:9-15),[139] suggests that its significance is for a future community whose members will be witnesses (Isa. 43:10, 12) for the Lord in the trial that the Lord will conduct against the nations (Isa. 43:8-13). In the Book of Isaiah the Lord's words spoken in the past vision of the prophet Isaiah, originating in a period of Assyrian ascendancy, become audible in a future time when they read to a community at the time of Persian ascendancy.

4.3.2.2.1. Comments on Isaiah 6:10 in relation to Illness, Health and Healing

In the Book of Isaiah repentance or return (שׁוב) is seen as a pre-requisite for Yahweh's healing (Is. 6:10). However, this cannot be true for all the "healing" passages. Repentance is not always seen as a pre-condition for healing. Yahweh's healing and forgiveness are not occasioned by Israel's repentance or her good intentions, but springs solely from His generous and free grace.

According to Robert Carroll,

> There are many motifs, themes, and images running through the book of Isaiah which make it such a rich, dense book for readers in search of mind-bending encounters with the text. Inter-textuality is a dominant feature of the book as themes are woven and interwoven throughout it to form networks, which provide reflective puzzlement for modern readers. Most of all the many interwoven themes in the book the twinned topoi of "blindness and insight" in 6:10 is to be considered as utmost importance.[140]

---

[137] Edgar W. Conrad, "Reading Isaiah and the Twelve as Prophetic Books," in *Writing and Reading the Scroll of Isaiah: Studies of an Interpretive Tradition*, ed. Craig C. Broyles and Craig A. Evans (New York: Brill, 1997), 8.

[138] E. W. Conrad, *Reading Isaiah* (Minneapolis: Fortress Press, 1991), 137-138.

[139] Ibid., 9.

[140] Robert P. Carroll, "Blind sight and the Vision Thing: Blindness and Insight in the Book of Isaiah," in *Writing and Reading the Scroll of Isaiah in Studies of Interpretive Tradition*, ed. D. Craig, C. Broyles, and Craig A. Evans (New York: Brill, 1997), 79.

Words having to do with sight/seeing in physical and metaphysical senses (e.g. understanding, insight, disclosure, realization) abound throughout the book. Much of the book of Isaiah focuses on the dynamics of human action, perception, attentiveness and a perception: seeing, hearing, speaking, observing, exchanging, feeling, reflecting, touching and general somatic experience. Thus, the language of the body is writ large throughout the book especially in 1:5-6; 49:16; 53:1-6; 66:7-11. From such a corpus of language about the body comes the focus on activities and states of seeing and not seeing, perceiving and not perceiving and of understanding and not understanding. From 1:2-3 to 66:24 the book of Isaiah is about seeing and perceiving, lacking understanding and being blind.[141] Such kind of relationship may be explained as under:

4.3.2.2.1.1. Seeing (ראה)

In Isaiah 6:9-10, the importance with the infinitive absolute is used in the utterance, "Be ever seeing,[142] but never perceiving". The instruction to Isaiah to close their eyes is also added. This utterance sums up not only the content of Isaiah's public preaching, but its effect as intended by God. The commission to blind does not mean that the truth is merely withheld from the sinful people. It is proclaimed through the prophet but only in order to speed the coming judgment. Every word of the prophet would make them more determined not to abandon their own groups. However, they had to come to the point where one more rejection of the truth would finally condemn them to inevitable judgment.[143] The dilemma of the prophet was that there was no way of saving sinners but by the very truth, the rejection of which would condemn them utterly.

4.3.2.2.1.2. Hearing (שמע)

The primary meaning of שמע is to hear sounds with car, where words are heard, it implies an engagement with the mind and comes to mean listen.[144] Israel's failure to perceive God's revelation can therefore be expressed as the inability of their ears to hear. In Isaiah 6:9, the prophet is told to tell the people "Be ever hearing, but never understanding; be ever seeing, but never perceiving." Isaiah's task is to dull Israel's organs of perception, rendering them blind, deaf and ignorant so that they might not repent and be healed (v.10). In these passages,

---

[141] Ibid., 79-80.

[142] The dropping of the *waw* of וראו of the MT in 6:9 gives a better reading from the point of view of parallel structure and emphasis. The MT reading may be the result of a dittography. Joseph R. Robinson, *The Dead Sea Isaiah Scroll: A Literary Analysis* (Grand Rapids, Michigan: William B. Eerdmans Publishing Company, 1970), 13.

[143] Jackie A. Naude, "See," in *New International Dictionary of Theology and Exegesis*, ed. Willem A. Van Gemeren (Carlisle, Cumbria: Paternoster Press, 1996), 1011. In late Judaism, seeing gave way to hearing. The verb is used in the sense of meeting with/coming to; he who sees a place.

[144] K. T. Aitken, "Hear," in *New International Dictionary of Old Testament Theology and Exegesis*, ed. Willem A. Van Gemeren (Carlisle, Cumbria: Paternoster Press, 1996), 175.

God is the ultimate cause of human failure to perceive his revelation. Spiritual perception is a divine gift denied to Israel, while spiritual deafness is an act of divine judgment.[145] Such judgment, however, confirms Israel in the blindness and deafness of their own perverse refusal to hear God's word and to seek his work (cf. Isa. 1:2-3; 5:12-13; 30:9).

4.3.2.2.1.3. Understanding (/ב)

/ב is connected quite naturally with terms meaning "to hear" and "to see," and in such instances, it obviously denotes the act of perceiving.

In Isaiah 6:9ff the prophet receives the command to preach to the people, "hear and hear, but do not 'perceive;' see and see, but do not 'understand.'"[146]

Such an ironical declaration presents a challenge to any commentator. The divine declaration indicates what must be done for redemption of the people at a moment when there are no longer any prospects of success. God sees that the obduracy of the people is already complete and irrevocable; nevertheless, he still sends a prophet to proclaim the penitence that is the sole possible route to life.[147] The idea is that the external seeing and hearing will not lead to a deeper understanding of the situation; the heart of the people will become hard so that they see, hear and understand nothing that God might heal them. The prophets' use of the verb שׁוּב may point to the idea of conversion, but it is also possible to translate: 'that they may be healed again.'[148]

This text talks about the relationship between spiritual understanding, conversion, and healing. Isaiah 6:9-10 notwithstanding, it is going too far to say that Isaiah did not preach repentance. There are indications throughout Isaiah's preaching that the prophet expected the people to repent. Such expectation would imply a hope for a remnant and, perhaps, for restoration. The following examples may be noted. Despite the blows delivered against them (as described, for example, in 9:8-12), "the people did not turn to him who smote them, nor seek the Lord of hosts" (9:13). In 30:15 opportunity for repentance and salvation are offered: "In returning [i.e., repenting] and rest you shall be saved; in quietness and in trust shall be your strength." Perhaps the best example is found in 31:6: "Turn to him from whom you have deeply revolted, O people of Israel."[149]

Linguistically, there are some basic differences between the Hebrew and the LXX rendering of Isaiah 6:9-10. A translation of the Hebrew reads as follows,

---

145 Ibid., 175-176.

146 Rinngren, "Understanding," in *Theological Dictionary of the Old Testament*, ed. G. Johannes Botterweck and Helmer Ringgren (Grand Rapids, Michigan: William B. Eerdmans Publishing Company, 1975), 101.

147 Joze Krasovec, *Reward, Punishment, and Forgiveness: The Thinking and Beliefs of Ancient Israel in the Light of Greek and Modern Views* (Leiden: Brill, 1999), 378.

148 Rinngren, "Understanding," 101.

149 Evans, "Isaiah 6:9-13 in the Context of Isaiah's Theology," 145.

> [And the Lord said] Go, and say to this people: "Hear and hear, but do not understand: see and see, but do not perceive. Make the heart of this people fat, and their ears heavy, and shut their eyes, lest they see with their eyes and hear with their ears, and understand with their hearts, and turn and be healed." (RSV)

The LXX reads:

> And he said, go and say to this people, by hearing you will hear and not understand and while seeing you will see and not see, for the heart of this people has become fat and with difficulty they heard with their ears, and their eyes grew tired lest they should see with the eyes and hear with the ears and understand by the heart and turn and I will heal them.

Even a superficial comparison reveals some striking differences between the two texts. The imperative in the Hebrew, "hear" and "see," are rendered into Greek using the future tense, "you will hear" and "you will see." The change in tense shifts the cause of Israel's stubbornness from God (Hebrew) to Israel herself (LXX). Consequently, instead of God being the direct cause of making the people's heart grow fat or dull, which prevents hearing and seeing, it is the people themselves whose heart prevents hearing, seeing and understanding (ἐπα-χύνθη γαρ ἡ καρδία του λαοΟ τούτου). Unlike the Hebrew text where the emphasis is placed on God, who prevents repentance as part of his judgment, the μήποτε (lest) clause of the LXX refers the inability to repent back to the prophet's audience.[150]

4.3.2.2.1.4. 'Deafness' and 'Blindness' as a Metaphor for Spiritual Illness

Using the Hebrew text, Gerhard Von Rad offers some excellent insights into Isaiah 6:9-10 and its relationship to eschatology. For Von Rad there is no way to remove the sting from the Hebrew version. The word of God spoken through the prophet does precisely what it says. God indeed hardens the hearts of the people in order to reveal his power (cf. Exod. 9:16). In the case of Israel, God will destroy the nation he formed in order to rebuild it anew in the future. This historical/ eschatological dimension derived from Isaiah 6:9-10 shows that the harshness of the saying, rather than being a closed fiat intended to punish an unfaithful people, opens up to the future. By treating Is 6:9-10 as a prelude to what is to come, Von Rad rightly, perceives the ongoing creative activity of God's Word which rebuilds a new nation comprised of Jews and Gentiles. According to him,

---

[150] Craig A. Evans, "To See and Not Perceive: Isaiah 6:9-10 in Early Jewish and Christian Interpretation," *Journal for the Study of the Old Testament* 64, no. Supplementary Series (1989): 61-64.

> We must learn to read the saying about the hardening of the heart with reference to saving history. Any psychological or devotional explanation or any understanding of it merely as punishment, means understanding it as the end, the final stage of a process which operates in a greater or lesser degree according to fixed laws. This is not consistent with the plain evidence found in Isaiah; for paradoxical as it may be, its position there is emphatically at the beginning of a movement in saving history. It was at the beginning, at his call, that Isaiah was given this word, and in Isaiah 8:17 he says paradoxically that his hope is founded precisely in this God who hardens the heart; here too, hardening of the heart is an event, from which the prophet looks out into the future; and in Isaiah 30:8ff the position is no different. . . Absolutely everything in Isaiah points out into the future—even the saying about the hardening of Israel's heart which is the action of Yahweh himself.[151]

The person being described here might be a leper, but the primary connotation is metaphorical. John N. Oswalt rightly points out that, "This Servant has taken on himself the sin-sickness of humanity. All the grief, all the sorrow, all the diseased relationships, all the disease that sin has brought to the human race, as typified by Judah, he has taken into himself."[152]

The text emphasized is a command for hardening. The discourse about the ears hardening and the eyes sticking shut is equal to the "seeing" and 'hearing" in v.9b. The heart is mentioned as the residence of that insight and understanding, which is identified as missing in v.9b. The phrase השמין לב (make the heart of this people fat) seems to be a phrase which Isaiah himself has formulated. Hence, the meaning, which is given as 'heart' in this passage, corresponds completely to the wisdom tradition, which is detected repeatedly in Isaiah. It is the highest goal of a pious Israelite to get a "wise heart" (Ps. 90:12; Prov. 16:23).[153]

It is argued that the motif of deafness and blindness is a metaphor for a spiritual condition that (1) is brought on by the people themselves, (2) comprises a judgment from God, and (3) will ultimately be rectified by God himself "in that day" of salvation. Hence, the spiritual condition of the nation is described by

---

[151] Gerhard Von Rad, *The Message of the Prophets* (New York: Harper & Row Publishers, 1967), 126.

[152] John N Oswalt, "Isaiah 52:13-53:12: Servant of All," *Calvin Theological Journal* 40, no. 1 (April 2005): 92.

[153] Wildberger, *Isaiah 1-12: A Commentary*, 272. The hardening of heart is used only by Isaiah as a verb שׁעע. The prophet is well aware of the hardening of heart of the people. However, it was noted already by Yahwist (Exod. 7ff), about not only Pharaoh's hardening of heart but Yahweh hardening it. The other prophets did use the hardening of heart though they did not use this terminology. Therefore, it is to be understood here that Israel hardened the heart in its opposition to God because of Yahweh's judgment.

Isaiah as deaf and blind. In this, the creation is called to listen and give ear to the fact that Yahweh's own people have rebelled (1:2), acted corruptly, abandoned, despised, and turned away from God (1:4). In consequence, the rulers and people are urged to repent and to return so that they may be healed.

In its development, 1:2-9 clearly parallels 6:9-10. In both passages, each of the following conditions hold:

1. Israel has a failure of understanding and knowing (1:3; cf. 6:9).
2. Israel has turned away from Yahweh (1:4; cf. 6:10).
3. Israel is sick from the head to feet and, by implication, in need of healing (1:5; cf. 6:10).
4. Yet Israel continues to rebel and refuses to turn and be healed (1:5; cf. 6:10).
5. Destruction follows (1:7-8; cf. 6:11), but a remnant remains (1:9; cf. 6:13).

The people of Judah and Jerusalem failed to see God's hand of judgment in the Assyrian invasion and dispersion of the Northern Kingdom in 722 BC, and in the destruction already experienced in Judah (1:7-8).[154] In other words, "This is the height of blindness: not to recognize that Yahweh is God in judgment as in deliverance, and that nothing happens to them that is not his will."[155] The reality and extent of the people's sin, their hardness of heart, and their blindness to the work of God in their midst, all point to the fact that "the Israelites had not yet perceived the reality of God, and so they were messengers who cannot hear the message nor see where they are going."[156]

The text is also expressed as God's Judgment upon Israel as deafness and blindness. It is this aspect, judgment that is being emphasized in 6:9-10. These verses must be understood in the light of God's nature as both loving and holy and in the light of God's actual dealings with his people in patience and with much warning to repent. Additional interpretive contexts include the divine response to human stubbornness and wilful blindness, the way in which other texts apply this passage, and the irony inherent in the message. Only when all these factors are carefully considered can the full meaning be ascertained. The seriousness of illness is seen in the way the Israelites close their eyes, stop their ears and refused to understand and receive healing. The nature of God's love is associated with the word שׁוּב, which is culminated in healing.

[154] John D. W. Watts, "Isaiah 1-33," in *WBC* (Waco, Texas: Word, 1985), 4-7.

[155] J. L. McKenzie, *Second Isaiah* (New York: Doubleday, 1968), 47.

[156] Ibid., 48.

Summary

Hosea and Proto-Isaiah give the picture of a sickly state of the community. This sickly state is because of the non-commitment of the people to the covenant relationship with God. Illness or sickness in these passages is seen as psycho-physical and socio-religio-economic reality. That raises the question whether it is only a spiritual sickness? The understanding of sickness does not merely confine to the physical aspect especially in Hosea and proto-Isaiah. As discussed above, their idea of sickness is in terms of socio-economic and political sickness, which has crippled their very existence of life and therefore, is in need of healing. The sickness metaphors in both the prophets are seen in the way the people have turned their way to Assyria, Egypt and to other gods for remedy and healing.

Proto-Isaiah's description of apostate Israel as a disease-ridden body is expressed in terms of repentance that could bring cure. The Isaianic material continues to expand on this theme. Concepts such as health and healing were more wide reaching in their import and the idea of Israel being sick and in need of healing might not have been perceived strictly as metaphorically by the ancient hearer. The terms could have simply conveyed the wider concepts of suffering and affliction on the one hand, and restoration and rehabilitation on the other hand, with everything those words entailed.

In Hosea the concept of "turning back the captivity of Israel" equates national restoration with the root רפא. The richness of the metaphors and similes employed in referring to God's being and activity unsurpassed in other Biblical writings. Hence, the metaphor of God as רפא is best expressed in the words of Hosea to a nation that is in need of healing.

Another important aspect evident is that Yahweh is the source of illness. The prophets in a context of religious apostasy and people's stubbornness to turn to God reminded the people that it is God who is able to bring disaster and also heal them. This is seen in a context where God has concern for the health and well being of the people in terms of establishing the right relationship with Him. The cure from sickness is to maintain the right relationship with God. Healing means restoration of health and relationships. The passages discussed above make things quite clear that sickness, health and healing is to be seen wholistically and a wholistic approach to the problem will help us understand these texts in a better way.

Chapter 5

Illness, Health and Healing in Exilic Prophecy of Jeremiah and Deutero-Isaiah

Introduction

Disasters inflict wounds without words, or at least without words adequate to the harm that has been done.[1] The people of Judah underwent destruction, traumatic violence and violent loss during three invasions that overwhelmed the senses that led to deportations, and occupation at the hands of the Babylonian Empire in the sixth century B.C.E.

The envisioning of a healed community does not arise out of the comfort zones of the prophets. However, the cries and pains voiced out by people who found themselves in a foreign land led to the hope of restoration and healing. The event of "the Exile" was a traumatic experience, a time of crisis for the people of God. The cry of the people was the lament that questioned the health of a conquered people who had suddenly lost freedom, land, king and Temple, and in that catastrophe, experienced the loss of their God.[2] Keeping in mind this context, the chapter will explore the understanding of illness, health and healing in Jeremiah and Deutero-Isaiah.

5.1. The Socio-Historical Context of the Exilic Period

In the sixth century, B.C.E., the Babylonian army devastated Judah and Jerusalem. It invaded Jerusalem three times, it occupied the land, and it deported leading citizens to Babylon. The nation of Judah faced extinction. The people underwent traumatic violence in a series of disasters, after which lingered theological and emotional layers of harm for decades.

[1] W. G. Sebald, *On the Natural History of Destruction* (New York: Random House, 2003), 25.

[2] Eileen Schuller, *Post - Exilic Prophets* (Wilmington: Michael Glazier, 1988), 13.

One layer of harm involves traumatic memories of violence. Violence overwhelms its victims, leaving them with memories of the traumatic blows that cannot be incorporated into their daily lives, into their sense of themselves. Often memories haunt victims like a ghost who take up residence in the mind to disturb and interfere with life. Because the experience overwhelms the psyche, victims usually cannot find language adequate to their experience of the violence. Without the ability to speak about it, community is shattered and its members often feel isolated and unmoored from their world. Accompanying these effects is the loss of confidence and trust in the world.[3]

The people of Israel who were called as God's chosen people were left in a situation where they started to question the promise of God that "I will take you as my people, and I will be your God (Exod. 6:7)." They had been delivered with mighty hand and an outstretched arm from slavery and oppression in Egypt to freedom in the land promised to their ancestors. The Law of the Lord was received by Moses at Mt. Sinai, which instructed them how to live their lives in response to the covenant, which God had initiated. In time, the Lord had chosen for them a king, David, and given the assurance 'your house and your kingdom shall be made sure forever before me; your throne shall be established forever' (2 Sam. 7:16). Over the centuries, the prophets had spoken to them the word of God in judgment and promise. Then, suddenly in the year 587 B.C.E., all was called into question when the mighty Babylon Empire conquered the tiny and vulnerable kingdom of Judah. Many of the people, especially the leaders and the elite, were carried off to the foreign land of Babylon as exiles; the Temple, the sacred site of divine presence, was burned; King Zedekiah was blinded and taken away in fetters.[4] Hence, the question 'what kind of God could do this to a people who were chosen to be kingdom of priests and a holy nation?'

Like the Exodus, the exile was a turning point in God's relationship with the chosen people. On the surface, it looked as if the kingdom of Judah might disappear totally, as the ten lost tribes of the Northern Kingdom had vanished a century earlier. However, in spite of the tremendous suffering involved and the profound crisis of faith engendered, this was ultimately to be not a time of destruction but of reconstruction. It became a time for re-examination of old traditions and the discovery of new, hitherto unimagined ways of being God's people. Throughout the whole Exile experience, the prophets (Jeremiah, Ezekiel, and Second Isaiah) spoke a new message of hope in the midst of hopelessness.[5] The experience of exile became the beginning of new hope for the people of Israel. In the days of deepest despair, a prophet who was living in exile in Babylon, was

---

[3] Kathleen M. O'Connor, "Rekindling Life, Igniting Hope," *Journal for Preachers* 30, no. 2 (2007): 30.

[4] Schuller, *Post - Exilic Prophets*, 13-14.

[5] Ibid., 14.

called to speak powerfully and he appeared on the historical scenario with poetic words of consolation, "Comfort, comfort my people" (Isa. 40:1).

The Book of Jeremiah and Deutero-Isaiah is marked with full of promises. However, those promises are addressed only to people in exile who have seen the city destroyed and have suffered the loss of their entire world of faith.[6] Both of their vision of 'new thing' cannot be considered without taking into account the experience of the exiles. The poetry of Jeremiah and Deutero-Isaiah is shaped by powerful poetic metaphors. The social, historical setting for this poetry is exile. The poet thus, must be heard through the metaphor of exile.

5.2. Health and Healing in Jeremiah

The book of Jeremiah is a quest for language to name this world of catastrophe and misery. Its wide, chaotic collection of poems, stories, and sermons over and over again depicts a shattered world, usually in symbolic form as, for example, in the ruin of Jeremiah's buried loincloth (13:1-11), the destruction of the pot by the divine Potter (18:1-12), the breaking of the vase (19:1-15). For the book's audience, these and other symbolic events retell what happened to them. They do so indirectly in symbolic form to help them re-enter the experience but not re-traumatize them by literal renderings.[7]

In this way, even Jeremiah's most horrifying imagery helps survivors of the disaster to come to grips with it, to grieve it, to understand how God was present through its many manifestations. Only then is it possible to believe in God's intervention, to make room for hope and to rebuild community. The passage, which refers to violence in the book, reflects back to the community that was destroyed and lost. It also refers in horrendous scenes that give them their story of terror and destruction, of pain and disaster. Against common perception, by re-immersing them in the calamity, Jeremiah creates words that are a healing balm for wounds without words.[8]

First and foremost, the book of Jeremiah names the disaster, reveals its contours, and mirrors it back to its audience. It depicts the totality of the destruction, speaks of pain and bitter grief, and articulates the rawness of the world in which survivors find themselves. It first names the disaster as a coming event, an onrushing attack upon Jerusalem, by the mythic "foe from the north" (1:14; 4:6).[9]

The book's poetic world mirrors their predicament. It enables survivors to see the overwhelming nature of the catastrophe they have gone through. Its

[6] Walter Brueggemann, *Hopeful Imagination: Prophetic Voices in Exile* (Philadelphia: Fortress Press, 1986), 90.

[7] O'Connor, "Rekindling Life, Igniting Hope," 31.

[8] Ibid.

[9] John Hill, *Friend or Foe? The Figure of Babylon in the Book of Jeremiah MT*, Biblical Interpretation Series, vol. 40 (Leiden: J. E. Brill, 1999), 239.

truthful, bitter, depiction of disaster is a survival tactic because it brings pain out of numbness, gives it a language, and makes it visible. By showing them their losses, it validates them in their suffering, lets them know they are not alone in it, and provides words for them to begin to speak of it. When they accept the magnitude of their disaster, healing can begin.

5.2.1. Exegetical Study

5.2.1.1. Jeremiah 3:22

V. 22 "Turn back, backsliding children;
let me heal[a] your backsliding!"
"Here we are! We have come to you,
for you are the LORD our God."

Form Critical Notes

There is no agreement among scholars as to the extent of the pericope involving Jeremiah 3:21-4:4. Some reduce it to 3:21-25,[10] while others expand it to as much as 3:1-5; 3:19-4.4.[11] Admittedly, there are points of contact with what precedes (as 'sons' in 3:19 and 21, 22; and in 3:1 [twice] and 22; 4:1 [twice]; etc.) and with what follows (Judah and Jerusalem in 4:3 and 5), but these appear to be redactional joints rather than integral parts of a common original pericope.[12]

Scholars have proposed three positions. First, in 3.22b-25 Jeremiah is envisioning events in the future, which he thinks or hopes will occur, and describing them as if they were present. Hyatt thinks that these are words, which the Israelites should say as they acknowledge their sin and return to Yahweh.[13] Harrison believes that in 3:21-25 the prophet is voicing what Judah will learn in the Babylonian captivity, namely, that man cannot serve Yahweh and Baal. Then in 4:1-2 Yahweh expresses his concern that Israel's repentance be genuine and lasting. These verses show that the situation envisioned in 3:21-25 was a prospect rather than a reality.[14]

According to this view, the protasis of the lines beginning in 4:1 indicates that Jeremiah is thinking of the future. Second, in 3:22b-25 either the people themselves actually repent sincerely or Jeremiah intercedes on their behalf by

[10] A. W. Streane, *The Book of the Prophet Jeremiah, together with the Lamentations* (Cambridge: Cambridge University Press, 1882), 32-33.

[11] Guy P. Couturier, "Jeremiah," in *The Jerome Biblical Commentary* (Englewood Cliffs: Prentice-Hall, 1968), 307.

[12] John T. Willis, "Dialogue between prophet and audience as a rhetorical device in the book of Jeremiah," *Journal for the Study of the Old Testament* 33 (October 1985): 66.

[13] J. P. Hyatt, *The Book of Jeremiah: Introduction and Exegesis*, The Interpreter's Bible, vol. V (Nashville: Abingdon Press, 1956), 829-30.

[14] The Tyndale Old Testament Commentaries Roland K. Harrison, *Jeremiah and Lamentations: An Introduction and Commentary* (England: InterVarsity Press, 1975), 67-68.

putting sincere words of repentance in their mouth. Then, in 4:1-2 (or 4) Yahweh assures them that he will restore them as they return to him with their whole heart.[15]

Vv. 21-25 is a third element of the summons to return now which follows after 12-14 and 19-20. The invitation is offered in v. 22, a summons and an assurance of God will heal. Walter Brueggemann argues that it is however not clear if this summons is to be taken at a face value, or if this is a mocking at Israel's too-easy presumption upon Yahweh.[16] However, in any case, vv. 21, 22b, 23 are an articulation of repentance, an acknowledgment of guilt, and a recognition that trusts in other gods has been an exercise in futility. It is only Yahweh who is the divine deliverer or a healer.

Setting

The poem in chapter 3 resembles the metaphor of marriage in chapter 2. The section Jeremiah 3:1-4:4 has a long complex redactional history.[17] The purpose of this unit is an accusation of Judah and a strict invitation to return to Yahweh. The analysis of this section is by no means an easy one, and different scholars have produced a variety of versions of the poem and its additions.[18] The original poem is most likely to be found in 3:1-5, 12b-13, 19f, 21-23; 4:1f. A different set of metaphors is seen in 4:3f, which is contrary to the motif of repentance. Thus, the brief section is seen as a transition between repentance material and the collection of judgment oracles in chapters 4-6.[19]

The section 3:1-4:4 focuses changes from accusation and indictment to appeal for Israel to return to Yahweh or to the land following the exile.[20]

---

[15] John Paterson, *Jeremiah: Peake's Commentary on the Bible* (London: Thomas Nelson and Sons, 1962), 543.

[16] Walter Brueggemann, *A Commentary on Jeremiah: Exile and Homecoming* (Grand Rapids, Michigan: William B. Eerdmans Publishing Company, 1998), 48.

[17] John Bright, *Jeremiah*, 2nd ed. (Garden City, New York: Doubleday, 1978), 25-27.

[18] Robert P. Carroll, *From Chaos to Covenant: Prophecy in the Book of Jeremiah* (New York: Crossroad, 1981), 73.

[19] Ibid.

[20] Apparently, Jeremiah called for the northern exile to return to Yahweh and for repentance on the part of Judah in the early days of his ministry, but this call went unheeded. The language of promise inserted in the middle of the calls to repentance (3:14 18) assumed the fall of both Israel and Judah. Fretheim writes, "And so the call to repentance, whatever its force as an earlier message of Jeremiah is now represented as a word to exiles, for whom repentance is possible." Terence E. Fretheim, *Jeremiah: Smith & Helwys Bible Commentary* (Macon, GA: Smith & Helwys, 2002), 81. This focus on the final exilic (or postexilic) audience in Jeremiah may explain the use of prose to relay the prophet's message in 3:6-11, 14-18. Stulman has noted that prose passages like those in Jeremiah 7, 25, and 26 play, a key role as signposts and interpretive summaries for the reading of the prophet's poetic oracles in the book as a whole and one can imagine a similar role for these prose passages within the smaller unit of 2:1-4:4.Louis Stulman, *Order Amid Chaos: Jeremiah as Symbolic Tapestry* (Sheffield: Sheffield Academic, 1998), 57-58. In their prose form the messages

In 3:1-11 the prophet argued that Israel (and particularly Judah) had forfeited the opportunity to return to Yahweh, but then he closed in 3:12-4:14 with repeated calls for the people to return. By appearing to shut them off from the opportunity to repent, the prophet motivated his audience to respond to the gracious offer of a restored relationship with Yahweh.[21] The divorce law in Deuteronomy 24 stated that if a man divorced his wife, he was not allowed to take her back if she married another man and was later divorced or widowed. Remarrying the first husband after the woman had married another man would bring defilement on the land. The rhetorical questions in Jeremiah 3:1-5 seek to bring the prophet's audience to an understanding of their precarious position as Yahweh's wife. The questions in verse 1: "Will he still return (שׁוב) to her?" and "Will not that land be completely polluted?" call for no and yes answers. The following ושובאלי in verse 1c is more ambiguous in both construction and intent. The infinitive absolute could be translated as an imperative ("return to Me"), but this understanding seems to be doubtful in light of the previous questions. More likely, the construction should be read as another question, "Would you return to Me?" As Fretheim explains, the question suggests, "no renewal of the relationship between Yahweh and Israel is possible."[22] In fact Israel's flagrant and repeated infidelity went beyond the circumstances set forth in Deuteronomy 24, making the possibility of return even less likely (Jer. 3:2-3).[23]

The standing of the marriage becomes more precarious in the prose message in verses 6-11. Yahweh is portrayed as the husband of sisters "Faithless or apostate (משׁבה, in v.6) Israel" and "Treacherous (בגודה in v.7) Judah," when Israel refused to "turn" (שׁוב) to Yahweh. He divorced Israel and sent her away into exile (v. 7)". Despite observing what happened to her sister Israel, Judah also refused to "return' (שׁוב) to Yahweh genuinely ("with all her heart," v.10), making her more culpable

---

provide a historical object lesson that invites Israel to learn from the mistakes of the past and to begin the process of restoration. Allen stresses the Importance of being attentive to both the "now" of Jeremiah's message for the intended reader and the "then" of Jeremiah's message in its original historical setting. *Leslie C. Allen, Jeremiah: A Commentary* (Louisville: Westminster John Knox Press, 2008), 14-16.

[21] Michael Fishbane, *Biblical Interpretation in Ancient Israel* (Oxford: Clarendon, 1985), 307-312.

[22] On the other hand, J. A. Thompson argues that the fact that Judah had not "married a particular lover" provided a "loophole" to the Deuteronomic provision. J. A. Thompson, *Jeremiah: New International Commentary on the Old Testament* (Grand Rapids: Michigan, 1980), 191. However, Jeremiah's rhetoric here made the opposite point, namely, that Judah's behaviour was worse than anything envisioned in Deuteronomy 24. Moughtin-Mumby comments, "According to 3:1, Judah has already done worse than the hypothetical wife." Sharon Moughtin-Mumby, *Sexual and Marital Metaphors in Hosea, Jeremiah, Isaiah and Ezekiel* (Oxford: Oxford University Press, 2008), 99.

[23] Fretheim, *Jeremiah: Smith & Helwys Bible Commentary*, 73.

than Israel.[24] If Yahweh had already divorced Israel, and Judah was even worse than Israel, the only logical expectation is that Yahweh would also divorce Judah and send her away into exile.

After seemingly to arguing quite emphatically that a return was not possible, it is even more surprising that Yahweh repeatedly called for the return of His people in 3:12-4:4. After the negative uses of the root (שׁוב) in 3:1-11 and the appearance that the covenant was irrevocably broken, several imperatives calling for Israel's return dominate this section.

3:12, "Return" (שׁוּב) directed to the exiles from northern Israel
3:13, "Acknowledge" (feminine singular imperative of ידע)
3:14, 22, "Return" (שׁוּבוּ)
4:3, "Break up (נירו) your fallow ground" (cf. v. 3c, "do not sow among thorns")
4:4, "Circumcise (המלו) yourselves to the Lord"

4:4, "Remove (הסרו) the foreskins of your heart"

5.2.1.1.1. Comments on Jeremiah 3:22 in relation to Illness, Health and Healing

The placement of the metaphor of Israel as unfaithful wife in Jeremiah 2-3 means that this understanding of Israel's relationship stamps the entire book to Yahweh.[25]

The prophet's call for Israel to return to Yahweh in 3:14-4:14 reflects a significant shift from the prevailing husband-wife metaphor in 2:1-3:3 to the portrayal of Yahweh's relationship with Israel as that of father-child (son). Yahweh called for the "sons" to return (3:14) and longed for the time when He could reward them as faithful sons rather than punish them as an unfaithful wife (vv.19-20). This overlapping of family metaphors may seem strange but the portrayal of Israel's relationship to Yahweh as both spouse and child stresses the closeness of their bond and the fact that Yahweh had been intimately associated with His people from their inception (cf. Ezek. 16:1-14).

In the portrayal of Israel as a child, the prophet first employed female imagery in Jeremiah 3:19-20 as Yahweh expressed the desire to give His daughters an inheritance. As Lundblom observes, the passage reflects an honoured status for the female in that daughters normally did not receive an inheritance (cf. Num. 27:1-8; 36:1-12; Job 42:15).[26] The honoured status Yahweh wished to confer on

---

[24] The repeated root בגד ("treacherous") stresses the refusal of Judah to turn from her sinful ways (3:7-8, 10-11; cf. בגדה "treacherously" in v. 20).

[25] Gerlinde Baumann, *Love and Violence: Marriage as Metaphor for the Relationship Between YHWH and Israel in the Prophetic Books*, trans. Linda M. Maloney (Collegeville, MN: Liturgical, 2003), 105.

[26] Jack R. Lundblom, *Jeremiah 1-20: A New Translation with Introduction and Commentary* (New York: Doubleday, 1999), 318.

Israel, made her betrayal of Him, all the more deplorable. After the final reference to Israel as unfaithful wife in Jeremiah 3:20, Israel is addressed or described only as the male "son(s)" of Yahweh in 3:21-4:4. The anticipated confession when Israel returns to Yahweh in 3:22-25 is that of rebellious sons returning to their father in verses 21-22. The image of male circumcision symbolically represents Israel's repentance in 4:4. The call for the people of Israel to "circumcise" themselves to Yahweh results in the unusual image of a circumcised prostitute.[27]

The context of this text portrays Israel as sinning again. This time their sister, Judah, followed their example and became even more perverse than Israel (3:7-8). Repeatedly the Lord implores Israel and Judah to return to Him (5 times in chapter 3 alone). Although Israel made an effort to return, Judah would not return with her whole heart but only in pretence (3:10). Not wanting His anger to fall (3:12), National Israel's history is marked with numerous wanderings from the will and Word of God, God tells them again to return to Him. Reminding them of His mercy, He assures them that His anger will not remain if only they would return.

The dialogue between Israel, Yahweh, and Jeremiah that begins in 2:1-4:4 carries over into the rest of the book. Yahweh would restore Israel so that she would move from empty expressions of covenant fidelity to the proper confession of past sin and true loyalty (envisioned in 3:22-25; 4:2). However, to the very end of this book Israel continued to say the wrong things and to defy Yahweh or to profess loyalty to Him with empty words. By hearing these quotations, the reader can almost visualize the entire book as a debate between Yahweh and His people with Jeremiah as the intermediary. Jeremiah 3:22-25 looks forward to Israel acknowledging that it was their worship of Baal that took away their blessing and prosperity.

In this text, Kimchi explains the medical metaphors in v. 22; just as a wound caused by a blow is healed by the medical care which it receives, so is it

[27] Some feminist studies object that the female is marginalized in the promises of salvation. Moughtin-Mumby comments, "While this passage has a positive impulse, the female Judah is excluded from such 'redemption.'" Moughtin-Mumby, *Sexual and Marital Metaphors in Hosea, Jeremiah, Isaiah and Ezekiel*, 111. J. Cheryl Exum notes the incongruity of the circumcision of the male as a symbol of covenant fidelity, while the female body and womb is associated with *uncleanness*, defilement, and death. J. Cheryl Exum, *Fragmented Women: Feminist (Sub) Versions of Biblical Narratives* (Valley Forge, PA: Trinity Press, 1993), 24-28.The shift from female to male imagery in this passage is the prophet's attempt to deliver the punch line of his controlling metaphor. Israel as a woman is a literary metaphor, whereas the "sons of Israel" represent the actual people and leaders in the prophet's predominantly male audience who are called to repent of their sinful ways. Jeremiah must move beyond the metaphor of the unfaithful wife in order to address the need for his male audience to change their sinful ways, turn and be healed.

with a wound of the soul; the remedy for sin is a forgiveness which is a response repentance.[28]

The tone of vv. 21-25 is very different from the denunciations of the nation in the discourse. Here, the awareness of their perverted ways makes them to seek Yahweh's healing. The poem depicts a nation deeply conscious of the wrong it has done, hence the divine invitation to turn and the promise of healing for such waywardness. In Jeremiah 3:22 רָפָא is used for the healing of sin and apostasy, presupposing the figure of sin as a serious illness (cf. Hos. 14:3). Thus, Israel's מְשׁוּבָה (unfaithfulness, waywardness, backsliding) is a dangerous condition that only God can cure. In this case, the translation of "heal" should be retained (as opposed to forgive, as per some translators and commentators), although it is acceptable to speak of figurative usage here, since the specific object of רפא is abstract viz., the people's sinful condition is pictured as an illness, rather than the people and nation are pictured as ill.[29] In Hosea 14, the central point is the healing motif;[30] here it is one element, and the acknowledgment of past mistakes is the central feature. A very important principle needs to be recognized. In nearly every case - there is "Pain which precedes Healing." Ehud Ben Zvi gives a clear picture of the prophet giving hope in the midst of hopeless and sickly situation. According to him, "the Old Testament prophetic books are generally "variations on a tripartite structure" of punishment for Israel, punishment for the nations, and salvation for Israel (or Israel and the nations).[31] Therefore, words of judgment ultimately give way to words of hope. In the case of Israel's backslidings, there is much pain and wound incurred by the people by turning away from God, but a condition is made for the people to be healed. The condition that the pain will be removed if only Israel turn (שׁוב) back to God. There is no denial that physical healing is referred to in the above text, yet the aspect of spiritual healing is at the heart of this statement.

[28] As quoted in William McKane, *A Critical and Exegetical Commentary on Jeremiah: Introduction and Commentary on Jeremiah 1-XXV*, vol. 1 (Edinburgh: T & T Clark Limited, 1986), 80. cf. Targums interpretation, 'I shall forgive you when you repent,' a rendering of ארפהמשובתיכם is apparently taking משוכתיכם in the sense, 'your acts of repentance.'

[29] Alan Kam-Yau Chan, Thomas B. Song, and Michael L. Brown, "*RAPHA*," in *New International Dictionary of Old Testament Theology and Exegesis*, ed. Willem A. VanGemeren (Cumbria, UK: Paternoster Press, 1997), 1165-1166.

[30] Hans Walter Wolff, in *Hosea*, ed. P. D. Hanson (Philadelphia: Fortress Press, 1974), 233.

[31] Ehud Ben Zvi, "The Prophetic Book: A Key Form of Prophetic Literature," in *The Changing Face of Form Criticism for the Twenty-First Century*, ed. Marvin A. Sweeney and Ehud Ben Zvi (Grand Rapids, Michigan: William B. Eerdmans Publishing Company, 2003), 285.

5.2.1.2. Jeremiah 6:7, 14

V. 7. As a well keeps fresh its water,
so she keeps fresh her wickedness;
'Violence! And Destruction are heard within her;
sickness and wounds are ever before me'
V. 14. They have treated the [a]wound of [a] my people carelessly,
saying: 'Peace, peace,'
[b]when there is no peace.[b]

Form Critical Notes

Vv. 6b-7 contains the indictment that is the motivation for the invasion. Six terms are used: "oppression," "wickedness," "violence," "destruction," "sickness," 'wounds,". The terms 'sickness" and "wounds," state the consequences of exploitation: a society that does not function is immobilized and under judgment (cf. Isa. 1:5-6).[32]

The structure of this poetic warning oracle may be set out as follows:

(i) A portion of a "call to alarm" (v 1; cf. 4:5–8).
(ii) A brief pastoral scene (vv 2–3), converted into a battle scene (vv 4–5), characterized by a note of urgency.
(iii) A divine oracle (vv 6–8), in which an enemy is instructed to lay siege to Jerusalem, but a final warning to Jerusalem (v 8) is also issued. The theme of the poem as a whole is similar to that in 4:5–10, although it is developed in a new direction.

Although, parts of this poem may have been drawn originally from separate sources, in its present form it is an effective poetic unity. The structure of the whole is bound together by the use of assonance, word play, and repetition. The following are the characteristics of the poem, which give the whole, a sense of literary unity:

(i) Assonance/word play on תקע
v 1תקוע "Tekoa"
v 1 תקעו "toot, blow"
v 3 תקעו "pitch"
v 8 תקע "be alienated," from
(ii) Assonance/word play on רעה
v 1 רעה "evil"
v 3 רעים "shepherds"
v 3 רעו "graze"
v 7 רעתה "her evil"

[32] Brueggemann, *A Commentary on Jeremiah: Exile and Homecoming*, 72-73.

(iii) Repetition
(a) קרב (vv 1, 6)
(b) קומו ונעלה (vv 4, 5)

The passage is similar to the dialogue in 5:1–9; it is possible that originally both passages belonged to a larger text in which a more comprehensive record of the dialogue was preserved. The following points of contact between 6:9–15 and the earlier dialogue (5:1–9) are worthy to be noted.

(i) In each passage, the dialogical sequence is the same:
(a) the Lord speaks, (b) Jeremiah responds with question and comment, and (c) the Lord speaks again.
(ii) In both passages, certain key words or themes are repeated (or continued): e.g., (a) the "streets of Jerusalem" (חוצות) may be alluded to again in 6:11 (חוא). (b) The people's capacity for "falsehood" (5:2, שקר) is repeated in 6:13 (שקר). (c) In both passages, there is reference to the "great, noble."

The data summarized above provide reasonable grounds for presupposing an original link between 6:9–16 and 5:1–9, prior to the editorial arrangement of the passages in their present position. Certain of the themes of the text separating the two dialogues are taken up and developed in this unit (6:9–15), suggesting perhaps reasons for the overall editorial arrangement. Thus the imagery of the vineyard contained in an earlier poetic fragment (5:10) is resumed in the Lord's opening words of the dialogue (6:9). In addition, the prior critique of prophets and priests (5:31) is developed further in the Lord's response to his prophet (6:13–14).

Setting

The general setting of the prophetic words was almost certainly Jerusalem, here pictured as a vineyard ready for harvest, though the harvest is a metaphor for judgment. The references to Benjamin, Tekoa and Beth-hacherem must be interpreted in the context of Jerusalem. However, there are different opinions of scholars with regard to this setting. The question about the metaphors of judgment leads to a quest of which two judgments are referred to. Are they the fall of Samaria and then the fall of Jerusalem, or the death of Josiah and then the fall of Jerusalem, or the first and second sieges of Jerusalem? Volz and Rudolph, adhering to a higher chronology, opt for the period 625-622 here,[33] so that the second and third options are eliminated. Bright, seemingly suggests a time after 597 B.C.E. for all of chapter 6.[34] The poem breathes an atmosphere of urgency and imminence, but the warning note of the end (v.8) suggests of a time that is

[33] W. Rudolph, *Jeremia* (Tubingen: Mohr, 1968), 45.

[34] John Bright, *Jeremiah* (New York: Doubleday, 1965), 51.

still there before the city's fall.[35] Nevertheless, an enquiry in this direction does not bring assurance. It has already been determined that this passage was one of the additions in Jeremiah's second scroll. Hence, the data is summarized as follows: The present passage is closely similar to 5:10-17; Israel is depicted as a vine, 5:10; 6:9; there are falsely optimistic prophets, 5:12-13; disaster, 5:14; 6:11. The setting hence is close to 5:10-17 and 14:13. There is also the possibility that the phrase "from the least of them to the greatest" (v.13) is an indirect reference to the sequence of events leading to the reading of the first scroll to the king (36:9-26), given reference in 22:17 to the king's concern for his own "cut," the same term that appears here.. There is also possibility that the mention of corrupt priest and prophets in v. 13 can be tied to the setting of 5:30-31 and 23:13-14. All these suggest a setting in 601 or early 600. The two judgments are likely to be the fall of Samaria and Jerusalem.[36]

The date cannot be pinned down precisely, though the later years of Josiah's reign are the probable period reflected in these verses. The dialogue represents the personal encounter between the prophet and God; it implies that the prophet's ministry had not been going well, and that he had turned to the Lord for direction and help.

5.2.1.2.1. Comments on Jeremiah 6:7, 14 in relation to Illness, Health and Healing

A well keeps its water cool, fresh, and available, a concern particularly in the context of a siege, (v. 6a) in the same way the city keeps the sin fresh and available. Two features of v.7 are worth noting. One is the use of water imagery (cf. 2:13; 17:13). Here, the similes are disorienting, since the positive picture of water kept purely and freshly in a well is used to depict the people's wickedness. They store it up and keep it fresh, ready to pour it out at the first opportunity. The congruity of fresh well water ready and available to drink and pent up wickedness ready to be vented on someone is one of the many jarring poetic features in the rhetoric of this prophet. Here, the water imagery is accentuated as the metaphor to point out the sickness of people. The paradoxical assertion in Jeremiah 6:7 "As a well keeps its water fresh, so she keeps fresh her wickedness" is contrary to the prophetic usage of "a well dries up" (Hos. 13:15) to the impending judgment. The sins of God's people in Jeremiah's day are often as fresh as the well that keeps fresh water. In their vain attempts to satisfy their thirst, deep within, they look in all the wrong places.

---

[35] Peter C. Craigie, Page H. Kelley, and Joel F. Drinkard Jr., "Jeremiah," in *Word Bible Commentary*, ed. David A. Hubbard (Dallas, Texas: Word Books, 1991), 99.

[36] Holladay, *Jeremiah 1: A Commentary on the Book of the Prophet Jeremiah Chapters 1-25*, 213.

5.2.1.2.1.1. 'Violence' (חמם) and 'Destruction' (שׁד) as the Loss of Health and Well-Being

The prophet uses the image of "violence" and "destruction" to that of the city's sinful and corrupted state. The phrase "sickness" and "injury" refers to outer manifestations, leading one to construe the present phrase as parallel. If the reconstruction of the last colon of v.7 is correct, then "violence" and "destruction" is metaphorically understood as some kind of treasure. It is difficult to distinguish clearly between חמם (violence) and שׁד (destruction). Wolff proposes that the former is violence against property.[37] However, the matter is not so simple. A recent study shows that µmj (violence) involves brutality, which may involve violent rift and plunder as well as devastation. The former is the larger semantic field and tends to refer to violence that is passing.[38]

The understanding of "sickness and injury" is not very clear. Masoretic text construes the words with what precedes: "before me continually are sickness and injury." LXX and Syriac version construct them with what follows: Syriac version reads "with pains and injuries be instructed, O Jerusalem." While violence and destruction is a phrase describing Jerusalem's evil, the pair of "sickness and injury" is evidence of Yahweh's warning of possible judgment. Sickness and injury are thus the disciplinary or warning blows, which the people have suffered from Yahweh.[39] The mention of a "wound" *(šeber)* in this context presupposes a "break" *(šbr)* in the existing order of creation, that is, a violation of that order on the part of the community resulting in their collective injury. Although there is no evidence connecting the text with a liturgy of intercession, there can be no doubt that the healing activity *(Rapha)* of the prophets mentioned in 6:14a refers to their mediatory role in securing a *Shalom* oracle.

In 6:l-12 we read a description of the dispossession and enslavement of large portions of the population, which suggests that the "wound" itself consisted in the ravages of war. As such, it had the character of divine punishment for the misdeeds of both the community at large and their representatives, the priests and the prophets.

The ambiguity in the final line is further evidence of the poetic force in this speech. In the Hebrew and Masoretic text, the sickness and wounds are connected to the preceding lines and thus are a part of the portrayal of the moral sickness of the people or of the consequences of their social violence. In the Greek and Syriac translations, however, "sickness' and "wounds" are connected to v.8 and refer to the attacks of the invading army, which ought to serve as a corrective, evolving a more moral and covenantal behaviour on the part of the people. This latter

---

[37] H. W. Wolff, *Joel and Amos* (Philadelphia: Fortress Press, 1977), 194.

[38] Jacques Pous as quoted by Holladay, *Jeremiah 1: A Commentary on the Book of the Prophet Jeremiah Chapters 1-25*, 208.

[39] Ibid.

alternatives is what is suggested by other uses of these terms in Jeremiah (e.g., Jer. 10:9; 30:12-15), but neither possibility can be ruled out. The imagery of illness and battle wounds speaks as powerfully the condition of a morally corrupt society as it does to a besieged and devastated city.

The context of verse 14 is close to that of 4:10 where the phrase saying "peace" is in the context of a threat to life. For שלם (here "fracture") suggests the collapse of roof-beams of a house onto pottery storage-jars; here given the medical connotation of רפא 'heal, treat', it is best to translate 'fracture', as metaphor for the violent break-up of community, for verb רפא does not always mean 'heal'. Healing is a process implying success, but in this instance, success is not predicted.[40]

To this Holladay rightly observes,

> The noun *šeber* in Jeremiah appears to center around three usages: the fracture of a bone (metaphorically in 6:14; 8:21; 10:19); shattering of pottery (cf. Isa 30:14); and the breaking of walls (cf. Isa 30:13). When a village or city is destroyed, walls collapse, roof-beams fall and break pottery storage jars, and these images are here in the forefront: the nation crashes with the totality of numberless crashes and so itself collapses in a heap.[41]

The promised restoration of Judah and Israel primarily described by *Rapha* and שוב could be no less comprehensive in its overall healing effects than the tragic, devastating collapse. Thus, what the Lord "broke/shattered/smashed" could only be "repaired/healed/restored" by his hand.

The appearance of מי in v. 14 might be thought more appropriate to Yahweh than to Jeremiah, but it should be taken as a mark of the intensity of the prophet's identification with his people and compared with 8:23, where Jeremiah is the speaker. Prophet and priest lack integrity and their words and deeds have the hollowness of falsehood: "they have prescribed superficial cure for the wounds of my people, saying, 'health, health,' when there is no health". One feels this need to sustain the medical imagery in the translation of שלם ('wholeness' or 'health'), rather than to interpret the imagery and render שלם as 'well-being" or "prosperity."[42] Hence, according to McKane, שלם is explained not as superficial treatments of wounds but as superficial talk שלם prophecy which has no substance in it.[43]

---

[40] Ibid., 216-217.

[41] Ibid., 202-203.

[42] McKane, *A Critical and Exegetical Commentary on Jeremiah: Introduction and Commentary on Jeremiah 1-XXV*, 147.

[43] Ibid. several images are used in Hosea 5:13-15: the people are ill (חלי and מזור). However, they expect healing from a wrong doctor. The same images are found in 6:1; 7:1; 11:3; 14:5. The name אפרים occurs frequently in this passage (5:9; 11, 12, 13 twice, and 14), that there seems to be a sort of word-play with רפא. In 6:1שוב, טרף and רפא are repeated so that the images from the above

Andersen and freedman suggest that recovering from illness does not mean resurrection from death.[44] The piel of היה normally means, "to make alive" and not 'to let live", which is a secondary derivative. Especially 1 Sam 2:6 supports the sense of "making alive". In addition, even if recovery from illness is pictured as a return from death, it is improbable that this imagery is not at all grounded in reality.[45] In Hosea 6:3 the verb [dy is used, which is of much importance in Hosea 2:19; 4:6; 6:6. This also contributes to the conclusion that 6:1-3 is an integral part of the prophetic message, and not an inadequate reaction of the people.[46]

5.2.1.2.1.2. 'Injustice and Corruption' resulted in Sickness, Wounds, and the Loss of Well-Being

The prophetic books also portray the "sickness and wounds" (חלי ומכה) of the city and its people (Jer. 6:7b). Six times Jeremiah referred to the immanent שׁבר גדול (great collapse). The Hebrew term שׁבר (disaster/ collapse) is the central word used to describe the people's broken condition and one third of the Old Testament occurrences are found in the book of Jeremiah. Fortunately, the Bible does not only focus on sin and the consequences of sin, but portrays Yahweh as healer of sins and broken relationships.

Having commanded Jeremiah to address all sections of his society, the Lord continues to elaborate upon the reason; all sections were equally guilty, "from the least of them to the greatest of them" (v 13). Even the clergy ("prophet and priest," v 13) were responsible for the national crisis in Judah. Having seen the nation's "wound" (viz. that not all was well), they offered only with no power to cure. They spoke of peace, when there was no peace. (It is possible they spoke of peace with reference to a period of temporary calm in international affairs, failing to see that there can be no real peace when a nation is sick at heart.) Indeed, the clergy were so far gone in their abominable acts that they no longer knew the shamefulness of what they were doing. When evil is pursued and practiced regularly and devotedly, it produces eventually a moral blindness in the perpetrator. Therefore, the divine oracle concludes, given the widespread and rampant nature of the whole nation's evil, all would fall in the coming Day of Judgment.

Vv. 13-15 makes specific the ways in which Judah has rejected God's word. The Jerusalem leadership is deeply involved in social injustice through acquiring unjust germ (v.13). While false dealings most evidently refer to the unsavoury economic practices (c.f., 2:34-35, 5:27-28), the prophetic and priestly falseness indicated in verse 14 suggests another dimension of this problem. Not only have

---

mentioned verses are taken up. The words of 6:2 (life again) are in the same line. They also belong to the images of sickness and healing. Healing can be seen as recovering from death.

[44] As quoted by Wolff, 151.

[45] Francis I. Andersen and David Noel Freedman, *Hosea*, The Anchor Bible (New York: Doubleday, 1998), 421.

[46] Ibid., 427.

there been false dealings socially and economically, but there is also falsehood in the subsequent response of the Jerusalem leadership to the seriousness of such dishonest economic practices, a cover-up if you will. The duty of the prophets and priests is to call Judah to be faithful to their covenant with God, who had freed Israel from slavery in Egypt. Instead, this text suggests that the Jerusalem leadership have either ignored the situations or, worse, found a way to justify the unscrupulous economic practices in the name of God, who had deep concern for the poor and disadvantaged. So, Jeremiah challenges that the "wound" of God's people (6:14) is being treated "carelessly" by announcing "'peace, peace' when there is no peace."[47] The exploitative economic schemes being practiced in Judah are a festering wound that threatens Judah's life that will lead to defeat and exile.[48] To ignore the symptoms of illness and to pretend that all is well, can seriously imperil our health and even lead to death. Jeremiah accuses Judah's prophets and priests of ignoring the social symptoms of a disease, a broken relationship with God that threatens Judah's existence.

5.2.1.2.1.3. '*Shalom* (שׁלוֹם) Vision' as an Eschatological Hope for Health and Well-Being of the Cosmos

The context of v.14 is close to that of 4:10: the phrase "saying, 'peace'" is in the context of a threat to life. For in 4:6, שׁבר means (fracture) where as in 6:1 it means the collapse of roof-beams of a house onto pottery storage jars. Here given the medical connotation of רפא piel "heal, treat," it is best to translate as 'fracture', as a metaphor for the violent break-up of community.[49] The verb רפא does not always mean, "heal". Healing, which is a procedure implying success is not predicted in this text, but implies the translation of שׁלוֹם as means of safety and security and in the context of medicine and health, the expression means "well-being".

According to Walter Brueggemann, there are four points that can be taken out from this text.

1. First, at the center of the text the leaders say, "peace, peace," when there is no peace. The poet insists that the kings, priests, and leaders in Jerusalem are engaging in an enormous deception.
2. The Hebrew word for peace, which is שׁלוֹם, means a harmonious, properly functioning, life-giving order to society. The leadership asserts in its policies and propaganda that society is harmonious, properly functioning and life-giving. However, says the poet: "It is a lie. It is not so". The opposite of *Shalom* is not war but chaos. The poet wants his

---

[47] John M. Bracke, *Jeremiah 1-29* (Louisville, Kentucky: Westminster John Knox Press, 2000), 65.

[48] Ibid., 66.

[49] William L. Holladay, in *A Commentary of the Book of the Prophet Jeremiah Chapters 1-25*, ed. Paul D. Hanson (Philadelphia: Fortress Press, 1986), 216.

community to notice chaos, to experience destructive disorder that is everywhere in the life of the community

3. The poet's judgment of why such things are happening among his people is because everybody has been sold out. The prophets in Israel had always been hard on the leadership, not common folk. It is the leadership who use position for self-advantage, who use office to feather their own nest, who form alliances for personal gain.
4. The passage culminates in verse 15 with a massive, ominous "therefore." The word "therefore" always means that a judgment is coming: therefore a time to fall, of overthrow, of punishment.[50]

Walter Brueggemann describes the '*Shalom* vision' as "the central vision of the world history in the Bible, according to which all creation is one, every creature in community with every other, living in harmony and security toward the joy and well-being of every other creature."[51] Such a vision has deep significance for a world characterized by great disparities between the rich and the poor, the satisfied and the hungry, the powerful and the powerless, or the human and the non-human.

Shalom, which encompasses the health for all is not realized if economic justice is denied to the poor and the needy, and if there is judicial perversion and political exclusiveness. The link between justice and *Shalom* which is the fundamental theme in the Old Testament is seen here. According to McAfee Brown, "we need to measure our world and the imperative for peacemaking, with an eye to justice. Whatever is unjust threatens peace. Whatever fosters justice is an act of peacemaking."[52] Peace is to be understood not as a static condition but as a dynamic realty intimately related to human beings' constant search for human dignity.[53] It is clear that no individual fulfilment was possible apart from seeking the welfare of the whole community. This is perhaps the reason why the prophet Jeremiah advised those in exile to seek *Shalom* even in the midst of one's enemies (Jer. 29:7). Whatever establishes wholeness and harmony in the social and political community works for health of all.

The poet speaks here of the hard truth which asserts that peace is not present, health not available, and that the community is engaged in a big lie. Hence, he announces punishment and devastation. However, the text here also implies that the lack of peace in the community can be healed and restored if only people

[50] Walter Brueggemann, "A World Available for Peace: Images of Hope from Jeremiah and Isaiah," *Sojourners* 17, no. 1 (1988): 22-23.

[51] Walter Brueggemann, *Peace* (Missouri: Chalice Press, 2001), 13.

[52] Robert McAfee Brown, *Making Peace in the Global Village* (Philadelphia: Westminster Jhon Knox Press, 1981), 15.

[53] Daniel S. Thiagarajah, "Shalom: A Central Vision for Holistic Healing of Humanity," *CSI Life: Magazine for the Church of South India* X, no. 2 (2011): 3.

will repent. Peace begins in the communities of bleeding that will give life to all. That bleeding may indeed lead to repentance, then to healing, and finally to homecoming and with it, peace.

5.2.1.3. Jeremiah 8:11, 15, 18, 22

V. 11 And they have healed my people[a] superficially,
saying, 'Peace, Peace,'
but there is no peace!
V. 15. We hoped for peace, but no good came;
for a [a]time of healing, but saw terror.[a]
V. 18. [a]Sorrow has overwhelmed me;
my heart is sick[a] within.
V. 22. [a]Is there no balm in Gilead?
Is there no healer there?[a]
Why then is there no restoration
of the health of my people?

Form Critical Notes

It is almost universally agreed among scholars that one pericope ends at Jer. 8.17, and another begins at 8.18. However, there is little agreement as to whether the first begins with v. 4, 10, 13, or 14. However, for John T. Willis "the most likely beginning is v. 13. Then the pericope would begin and end with נאם היוה (vv. 13, 17)". Furthermore, the root אסף connects vv. 13 and 14.[54]

If this is the correct analysis, Jer. 8.13-17 contains some sort of dialogue. Paterson believes v. 14 contains the people's cry of distress which Jeremiah hears in his imagination.[55] While John Bright thinks vv. 14-16 represent a soliloquy placed in the mouth of the people by the prophet to indicate their terror at the approaching invader.[56] It seems more likely, however, that the picture is that of a dialogue between the prophet (speaking in Yahweh's name) and the people. While it is assumed that the people are the speakers in v. 16,[57] it appears to be more in keeping with the flow of the context to take Yahweh as the speaker here.[58]

Accordingly, the pericope may be analyzed in this way. Yahweh begins by expressing his desire to have an intimate relationship with his people and bring them near him as a gleaner would gather grapes or figs, but he found this impossible because they had produced no fruit even though he had blessed them richly

---

[54] Willis, "Dialogue between prophet and audience as a rhetorical device in the book of Jeremiah," 70.

[55] Paterson, *Jeremiah: Peake's Commentary on the Bible*, 545.

[56] John Bright, *The Anchor Bible: Jeremiah* (New York: Doubleday & Company, 1965), 65.

[57] Ibid.

[58] William L. Holladay, *The Architecture of Jeremiah 1-20* (Lewisburg: Bucknell University, 1976), 110.

(v. 13). The implication clearly is that they are doomed to destruction. The people respond by encouraging each other to flee for safety to the fortified cities, since Yahweh had doomed them (vv. 14-15). Yahweh replies that the enemy is indeed approaching from the North, because he is sending him to punish his people for their sins; therefore, it is hopeless for the people to try to escape (vv. 16-17).[59]

Scholars are virtually in unanimous agreement that the pericope which begins at 8.18 continues through 8.23. This passage contains several abrupt changes of speakers, a 'kind of quick conversational interchange'[60] similar to that found in 6.4-5 and 6.16-17. Some believe that this is not a genuine dialogue, but it arises from Jeremiah's imagination.[61] However, the sudden change of speakers and the liveliness of word exchange suggest at least a literary presentation of the kind of oral interaction, which actually occurred during Jeremiah's career. Holladay's analysis seems to be correct: Jeremiah begins by expressing his grief over the sin and punishment of Judah, and by quoting the cry of the people, that Yahweh is in Zion (w. 18-19b). Yahweh declares that the Judeans have aroused his anger by turning away from him to idols (v. 19c). The people concur sadly, probably quoting a well-known proverbial statement, that even though Yahweh had given them many opportunities, they had not returned to him (v. 20). Jeremiah immediately takes up the people's remorse, yearns for some means by which they could be healed, and declares that he will weep over them incessantly, in spite of their apparently irreversible condition (vv. 21-23).[62]

A pericope such as this reveals the manner in which dialogue can be used effectively in prophetic literature to indicate the beliefs and emotions of various personalities and groups involved in a conflict or crisis situation.

Setting

The life setting of these texts are divided into two parts: Jer. 8:4-13 and 8:14 23.The life setting of v.7 and the second half of vv 8-13 points to a life setting in the autumn of 601, more specifically to the time of the feast of booths were celebrated. The onset of the great drought in v.13 dated in the present study to 601-600 B.C.E. The word play of "in gathering" in v.13 implies the celebration of the feast of booths and the mention of "law of Yahweh" "scribes" and "pen" in v.8, and "order of Yahweh" in v.7 implies the recitation of the law of Deuteronomy, and the autumn of 601 was one such occasion.[63]

[59] Willis, "Dialogue between prophet and audience as a rhetorical device in the book of Jeremiah," 70.

[60] Holladay, *The Architecture of Jeremiah 1-20,* 111.

[61] Paterson, *Jeremiah: Peake's Commentary on the Bible*, 545-546.

[62] Holladay, *The Architecture of Jeremiah 1-20,* 110-111.

[63] W. L. Holladay, *Jeremiah 1: A Commentary of the Book of the Prophet Jeremiah Chapters 1-25* (Philadelphia: Fortress Press, 1986), 278.

The second part consists of 8:14-23 where the setting is attributed to the time when this passage took shape in the autumn of 601 B.C.E, just before the king burned Jeremiah's scroll. Verse 23 offers diction similar to that of 14:17, part of liturgy to the drought, to be dated to that period. The phrase "the harvest is past, the summer is gone" may be understood metaphorically in the drought. The rhetorical questions of Yahweh in verses 19 and 22 perhaps suggest a time before Jeremiah became convinced of the irrevocability of Yahweh's punishment of the people.[64]

Jeremiah 8:18-9:3, inverts the problem of theodicy. Instead of attempting to justify the ways of God to humans, Jeremiah poses the question in reverse order: how can you justify the ways of humans to God? The response the prophet offers is that human evil causes God great pain.

There are a few passages in the Bible that express grief as pointedly and passionately as Jeremiah 8 and 9. "My joy is gone, grief is upon me, my heart is sick," says the prophet. There is actually a question about who is speaking in this passage. The phrase, "says the Lord," at the end of this unit of Scripture is "textually insecure."[65] It does not appear in all ancient manuscripts. Yet whether it is about the pathos of God or of the prophet, the grief here is surely inclusive of both. Indeed, the grief of God and the prophet appears to be beyond healing, for as the question is posed, "Is there no balm in Gilead?" (v. 22)."

5.2.1.3.1. Comments on Jeremiah 8:11, 15, 18, 22 in relation to Illness, Health and Healing

In verse 15, the condition of the people is compatible with the condition of hopelessness. The text does not indicate that hope is still entertained, but that hope, which was entertained in the past has been disappointed and that nothing is left but despair. The people hoped that the wounds of the community would be healed, but what they experienced was terror and great afflictions, the exhausting effects of a fear that the worst was about to happen to them. The version supports the view that v. 15 describes the dashed hopes of the community and interprets קוה as first person plural.

Jeremiah 8:18-9:3, inverts the problem of theodicy. Instead of attempting to justify the ways of God to humans, Jeremiah poses the question in reverse order: how can you justify the ways of humans to God? The response the prophet offers is that human evil causes God great pain. There are few passages in the Bible that express grief as pointedly and passionately as Jer. 8 and 9. "My joy is gone, grief is upon me, my heart is sick," says the prophet (or God, or both). The familiarity of these words diverts attention from the real problem indicated by this question, because everyone who knew the Judean geography of Jeremiah's day

---

[64] Ibid., 291.

[65] Brueggemann, *A Commentary on Jeremiah: Exile and Homecoming*, 91.

would immediately catch the allusion. Gilead was outside the normal channels of religious and political authority.

The source of their grief is clear. The people are sick (8:22). They have assumed that God was their patron (8:19) and made fickle allegiances designed to enhance their own political destiny (Chs. 36-39). They have forgotten the poor and the outcast in their midst (7:5-7; 8:10; 22:16-17). They have abused the resources of the earth that were given to them for the flourishing of all the peoples of the land. They have, in other words, abandoned their covenant with the God who brought them out of slavery into a land of abundance in order that they might be a light to all nations (2:4-7; 3:17).[66]

The brokenness of Judah is not a condition of which he has a spectator's view; it is a suffering and sickness in which he is immersed. His heart is sick and his spirit dissolves or perhaps קדרתי is rather an indication that he is afflicted by the sadness of a mourner and wears a mourner's garb.[67]

5.2.1.3.1.1. The Metaphorical Image of the 'Balm of Gilead' for Health and Healing

Although, the text is well known, many of the interpretations of the words of the prophet do not reflect the true intent of Jeremiah's message to the people of Judah. The balm of Gilead, which is a strong metaphor in this text implies different meanings. According to Keil, "To these questions a negative answer is given: if there were balm in Gilead and a physician there, then a plaster would have been laid on the daughter of my people, which is not the case."[68] Terrence Fretheim, in his commentary on Jeremiah wrote, "The first two questions are rhetorical; there is balm in Gilead; there are physicians there; but, it is implied, they are powerless to restore health to a patient with this kind of illness."[69]

The balm of Gilead, which the prophet implies here was an ointment made from the resin of a tree that was used as a healing ointment. The identity of this tree is unknown although many solutions have been proposed. In the Old Testament, the balm of Gilead was used for medicine, perfume, and body ointment. In Genesis 37:25, an Ishmaelite caravan travelled from Gilead carrying spices, balm and myrrh to sell their merchandise in Egypt. Jeremiah tells the Egyptians to go to Gilead and use its balm because they had used many medicines without finding healing for their sickness (Jer. 46:11).[70] The balm of Gilead is a

---

[66] Roger J. Gench, "Jeremiah 8:18-9:3," *Interpretation* 62, no. 1 (January 2008): 74.

[67] McKane, *A Critical and Exegetical Commentary on Jeremiah: Introduction and Commentary on Jeremiah 1-XXV*, 195.

[68] C. F. Keil, *The Prophecies of Jeremiah*, vol. 1 (Grand Rapids: William B. Eerdmans Publishing Company, 1950), 182.

[69] Terence Fretheim, *Commentary on Jeremiah* (Macon: Smyth & Helwys, 2002), 154.

[70] A balm is an ointment used to heal the wounds and soothe pain. In the Old Testament, the "balm of Gilead' referred both to powerful healing ointment from the land of Gilead and,

metaphor used by Jeremiah to explain how the people could find a cure for their spiritual illness. The balm that Jeremiah was talking about was not repentance, even though repentance was the first step toward the healing of their wound. The prophet means by this metaphor that there are still means available for healing the spiritual ills of his people, mainly repentance, obedience to the law, and sole allegiance to God, and still people available who will apply this medicine to them, namely prophets like himself.

Thus, in Jeremiah 8:22, the prophet is saying that there were plenty of physicians in Gilead who could heal the spiritual sickness of the people of Judah, for the physicians were the prophets. There was plenty of balm in Gilead, for the balm of Gilead in the mouth of Jeremiah is a metaphor for the word of God being preached by the prophets to a rebellious people. However, there was no healing because the prophets were preaching a message that did not bring healing. No new skin will grow over the wounds to close them and give proof of an effective process of healing.

The wound of the people is the city's wound, and she mourns their loss. Again, the image changes in v. 22, and the figure of the wound (*seber*, 'breaking') conjures up its healing process. Is there neither balm nor physician in Gilead? The rhetorical questions reflect the trade with Gilead and the belief that balm helped pain. Whether the balm was used to heal wounds or to conceal the smell of festering wounds is a debatable point. The questions are rhetorical because the wound is incurable (i.e., the city is destroyed), as the intense of emotion of 9:1 shows. Such strong response to the people's wound highlights the triviality of the nostrums used by the prophet and priest.[71] As Brueggemann points out, the prophet observed a "fundamental distinction between social prospect and divine promise."[72] Thus, as deep and pervasive as God's despair about human sin may be, there is also God's promise. The promise is hardly rooted in our goodness. Indeed, as Brueggemann says, "We need to be saying to each other that our energies are rooted in and aimed toward God's promise and not our social prospects... [for] Jeremiah was more than a social critic. He is the holder of a vision rooted in nothing other than God's promise."[73] Accordingly, Brueggemann suggests pairing Jeremiah 8:18-9:3 with 32:1-15, the story of the prophet's purchase of a field in occupied territory. The year is 588 B.C.E., and the

metaphorically, to the power of God to heal and save the soul. Gilead was an area of ancient Palestine, east of the Jordan River. Now north western Jordan, it was bounded to the north by the Yarmuk River and to the southwest by what were known then as the plains of Moab. Sometimes the name is used in a more general sense to describe the entire region east of the Jordan River and west of the Arabian Desert.

[71] Carrol, *Jeremiah; A Commentary*, 237.

[72] Walter Brueggemann, *Like Fire in the Bones: Listening for the Prophetic Word in Jeremiah*, ed. Patrick D. Miller (Minneapolis: Fortress Press, 2006), 182.

[73] Ibid.

Babylonian armies encircle Jerusalem. Judgment is at hand, and Jeremiah is under house arrest for treasonous proclamations against king and priest. King Zedekiah was not pleased when Jeremiah prophesied that the Babylonians would sack the city and take its inhabitants into exile, and the temple priests probably did not care for Jeremiah's question: "Is there no balm in Gilead?" Nonetheless, amid this hardship, the Word of the Lord comes to Jeremiah and tells him about a cousin who will come and say, "Buy my field which is in Anathoth, for the right purchase is yours" (32:6). In a grand gesture, Jeremiah purchases the field before witnesses and signs the deed. Then he instructs that the deeds be put in earthenware jars so they will last. Finally he says, "For thus says the Lord of Host, the God of Israel: Houses and fields and vineyards shall again be bought in this land" (32:15). By all human standards, the gesture is absurd because the Babylonians occupied the land

The prophets of Israel were never dispassionate observers of their people's suffering and were known to enter deeply into and share in the anguish and suffering of their people. They had to deliver a message of divine judgment to people whom they knew, loved and cared for. In the same manner, caught up in an uncomfortable situation and torn asunder between God and the people, Jeremiah had to cope with the combination of love and anguish. The people were wondering if Yahweh had forsaken them and were fast beginning to believe that there was no hope for deliverance. Jeremiah then voiced his passionate grief along with the people. Despondent and desperate, he mourned their plight and wondered if there is no balm in Gilead; Gilead located on the eastern side of the river Jordan and was known for its balsamic trees and their healing balm. He realised that no balm could bring healing as long as the people were filled with a rebellious spirit and would not repent. The balm that would bring healing was repentance, a return to Yahweh, on the part of the people. We find here a metaphor based on the physical imagery of a 'physician' providing help to the afflicted. Hence several basic insights may be gleaned from this poetic, metaphorical cry: (1) the *rôpē'* was viewed positively. (2) His presence in a typical village/city was expected (3) He was recognised as a professional (i.e., either as a known practicing folk healer or as a member of a professional class. (4) He was expected to promote the healing of wounds. (5) Balm was commonly utilized in this process.

5.2.1.4. Jeremiah 14:18, 19

V. 18. "When I [a]go out into the field,[a]
I see those slain by the sword.
And when I enter the city,
I see the ravages of famine.
Yet both prophet and priest ply their trade
in the land, and have no knowledge.[b]

V. 19. Have you completely rejected Judah,
or does your soul loathe Zion?
Why have you smitten us,
so there is no healing for us?
We looked for peace and there was no good,
and for a time of healing, but behold terror."

Form Critical Notes

Jeremiah 14:1-15:9, is assumed as a collection of disparate pieces, "a mixed collection of oracles."[74] Jeremiah 14:1-10 and 14:17-15:4 are strikingly similar in form and content, and should be examined together. Several scholars have correctly argued for the coherence of Jer. 14:1-15:4[75] or 15:9.[76] However, this is a redactional unity, and thus does not necessarily indicate that this whole section comes from the same occasion or even the same time period. In fact, the crisis of 14:17-15:4 apparently was decidedly more intense than that of 14:1-10. Whereas the problem in 14:1-6 is a drought, that in 14:18-19 and 15:2-3 is military invasion with its attendant devastations. It appears that the redactor of this section of the book or the whole book has arranged this material in a chiastic fashion:[77]

A 14:1-10
B 14:11-16
C 14:17-15:4

The first and last sections follow the same sequence:

(1) Yahweh instructs Jeremiah to describe for his hearers the calamity to come upon them (14:1-6 and 17-18);
(2) His hearers respond, confessing their sins and asking God for deliverance (14:7-9 and 19-22);
(3) The Lord rejects their pleas because he sees they are insincere (14:10 and 15:1-4).

The text is understood as Jeremiah's intercession for the people, citing 14:11 and 15:1.[78] However, Yahweh's prohibition against the prophet interceding for the people and the reference to Moses and Samuel as intercessors for Israel does not necessarily refer to the controversial verses under consideration. They

[74] John Skinner, *Prophecy and Religion, Studies in the Life of Jeremiah* (Cambridge: Cambridge University Press, 1922), 128.

[75] Hyatt, *The Book of Jeremiah: Introduction and Exegesis*, 929-937.

[76] Paterson, *Jeremiah: Peake's Commentary on the Bible*, 548.

[77] Willis, "Dialogue between prophet and audience as a rhetorical device in the book of Jeremiah," 74.

[78] Arthur S. Peake, *Jeremiah I: The Century Bible* (Edinburgh: T.C. & E.C. Jack, 1910).

could be simply forthright instructions designed to emphasize that God's people had gone so long and so deep in sin that it was vain to pray for their deliverance in view of the present condition of their hearts. Others regard these passages as the prophet's concept of the ideal confession, which the people should make if they are to be accepted by God.[79] However, the language appears to be stronger than what would be expected if one were suggesting to others what they should do. Consequently, it seems best to understand 14:7-9 and 19-22 as a literary representation of the response of Jeremiah's hearers to what he had just said in Yahweh's name.[80]

In 14:17-18, these verses make up a lament spoken by Jeremiah. The lament employs what might be called the 'motif of alternative deaths" in v. 18. According to Von Rad, this motif has its origin in real-life situations but is shaped by folk wisdom (1 Kgs. 14:11; 26:4; 21:24).[81] 14:19-22 is a communal lament. The first two cola of v.19 are reproachful questions to Yahweh. Similar diction is to be found in Lam 5:22, though the syntax there is difficult, and it is by no means certain that these verses embody a question, as RSV has it.

Setting

In Jeremiah 14:2-15:4 we have an example of a liturgy of intercession occasioned by a drought.[82] The liturgy itself consists of a description of distress (14:2-6) and a series of laments, two of which, 14:7-9 and 14:19-22, are songs of collective lament. Following the elements of confession, complaint, and a plea for help in the first song of collective lament, we expect prophetic intercession and a salvation oracle. In fact, the divine response is negative (14:10) and intercession is forbidden (14:11-12). A complaint by Jeremiah follows (14:13a*)* in which he argues that the people have been misled by the salvation oracles of the prophets. He cites as an example the expanded formulation of a *Shalom* oracle: "You shall not see the sword, nor shall you have famine, but I will give you assured peace in this place."

Jeremiah's attempt at intercession on behalf of the community failed. The people and the prophets in whom they trusted will fall to sword and hunger alike (14:14 16). Nevertheless, the significance of these verses within the liturgy as a whole is clear. The intercession of the prophet was designed to induce a positive response from the deity. The reference to the salvation oracles of the prophets in 14:13 comes at a point in the liturgy when just such a positive response is expected, which suggests that their prophecy of *Shalom* was itself originally part

[79] Hyatt, *The Book of Jeremiah: Introduction and Exegesis*, 931.

[80] Paul Volz, *Der Prophet Jeremía übersetzt und erklärt, 10; 2nd edition* (Leipzig A. Deichen, 1928), 163.

[81] Von Rad, *Studies in Deuteronomy* (Naperville: Allenson, 1953), 82-83.

[82] O. Eissfeldt, *The Old Testament: An Introduction* (New York: Harper & Row, 1965), 356.

of an intercession liturgy. Jeremiah's own efforts at intercession, however, resulted in a negative oracle and in the recognition that further intercession was futile.

5.2.1.4.1. Comments on Jeremiah 14:18, 19; in relation to Illness, Health and Healing

The contents of these psalms reveal a discrepancy between the *Shalom* of the order of creation and the well-being of the individual within that order, who is often described as suffering illness, economic distress, or the animosity of personal enemies. It was the aim of the lament to restore the petitioner to a condition of wholeness in relation to the cosmic order. Criteria of form and content in these psalms lead us to believe that this restoration was accomplished in connection with cultic activities probably in the form of a salvation oracle delivered as part of a liturgy following the elements of complaint and a plea for help.

5.2.1.4.1.1. '*Shalom*' as Restoration of the Community's Health and Well-Being

The *Sitz im Leben* of the salvation oracle in the songs of individual lament and the function of the genre within the framework of the Jerusalem conception provide the basis for our own interpretation of the use of שלום by Jeremiah and his prophetic opponents. When we refer to the use of a שלום oracle in this regard, it is to be understood as a salvation oracle whose wording employed the term שלום to describe the restoration of the community to a condition of health and well-being. In proposing this, there are two difficulties. On the one hand, we must describe the possible formulation of that oracle and on the other hand, we must account for its use as a formal element belonging to the genre of lament. Evidence of both the content and the formal usage of the שלום oracle support the conclusion that it formed a part of a prophetic liturgy of intercession.[83]

Of the 26 (31) references to the word שלום in the book of Jeremiah, 17 (22) references are relevant to our topic.[84] Of these 17 (22), there are only 11 (15) references to what might be construed as oracular usage of the term.

With regard to its wording, we have 3 examples of an apparent quotation of a שלום oracle in 4:10 (23:17); 14:13; and 29:7b, whereby both the doublet in 23:17 and the formulation of the oracle in 14:13 stem from the Deuteronomic redaction. The wording of the oracle in 4:10 is given as follows: *Shälom yihyeh läkem* יהיה לכם

[83] This thesis was put forward by H. Graf Reventlow, *Liturgie und prophetisches Ich bei Jeremía* (Gütersloh: Mohn, 1963). 121-40. Although, the present writer differs with his analysis in a number of points, he shares his opinion concerning the *Sitz im Leben* of the *Shalom* oracle in a liturgy of prophetic intercession. Noteworthy also is Reventlow's argument that the use of the liturgy did not necessarily result in a favorable divine response A negative oracle was also possible, if the efforts at intercession failed to influence the deity favorably.

[84] The numbers in parentheses represent the total sum of references to *Shalom* including the doublets. The number without the parentheses shows the sum of references to the word minus the doublets.

שׁלום ("it shall be well with you"). In 29:7, there is a similar formulation of the oracle with a slight modification. It is important to note that in 4:10 the oracle is ascribed to the false prophets, whereas in 29:7 Jeremiah himself is its author. The dual reference to שׁלום in 6:14 (8:11) has been variously explained as either an abbreviated formulation or a designation of the oracle. In any case, it seems certain that reference is being made to oracular activity of the prophets. This same assumption is applicable to the use of שׁלום in connection with three different terms of oracular inquiry: in 15:5, 28:9, 29:7 and 38:4. The expression *qaw-wēhlē šhalôm* קוה ולשׁלום ("to look for peace") in 14:19 (8:15) seems to refer both to the expectation of a *Shalom* oracle itself and to the positive condition of welfare following from such an oracle.

Chapters 14:7-9 and 14:19-22, are songs of collective lament. Following the elements of confession, complaint, and a plea for help in the first song of collective lament, we expect prophetic intercession and a salvation oracle In fact, the divine response is negative (14:10) and intercession is forbidden (14:11-12). A complaint by Jeremiah follows (14:13*)* in which he argues that the people have been misled by the salvation oracles of the prophets. He cites as an example the expanded formulation of a שׁלום oracle: "You shall not see the sword, nor shall you have famine, but I will give you assured peace in this place."[85]

Jeremiah's response of (*'ên-šhālôm)* אי/ שׁלום is significant in two respects. It is implied not only a negation of the claims of peace for Jerusalem but also a reversal of the motifs associated with those claims, particularly those regarding Zion's inviolability. In 16:5, it is stated that the deity has removed his *Shalom* from the Jerusalem community. The loss of *Shalom* had far-reaching consequences for the understanding of Jerusalem as the center of the order of creation. On the one hand, it meant a disruption of the natural and social spheres of life vegetation and animal life languished. Hunger and plague visited its inhabitants, and the exercise of justice was neglected. In addition to (*'ên-šhālôm)* אי/ שׁלום, the expressions (*'ên-marpē')* אי/ מרפא *and* (*'ên-tôb)* אי/ טוב were used to describe the lack of well-being and prosperity within the cultic community.[86] On the other hand, the removal of *Shalom* from Jerusalem marked deterioration in the political situation and signalled an upsurge of hostilities against the city and the surrounding population.

The prophet played an important role in securing the health of the individual and the community in Israel.[87] In this role, the prophet functioned both as the representative of the people in the divine council and as the speaker of the divine oracle. The proximity of Jeremiah's prophetic opponents to the cult in Jerusalem

---

[85] Jonathan Paige Sisson, "Jeremiah and The Jerusalem Conception of Peace," *Journal of Biblical Literature* 3, no. 105 (1986): 434.

[86] Ibid., 437.

[87] A. R. Johnson, *The Cultic Prophet in Ancient Israel*, 2nd ed. (Cardiff: University of Wales Press, 1962), 49-50, 75.

has led many scholars to interpret their prophecy of *Shalom* in light of the complex of traditions associated with that city.

According to this view, their assurances of peace were grounded in a false sense of security motivated by the traditions of Zion's inviolability and the election of the Davidic dynasty.[88] One of the more promising developments in this regard has been the recent line of research linking *Shalom* to a broad conception of peace formulated and transmitted in the Jerusalem cultic community.

Within the limits of this conception, *Shalom* was employed to describe both the welfare of the cultic community and the manner of conduct that led to such welfare.[89] The person who sought to understand the order of creation and by means of his or her deeds to aid in maintaining it was known as *(tsaddÎq),* צדק righteous or wise. Justice here means to maintain the general health, the strength and well-being of the community. An unjust deed, on the other hand, was viewed as a violation of the world order, indeed, as an objective injury to that order and demanded restitution.[90] *Shalom* thus came to connote both the positive condition of restored world order and the well-being and prosperity resulting there from.

Both in the tribal period and in the national period *shalom* broke down. Actually, the vision of *Shalom* failed to be realized. Jeremiah weeps over the situation denouncing the false prophets.

While definitions of health are almost as hard to come by as definitions of *Shalom*, we focus on the physical and psychological well-being of persons, which enables them to function in the context of their own personhood and community. Moreover, the prophets freely use sickness/health images metaphorically, applying these both to individual persons and to the covenant people as a whole.[91]

5.2.1.5. Jeremiah 15:18

V. 18. Why is my pain unceasing,[a]
and my wound incurable, refusing to be healed?
You are to me like a dry wadi,
whose waters have failed.

---

[88] John Bright, *Covenant and Promise* (London: SCM Press Ltd., 1977), 136-139.

[89] Similar to the cultic understanding of *Shalom,* a distinction was made in wisdom circles between *sedeq* and *sĕdaqâ. Sedeq* was used to describe the order of creation itself, and *sĕdaqâ* the proper conduct in conformity with that order.

[90] Sisson, "Jeremiah and The Jerusalem Conception of Peace," 431.

[91] Isaiah for example laments, "The whole head is sick, and the whole heart faint. From the sole of the foot even to the head, there is no soundness in it, But bruises and sores and bleeding wounds; they are not pressed out or bound up, or softened with oil" (1:5b-6). Jeremiah likewise asks, "Is there no balm in Gilead? Is there no physician there? Why then has the health of the daughter of my people not been restored?" (8:22).

Form Critical Notes

In judging its form and structure, the strong resemblance of our text to the complaint-psalms has long been noted.

To this point, the convention of attributing this prayer to Jeremiah has been followed. Certainly, the present shape of the Book of Jeremiah invites the reading of this text against the portrait of the prophet presented there.[92]

Setting

Understood in that way, the prayer of Jeremiah 15:15-18 is heard as the cry of the prophet persecuted by the leaders of Judah. Yet, the similarity between the language of Jeremiah's prayer and the language of the psalms of lament suggests that the meaning of Jeremiah 15:15-21 moves beyond its sense as an event in the life of the prophet Jeremiah. The language, like that of the laments, is imprecise, difficult to relate to specific events in the prophet's life, and open for use by others who might find that it expresses to God their plight. In fact, certain phrases (e.g., "called by thy name," "why is my pain unceasing . . .") are most frequently applied to the whole community of God's people in the Book of Jeremiah; and their use in our text suggests that at one level of meaning, the prayer of Jeremiah is an intercession on behalf of the community (cf. Jer. 7:16; 11:14; 14:11; 15:11). Verses 19-21 stand beside Jeremiah's prayer as God's response. Like the prayer, the response also has both personal and communal dimensions. Because the prophet's petition is much like a lament, one almost expects a salvation oracle to follow. That is only partially characteristic of God's actual response. God's response is introduced by a formula (v. 19a, "Therefore, thus says the Lord") which is most frequently associated in the Book of Jeremiah with oracles of judgment (5:14; 6:21; 11:11; 23:2), and the response's first phrases, unlike any salvation oracle, are a call to repentance.[93] Evidence suggests that there are two strata of vv.10-21: (1) a lament of Jeremiah (vv. 15-18) and Yahweh's reply (v 19); and (2) a supplement to that early lament (vv. 20-21).

5.2.1.5.1. Comments on Jeremiah 15:18 in relation to Illness, Health and Healing

In one respect, however, it is unique in that it has so much "confessional material", sometimes called "the intimate papers of Jeremiah." These passages do not appear to have been a part of the prophet's public proclamation, but they were recorded nevertheless, and they have come down to us as a precious legacy. The form of these confessions is that of monologue or soliloquy or, perhaps more correctly, "colloquy," for they come out of communion with God.[94]

[92] John M. Bracke, "Jeremiah 15:15-21," *Interpretation* 37, no. 2 (April 1983): 176.

[93] John M. Brake, "Jeremiah 15:15-21," *Interpretation* 37, no. 2 (1983): 174.

[94] David Ewert, "The Confessions of a Prophet," *Direction* 4, no. 4 (1975): 383.

5.2.1.5.1.1. The Image of 'Sickness' and 'Wound'

The rhetoric of v.18 introduces a new metaphor- sickness and incurable wound.[95] Verse 18, is referred by most scholars to medical terminology frequently for the sickness of the people, and for the sympathetic symptoms he manifests because of his people's plight, and here for his own disability in the face of persecution. The word 'pain' (כאב) occurs here for the only instance in Jeremiah. The related verb is used in Genesis 34:25 of the pain experienced by the Shechemites the third day after their circumcision-that is, the word may refer purely to physical pain as well as psychic pain.[96]

In 15:18, the full force of the accusation against God as false and unreliable is removed by reading the verb as either the third person feminine singular or the third person masculine singular with "my wound" as the subject. This also effaces the ironic play on the divine description.[97]

The phrase "And he can no longer endure it (v. 18a)" depicts the condition of the person who is in constant pain, suffering from an incurable wound (cf. 10:19; Ps. 38:5-8; 42:10). Does the wound endure forever? Will it never end? He sees no hope; nothing helps. In addition (v. 18b), he finds no help in God. Here Jeremiah's complaint goes far beyond the bounds of a conventional lament and becomes a flat accusation directed at God. Jeremiah declares that God has been to him like a brook to which the thirsty traveller comes in search of life-giving water, only to find that it has run dry.[98] In verse 19, the rhetorical questions express a traditional belief and seek to establish a basis of which appeal can be made.[99]

Jeremiah complains that his pain is persistent; it is like an incurable wound. He wonders why he has to endure so much. Earlier in the book, he accuses Israel of forsaking God, the fountain of living waters, and making for themselves cisterns that do not hold water, cracked cisterns, which deceive the thirsty. Now he accuses God of deceiving him. "Wilt thou be to me like a deceitful brook, like waters that fail?" He feels like a thirsty traveller who sees a *wadi* in the distance and rushes forward to slake his thirst, only to find it has gone dry in the summer drought.

---

[95] James Muilenburg, "The Terminology of Adversity in Jeremiah," in *Translating and Understanding the Old Testament*, ed. Harry Thomas Frank and William L. Reed (Nashville: Abingdon Press, 1970), 42-63.

[96] Holladay, *Jeremiah 1: A Commentary on the Book of the Prophet Jeremiah Chapters 1-25*, 460-461.

[97] A. R. Pete Diamond, "Jeremiah's confessions in the LXX and MT: a witness to developing canonical function?," *Vetus Testamentum* 40, no. 1 (January 1990): 37-38.(MT: "surely, you have been as a falsehood to me, unreliable water"; cf. Jer.2: 13).

[98] John Bright, "Prophet's lament and its answer, Jeremiah 15:10-21," *Interpretation* 28, no. 1 (January 1974): 66.

[99] Walter Brueggemann, "Jeremiah's Use of Rhetorical Questions," *Journal of Biblical Literature* 92, no. 3 (September 1973): 363.

According to William McKane,

> [T]he medical vocabulary in v.18 is metaphorical, but profoundly metaphorical; the two complexities of imagery are used to describe the intense, spiritual anguish of Jeremiah: pain from which there is no relief and wounds for which no treatment will avail, on the one hand, the failure of the spring of water through whose constant and ample supply he had hoped to endure on the other. His loneliness, his tortured and irreconcilable loyalties, the nadir of his hope and the brokenness of his spirit are gathered up in the language of v.18. Why should he have been brought to such a point of contradiction, where the wholeness of his life was destroyed and where he could not fulfil his prophetic calling and be a man among his people?[100]

The words "sickness" and "wounds" are not frequently associated in the Old Testament, and for good reason to the ancient Hebrew, the wounded person is understood to be sick (cf. 6:7; 10:19). Chief among the words used for wound is the noun שֶׁבֶר, which appears frequently and always in strategic collocations.[101] The verb form is one of the most commonly employed in the Old Testament, most often with the meaning of break or shatter. Even Jeremiah uses this term in relation to breaking and shattering. According to Brueggemann, it is useless to speculate the metaphor of sickness and incurable wound in 15:18 as illness because the sickness metaphor is only conventional.[102] According to him, the reason being that sickness follows sin is found to be very good by the prophet where he considered himself as a faithful servant of God who has not sinned. This statement of the problem anticipates the poem of Job. In both Jeremiah and Job the problem of theodicy is raised because there is "punishment" for which there is no identifiable sin. Ludwig states: "we must, however point out here that the Old Testament contains no expression of opinion at all as to what is healthy and what is sickness.... Furthermore the language of illness is very lately developed."[103] However, illness, health and healing are not always about physical elements, it connotes the wholistic aspect of one's life. Wholeness has to do with the totality of things and the relationship of all things within that totality, with the harmony of all things, human and otherwise in God's creation, the harmony of relationships, the coming together in gentleness of that which shares participation in the creation of Yahweh. It has to do with well-being of the community at large.

The Old Testament understanding of health is not about dualism but it includes the physical as well as spiritual realm of life. The emphasis is on the

---

[100] McKane, *A Critical and Exegetical Commentary on Jeremiah: Introduction and Commentary on Jeremiah 1-XXV*, 356.

[101] Muilenburg, "The Terminology of Adversity in Jeremiah," 46.

[102] Brueggemann, *A Commentary on Jeremiah: Exile and Homecoming*, 147.

[103] Ludwig Kohler, *The Hebrew Man* (London: SCM Press Ltd., 1956), 18.

relationship of the one with the other. The prophet may not be sick physically or be wounded, but it is obvious as the leader of Israel's community, he can relate to people's sin and their wounded state. Therefore, the prophet here might not be talking about his sin and his physical sickness, but it can mean that he is representing the community by bemoaning its incurable state.

The description of the wound as being incurable (*ʾanûšāh*) אנושה and the pain being permanent includes the motif of incurableness (*ʾanûš*) אנוש.[104] The use of ʾ) *anûš)* אנוש suggests that the role of Jeremiah in 15:18a might be a representative of the community. The community's wound is incurable, so the prophet's wound is incurable. Standing for the community, the prophet assumes the role of the people. Illness or wounding as metaphors for the state of the community whether of corruption or disintegration is the common agenda for the prophet.

5.2.1.6. Jeremiah 17:14

V. 14. Heal me, O LORD, let me be healed,
Deliver me, let me be delivered,
For you are my (object of) praise!

Form Critical Notes

This confession, like any others, offers phrasing characteristic of personal laments. Verse 14a is a plea for help: For "heal me, Yahweh," and "save me". The latter imperative of two stems of a verb is found in Psalm 69:14b is compared to Psalm 71:6. In both cases, the phrase is an affirmative of confidence.

Most scholars accept vv.14-18 in relation to individual lament. The following structure is seen as:

v. 14 introductory address and petition (with expression of confidence)

v. 15 lament is a description of the suffering: for 'many are saying" in Psalm 3:3 and 4:7, but even closer is the phrase with an infinitive, "while they say to me," "where is your God?" in Psalm 42:4, 11.

v. 16 profession of innocence like 15:17. Verse 16b is an affirmation of confidence.

v.v. 17-18 is petition-17a is a plea and v.17b is an affirmation of confidence. verse 18 embodies wishes against the enemies of the prophet.[105]

Setting

The confession of Jeremiah is intentionally concerned to reflect problems related to a prophetic situation-i.e., conflict arising out of the delay in fulfilment of prophetic proclamation (v. 15). Then if one proceeds to consider the confession from the standpoint of its inclusion in the book of Jeremiah, it seems that it is meant to be read in terms of Jeremiah's prophetic situation. This is seen in the

---

[104] Carroll, *From Chaos to Covenant: Prophecy in the Book of Jeremiah*, 118.

[105] Holladay, *Jeremiah 1: A Commentary on the Book of the Prophet Jeremiah Chapters 1-25*, 505.

call narrative in v. 18 with the double use of which would seem to provide strong warrant to search for a setting within the prophetic mission of Jeremiah.[106]

The structure and content of the passage indicate that there are difficulties pertaining to the question of determining the specific setting. The reason being that the confession as a constituent part of the prophet's public proclamation does not seem to be very workable. Another problem is that there is the lack of an afffirmatory answering oracle (cf. 11:21-23). Furthermore, the mix of challenge and promise (cf. 15:11-14; 15:19-21) constitutes a serious problem for this approach. For it does not seem to be likely that the bare lament petition for vindication would provide any type of effective defence before his opponents, unless one assumes that the lament is functionally equivalent to a curse uttered for the benefit of one's opponents. However, there is the negative petition in verse 17 with the element of uncertainty. It introduces a relatively divine-prophetic solidarity and it is to be assumed as an odd approach to defending one's legitimacy as a prophet before those who question this very legitimacy.[107] Moreover, in the book of Jeremiah, a lament is formally addressed to Yahweh, which is used in a way functionally equivalent to a curse, and it is uttered for the benefit of one's opponents in a dispute or a conflict.

If the setting of this confession in the life of the prophet is accepted then it entails the rejection of the theory of origin as editorial composition. John Maclennan rightly points out that,

> [T]o see this passage as a transfer to the prophet of a normal individual lament-which originally had nothing to do with a prophetic figure, but whose stereotyped idioms provided the necessary ambiguity to make such a transfer possible. While some of the idioms of this confession are ambiguous (for example: יום רעה allusion to call narrative, חתת) and their character as prophetic could be a factor solely of the context, the attempt to argue that the presence seems very unlikely.[108]

If one is going to argue that the presence of such features is the result of editorial adaptation to make the lament more applicable to prophetic concerns, then on what basis can the very same process be denied to the prophet himself? [109] The examination of this passage so far indicates that none of its features necessarily excludes its connection with a prophetic and Jeremianic setting.

---

[106] A. R. Diamond, *The Confessions of Jeremiah in Context: Scenes of Prophetic Drama* (Sheffield: JSOT, 1987), 83.

[107] Ibid.

[108] John Maclennan, *Prophet, People, and the Word of Yahweh* (Zurich: EVZ-Verlag, 1970), 138.

[109] Diamond, *The Confessions of Jeremiah in Context: Scenes of Prophetic Drama*, 84.

5.2.1.6.1. Comments on Jeremiah 17:14 in relation to Illness, Health and Healing

The introductory petition, which could be understood totally in traditional lament categories, receives a more pointed force, since the 'healing' requested should be understood in terms of the crisis arising from delayed fulfilment (v. 15), and so consists essentially of the realization of the announced judgment (v. 16). That this is the concern of the petition is indicated further in the petitions of vv. 17-18, which appear to contain allusions to the call narrative (1:17) through repeated use of the root חתת. The healing of the prophet is essentially his vindication over against his opponents through bringing on the Day of Judgment. (v.18). The veiled complaint of the negative petition (v. 17) is enhanced further by the mini-confessions as Psalm 94:22 –ויהיה והלילמשגב or Psalm 118:14, 21- ותהילילישועה/ויהי. Further, special nuances which probably are to be detected relate to the vocabulary cluster of רפא, ישע (v.14); אנוש (v.16). This block of vocabulary which is especially associated in the book of Jeremiah with the destruction/judgment that the opponents referred to so obliquely, is in actuality to be identified as the whole nation.[110] This lends even more force to the prophet's petition, for his healing will mean the breaking of the nation.

The words, "Heal me, oh Yahweh, and I shall be healed" in Jeremiah 17:14 is a statement, which is part of the meditation that contrasts trust in Yahweh with trusts in humans. In this light, one can see that the theology expressed in this implies that healing is one thing for which Yahweh and his rightful intermediaries, not other professions, should be consulted.[111]

5.2.1.6.1.1. The Metaphor of Refuge

The metaphor of "refuge," in this text has both positive and negative connotation. The motif stands for both salvation and terror. Where Jeremiah pleads with God- "save me and I shall be saved" (Jer. 17:14), the Hadayot poet praises God for "saving" him from "the zeal of the mediators of deceit" and "redeeming my soul from the pit." Rarely in IQH will the poet ask for "salvation" ישע) or "redemption" (פדה) or "help" (עזר); more often than not he simply acknowledges these gifts as already received. This does not mean, however, that JL and IQH present fundamentally different portrayals of God. Where Jeremiah plaintively begs, "Do not become a terror to me" (מחתה), the Hadayot poet also describes himself as someone quite "terrified' by God's "just judgments" (נבעט המשפטיצדק, IQH 9:23).[112]

---

[110] One could also argue that his opponents are prophetic ones (14:15; 27:9). However, the broad usage of the 3rd pers. Pl. pronoun in Jeremiah permits the view, for it is more generally used either of Jeremiah's opponents or in accusation of the nation.

[111] Hector Avalos, *Illness and Health Care in the Ancient Near East: The Role of the Temple in Greece, Mesopotamia, and Israel* (Atlanta, Georgia: Scholars Press, 1995), 287.

[112] Michael S. Moore, "The Laments in Jeremiah and IQH: Mapping the Metaphorical Trajectories," in *Uprooting and Planting: Essays on Jeremiah for Leslie Allen*, ed. John Goldingay

One of the major divergences within this metaphor focuses on "healing" verses "disease". Jeremiah begs God to "heal him" so that "he shall be healed" (רפא, Jer. 17:14), even as he acknowledges the "pain" he suffers something "incurable." In Hadayot, the poet praises God for turning "affliction: into "eternal healing" (מרפע ולם, IQH 17.24-25), but using Jeremiah's exact words, he twice speaks of "incurable pain" (כאיבאנוש, IQH 13.28; 16.28). When it comes to describing pain, Jeremiah tends to blame God for his pain, IQH singles out the "men of Belial" as the source of his pain (13.26).[113] Therefore, the metaphor of refuge is seen as "salvation" and "healing."

5.2.1.6.1.2. The Lament of 'Pain' and 'Suffering'

The pain and suffering which are indicated by the prayer for healing (רפא) refer, to contempt. Jeremiah's soul is scarred by rejection and scorn, by hostility and misinterpretation, and he asks for healing and salvation. He uses language that is appropriate to a sick person in the style of individual lament, but his sickness is of the spirit rather than the body. Reventlow has noticed that an analogous metaphorical use of רפא is found in Jer. 8:22 and 14:19, where the "health" or "wholeness" of the body politic is the antithesis of its condition of brokenness and disease.[114] However, the circumstance in which רפא (14:19) and ישע (14:8) are found in corporate laments, in connection with the brokenness of the body politic, is not a demonstration that they would be inappropriate in an individual laments in connection with the brokenness of an individual. The combination of רפא and ישע in v. 14 does indicate that the verse refers to a condition of bitterness, despair and spiritual defeat, rather than to physical disease.[115]

The medical vocabulary is being used metaphorically to describe a special kind of sickness. The person who prays is not a pious man stricken with bodily disease, but a prophet trembling with anguish and near to physical collapse in the face of the sorrows and contradictions of his vocation. The prophet, in a condition of bitterness and brokenness, calls out for healing and for the strength to endure, however hard and cruel the circumstances of his life and vocation are.

The prayer of healing in v.14 echoes a common motif in the Psalms (Ps. 6:2; 41:14; 60:2 and also to be found in the Jeremiah tradition.[116] The brief prayer contains elements familiar in the Psalms of lament:

(a) petition (v. 14a),
(b) motivation (vv 14b-16),
(c) petition (v. 17a),

(New York: T & T Clark, 2007), 247.

[113] Ibid.

[114] Henning Graf Reventlow, *Liturgie und Prophetisches Ich bei Jeremia* (Gutersloh, 1963), 235ff.

[115] McKane, *A Critical and Exegetical Commentary on Jeremiah*, 408-409.

[116] Carroll, *From Chaos to Covenant: Prophecy in the Book of Jeremiah*, 122.

(d) motivation (v. 17b),
(e) petition (v. 18).[117]

Such occurrences of the healing motif in Jeremiah are either liturgical or consolatory, and are addressed to the community rather than the individual. So the use of the motif in 17:14 should be understood as a prayer for the community's healing. Again, the prophet is presented as a community engaged in prayer for restoration. The redactional shaping of the passage has made the quest for salvation the contextual meaning of confession (12, 14), so the question must be treated in relation to the community's expectation of salvation in terms of healing. Such an expectation of deliverance may be pre-exilic in origin, but probably should be seen here as the prayer of the exiled community waiting for divine restoration.

5.2.1.7. Jeremiah 30:13-18

V. 13. There is no one judging your case[a] concerning a running sore.
There is no healing of new flesh for you.[b]
V. 14. All your lovers have forgotten you.
They will not take care of you.
Indeed, with an enemy's blow[a] I have struck you,
with a cruel one's discipline,[b]
Because[b] of the abundance of your iniquity,
V. 15. Why do you cry out[a] about your shatteredness?
An incurable wound is your anguish.
Because of the abundance of your iniquity,
(because) your sins are so numerous,
I have done these things to you.
V. 16. Therefore all the ones eating you will be eaten,
and all[a] your adversaries, all of them, shall go into captivity;
and all your plunderers shall become plunder,[b]
and all your despoilers I will make spoil.
V. 17. For I will bring healing over you,
and from your wounds[a] I will heal you
For they have called you "Banished:
She is Zion;[b]
No one cares for her.

Form Critical Notes

This poem announces salvation in the form of divine healing for the people personified as Zion. The speaker throughout is the LORD, and the addressee is second person feminine singular. Verse 17 identifies her as Zion. The beginning of the unit, however, is devoted to a description of the people's hopeless condition

[117] Brueggemann, *A Commentary on Jeremiah: Exile and Homecoming*, 163.

(vv 12–14a) and the reasons for it (vv 14b–15). The salvation promise includes destruction of the enemies (v 16) and healing for Zion (v 17a). Following the oracle formula (נאם יהוה, "oracle of the LORD"), a report of the enemies' taunt against Zion (v 17c) functions as an explanation for the LORD's promise to bring healing.

The vocabulary, motifs, and order of this poem mirror the lament psalm form. Shatteredness, wounds, pain, abandonment, enemies, and taunts are all features compatible with a lamenter's complaint. Yet in this passage, it is the LORD who describes the suffering, not the human victim. This change of voice continues in vv 14–15, where the LORD acknowledges, "I have done these things to you." Lament psalms sometimes charge the LORD with being the source of suffering (e.g., Ps. 44:10–15, 23; 60:5, as does Jeremiah's "confession" in 15:17–18. Here the truth of the charge is acknowledged. The wound inflicted by the enemy came from the LORD by reason of the people's guilt. A few lament psalms do include the psalmist's confession of sin (Ps. 32, 38, 41, 51, 102, 130, and 143). Psalm 38:4; and 41:4 make the connection between loss of health and sin. Therefore, at the beginning of v 16 typically signals the beginning of a judgment announcement following an indictment. In this passage, however, it introduces judgment on the enemies, which, by implication, means deliverance for Zion. The salvation announcement in vv 16–17 promises answers to two typical categories of lament petitions by removing the enemies (v 16) and healing injuries (v 17a). Such an oracle given in answer to a psalmist's complaint is implied by many Psalms, but it is rarely included in the text (e.g., Ps. 12).

The literary features that establish the unity of the poem in its present form do not confirm in themselves whether the unit was composed in a single stage or in two or more. The imagery suits the condition of Judah and Jerusalem resulting from conquest by the Babylonians, but the personal connotations of the motifs typical of the individual lament genre free this poem to address readers long after the sixth century B.C.E.

Words repeated in different parts of the poem form the links in its unified structure. The diseased wound (v 12) was from the LORD's hand (v 14), but the LORD will heal their wounds (v 17). No healing (v 13) will be replaced by healing (v 17). The people's former lovers do not "seek" or "care for" them (v 14), but when the enemies taunt them with their abandonment ("No one cares for her," v 17c), the Lord takes action against the taunters (v 16). This structure corresponds to the theological logic of the lament, discussed above, and with the canonical shape of the book of Jeremiah. According to Jeremiah 1:10, "to pluck up and tear down ... to build and to plant" and "wound" and "heal" in 30:12–17 make an analogous pair. Furthermore, the destruction of the Babylonians in chaps. 50–51 is based upon what they had done to Israel, Judah, and Jerusalem, as promised in v 17. This unit ends with the citation of the enemies' taunts, which serves to prepare for the next unit by calling attention to the people's location in exile. 30:18–31:1 begins with a promise of restoration and rebuilding for Jerusalem.

Setting

This poem announces salvation in the form of divine healing for the people personified as Zion. The speaker throughout is the Lord and the addressee is second person fem sing. Verse 17 identifies her as Zion. The beginning of the unit however, is devoted to a description of the people's hopeless condition (vv 12-14a) and the reasons for it (vv. 14b-15). The salvation promise includes destruction of the enemies (v.16) and healing on Zion (v. 17a). Following the oracle formula נאם יהיה, "oracle of the Lord": a report of the enemies taunt against Zion (v. 17c) functions as an explanation for the Lord's promise to bring healing.[118]

Contemporary analysts of this poem typically divide it into an early or original part vv. 12-15, and later addition of vv. 16-17. Holladay for example, gives the setting of vv. 12-15 in Jeremiah's preaching to the survivors of the Northern Kingdom in the period 615-609 B.C. and he assigns vv. 16-17 to a much later Judean edition prepared just prior to the fall of Jerusalem. The literary features that establish the unity of the poem in the present form do not confirm in themselves whether the unit was composed at a single stage or in two or more.[119] The imagery suits the condition of Judah and Jerusalem resulting from conquest by the Babylonians, but the personal connotations of the motifs typical of the individual lament genre free this poem to address readers long after the sixth century B.C.

5.2.1.7.1. Comments on Jeremiah 30:13-18; in relation to Illness, Health and Healing

The theme of exile and return is here considered afresh through a different metaphor, that of sickness and healing. The most interesting fact about this poem is that it is bound by two statements that blatantly contradict each other. The beginning point is a ruthless, candid diagnosis of diseased Israel (v.12). God's people is terminally ill, beyond healing, sure to die. The end of the poem is a promise that God will indeed heal and restore (v. 17). Taken together, vv. 12 and 17 affirm that the one who is utterly beyond healing will be healed. The work of the poem is to trace the way in which Israel's faith and imagination move from the hopeless condition of v. 12 to the astonishing assurance of v. 17.[120]

---

[118] Gerald L. Keown, Pamela J. Scalise, and Thomas G. Smothers, *Jeremiah 26-52*, vol. 27 (Dallas, Texas: Word Books, 1995), 96.

[119] Holladay, *Jeremiah 1: A Commentary on the Book of the Prophet Jeremiah Chapters 1-25*, 97.

[120] Walter Brueggemann, "The "Uncared For" Now Cared for (Jer. 30:12-17): A Methodological Consideration," *Journal of Biblical Literature* 104, no. 3 (September 1985): 419-428.

Within vv. 1-16 P. D. Hanson sees six sub-divisions, each of them 'a tightly knit unit of thought held together by parallelism, repetition of grammatical elements, assonance, paronomasia, and similar poetic devices.'[121]

The prophetic dream was to restore and heal the land and the people. As H. M. Wolf notes,

> The most remarkable descriptions of curse reversals in the Hebrew Bible appear in those passages in the prophets that deal with the restoration and rebuilding of Israel after a long period of shame and disgrace in exile. The once-battered nations now achieve a level of prosperity and blessedness that more than compensates for her great suffering and degradation. The curses of famine, disease, and war give way to unprecedented blessings of health, fruitfulness and peace.[122]

Verses 12-15 revolve around the twin themes of guilt and illness. The sickness of Israel is beyond help. Israel, in its disease, is utterly abandoned, disregarded by former allies. The figure suggests abandonment by fair-weather friends who will not stand by a loser, and who leave of friendship when sickness strikes. Walter Brueggemann here rightly argues that, in verse 12, the verdict is announced. The sickness of Israel is terminal. The rest of the poem is derived from the unquestioned premise. That is not negotiable, nor is reason for it given. The vocabulary of sickness is rich and diverse. In v 15 the verdict is announced again, only now Israel is chided for crying out in pain or protest. The verdict is sure. The situation is hopeless and it is futile to protest it.[123]

The intensification of terminal illness with the double use of (*'ên*) /אין to strengthen the absolute negation is seen. This is matched by moving the metaphor of sickness in verse 14 into the political arena.

5.2.1.7.1.1. The Image of the 'Judge'

The mixed metaphor in verse 13 has called forth various proposals for rearranging or emending the text. "Judging your case" (13a) seems at first to have nothing to do with a sore that will not heal. Therefore, Rudolph replaces the phrase with מַבְכִּיר, "soothing things," as in Isa 1:6.[124] Carroll[125] and NRSV set aside the Masoretic accents and divide the verse into three cola:

---

[121] Paul Hanson, *The Dawn of Apocalyptic* (Philadelphia: Fortress Press, 1975), 47.

[122] H. M. Wolf, "The Transcendent nature of the Covenant Curse Reversals," in *Israel's Apostasy and Restoration*, ed. A. Gileadi (Grand Rapids: Baker, 1988), 321.

[123] Brueggemann, "The "Uncared For" Now Cared for (Jer. 30:12-17): A Methodological Consideration," 420.

[124] W. Rudolph, in *Jesaja XV-XVI*, ed. D. W. Thomas and W. D. McHardy (Clarendon Press, 1963), 175.

[125] Carrol, *Jeremiah; A Commentary*, 580.

"There is no one judging your case.
(You don't have) remedies for your open wound;
You don't have new skin."

Bozak likes the mixed metaphor, however, finding in the tension a stimulus to reflection and increased understanding.[126] She concludes that the presence of the courtroom image indicates that the wound is spiritual.

The lack of one to judge might also be understood as a form of lament and thanksgiving motif of sufferers who need someone to vindicate them. The wounded wanted justice as well as healing. The cognate accusative construction in v.13 occurs only two other times, both in the book of Jeremiah (5:28, concerning orphans) and 22:16 (concerning the poor and the needy). Jeremiah 22:16 describes Josiah, so 30:13 alludes to the absence of a just king or ruler, like the one promised in v. 21. Another point can be that such a ruler lacks because no human could sit in judgment on a case against the Lord, who is the one who has wounded Zion (vv. 14-15). The clinical details of wound that does not heal (v. 13a) include the lack of new skin to cover and close it (v. 13b).

5.2.1.7.1.2. The Image of a 'Lover'

In verse 14, it combines the vocabulary of prophecy with the language of lament. "Lovers" is a metaphor for foreign allies. The connection with the medical image in v 13 may have been prompted by reflection upon Hosea 5:13, in which Ephraim has sent messengers to Assyria and her emperor for help, but he was not able to heal their מזור, "open wound." (Hos. 5:13 and Jer. 30:13 are the only occurrences of this word in the Old Testament). The particular nations referred to as "lovers" may have been the ones listed in 27:3, or the Egyptians, who caused a temporary interruption of the final siege of Jerusalem (37:5), or some other alliance not mentioned in the OT In Ezekiel 23:5, 9, the "lovers" are also the Assyrians, but elsewhere in Hosea and Ezekiel the term stands for foreign deities. Israel's "lovers" are to abandon her, according to Hosea 2:9a and in Jer. 30:14 they have forgotten her. The final colon converts the complaint heard in Psalm 142:5 from first to second person, "No one cares for you." דרש, "care for," includes the senses of care for the sick as well as searching for one who is lost.[127]

5.2.1.7.1.3. The Image of 'Sickness' and 'Wounds'

Verse 15 alludes Judah's sins to sickness that is equivalent to death. The poet sees the sickness so clearly, grieves the death so passionately. Judah seems not to have noticed the stench of death in the streets of Jerusalem.

---

[126] B. Bozak, *Life Anew: A Literary-Theological Study of Jeremiah 30-31* (Rome: Pontifical Biblical Institute, 1991), 49-50.

[127] Brueggemann, "The "Uncared For" Now Cared for (Jer. 30:12-17): A Methodological Consideration," 421.

In Verse 16, the LORD's acknowledgment that "I have done these things" at the end of v 15 is the basis for the promise of vindication. God, who had used their enemies to discipline Israel, will now judge the case of Israel's wound (v 13) and will give those same enemies punishments that correspond to their actions of eating, being adversaries, plundering, and despoiling. The foe from the north is described in 5:17–18 as eating every plant, animal, and person in the nation. Perhaps this metaphor is derived from the imagery of the locust plague.

5.2.1.7.1.4. The Image of 'Health' and 'Healing'

This is followed by healing in v. 17 that accompanies with vindication for Israel, because the wounded one receives justice, restored health, and forgiveness of sins. Taunting by enemies is typically one aspect of a lamenter's sufferings.[128]

The Poet asks about health. The prophet is a medicine man who knows what makes for healing. Judah had lulled itself into reinterpreting symptoms of sickness as marks of health.[129] Medical images are used in this passage, which continues the theme of God's judgment and restoration of Judah and Israel. As these verses begin, the diagnosis for God's people is bleak and shared forthrightly with then: "your hurt...incurable", "your wound...grievous, no medicine...no healing for you" (vv. 12-13). Jeremiah announces to God's people that they are abandoned and without support. Their "lovers", their political allies to whom they have turned for help, have forgotten them and no longer care for them (v. 14). Jeremiah links ominous medical images with political realism to describe God's judgment.[130] In Jeremiah 30:17, the phrase ארוכה, "I will restore health" is employed, and a similar phrase occurs in Jeremiah 8:22 and 33:6. The prophets frequently use the metaphor of "Yahweh heals" with the root רפא to convey God's restorative work. This restorative effort often focuses on Israel, but not exclusively so. Jeremiah 30:17 clearly states that Yahweh will restore the health of his people and heal their wounds not because they repented, but because others had called them outcasts and no one cared for them.

The verse is an expression of hope, a promise that God makes to all those who experience physical ill health, rejection, stigma, discrimination and

[128] Jeremiah prays in 18:19, "listen to what my adversaries say," and lament psalms like Ps 35:24–26 pray that the Lord will silence the enemies who congratulate themselves, saying things like, "We have swallowed you up." Hearing such taunting is what motivates God's decision to heal and vindicate Israel (כי, "because," v. 17a), even though the enemies are saying just what God has already said, "There is no one caring for you" (v. 14). The shift in this passage from distress to deliverance is as dramatic as in the psalms of lament. The brief explanation of motivation in v. 17b hints that God does listen to the needy person's prayer and is moved by his or her suffering. God hears when the people cry out (v. 15) and when their enemies mock them (v. 17) and responds with a promise.

[129] Brueggemann, *Hopeful Imagination: Prophetic Voices in Exile*, 36.

[130] John M. Bracke, *Jeremiah 30-52 and Lamentations* (Louisville: Westminster John Knox Press, 2000), 6.

oppression. The incurable will become curable. On that day when the people repent, recognize God as the sovereign ruler, obey the covenant; God will remove the bonds of captivity. On that day, God will cause healing to come up for those who are considered as outcast. Thus the text, tells about God calling the Israelites to see beyond the destruction and hopelessness to new hope, new life in terms of healing the wounds.

Jeremiah 30:12-17 is an interesting poem focusing on healing after a time of judgment and punishment. The first part (Jer. 30:12-15) announces that the sickness and wounds of Israel is incurable be-cause of their sins and Yahweh's punishment. The second part (Jer. 30:16-17) focuses on Yahweh's healing of a nation called an outcast and not cared for.

The portrayal of Yahweh as healer is not limited to restoration of what Yahweh has damaged through his judgment. Yahweh's healing capacity pertains to whatever damage has been done, by whatever agent. The healer metaphor does not merely refer to the healing of people. There are a few prophetic texts portraying the healing of the land, city, temple and even God's creation. Sometimes it is difficult to distinguish between people and material things but one can say that Yahweh as healer offered a comprehensive healing of people and material objects. This comprehensive healing includes the physical rebuilding of Jerusalem (Jer. 30:17-18), abundance of prosperity and security (Jer. 33:6), and the restoration of the fortunes of his people (Hos. 6:11-7:1).

5.2.1.8. Jeremiah 33:6

V. 6. I am about to bring upon it[a] restoration and healing,[b]
and I will heal them.[c]
I will reveal for them a fragrance,
namely peace and faithfulness.

Form Critical Notes

Chapter 33 serves as a continuation and further development of chap. 32. It makes use of material from that chapter, from other parts of the book of Jeremiah, and from the rest of the Old Testament. The sense of continuation is clear from the heading in v 1, which locates the following revelation in the time during which Jeremiah was "still" incarcerated in the court of the guard at the temple, as in 32:1, and which says that the LORD's word came "a second time" (שֵׁנִית). The second and third headings, in vv 19 and 23, give no date or location, but vv 19–26 form an inclusion with 31:31–36. Messenger formulas appear in 32:36, 42 and continue in 33:2, 10, 12, 17, 20, 25. This series of oracles takes up again God's response, which begins in 32:26, to Jeremiah's prayer (32:16–25). Formally, they are private revelations to the prophet, which are now reported to the larger audience in written form.

The oracles in this chapter are written in prose, but they include two fragments of poetry. V 11 quotes part of a hymn as an illustration of the psalms that people will recite again in the temple. An earlier promise, in poetry, is cited, with modifications, in vv. 15-16 in order to add an expansion to it in vv. 17-18. Standard prophetic formulas mark off each section. Within some units, a judgment announcement or description is followed by a salvation oracle. The words "nevertheless" or "yet" indicate the transition from one to the other.

Setting

This chapter is a development, elaboration, and explanation of earlier promise themes. The focus upon Jerusalem and the king and priests who will lead and serve there is especially appropriate to the concerns of the Judean exiles and the restoration community. The form, style, and content of vv 1–13 have led to widely varying views of the time of composition. Holladay, for example, detects a core of material attributable to Jeremiah within vv 4–9.[131] Carroll, following labels the whole of vv 1–13 Post-Deuteronomistic.[132] He assesses vv 14–26, which are entirely absent from LXX, as a "minority report" from the Persian period, perhaps as late as the Chronicler.[133] Absence from LXX does not necessarily prove a late origin for vv 14–26 since the MT and LXX represent distinct text types. The passage is well integrated into its context.

5.2.1.8.1. Comments on Jeremiah 33:6 in relation to Illness, Health and Healing

What is interesting in Jeremiah 33:6ff is that this divine healing is translated into the return of the Judean and Israelite captives (v.7a), the rebuilding of the cities as of old (v.7b), and the purification from and forgiveness of past sins (v.8). Repentance would lead to the return of the wearied exiles, the rebuilding of their ruined cities, and the reconciliation of their spiritual lives. The fracture would be healed; the breach would be restored, "new skin" would arise. This was the promise of the divine healer. With the covenant curses lifted, the blessings of God could come. Thus, the promise and call that are undergirded in the prophetic message is seen.[134]

The promise for the city that is torn apart from within, "smitten" (נכה) by God, and polluted with unburied corpses is literally "new flesh" (ארוכה as in 8:22), healing, and the balm of peace and faithfulness (or "true peace"). The healing sought in several verses in the first part of the book (6:14; 8:11; 8:15; 14:19b; 8:22; 15:18; 30:13) is promised here. This promise echoes 30:17, a word of comfort after a description of the incurable wounds caused by Israel's sin and

[131] Holladay, *Jeremiah 1: A Commentary on the Book of the Prophet Jeremiah Chapters 1-25*, 222.

[132] Carrol, *Jeremiah; A Commentary*, 634.

[133] Ibid., 639.

[134] Michael L. Brown, *Israel's Divine Healer* (Grand Rapids: Zondervan, 1995), 194-195.

unfaithfulness (30:12–15), and adds the key term from 8:15; 14:19b, ארוכה, "restoration" (i.e., the new flesh that closes the wound). Two terms from 30:17a, רפא, "heal," and נכה, "smite," appear in 33:5–6. (30:17b deals with the same theme as the last oracle in chap. 33, vv. 23–26, the nations' claim that the LORD has rejected Israel.) The language of divine wounding and healing apparently has its origin in the image of the LORD as a lion who tears the people to pieces (Hos. 5:14–6:2). The lion is no longer present in Jer. 30:15, but the divine word says of the people's wound and pain that "I have done these things to you" (cf. Deut. 32:39). Wounds have also been inflicted by enemies (30:16), but only the LORD can heal (Hos. 5:13). Spiritual waywardness can be "cured" (רפא; 3:22; Hos. 14:4), but 33:6 has in view the damage done to land and people by God's judgment at the hand of the Babylonians. The pronouns "it" (feminine singular) and "them" have their antecedents in vv 4–5, the ruined city and the destroyed houses.

5.2.1.8.1.1. 'Yahweh as the Restorer' of Health and Healing

The phrase, "I shall restore your health, and I shall heal your wounds" in Jer. 30:17 is similar to Jeremiah 33:6 where it says: "Indeed, I shall bring restoration and healing". Although, these texts refer to Israel, the socio-political entity, as the patient, it is clear that these references are part of a theology that regards Yahweh as the only רפא that should be trusted.

The metaphorical imagery, powerfully expressed through vivid figures such as Israel's "new skin" arising in Jeremiah 30:17; 33:6, or a physician applying healing balm (8:22; 46:11; 51:8; cf. also Isa. 1:6), must therefore be seen as inclusive and not as exclusive (in other words, healing of physical diseases was certainly not excluded from the wider metaphor of national healing and restoration).

God now resolves to bring healing in the face of the destructive powers, which have wrought chaos, and to give to the city utter well-being, a well-being (*Shalom*) marked by God's security. The language of the promise envisions a complete inversion of the destruction of the past. Thus, the promise uses the programmatic formula, "I will restore", that is, renew the good conditions of old (v. 7). The formula is given substance that is more concrete by three verbs: "I will build, I will cleanse, I will forgive" (vv 7b-8).[135] The first verb refers to the physical reconstruction and rehabilitation of the city and the other two refer to making the city heal from their religious apostasy.

The promise in Jeremiah 33:6 has three images of forgiveness. The word *Rapha* (heal) in verse 6 has the image of 'cleansing' and 'forgiveness' in verse 8.There are three language used for guilt and sin. The words "sin" "guilt" and "rebellion" are used, however, these words were overpowered by the strong verbs which refer to God's newness. The outcome of God's resolve and God's action is the rehabilitation and healing of Jerusalem by forgiving their sins. The metaphorical image of forgiveness is used here. Therefore, the text requires twofold healing. (1)

[135] Brueggemann, *A Commentary on Jeremiah: Exile and Homecoming*, 314.

healing from dispersion, weakness, brokenness as a socio-religious community (33:6) and (b) healing from the stain of that which causes God to turn his face from them. His defilement is directly attached to the cultic image, 'cleanse', which is also used in Ezekiel. The healing, cleansing and forgiving taken together embrace some sense of transformation, so that God is now free to pour out his favour on Judah and Jerusalem.

Summary

The graphic imagery of restoration and repair is found throughout the book of Jeremiah. Jeremiah was part of a tradition that viewed Yahweh as the only genuine רפא. Jeremiah emphasizes elsewhere that it is Yahweh who will heal. The book of Jeremiah intervenes in a national disaster and moves the nation toward healing.

Jeremiah's oracles are oracles of hope and healing, a healing intervention into a world destroyed. Jeremiah's fire and brimstone theology, graphic depictions of warfare and its horrors, and theology of blame help the people of Judah survive and face the future, but not until they have revisited the historical disaster by means of Jeremiah's poetry. Jeremiah wants to see "the wound of my people" (Jer. 6:14), by remaking the language.

Jeremiah uses the imagery of *Shalom*, a vision that he hoped to achieve in the future without any discrimination and injustice but an inclusive *Shalom* community.

In this way, even Jeremiah's most horrifying imagery helps survivors of the disaster to come to grips with it, to grieve it, to understand how God was present through its many manifestations. Jeremiah's message of health and healing was to make room for hope and to rebuild community. The violence of passages in the book of Jeremiah reflects back to the community all that was destroyed and lost; in horrendous scenes it give them their story of terror and destruction. Against common perception, by re-immersing them in the calamity, Jeremiah creates words that are a healing balm for wounds without words.

5.3. Health and Healing in Deutero-Isaiah

5.3.1. Socio-historical Setting of Deutero-Isaiah

The collection of oracles ascribed to Deutero-Isaiah (Chaps. 44-55) is usually designated as the book of consolation, and many of them are prophecies of salvation. Thematic and literary consistency, allied to some clear historical facts and allusion, shows that at least most of these oracles were written by one person who lived in the period after the fall of Jerusalem (587 B.C.E). The anonymous prophet addresses a despairing people in exile, announcing an imminent turning point in Israel's fortunes; its people will return to their homeland even more gloriously than did their fathers after leaving Egypt. This orientation towards the future is, however intimately linked with a harking back to the origin of the world of Israel, and of the nations. The will of the only ruler over Israel and the nations is to deliver the chosen people. The desolation of earlier years was caused by their guilt, which has now been expiated. The prophet sees the whole of history as a unity. In face of self-pitying lamentation of the Jews in exile, the prophet points to the reason for punishment and to the possibility of forgiveness, restoration and healing. The message to the people is summarized at the beginning of the account of the prophet's commission.[136]

Deutero-Isaiah comprises over 50 sayings, most of them addresses to the Jews in exile. The proclamation of salvation leads to comment on the Persian King Cyrus and on Babylon. Cyrus is sometimes referred to obliquely (41:2, 25; 45:13; 48:14) while in 44:28 and 45:1 he is named and greeted as God's "shepherd" and "his anointed" respectively because he was called 'to subdue nations before him and ungird the loins of kings, to open doors before him that gates may not be closed" (45:1). On Babylon however, the severest of judgment is pronounced. The dominant theme that runs out is proclamation of forgiveness and recognition of atonement for guilt.[137]

Deutero-Isaiah begins with the contemporary historical situation. The Exile is almost over; God commands the angelic forces to comfort Israel with the assurance that her iniquity that brought about the exile is pardoned. Deutero-Isaiah's message consistently describes how God was about to heal a torn creation and restore a broken community.[138]

5.3.2. Exegetical Study

5.3.2.1. Isaiah 53:4-5

V. 4. Surely[a] he has borne our infirmities
And carried our diseases;[b]
Yet we accounted him stricken
Struck down by God, and afflicted.
V. 5. But he was wounded for our transgressions,
Crushed for our iniquities;
Upon him was the punishment that made us whole,
And by his bruises we are healed.

Form Critical Notes

Unlike scholarly opinions on the other Servant songs, there is a general agreement among scholars to treat 52:13- 53:12 as a unit. Chapter 52:13-15 is constituted as an introduction or prologue to 53:1-12. Although, the unit as a whole confines itself to humiliation-exaltation sequence in the life of the servant, the song has

---

[136] Joze Krasovec, *Reward, Punishment, and Forgiveness: The Thinking and Beliefs of Ancient Israel in the Light of Greek and Modern Views* (Leiden: Brill, 1999), 484.

[137] Ibid., 485.

[138] Paul D. Hanson, *Isaiah 40-66, Interpretation: A Bible Commentary for Teaching and Preaching* (Louisville: Westminster John Knox Press, 1995), 10.

an indirect relationship to the contents of the preceding unit (is 52:7-12) and the following unit (Is 54:1-3), while Is 52:7-12 portrays the theophanic coming of Yahweh and the assumption of Yahweh's kingship on Zion and consequent manifestation of Yahweh's salvific action of deliverance in favour of Zion-Israel, Isaiah 54:1-3 narrates the future exalted state of Zion. In Is 54:13-53:12 the focus is on the servant's exaltation and its effect in the world of the nations.[139] The message of 52:13—53:12 thus materializes: Yahweh announces the exaltation of His Servant because of His satisfactory substitutionary death for the sins of both His guilty people and the Gentiles. The passage consists of five strophes, the central three of which compose the body of the report. Thus, the message has three units: (1) an introductory appraisal in which Yahweh promises to exalt His Servant supremely, who though deeply degraded, will both purify and receive the worship of nations (52:13-15); (2) a confessional report in which believing Israelites contrast their past rejection of the Servant with the true meaning of His death (53:1-9); and (3) a concluding epilogue in which Yahweh promises to exalt His Servant because He did His will in dying as a guilt offering (53:10-12).

J. Begrich has suggested that the song is a combination of a psalm of thanksgiving of the individual and lament.[140] Whybray has defended the entire poem (53:1-12, but not 52:13-15) as being an individual thanksgiving psalm, not in form only, but also in fact, the unusual feature in his view being that the sufferer is Deutero-Isaiah himself who is described in the third person by a group of persons who "confess their own guilt, which was at least partly the cause for his suffering."[141] However, Westermann has more correctly recognized that the genre of the individual thanksgiving psalm "does no more than form the background" for Isaiah 53 which "contains a second strand which is closely woven into it ... a confession on the part of those who experienced salvation."[142] Whybray's dissenting opinion that 52:13-15 is a separate and unrelated poem is based on his unwarranted view that chapter 53 is "a song of thanksgiving for the deliverance of God's servant, Deutero-Isaiah, from mortal danger."[143] But scholars disagree on nearly everything else in the song. Problems abound regarding the text, translation, and interpretation of virtually every verse in the song. Therefore, it is very difficult to ascertain the setting of this song. However, according to Daniel Jones Muthunayagom,

---

[139] Daniel Jones Muthunayagom, *The Relationship Between Election and Israel's Attitude Towards the Nations in the Book of Isaiah* (Delhi: ISPCK, 2000), 131.

[140] J. Begrich. As quoted by Muthunayagom, *The Relationship Between Election and Israel's Attitude Towards the Nations in the Book of Isaiah*, 180.

[141] R. N. Whybray, *Isaiah 40-66: New Century Bible Commentary* (Grand Rapids, Michigan: William B. Eerdmans Publishing Company, 1981), 110-112.

[142] Claus Westermann, *Isaiah 40-66* (Philadelphia: Westminster John Knox Press, 1969), 257.

[143] Whybray, *Isaiah 40-66: New Century Bible Commentary*, 169.

> It is very likely that this song has the form of royal liturgy where the just executed royal figure is liturgically presented by Yahweh with the assurance that the royal figure will be exalted as a well-respected king among the nations of the world. The main part (Isa. 53:1-11) is formulated as a liturgical confession by the member of the community among whom the servant was born, brought up, humiliated, and executed. Although, in this confession Deutero-Isaiah has used the form of a psalm of thanksgiving and the language of individual laments, this confession cannot be categorised as either of them. The reason that the perception of their understanding about the servant's task is different. Their previous understanding was that he suffered for his sins and was smitten by God whereas their present understanding is that the servant was smitten for their sins, and it was Yahweh's own initiative.[144]

One major problem is the identification of the speakers. It is clear that Yahweh is speaking in 52:13-15 and again in 53:10 or 11-12. The intervening verses (53:1-9 or 10) are a report about the humiliation, sufferings, and sacrificial death of the Servant. Thus, the song is a report within a divine utterance, beginning and ending with Yahweh speaking. However, who are the speakers of the report? Three groups have generally been suggested: (1) the prophet Isaiah (some say "Deutero-Isaiah") as representative of a group (usually the prophets),[145] (2) the Gentile kings of 52:15,[146] or (3) the believing Jewish remnant.[147] Since no addressees are indicated in the text, it is probably best to assume that both the divine utterance and the report of the believing remnant are addressed potentially to all humankind, similar to the first Servant song (42:1-4).

In refutation of the view that the speakers are Gentiles, Skinner has pointed out that "the 'nations' and 'kings' [of 52:15] are surprised by the Servant's exaltation [better, atoning death] because they had not previously heard of it; whereas those who now speak (v. 1) have heard but could not believe."[148] There is substantial positive evidence for the identity of the speakers as repentant Israelites. Paul quotes Isaiah 53:1 in Romans 10:16 as a complaint against the unbelief of Israel. Also in Isaiah 53:8 it is declared that the sins for which the Servant is

---

[144] Muthunayagom, *The Relationship Between Election and Israel's Attitude Towards the Nations in the Book of Isaiah*, 134.

[145] E. W. Hengstenberg, *Christology of the Old Testament and a Commentary on the Messianic Predictions* (Grand Rapids: Kregel Publications, 1970), 234.

[146] James Muilenburg, in *The Book of Isaiah: Chapters 40-66, The Interpreter's Bible*, ed. George R. Buttrick, 12 vols. (Nashville: Abingdon Press, 1956), 614.

[147] Franz Delitzsch, *Isaiah, Commentary on the Old Testament,* vol. 2 (Grand Rapids, Michigan: William B. Eerdmans Publishing Company, 1973), 310-11.

[148] J. Skinner, *The Book of the Prophet Isaiah: Chapters XL-LXVI* (Cambridge: University Press, 1951), 136.

stricken are those of "my people," that is, Israel. Delitzsch has argued, "whenever we find a 'we' introduced abruptly in the midst of a prophecy, it is always Israel that speaks."[149] The NIV has correctly translated the verbs in 53:1-9 in the past tense, suggesting that the speakers are looking backward to the Servant's sufferings and death. Leupold has painted this interesting picture: "So to speak, here we seem to hear two disciples standing on the street corner in Jerusalem reviewing the things that happened on Good Friday in the light of the better insight that came after Pentecost."[150] It should be noted however, that the speakers in the fullest prophetic scope [are] the remnant of Israel, who will turn in faith to the Messiah at His second advent (Zech. 12:10-13:1; Rom. 11:26).

Setting

The exilic period was a time of testing for the Jewish community. The exilic composition Isaiah 40-55 takes its place among a number of writings at the time that struggle with the question of how to make theological sense out of the devastating events that had led to banishment of much of the population from the Jewish homeland.[151] The attempts of Ezekiel and Jeremiah to explain the devastating events of 587 B.C.E. from the perspective of the faith of Israel shed light on the conditions within which the anonymous author of Isaiah 40-55 wrote his prophetic message and sketched his portrait of the Servant of the Lord. The viability of an official national worldview has been called into question by calamitous events. A spiritual struggle was underway to reformulate the conceptual underpinnings of the Jewish people. Secondly, Deutero-Isaiah, in addressing the wavering Jewish audience living in the shadow of pagan temples and under the din of Marduk festivals, mounts a counteroffensive. He is polite neither to pagan challengers nor to the stubborn defenders of national traditions. Boldly he speaks out the name of the God who called him to service.[152]

Issues that cried out for explanation in his counter offensive were kingship, temple, the remedies for the removal of sins that led to divine judgment of the nation, and the status of Israel's God among rival gods, especially those who in view of many had demonstrated their superior power in Babylon conquest and then in the meteoric rise of Cyrus. These issues stand in the background of Deutero-Isaiah's ministry to the exiles.

---

[149] Franz Delitzscht, *Isaiah, Commentary on the Old Testament* (Grand Rapids: William B. Eerdmans Publishing Company, 1973), 136.

[150] H. C. Leupold, *Exposition of Isaiah,* 2 vols. (Grand Rapids: Baker Book House, 1971), 225.

[151] Paul D. Hanson, "The World of the Servant of the Lord in Isaiah 40-55," in *Jesus and the Suffering Servant: Isaiah 53 and Christian Origins*, ed. William H. Bellinger and William R. Farmer (Harrisburg, Pennsylvania: Trinity Press International, 1998), 16.

[152] Ibid., 15.

5.3.2.1.1. Comments on Isaiah 53:4-5 in relation to Illness, Health and Healing

Isaiah 53 serves indispensably as the heart of anyone's healing theology. One's biblical expectations for eventually restored health rest on this biblical bedrock. Clearly the emphasis of Isaiah 53 centers on spiritual as well as physical salvation.[153]

Since sin is the moral cause of physical infirmities,[154] it is not surprising (1) that sin and sickness are related and (2) that dealing with sin (the cause) eventually addresses sickness (the effect). Isaiah 53 raises the question then, "What, if anything, does the prophet promise about physical restoration?"[155] Or, "Is Isaiah 53:4-5 limited to dealing only with sin and salvation?"

Contextually, Isaiah 53 uses three different words for sin like "sin," "iniquity," and "transgression". The Hebrew words[156] translated "griefs" (חלי, *holi,* sick, weak) and "sorrows" מכאוב *makob* "pain")[157] in Isaiah 53:3, 4, 10 can legitimately refer to either physical infirmities, mental pain, or spiritual problems. Those who limit this language only to physical problems should more accurately say that the words might refer to physical problems, but not necessarily.[158] In this context, none of

---

[153] The New Testament consistently presents Christ as the Christian's substitutionary sin bearer in His atonement. See Matt. 20:28; John 1:29; Rom. 4:25; 5:6-8; 8:3; 1 Cor. 15:3; 2 Cor. 5:21; Gal. 1:4; 3:13; 4:4-5; Heb. 9:28; 1 Pet. 3:18; 1 John 2:2; 4:10.

[154] But this is not to say that all disease can be related to specific sins committed by the ill person. But neither can we say that there is no relation between the two. John N. Oswalt, *The Book of Isaiah: Chapters 1-39,* New International Commentary of the Old Testament (Grand Rapids, Michigan: William B. Eerdmans Publishing Company, 1986), 605.

[155] This is a legitimate question in light of other passages in Isaiah which point to a time of physical healing, e.g. 29:18; 33:24; 35:5-6; 65:20.

[156] The language of Isaiah 53 is decidedly that of the atonement in Leviticus 16, which points strongly to a primary, if not exclusive, focus on the atonement's relationship to sin, not sickness. Read Douglas MacCallum Lindsay Judisch, "Propitiation in the Language and Typology of the Old Testament," *Concordia Theological Quarterly* 48, no. 2-3 (April-July 1984): 221-243; Douglas MacCallum Lindsay Judisch, "Propitiation in Old Testament Prophecy," *Concordia Theological Quarterly* 49, no. 1 (January 1985): 1-17; W. Kay, "Isaiah," in *The Bible Commentary,* ed. F. G. Cook (Grand Rapids, Michigan: Baker Books, 1981), 266; F. Duane Lindsey, "The Career of the Servant in Isaiah 52:13-53:12 "*Bibliotheca Sacra* 140, no. 557 (January-March 1983): 21-39; F. Duane Lindsey, "Isaiah's Songs of the Servant," *Bibliotheca Sacra* 139, no. 556 (October-December 1982): 312-329.

[157] See Ps. 32:10; Jer. 30:15; Lam. 1:12, 18 for examples other than actual sickness.

[158] "The terms "infirmities" and "sorrows," each of which should be identified as a metonymy of effect for cause, are used generally for all suffering which is viewed as the result of sin. This does not mean that Christ became sick or infirm in a substitutionary sense, nor that divine healing is guaranteed through the atonement (except in the ultimate sense of a resurrection body)" Lindsey, "The Career of the Servant in Isaiah 52:13-53:12": 23. See E. W. Bullinger, *Figures of Speech in the Bible* (Grand Rapids, Michigan: Baker Books, 1968), 538, 560. For a discussion of metonymy in general and metonymy of effect in particular. Certainly, if metonymy is not the speech figure

the primary translations reflects the physical idea, but rather all translate with the spiritual in view.[159]

Isaiah 53:4 reads that he "bore" (נשׂא,*nasa)* our griefs and "carried" (סבל,*säbal)* our sorrows. Deutero-Isaiah used these same verbs in v. 11 and 12. As one compares v. 3 with v. 4 and then v. 4 with v. 11 and v. 12, such usages of words can be seen as an emphasis that is related to salvation.[160]

5.3.2.1.1.1. *Rapha* in Deutero-Isaiah

The word רפא *(Rapha,* "heal, make healthful") is used six times in Isaiah (6:10; 19:22; 30:26; 53:5; 57:18; 57:19). While *Rapha* can either be literal with regard to physical healing (Gen 20:17) or figurative in the OT, in each of the use of רפא in the book of Isaiah other than 53:5. The author employs it figuratively of healing from sin. In light of (1) this otherwise exclusive figurative use by Deutero-Isaiah, (2) the previous discussion concerning metonymy of effect, and (3) the figurative use of "wounds," it is reasonable to conclude that Deutero-Isaiah intended the use of *Rapha* in 53:5 to be figurative also.[161] The word "healed" is used in *niphal* of רפא which means to be repaired; to be healed, cured; (of waters) to be made wholesome; (metaphorically) to be restored [to prosperity].[162] These words are used metaphorically in Isaiah 53:5, thereby meaning "to be restored to prosperity."

5.3.2.1.1.2. 'Infirmity' (חלי) and 'Disease' (מכאב) as Wounds

Two verbs are used in Isaiah 53 with the meaning "to carry", namely נשׂא and סבל. The verb נשׂא, "to carry", is rather common word and it does not in itself refer to a sacrifice, even if it is often used in connection with sacrificial language and issues about guilt.[163] Furthermore, in this verse it is not a form of guilt or transgression that is carried, but "our infirmities" (חלינו) and "our diseases" (מכאבינו). The two words חלי, "infirmity", and מכאב, "disease," are frequently used to describe the

intended in 53:4-5, then metaphor easily explains the use of "healing" in 53:5 (cf. J. Ramsey Michaels, *1 Peter*, Word Biblical Commentary, vol. 49 (Dallas: Word, 1988), 149. who opts for metaphor in both Isa 53:5 and 1 Pet. 2:24). Heb. 12:12-13 provides a fine example.

[159] Richard L Mayhue, "For What Did Christ Atone in Isa. 53:4-5," *Master's Seminary Journal* 6, no. 2 (Fall 1995): 127. Words should always be understood in a context and with a meaning intended by the author. Normally, the surrounding context indicates what the author meant by the words he used.

[160] Ibid.

[161] Ibid., 128.

[162] John D. W. Watts, "Isaiah 34-66," in *Word Biblical Commentary* (Waco, Texas: Word Books), 689.

[163] Kaiser's traditional interpretation of this statement asserts that these words refer to the servant's suffering as sacrifice. Most important for such understanding, the verb נצא, "to carry" Kaiser believes that this verb derives its meaning from the priestly language and that it describes the cause of guilt and how the effect of it is taken over.

condition of earlier disasters.[164] The word חלי is used, together with other words that describe wounds, in Isa. 1:5-6. Infirmities and diseases lie at the heart of the crisis, for they have accumulated without relief or sure to the point of dragging the nation to the brink of extinction.[165]

There are several problems in verse 8 that need to be addressed:

(1) The first problem regards the meaning of עצר. Several interpretations are suggested. A common translation of the word עצר is "oppression."[166] But this translation is considered as problematic. Following the rest of the declaration "we", it is more probable that it should be understood as negative statement. The servant is taken away from something positive and not from oppression. The word עצר is read as "protection" because it fits the context. Isaiah 53 in its entirety emphasizes the servant's loneliness. The rendering "protection" also agrees with a probable meaning of the line itself.[167] The parallel word משפט often has the positive value of justice in Isaiah 40-55 and especially in the servant songs. This is what the servant of Isaiah 53 is deprived of. Following this, the first colon of v. 8 is an expression of a miscarriage of justice.[168]

(2) The next problem is regarding the word. The word vocalised as in the MT is explained as hiphil pefect of חלה with the meaning "he brought sickness to him". According to BHS, the reading "he healed him who made", has been proposed. It is difficult to understand why such a statement should be changed to a much more complicated statement regarding God's part in the suffering. IQIsa has ויחללהו, "and he pierced him" or "he profaned him". However, החלי and דכאו should be understood together in the sense of "and it pleased Yahweh to bruise Him painfully".

Interestingly, each of its appearances in Isaiah clearly conveys the concept of spiritual restoration from such "illnesses" as idolatry, national self-reliance, and other sins (6:10; 19:22; 30:26; 57:18-19), with 19:22 referring to Egypt (not Israel), while 30:26 also implies a restoration from agricultural devastation. As Westermann rightly observes, the servant's wounds represent the totality of his

[164] The words are also used to describe other forms of wounds and diseases. This use is the most common use in the book of Isaiah and Jeremiah by which to describe the condition of the land, both after the fall of Jerusalem and after earlier disasters. These texts are most important with regard to the interpretation of Isa 53. The word מכאב, "disease", is also used of Babylon in Jer. 51:8. This is understandable, since the figure of Babylon is opposed to Jerusalem and the two images also carry significant resemblance. Hill, *Friend or Foe? The Figure of Babylon in the Book of Jeremiah MT*, 191-192.

[165] Hanson, "The World of the Servant of the Lord in Isaiah 40-55," 17.

[166] David P. Wright and Jacob Milgrom, "atsar," in *Theological Wordbook of the Old Testament*, ed. G. Johannes Botterweck and Helmer Ringgren (Stuttgart: Kohlhammer, 1993), 336.

[167] Sigmund Mowinckel, *He that Cometh* (Oxford: Blackwell, 1956), 198.

[168] The suffix in ע אם "my people", should probably be emended ע ום "his people," with Dead Sea Scroll of Isaiah (IQIsa). It seems unlikely that a singular person, for example that the servant or God, speaks in the middle of the confession of the "we".

suffering.[169] As those pre-exodus suffering led to Israel's deliverance, so now the sufferings of the Servant and his fellow exiles are preparatory to a new exodus."[170] In many cases of the use of רפא it is God who causes healing or afflicts with disease or catastrophes which cannot be healed but by divine intervention. This understanding that God is the healer is found in Jeremiah and even in Hosea.

5.3.2.1.1.3. Yahweh as the 'Restorer of the Nation'

The prophetic usage is most fully developed in Isaiah 53, where the figures of sin, sickness, and suffering are so beautifully intermingled that some Christian commentators, in applying this chapter to Jesus, have sought to read this chapter in exclusive terms of either spiritual redemption or physical redemption, but not both.[171] Yahweh as the one who is interested in the nation's health and well-being centers on the whole of prophetic literature especially in Isaiah 53. The understanding of health and healing in Isaiah 53 as physical cannot be ruled out, but it is also to ascertain the fact that Yahweh is not interested to heal the physical ailments of an individual but the spiritual aspect or the wholistic aspect of the nation in terms of restoration. However, this either-or tendency is ancient[172] and should not be taken at a face value. Motyer notes that, 'Isaiah uses healing in 53:5, in a total sense: the healing of the person, restoring fullness and completeness, a mark of the Messianic day."[173] J. MacArthur fails to understand this. He asks referring to Isaiah 53:5, "was Isaiah talking about physical healing?" answering with the claim, "A study of the book of Isaiah shows that the prophet was talking about the spiritual healing that Israel needed so desperately.[174]

Isaiah 53:5 describes foe healing of Israel at the cost of the servant's wounds and bruises. The prophetic hope was for the whole man to be wholly healed.

This is underscored by the prophetic expectation of the in breaking of the kingdom of God. Not only would righteousness and peace prevail, but sickness would also disappear (cf. Isa. 33:24; 35:1-6; 58:8). The future healing and restoration will not he only he for Israel but also for Egypt (Isa. 19:22).

---

[169] Westermann, *Isaiah 40-66*, 265.

[170] Anthony R. Ceresko, "The Rhetorical Strategy of the Fourth Servant Song (Isaiah 52:13-53:12): Poetry and the Exodus-New Exodus," *Catholic Biblical Quarterly* 56, no. 1 (January 1994): 43.

[171] H. H. Rowley, *The Servant of the Lord and Other Essays on the Old Testament* (Oxford: Blackwell, 1965), 1-94.

[172] This is reflected in AV's Translation of verse 4, "Surely he hath borne our griefs and carried our Sorrows." This emphasis on "grief's" and "sorrows" i.e., spiritualizing interpretation of *choli* and *makob*, follows both the LXX and Targ "this man bore our sins and was pained because of them"; "then for our sins he will pray and our iniquities will be forgiven because of him".

[173] J. Alec Motyer, *Isaiah: an Introduction and Commentary* (England: InterVarsity Press, 1999), 436.

[174] J. MacArthur, *Charismatic Chaos* (Grand Rapids: Zondervan, 1992), 103.

Therefore, interpreters of Isaiah 53 recognise both the servant bearing sickness and pain, by taking his people's guilt, he thereby incurred that total healing. There is no artificial dichotomy here. The whole human has been wholly healed. The straying and sickly nation has been completely restored and made well.

R.E. Clements states,

> By looking at certain role in other areas of Hebrew literature we may hope to find some explanation for the fluctuation between the experience of the individual and the community which appears in the Songs. In this fluctuation the fate of one individual in some way both embodies, yet redeems, the fate of the larger group.[175]

Such ideas are related to H. Wheeler Robinson's proposition, to accept that Israelite thinking displayed characteristics so fundamentally different from our own that individuality of a person was merged into that of the group to which he or she belonged.[176] This is described as a concept of corporate personality.

Summary

The above discussion cautions us against restricting Deutero-Isaiah's message in the fourth Song on narrowly conceived notions of spiritual healing and personal salvation. It must be seen as part of a larger proposal seeking to redefine the basis upon which the Jewish people were to re-establish themselves as a nation within the family of the nations of the world. In this proposition, political deliverance is addressed, as is physical reconstruction of the land, as is the restoration of the cult center, the temple. In the same manner, it must be also added, that the socio-political-economic restoration is inseparably tied to spiritual health. Underlying the entire calamity suffered by the nation was a spiralling legacy of sin and an accumulation of guilt. Political health could not be regained until the problem of spiritual disease has been resolved. The unexpected but apt use of a medical metaphor casts the political emergency as an issue of healthcare. Just as a wounded body needs a skilled medic to administer bandages, the disordered nation needs effective leaders to enforce stability. The trouble, then, lies not with the injured person or chaotic populace itself, but rather with foe absence of qualified individuals to restore health or social order.

---

[175] R. E. Clements, "Isaiah 53 and the Restoration of Israel," in *Jesus and the Suffering Servant: Isaiah 53 and Christian Origins*, ed. William H. Bellinger and William R. Farmer (Harrisburg, Pennsylvania: Trinity Press International, 1998), 42.

[176] H. Wheeler Robinson, *Corporate Personality in Ancient Israel*, ed. C. S. Rodd (Edinburgh: T & T Clark, 1981), 37-41.

Chapter 6

Health and Healing in the Post-Exilic Strata of the Book of Isaiah

Introduction

In this chapter, we will study the concept of health and healing in the Post-Exilic period. The study will include Isaiah 19 and 33 in the Post-Exilic time with the evidence of different representations of scholars. It will also study the concept of health and healing in Trito-Isaiah, especially on Isaiah 57 and 58 followed by the text critical note, form, setting and comments on the text.

6.1. Post-Exilic Prophecy

The book of Isaiah includes stories of conflict and war between communities or Nations, spanning from 8 to 6 B.C.E. Stories include the Assyrian threat upon the Northern kingdom (Israel) and Southern kingdom (Judah), the fall of Samaria and Jerusalem to Assyrian empire, the subsequent exile in Babylon, then the period when the Israelites were permitted to return to their homeland under Persian ruler, King Cyrus. Prophets who lived in the eighth century B.C.E. generally undermined the false security of the Israelite people. Isaiah was one among them (7:9; 8:5-8). When the Israelites became established in the Promised Land, they felt secure in their possessions, their victories, their way of doing things, even in their faith. However, from the moment that Israel believed it was "the master of its fate," it began to lose its own soul. It was subtly corrupted by its Canaanite surroundings - compromising with Canaanite gods, customs, and way of doing things. It sought military security by the number of its chariots, political security by alliances with foreign nations (e.g., Assyria, Egypt), and spiritual security by sacrifices offered, on the one hand, to foreign gods (the Baals) and, on the other hand, to God. Thus, the prophet called the people to repentance, to return to

God. Unfortunately, the call was not heeded, and thus judgment followed. The experience of exile in Babylon was declared beforehand by the prophet as God's punishment for iniquities committed by the Israelites, especially by its leaders or decision-makers (3:15), both politically and spiritually.

The context of restoration as witnessed by the Post-Exilic prophets was marked by the struggle of the Israelites to rebuild their homeland, including the temple of Jerusalem as symbol of their religious identity or spiritual life.

Although, certain themes and vocabulary remind us of second Isaiah (and even First Isaiah), the context is clearly different. It is evident that the people are back in their land (i.e., after 515 B.C.E), although it is difficult to know if all or any of the material dates from after rebuilding the Temple (515 B.C.E). If second Isaiah portrayed a magnificent vision of a glorious return, Third Isaiah confronts the harsh reality of conditions after the Restoration and seeks to explain why salvation has not come. Throughout, the prophet maintains a lively sense that God will again intervene in a wondrous way. Hope lies not in the present, but in the eschatological expectation that salvation will come.

The prophets not only use God's saving acts of the past to describe how he will act in the future; they also describe the future kingdom using conventional language and imagery that were appropriate to the place and time in which they ministered. Thus, the portrayal of what God has planned for his people in the kingdom is shaped in many ways by Israel's history and experiences in the Old Testament. Routledge explains:

> The OT points to the glorious future God has prepared for his people, using language and imagery appropriate to those who first announced and received the message. The world view of much of the OT focuses on the physical world, and so future hope is also portrayed in those terms. To describe the overflowing blessings of the coming age to a largely agricultural community, the prophets talk in terms of an abundant harvest. To give assurance to those who for the most of their lives have experienced oppression and injustice, they emphasize God's victory over attacking nations, and future freedom and security. To describe restoration, they talk about the reversal of the tragedies the people have suffered, such as the return of exiles and the future exaltation of Jerusalem. To describe the spiritual renewal of the nation, they again use familiar ideas, and talk about a purified and restored temple, about sacrifices offered sincerely and the meaningful celebration of festivals.[1]

[1] Robin Routledge, *Old Testament Theology: A Thematic Approach* (Downers Grove: InterVarsity Press, 2008), 278-279.

This use of conventional language introduces several complications and tensions regarding the canonical development of the prophetic promises concerning the future.

The aftermath of exile devastated the people beyond repair. The wounds and the bruises of the experiences of exile made the people to lose their hope and be distressed. It was such a time as this that again, their hopes were rekindled and faith renewed and healed through the Post-Exilic prophecies. Keeping this context in mind in this chapter, we will study the understanding of health and healing in the Post-Exilic strata of Isaiah.

6.2. Exegetical Study

6.2.1. Isaiah 19:22

V. 22. And Yahweh will strike Egypt with a plague
smiting and healing, they turn to Yahweh
he will respond to them and heal them.

Form and Setting

Isaiah 19 consists of two very different parts; the first vv. 1-15 is a prophecy against Egypt composed in poetic form; the second vv. 16-25 moves from poetry to prose and from judgment upon Egypt to a sweeping and almost unparalleled promise that all nations will live in harmony because of their common submission to God. The first part depicts the effects of God's visitation upon Egypt in three sections: Political and social confession (vv.1-4); destruction of the entire country by the drying up of the Nile (vv. 5-10); and the futility of Egyptian wisdom (vv.11-15).

The second part consists of six oracles varying length, each introduced by the phrase: The results are pictured with five "in that day" announcements:

(1) Judah will terrorize the Egyptians (16–17);
(2) Five cities will speak a Canaanite language (18);
(3) An altar to Yahweh will be set up in Egypt; Egyptians will worship Yahweh and he will respond to them (19–22);
(4) A highway between Egypt and Assyria; they will cooperate even in worship (23);
(5) Israel, Egypt, and Assyria under Yahweh's rule (24–25).[2]

Many interpreters have attempted to determine the historical background of the two parts, their date of composition, and their function in the overall scheme of Chapters 13-23, which deal with God's judgment on the nations.[3]

---

[2] Joze Krasovec, *Reward, Punishment, and Forgiveness: The Thinking and Beliefs of Ancient Israel in the Light of Greek and Modern Views* (Leiden: Brill, 1999), 526.

[3] Cf. T. K. Cheyne, *Introduction to the Book of Isaiah* (London: A & C Black, 1895). G. B. Gray, *A Critical and Exegetical Commentary on the Book of Isaiah* (Edinburgh: T & T Clark, 1912);

However, the very nature of the political allusion makes it difficult to come to any conclusion regarding the historical setting and the date of the chapter. This is particularly twice of the oracles in prose (19:16-23). As difficult as it is to date the time of this chapter, Isaiah 19:18-25 clearly does not date to the time of Isaiah. It conflicts directly with Isaiah's view of punishment against Egypt so clearly articulated in 18:1-7; Egypt, Israel, and Assyria, with Assyria as the dominant partner, flatly contradicts Isaiah's well-known opposition to Israelite or Judean alliances with foreign powers.[4]

The question of the form and content of Isaiah 19:16-25 have led most commentators to argue against the authorship of this prophetic vision of the future by Israel of Jerusalem.[5] Muthunayagom argues this view rightly too. He opines that in all form critical authentic passages of Isaiah, one sees the element of condition or punishment upon the addressee either as oracles of threat or salvation. However, this element is missing in this oracle of promise. Hence, there is the need to question the authenticity of this oracle.[6]

For Isaiah, God is a universal God who can be accessed by anyone even by the foreign nations. However, in this text the inclusiveness of God is seen "as the presence of God" to Egypt does not go with the conception of Isaiah's understanding of God. Moreover, Isaiah seldom used the Exodus tradition in his oracles in opposition to the author's use of Exodus elements in Isaiah 19:19-22. The classical patterns are God's striking of Egypt and the first Exodus of Israel as a metaphor for a variety of types of a new exodus, the tradition of the conquest of Canaan as image of a new conquest and God's fatherly correction of the rebellious people in order to bring about repentance and new covenant. All these patterns are based on a particular understanding of God, the creator and the ruler of the universe. The composition of the oracles in Isaiah 19:16-25 clearly reflects this theological background, as it is pervaded by the fundamental duality of divine punishment and salvation. Therefore looking at the themes mentioned above, A. S. Herbert writes, there is "an obvious progression of thought from hostility

---

R. B. Y Scott, G. G. D. Kilpatrick, and J. Muilenburg, *The Book of Isaiah* (Nashville: Abingdon Press, 1956).

[4] M. A. Sweeney, *Isaiah 1-39 with an Introduction to Prophetic Literature, Forms and Literature* (Grand Rapids, Michigan: William B. Eerdmans Publishing Company, 1996), 272.

[5] O. Eissfeldt, *Old Testament: An Introduction* (Oxford: E. T. P. R. Ackroyd, 1996); Otto Kaiser, *Isaiah 13-39* (London: SCM Press Ltd., 1980); Scott, Kilpatrick, and Muilenburg, *The Book of Isaiah*, 280 f. In addition, other scholars argue that these prophetic visions could have been originated by the disciples of Isaiah or by an Isaiahnic tradition. S. Erlandsson, *The Burden of Babylon: A Study of Isaiah 13:12-14:23* (Lund: C. W. K. Gleerup, 1970), 79 f.

[6] Daniel Jones Muthunayagom, *The Relationship Between Election and Israel's Attitude Towards the Nations in the Book of Isaiah* (Delhi: ISPCK, 2000), 237.

towards Egypt to a quite extraordinary vision of the whole world united as a people of God."[7]

With regard to the question of the date of composition of the passage, there is no consensus among scholars to have agreed to a period of time in Isaiah's authorship. Scholars have assigned it to various periods from the 8th to the 3rd century B.C.E.[8] The conception of an altar to Yahweh in the centre of Egypt and a sacred pillar on its border led scholars like Duhm, Otto Kaiser and others think of the time in the Greek period, i.e., 2nd century B.C.E.[9] There are also other scholars like H. Wildberger who think that both the style and the content of this part of the chapter would best suit the early or late Persian period.[10] Nevertheless, no attempt to adduce sufficient argument in favour of a particular period has gained broad agreement. One of the difficulties in interpretation lies in the considerable differences in rendering found in some places in the ancient version.[11] Krasovec continues to argue, "a close reading of the text supports those who are primarily concerned with the theological outlook of the passage rather than its historical allusions and accordingly interpret it against the background of the characteristic patterns of biblical typology."[12] However, the concept of the presence of Yahweh seems to have widened its horizon after Ezekiel's vision of the New Temple in chapters 40-48 and Deutero-Isaiah's view that Yahweh is present with his people in Babylon and he will lead them from Babylon (cf. Isa. 40:10f; 41:10f). Zephaniah in Zephaniah 3:11 widens such vision, where all nations shall worship Yahweh, everyone in his own place. Thus, Isaiah 19:9 reflects this view. Therefore, it is likely that a post-exilic date is more appropriate. However, the ascription to Assyria and Egypt of the predicates belonging to chosen Israel suggests that the passage was complied before the end of Persian rule.[13] Therefore, the fifth century is likely to be the period during which this passage would have been composed.

6.2.1.1. Comments on Isaiah 19:22 in relation to Illness, Health and Healing

This text shows the inter-relatedness of smiting and healing. Though the two verbs are of different representation, yet it connotes a relationship of smiting down to newness of life or healing.

---

[7] A. S. Herbert, *The Book of the Prophet Isaiah 1-39* (New York: Cambridge University Press, 1973), 125.

[8] The reason for the emergence of various proposals is the depiction of an altar in Egypt and the covenant relationship of the two warring nations Assyria and Egypt.

[9] Kaiser, *Isaiah 13-39*, 109.

[10] Hans Wildberger, *Jesaja 13-27* (Neukirchener Verlag: Auflage, 1989), 740-746.

[11] Krasovec, *Reward, Punishment, and Forgiveness: The Thinking and Beliefs of Ancient Israel in the Light of Greek and Modern Views*, 527.

[12] Ibid.

[13] Muthunayagom, *The Relationship Between Election and Israel's Attitude Towards the Nations in the Book of Isaiah*, 239.

The term נגף which means to "smite" (Exod. 12:23, 27) and רפא "to heal" (Exod. 3:9) is used most likely to highlight the helpless situation of the people of Egypt under the oppressive regime of a political opponent when this oracle was written. The author's depiction of the helpless situation of Egypt and Yahweh's immediate action of sending a deliverer implies that God's salvific action criterion is not the religio-ethnic factor but human suffering. The antithetic terms of striking/healing, or their synonyms also appears in a few passages elsewhere: Deuteronomy 31:39; Hosea 6:1-2, Isaiah 30:26; 53:5; 57:16-19. Healing alone in the sense of divine forgiveness and restoration is proclaimed in Hosea 14:5; Jeremiah 3:22 but denied in Isaiah 6:10; Hosea 5:13. The first two passages cited are especially illuminating for our treatment of the oracle in Isaiah 19:22. It is obvious that the two antithetic pairs function primarily as a rhetorical and stylistic device expressing the totality of God's sovereignty and power. However, the word also implies the reasons for the opposing divine actions, either punishment of human guilt or healing after repentance.

The word רפא "to heal" in Isaiah 19:22 mean healing no less literal than the effects of God's smiting. This usage is further underscored by the frequent metaphorical descriptions of "sin-sick" Israel as a wounded and diseased body (Is 1:5-6).[14] The Old Testament understanding of healing and sickness reflects God's dealing with the people of Israel. God as the one who smites and heals is reflected throughout the books of the Old Testament. Moreover, given the biblical association between the blessing of God and life and health, sickness serve as an ideal form of divine chastisement, since it clearly indicates that one has strayed from the path of life.[15]

The fact that sickness and disease are literal afflictions reminds that for the ancient Israelite, Yahweh's discipline was not simply envisioned as a spiritual concept or poetic figure of speech. In terminal cases, sickness literally leads to death. In chronic or temporary afflictions, it bears the mark of death. Instead of vigour there is weakness; instead of wholeness there is decay; instead of health there is disease; instead of rest there is pain. Thus, sickness could not only get the attention of the straying sufferer, it could remind one vividly of the error of his or her ways.[16]

The image of sickness and healing are also applied not only to the individuals but also to the nations with the concept of incurable illness. In Isaiah 19 the Egypt pronouncement in verses 1-17 describe the imminent destruction of the Egyptian people and their ultimate subjection to the people of Judah. Then, in verse 18,[17] the prophet foresees the day when the Egyptians, subjugated by the Judeans and

---

[14] Hempel as quoted by, Michael L. Brown, *Israel's Divine Healer* (Grand Rapids: Zondervan, 1995), 20.

[15] Ibid., 146.

[16] Ibid.

[17] Otto Kaiser, *Isaiah 1-39* (Philadelphia: Westminster John Knox Press, 1974), 104.

speaking the language of Canaan, will swear allegiance to the Lord of Hosts. As a result of their crying out to God because of their oppressors, the Lord will send a deliverer and champion and will rescue them in verse 20. Then in verse 21 the Egyptians will know God and worship him. All this is summarized in verse 22 where the Lord will smite and heal. When they turn back to the Lord, he will be entreated by them and will heal them. Significantly, the divine judgments are grouped under the heading "*Yahweh nagap*" יהוה ונגף and the bringing a new into divine favour is characterised by *rephaim* רפאם.

Isaiah 19:22 is perhaps the only prophetic text referring to "real" healing of another nation. Yahweh promises healing to Egypt after their repentance. In this passage one also finds the dual role of Yahweh as the one who both smites and heals

6.2.2. Isaiah 33:24

V. 24. No inhabitant will say
"I am sick";
The people dwelling in it
will be forgiven (any) guilt.

Form Critical Notes

Chapter 33 is a unit by itself and it is an example of the alternating prayers and prophetic oracles which were uttered at the service of entreaty in the temple as referred to in Jeremiah 14, 12;36, 6; Joel 2, 15-17;2 Chronicles 20:3-19; Psalm 12:20; 60;85 and elsewhere.[18]

Yahweh challenges those near and far to "hear" and "know" (v 13). The rest of the episode responds to that challenge, assessing what the results of God's intervention and rebuke will be. Vv 14–16 reflect on the tension inherent in "dwelling with the devouring fire," that is, in depending on and worshiping Yahweh who in his holiness is understood to devour whole nations. This issue was an old one in Israel. Abraham on Moriah (Gen. 22) first faced it. Then Moses wrestled with the issue on Sinai (Exod. 19–34). The liturgies used when entering the temple, where one experienced the presence of the holy God, are dealt with it (Ps. 15; 24:3–6). The answer given here may be compared to the Psalms.

Vv 17–19. Jerusalem is called to imagine what life will be like without the reminders of a life without the terrors of secret police, tax collectors, or strangers with foreign accents, who for more than a century had ruled over them.

Vv 20–22. In a different frame of mind, Jerusalem is called to think of herself as a city preparing for a festival in honour of Yahweh.

Vv 23–24. Return to the political and economic results following the withdrawal of the emperor's representatives.

---

[18] Sebastian Kizhakkeyil, *Isaiah: An Exegetical Commentary* (Bangalore: Asian Trading Corporation, 2006), 218.

Setting

The historical setting is the period, which ended effective Assyrian administration of Judah. The last decades of Assyrian suzerainty were chaotic. Babylon turned back an Assyrian army in 626 B.C.E. Scythian invasions of Palestine during the following decade cloud the picture. Historians have had difficulty determining whose side Egypt was on in these struggles between Babylon and Assyria between 626 and 609 B.C.E. If this is true at this distance, how much more confusing must it have been for those living at that time?

The historical setting of Chapter 33 has proved to be particularly problematic. Scholarly opinion runs the entire gamut of possibilities including the time of Isaiah, the time of King Josiah, the period the Babylonian exile,[19] the Persian period,[20] and the Hellenistic period.[21] The problem is rooted in the liturgical character of the passage and the absence of any definitive historical references. The passage clearly presupposes a situation of threat by a foreign oppressor, but the situation pertains to all the settings suggested above.[22]

Despite the difficulties involved, it seems best to maintain that chapter 33 stems from the Persian period: specifically, it is the product of the 5th century redaction that produced the final form of the book of Isaiah. A variety of considerations support this view, including its portrayal of the oppressor and of Yahweh as king, its liturgical setting, and its literary character as a mirror text within the book of Isaiah. The decisive arguments for the 5th century setting of Isaiah 33, however relate to its literary character and setting. In its present position chapter 33 concludes the first half of the book of Isaiah (chps. 1-33), which contains the announcements of the prophet's oracles concerning the Assyrian period. Insofar as chapter 33 stands as the conclusion of chapters 1-33, and before chapters 34-36, which proclaim the prophet's message for the Babylonian and Persian periods, it is an opportune position to summarize the first part of the book and to anticipate the second part, thereby serving as part of a literary bridge between the book's major component.

6.2.2.1. Comments on Isaiah 33:24 in relation to Illness, Health and Healing

Isaiah 33:23 is believed to be a misplaced oracle somehow found its way here. According to R.E. Clements, verse 23 seems to be misplaced because it does not have any continuity with the previous verse or make any sense in the context.[23]

---

[19] R. E. Clements, *Isaiah* (Grand Rapids, Michigan: William B. Eerdmans Publishing Company, 1980), 265.

[20] Wildberger, *Jesaja 13-27*, 1288.

[21] Kaiser, *Isaiah 13-39*, 342.

[22] Sweeney, *Isaiah 1-39 with an Introduction to Prophetic Literature, Forms and Literature* 429.

[23] Clements, *Isaiah*, 270.

Kaiser is of the opinion that these verses were added either by the apocalyptic author of the rest of the passage or by a later redactor taking up the theme of spoil first mentioned in v. 4 and developing in a new and fantastic direction.[24] Though there is no continuity, yet scholars have tried to figure out some meaning out of it, looking at the symbolism of a wrecked-ship as standing for the enemy. The author of this imagines that the ship that would sail up the river into Judah will get stuck, being unable to sail further and would be plundered with all its treasures. Even the handicapped would be able to share in the plunder and in the spoil. After adding this hope, the author adds further that in the future Zion, there will not be any sick people. This conclusion in 33: 24, is a later addition by a redactor to repair any possible damage caused by 33:23b which speaks of handicapped or sick people in Zion. In the coming age of salvation, sin the root cause of sickness will be removed and none will suffer from any evil any more. None will be sick on that day, or disadvantaged in the division of spoils. There will be a general amnesty for past crimes to celebrate the return of freedom. Hence, the texts attempt to portray a wholistic community where even the sick and the lame will receive healing.

Watts is of the opinion that the episode is an illustration of the close relation between religion and politics in ancient Judah. The event described is political. Assyria must relinquish sovereignty over the city, along with all privileges that it entailed. The result is described in terms of Yahweh's re occupation of the city, its defence, and its economic structure. The episode is also consistent with the vision's position. The futures for Jerusalem and for Israel will not include the reconstitution of the Davidic kingdom. It will bring recognition that Yahweh is present in Jerusalem and may be worshipped there.[25]

There is a new element of considerable interest, which is the promise in Isaiah 33:24. In Isaiah 33:17-24, there contains a contrast between the coming time of security and threats posed by foreign powers, and between the times of sickness and forgiveness. The promise of peace is not very different from the hopes that apparently were expressed regularly in the cult, as the Psalms indicate.[26] The river imagery also is not greatly different from the way it is used in cultic language. However, Isaiah 33:24 introduces something truly eschatological, indicating that this is more than idealizing of the Jerusalem of the present.[27] Most of the passages that deal with the future of Jerusalem are promise of restoration. The picture of the future city of God can be presented without any reference to judgment, destruction, or exile.

The absence of sickness is found in Isaiah 33:24, which reaches a climax as the conclusion of a future prophecy. In this text, we see God's vision of health and

---

[24] Kaiser, *Isaiah 13-39*, 349.

[25] John D. W. Watts, "Isaiah 1-33," in *WBC* (Waco, Texas: Word, 1985), 429.

[26] B. S. Childs, *Isaiah and the Assyrian Crisis* (London: SCM Press Ltd., 1967), 112-117.

[27] Donald E. Gowan, *Eschatology in the Old Testament* (Edinburgh: T & T Clark, 1986), 13-14.

wellbeing in the light of the sick and the lame receiving healing. The reference of the lame is probably important but not as important as the phenomenal promise that there will be no illness in that city. According to Walter Brueggemann, "verse 24 overrides even that good news win verse 23 with the more sweeping assurance that there will be no lame people in the new governance. All disability will be overcome. The new rule of Yahweh will be one complete health, utter forgiveness, full reconciliation, total rehabilitation, life as dreamed by Judah, life as willed by the creator God."[28] The understanding of the wholeness of life is seen here. Thus, we can say that the employment of the image of the sick person as a paradigm of God's healing is seen in this text. It is Yahweh who intervenes directly in human life; his actions display the characteristics either of punishment or of healing; human beings are put to a place where guilt becomes punishment and healing becomes salvation. Such kind of network of associations is based on the paradigm of sickness the prophets had before them, a paradigm worked out by cultic legal theology and theological wisdom ethics. Nonetheless they disremember it even as they embrace it, employ some detail as a partial piece, and thus illuminate it a new with their configuration of reprimand-threat-salvation pronouncement.

6.2.3. Background Study of Isaiah 56-66

Scholars have consistently pointed to the dependence of Trito-Isaiah on Deutero-Isaiah. Scholars like, Mowinckel, Elliger and Bonnard among others have argued that Trito-Isaiah is the product of Deutero-Isaiah's disciple who elaborated upon the message of the master. Jones, Ackroyed and Rendorff point to the influence of Trito-Isaiah in presenting the material concerning First Isaiah.[29] Isaiah 56-66 is less unified than Deutero-Isaiah from the thematic as well as the literary point of view. A new preacher addresses himself to his people in a new situation, after their return to Judah. He follows his predecessor in proclaiming deliverance (cf. 57:14-20; 60-62; 65:16b-25; 66:6-16). This nucleus has, however been expanded by additions dating from different times, and the following themes are treated in it; the people's complaints, the prophet's response with its charges of guilt, a recital of reasons for the present misery and a statement of the conditions for forgiveness and restoration, a confession of guilt, and a proclamation of forgiveness and salvation.[30]

Chapters 56-66 incorporate the remarkable self-contained units that can be characterized, in a very general sense, as a call to repentance (59:1-21; 63:7-64;

---

[28] Walter Brueggemann, *Isaiah 1-39* (Louisville, Kentucky: Westminster John Knox Press, 1998), 266.

[29] Douglas Jones, "The Tradition of the Oracles of Isaiah of Jerusalem," *ZAW* 67 (1955): 226-228. Peter Ackroyd, "Isaiah 1-XII: Presentation of a Prophet," *Vetus Testamentum Supplement* 29 (1978): 16-48.

[30] Krasovec, *Reward, Punishment, and Forgiveness: The Thinking and Beliefs of Ancient Israel in the Light of Greek and Modern Views*, 484.

and 65:1-25). Other sayings are on a smaller scale and they deal with different aspects of retribution, reward and forgiveness. In Isaiah 57:13, the prophet makes use of an antithetical structure to challenge idolaters in ironic terms and to promise blessing to those who take refuge in God. In 57:16-18, the speaker affirms that God will not be angry for ever; Israel was chastised on account of her wickedness, but now God is determined to turn and to bless the people. In the speech of admonition 58:1-14, the prophet is commissioned to proclaim to the disappointed people a conditional promise of blessing. Within the proclamation of salvation in chapter 60, God makes manifest the change in the divine attitude towards Israel. In 61:2 and 63:4, the traditional phrase "the day of vengeance", appears. The idea of God taking vengeance on Israel's oppressors is not made explicit in 61:2, but may be assumed in view of the prophetic vision of a universal divine judgment over foreign nations in 63:1-6. The concluding chapter 66 is a collection of disparate elements that either threaten judgment or declare universal salvation.[31]

While not everyone has accepted Duhm's proposal, it has gained a large measure of support. The reason for this degree of acceptance is clear: the theory succeeds in explaining the manifest differences between this section and the others. Recent study has carried Duhm's conclusion further, affirming that these chapters were not the work of an individual but of a community.[32]

Another important problem that was raised was why are these materials included in Isaiahnic corpus at all? The proposal that it is included because the authors were disciples of Deutero-Isaiah,[33] even if it could be true, still would not solve the dilemma. J. Blenkinsopp comments that there are so many gaps in our knowledge of Judaism in the post-exilic period 'that trajectories of this kind risk being too speculative to be useful."[34]

What was it about these writings, given their apparent differences in outlook from those of the author's supposed mentor, which caused the believing community to attach them to the larger collection?[35]

A historical connection is clearly not enough to say that these chapters have been included with the rest because they form a kind of informal reflection upon Deutero-Isaiahnic writings. The reflections on chapters 40-55 are neither

---

[31] Ibid., 499.

[32] Elizabeth Achtemeier, *The Community and Message of Isaiah 56-66* (Minneapolis: Augsburg Publishing House, 1982), 16; Paul Hanson, *The Dawn of Apocalyptic* (Philadelphia: Fortress Press, 1975), 32-41.

[33] Hanson, *The Dawn of Apocalyptic*, 99.

[34] Joseph Blenkinsopp, *A History of Prophecy in Israel* (Philadelphia: Westminster John Knox Press, 1983), 283-284.

[35] John N. Oswalt, "Righteousness in Isaiah: A Study of the Function of Chapters 55-66 in the Present Structure of the Book," in *Writing and Reading the Scroll of Isaiah in Studies of an Interpretive Tradition*, ed. D. Craig, C. Broyles, and Craig A. Evans (New York: Brill, 1997), 178.

so explicit nor so thorough going as to require, or even to suggest, inclusion with chaps 40-55 in a single book. But chapters 56-66 have been included with the rest of the book, despite their different focus and context, not that they are the reflection on chaps 40-55, which are in turn a reflection on chaps 1-39, but that chapters 56-66 are written in the full knowledge of the entire preceding corpus and function to unify that corpus.[36] Without these corpus chaps 1-39 and 40-55 stands in very serious conflict.[37]

It is generally recognized that modern critical study of Isaiah 56-66 begins with Bernhard Duhm's 1892 commentary on Isaiah. In his ground, breaking work Duhm suggested that the last eleven chapters of the book of Isaiah should be separated from the preceding section (40-55), and should be considered the work of an author living in the mid-fifth century B. C., just before the time of Nehemiah. Although, some have attempted to maintain the unity of authorship of chapters 40-66,[38] majority have followed Duhm in perceiving a significant caesura between chapters 40-55 and 56-66, whilst, at the same time, not denying the elements of continuity between the two sections or the possibility of later editorial activity within chapters 40-55 by the author/authors of Isaiah 56-66.[39]

The primary question concerning whether these chapters should be regarded as the work of one author or of a multiplicity of authors over a greater or lesser period of time is raised. While commentators such as Marti and Box followed Duhm in his ascription of these chapters to one author located in the mid-fifth century B.C.E,[40] it was not until 1928 that this position was agreed in detail. Producing the conclusion that the bulk of the chapters should be ascribed to one author working in the last quarter of 6th century B.C.E. Although, a number of commentators have in general term agreed to this proposal there were before significant voices raised in dissent against this thesis. Paul Hanson does denied the possibility of denying the unity of these chapters in terms of single author. Rather, he sees the unity of the collection in terms of the tradition and historical background of the material.[41]

Over a period, a new material was added in layers around this original nucleus to form the collection as we now have it. The first redactional layer

---

[36] R. E. Clements, "Beyond Tradition History: Deutero-Isaianic Development of First Isaiah's Themes," *Journal for the Study of Old Testament* 31 (1985): 95.

[37] Oswalt, "Righteousness in Isaiah: A Study of the Function of Chapters 55-66 in the Present Structure of the Book," 178.

[38] M. Haram, "The Literary Structure and Chronological Framework of the Prophecies in Isaiah XL-XLVIII," *Supplement to Vetus Testamentum* 9 (1963): 127-128.

[39] P. A. Smith, *Rhetoric and Redaction in Trito-Isaiah: The Structure, Growth and Authorship of Isaiah 56-66* (New York: E. J. Brill, 1995), 1.

[40] G. H. Box, *The Book of Isaiah* (London: Leipzig, 1905), 8.

[41] Paul Hanson, as quoted by, Smith, *Rhetoric and Redaction in Trito-Isaiah: The Structure, Growth and Authorship of Isaiah 56-66*, 2.

emphasized the division of the community between the pious and the apostates. The second was dominated by the theme of judgment against the nations, and was accompanied by a series of apocalyptic additions. Finally, a number of additions at the beginning and the end of collection served to join the two independent complexes chaps 56-58 and 60-66 together, and emphasized with openness of the community to gentiles and the importance of Sabbath observance. In this way, the chapters appear to consist of diverse material referring from pre-exilic oracles of judgment to post-exilic oracles of salvation to later post-exilic apocalyptic additions. This mélange was finally formed into a basically concentric structure around chapters 60-62.[42]

In spite of a dearth of information, Third Isaiah is commonly taken as a Post-Exilic piece of writing. Nevertheless, dating Third Isaiah to the post-exilic period does not exclude the possibility of the use of pre-exilic or exilic material. A reason for writing down pre-exilic prophecy concerning exile and return might be the conviction that this prophecy had been fulfilled (to a certain extent). Such a scenario allows for the possibility or maybe even plausibility (however not probability),[43] of the conservative position that the main part of or even the whole text originates from Isaiah of Jerusalem. Taken a less conservative scenario, it is a moment in the redaction history.[44] Having pointed out the importance of a post-exilic reading of third Isaiah, the Persian period acts as the historical background of this study. While there is a lot of discussion about the dating of specific texts or passages in Third Isaiah, there is very little discussion about the location. Jerusalem is generally accepted as the place of provenance for the text.

6.2.4. Isaiah 57:18-19

V. 18. "I have seen their ways, and will I heal him,
and I will lead them[a] and repay them with comfort,[b]
creating for their mourners the fruit of the lips.
V. 19. "Peace, Peace, to the far and near,
says the Lord; and I will heal them.

Form Critical Notes

This scene ends the act by repeating; "There can be no peace for the adversaries" (cf. 48:22 and 66:24). It combines the very optimistic encouragement to "build a way" with a clear recognition of the apostasy that is rampant. It summarizes the tension between God's anger over sin and his determination to heal his people and

[42] H. Robert O'Connell, *Concentricity and Continuity: The Literary Structure of Isaiah*, Journal for the Study of Old Testament Supplementary, vol. 188 (Sheffield: Sheffield Academic Press, 1994), 215-217.

[43] Izaak J. de Hulster, *Illuminating Images: An Iconographic Method of Old Testament Exegesis with Three Case Studies from Third Isaiah* (Utrecht: The British Museum, 2007), 275.

[44] Ibid., 276.

his city. This passage has sometimes been called as an oracle of salvation. However, the mixture of positive and negative elements hardly fits that genre.

The passage begins with imperatives: "Build up! Prepare!" (v. 14). Here, Yahweh, host to Jerusalem's festival, supports this command with three speeches beginning with כִּי "for, indeed" in vv 15, 16a, 16b. He continues with a complex explanation of his apparent inconsistency (vv 17–18) which makes his invitation and promise possible (vv 19). The scene closes with a disclaimer: that this promise does not apply to "the adversaries" (vv 20–21).[45]

There has been lots of confusion about the time when this was written. The speculation of whether it is Haggai or Zechariah after the death of Zerubbabel? Or is this an unknown leader near the end of Darius's reign or during the reign of Xerxes? (cf. parallel calls in 48:20 and in 52:11–12, although here the object is a highway, as in 40:3–4.). Perhaps the Temple is finished. Preparations are being made for pilgrims to come for festival.

Setting

The four units 56:1-8; 56:9-57:21; 58:1-59:20; 65:1-66:17 are most likely the work of a single author and reflect a developing situation of moral and religious disintegration and division within the early post-exilic community in Jerusalem and Judah. Chapter 56:1-8 is probably the earliest unit in the group, presenting no indication of a division within the community, but setting the promises of salvation in Deutero-Isaiah and Trito-Isaiah within a conditional framework (56:1-2). 58:1-59:20 is addressed to the whole people and assumes no definite division with the people, but does not anticipate the possibility that one might be created when Yahweh intervenes. Thus, the people as a whole are offered another chance to change their ways, upon which will depend their fate when Yahweh comes to judge. The criteria that are used to judge the people are the same as those of 56:1-8, so that the people's salvation and vindication are dependent upon their justice and righteousness.[46] Therefore, given the fact that the situation appears to have developed further with a deep split forming within the community itself, suggests that the situation was becoming ever more hostile and vitriolic.

6.2.4.1. Comments on Isaiah 57:18-19 in relation to Illness, Health and Healing

Isaiah 57:17-19 also portrays Yahweh's healing despite Israel's apostasy. The text depicts Yahweh's anger because of their wicked covetousness, but also emphasises that Yahweh will heal them and "repay them with comfort."

---

[45] John D. W. Watts, "Isaiah 34-66," in *Word Biblical Commentary* (Waco, Texas: Word Books), 262.

[46] Smith, *Rhetoric and Redaction in Trito-Isaiah: The Structure, Growth and Authorship of Isaiah 56-66*, 187.

More specifically, the two of the elements from the language of judgment in v 17 have corresponding counterparts in the restoration section of v 18, which can be presented schematically thus:

(v. 17 "I struck him") - (v. 18 "I will heal him")

(v 17 "he went wandering") - (v. 18 "I will lead him")

The correspondence between "striking" as divine punishment for sin followed by divine "forgiveness" in healing suggests that there might be a similar correspondence between Israel's sinful wandering and the concept expressed by "I will lead him", and consistency of metaphor would seem to require, as God's remedy for "he went wandering, not rest, but divine guidance (e.g., Ps. 5:9, 23:3)." So, the relevant phrases should be rendered: "I struck him . . . but he went wandering ... I will heal him, and I will lead him."[47] In the words of McKenzie commenting on this passage, "The issue of the wrath of Yahweh must not be destruction but healing."[48] In Isa 57:18 we find two words that link the section back to Isaiah 53, namely the verbs רפא, "to heal" and שלום, "to make/give peace." The roots of both these words occur in Isaiah 53:5. In Isaiah 53, it is the suffering of the servant that leads to peace and health. But here in Isaiah 57 that specific way seems to have vanished. Here, Yahweh himself heals and gives peace.

Isaiah 57:14-21 reflects this interplay of punishment and restoration-striking and healing-that are part of Yahweh's effort to redirect human behaviour. Except for the unrepentant wicked in vv. 20-21, Yahweh's goal is restoration of God's people.[49]

That restoration is depicted in term of healing, as well as of providing comfort and peace. Jeremiah 3:6-4:4 speaks of God's disciplinary work with Israel, but also relates God's mercy, generosity, healing and salvation.[50]

Isaiah's reference to *rapha* in 57:18-19, follows God's punitive measures against his disobedient people. The Lord's mercy will cause him to turn back and will say, 'I have seen his ways and will heal him...It shall be well, well with the far and the near..says the Lord... and I will heal him'. Hence, the pronouncement of *shalom* is the result of "I will heal him," in other words, "I will make him whole." Thus, bringing him into a state of *shalom*-complete well being.

---

[47] In the same general context, note Isa. 58: 8 "your wound will be quickly healed, and your vindication will go before you" and Isa. 58: 11 "and Yahweh will guide you always. Here, the connection is between healing and guiding in 57: 18.

[48] J. L. McKenzie, *Second Isaiah* (New York: Doubleday, 1968), 160.

[49] John Goldingay, *Isaiah* (Peabody: Hendrickson, 2001), 324.

[50] Sarah J. Melcher, "With Whom Do the Disabled Associate? Metaphorical Interplay in the Later Prophets," in *This Abled Body: Rethinking Disabilities and Biblical Studies*, ed. Hector Avalos, Sarah J. Melcher, and Jeremy Schipper (Atlanta: SBL, 2007), 119.

6.2.5. Isaiah 58:2-8

v. 2. Yet day after day they seek me
and delight to know my ways,
as if they were a nation that practiced righteousness
and did not forsake the ordinances of their God;
they ask of me righteous judgments,
they delight to draw near to God.
v. 3. "Why do we fast, but you do not see?
Why do we humble ourselves, but you do not notice?
Look, you serve your own interest on your fast day,
and oppress all your workers.
v. 4. Look, you fast only to quarrel and to fight
and to strike with a wicked fist.
Such fasting as you do today
will not make your voice heard on high.
v. 5. Is such the fast I choose,
a day to humble oneself?
Is it to bow down the head like a bulrush,
and to lie in sackcloth and ashes?
Will you call this a fast,
a day acceptable to the Lord?
v. 6. Is not the fast that I choose:
to loose the bonds of injustice,
to undo the thongs of the yoke'
to let the oppressed go free[a]
and to break every yoke?
v. 7. Is it not to share your bread with the hungry,
and bring the homeless poor into your house;
when you see the naked, to cover them,
and not hide yourself from your own kin?
v. 8. Then your light shall break forth like the dawn;
and your healing shall spring up quickly;
Your vindicator shall go before you,
The glory of the Lord shall be your rear guard.[a]
v. 9. Then you shall call, and the Lord will answer;[a]
you shall cry for help, and he will say "Here I am."

Form Critical Notes

The opening reference in v 5 is to אדם "a human being" is carefully portrayed rather than to Israel or Jerusalem. The requirements by Yahweh for worship apply to anyone who seeks him. Then in v 6 the address is in plural addressed to all those who hear him. Vv 7–14 consistently address individuals in 2nd masc. sg, yet they are clearly not always to the same individual, since the content applies appropriately to different persons. These are not spoken to Jerusalem, who is always addressed in the feminine.[51]

The scene has two parts. Vv 1–4 are a dialogue between those on the balcony and those on the lower stage. Vv 5–14 are spoken from the balcony. They are addressed to Israel (cf. v 1) as God's people and to the Persian authority (vv 10–12). The date is about 465 B.C.E.

A close reading of the chapter shows that vv 1–4 (and 6e) address a group in the plural. Vv 5–14 address individuals in the singular. The scene is unified around the subject of worship, specifically the nature and purpose of "the fast" and the will of God. The chapter parallels Zechariah 7 and 8 in theme and content.

This scene is set a half century later than Zechariah 7–8. A temple of sorts has been established in Jerusalem. Worship is performed there regularly, which includes fasting, "inquiring," and praying for justice. However, the result is satisfactory neither to God nor to the worshipers.

What is announced could be applicable to any person seeking Yahweh. This includes the Judean/Israelite worshiper, but it is also applicable to Yahweh's Persian leader. A new king named Artaxerxes has taken the throne in Persepolis. For him, this scene performs the same function that of Isaiah 44:24–45:13 did for Cyrus and Isaiah 49:5–12 did for Darius. All the conditions mentioned here (with the exception of the Sabbath) apply to him, as well as the promised benefits (vv 8–9, 10b–11a, 12, and 14b).

Jerusalem has become a place of violence (cf. 56:9–12; 57:1–10; 59:4). Judean leaders are responsible for that. Their penchant for rebellion and for obtaining personal gain at the expense of the poor runs counter to God's will that they co-operate with Persian authority. In this, the governmental authorities share the blame. So, now the appeal is made both to the worshipers in Jerusalem and to the authorities to recover a sense of order and to establish priorities in their policies.[52]

---

[51] Watts, "Isaiah 34-66," 271-273. Some of the admonitions and promises are suitable to any Judean worshiper. Others are consistent with the kind of promises Yahweh has made to Persian emperors in chaps. 44–45 and 49–52. Some of the admonitions might well fit either of them (v 7a–and v 9). The admonitions that fit Judah are: v 7 "your own flesh;" v 8 "your healing;" v 11 "you will be like a watered garden;" vv 13–14 on Sabbath observance; v 14 "the heritage of Jacob, your father." Those that are fitting to Artaxerxes, the Persian emperor are: v 8 "your light will break forth, v 8 "your legitimacy", and "your rear-guard" which fit the military character of the emperor; v 10 "your light will rise"; v 11 "guide, strengthen" which seem to refer to military campaigns; v 12 "Repairer," "Restorer," which fit the edicts spoken to Cyrus, Darius, and Artaxerxes (see Ezra and Isa. 44:28cd, 45:13c, and 49:8e); v 14 "ride the heights of land," a metaphor for triumph and conquest which fits the emperor.

[52] Ibid.

This stanza 58:6-14 constitutes the second section of the prophet's response to the question raised by the people in v. 3a, and it consists of three parallel strophes (vv. 6-9a, 9b-12, 13-14).

Setting

As a whole, Isaiah 58 may be taken as a rhetorical unit addressed to a section of society composed of people who are sincerely seeking God and genuinely trying to follow ways pleasing God (58:2).[53] The result, however, is a fractured community scarred by discord and discrimination. This situation arises as a consequence of the divorce from the practice of justice.[54]

The structure of the chapter appears in the closing words of 58:5, when the prophet, while underlying the discrepancy between religious observances and social injustice asks, "Is that what you call fasting, a day acceptable to Yahweh?" Then in the rest of the chapter (vv. 6-14), the prophetic voice rhetorically indicates the type of fasting that God chooses (58:6). The thematic center of the chapter is located in this section, in 58:9a, in the promise of God's presence with God's people.

Watts[55] and O'Connell[56] also locate the rhetorical center of Isaiah 58 in v. 9a, specifically in the divine announcement הנני. This is the point in the passage, they argue, that unifies the themes of social justice and God's presence in answer to the question raised in vv. 2 and 3a as to the reason for God's absence and cause for his ignoring the people.[57] Watts, structuring the chapter according to a symmetrical pattern, identifies v. 9 as the keystone that holds together the "arch structure."[58] O'Connell regards the phrase "Here am I' in verse 9a as the "axis…pivot" of the piece.[59] Other scholars lend their assent to this assessment, Brueggemann notes that "Yahweh's presence, attentiveness, and availability are exactly what is hoped for in verse 3", but that they are not manifest until "the ethical conditionality of vv. 6-7"[60] is enacted. The importance Brueggemann invests on v. 9 is reflected in the language he chooses to articulate its meaning. He says that it represents the possibility of "full communion with Yahweh,"[61] a comment which, given his insistence on 'ethical conditionality," strongly suggests that the fullness of God's

---

[53] Goldingay, *Isaiah*, 325.

[54] Thomas L. Leclerc, *Yahweh is Exalted in Justice: Solidarity and Conflict in Isaiah* (Minneapolis: Fortress Press, 1990), 141-142.

[55] John D. Watts, *Isaiah 34-66* (Waco, Texas: Word Books, 1987), 272.

[56] O'Connell, *Concentricity and Continuity: The Literary Structure of Isaiah*, 223.

[57] Mark Gray, *Rhetoric and Social Justice in Isaiah* (New York: T & T Clark, 2006), 73.

[58] Watts, *Isaiah 34-66*, 272.

[59] O'Connell, *Concentricity and Continuity: The Literary Structure of Isaiah*, 223.

[60] Walter Brueggemann, *Isaiah 40-66* (Louisville: Westminster John Knox Press, 1998), 198.

[61] Ibid.

presence is inextricably linked to and cannot be divorced from the practice of justice.

6.2.5.1. Comments on Isaiah 58:2-8 in relation to Illness, Health and Healing

Isaiah 58 is a passage characterized by challenging contrasts. The conduct of the community is contrasted with the intention of the community expressed in their worship.[62] Also contrasted are the interests of the people and the interests of God,[63] righteousness and ritual, and inclusiveness and exclusiveness.[64] These contrasts are introduced with a strong declaration as the prophet calls to shout out, announce with the trumpet the people's rebellion, and sin (v. 1). This strong language indicates that what is to follow is a matter of life or death.[65]

The fact of the matter of life or death is addressed to the community of Israel. Their significant problem described in vv. 2-5 appears on the surface to be a discussion of fasting, yet in reality the issue is much deeper and goes to the core of faith. Stated most simply, the fasting of the people is not strengthening their connection with God. From the people's perspective, God is not responding to their pious efforts at fasting (v. 3). They are looking for a "quick fix" through their religious observance of fasting while ignoring the more challenging religious discipline of care for one's neighbour. The religious practices such as fasting and observing the Sabbath are meaningless unless accompanied by work for a just and compassionate social order.[66] New beginning and personal restoration are offered as key promises when the true fest is observed.[67] The true fast and the desired Sabbath observance both nurture and reflect a right relationship with God. The right relationship reflected in a true fast represents the paradox of what one must give up to pursue righteousness and justice. J. Alec Motyer rightly points out that,

> A true fest is for correction of inhuman conditions, banishing mischief-making and meeting needs and it results in clear guidance in life's perplexities, renewal, durability, ever-fresh resources, restoration

---

[62] Ibid., 186.

[63] Paul D. Hanson, *Isaiah 40-66. Interpretation for Teaching and Preaching* (Louisville: Westminster John Knox Press, 1995), 204.

[64] Walter Brueggemann, *Using God's Resources Wisely: Isaiah and Urban Possibility* (Louisville: Westminster John Knox Press, 1993), 61.

[65] Brueggemann, *Isaiah 40-66*, 186.

[66] Joseph Blenkinsopp, *Isaiah 56-66: A New Translation with Introduction and Commentary* (New York: Doubleday, 2003), 88.

[67] J. Alec Motyer, *Isaiah: An Introduction and Commentary* (Downers Grove: InterVarsity Press, 1999), 362.

and continuance. What seems like deprivation—fasting—is actually enrichment when used according to God.[68]

Therefore, such an approach allows us to think of the mutual obligation of humanity and create awareness for the health and well being of others. Economics and the distribution of the basic resources for life are dimensions of the justice issues in Isa 58:4-5, which also includes health care and opportunities for health, food, and clothing.

After the description of the type of fasting that leads to violence, oppression, and disorder in verse 4, Oswalt notes that this negative and destructive manifestation of a supposedly religious event is linked to it's positively presented corrective means of two similar rhetorical questions. He observes that "verse 5 ended with a rhetorical question that made plain that people's vision of fasting was not God's vision" and argues that "God's vision" is introduced "through another rhetorical question."[69] Therefore, the concluding and condemnatory formulation in v.5 is hooked to its introductory and emphatically positive counterpart in v.6 after which the content of the type of fasting chosen by God is substantiated. Therefore, Westermann writes, "the remarkable accumulation of different ways of expressing one single act of proper fasting…shows that, in the eyes of the speaker here, of all the conceivable acts of help, one loosing from bonds and setting men [*sic*] free was of supreme importance."[70]

This sense of determined impetus of liberation in Isaiah 58:6 reaches a fitting climax in נתק, the very forceful form of which, meaning to "tear apart", concludes the verse. The relentless insistence on the need for freedom built up by the rhetorical deployment of פתח, נתר, שלח in relation to various dimensions of freedom's embodiment fittingly culminates in the summary statement that the ultimate purpose of all this liberative activity is the shattering of every yoke.[71] The image of the yoke being shattered, however, does not always bring beneficial consequences and is not always positively viewed.[72] However, in this context, the passage should be seen as a community that stands on the far side of exile,

---

[68] Ibid.

[69] John Oswalt, *The Book of Isaiah: Chapters 40-66* (Grand Rapids, Michigan: William B. Eerdmans Publishing Company, 1998), 502.

[70] Claus Westermann, *Isaiah 40-66* (Philadelphia: Westminster John Knox Press, 1969), 337.

[71] This type of power implied in use of the term is reflected in that it was chosen to depict Samson's breaking of the cords that bound him in judges 16:9 and 12.

[72] Quite the reverse is the case in Jer. 2:20, in which God after breaking the yoke of the people and bursting their bonds is met by the response "I will not serve you". Further in Jeremiah 5:5 Israel is portrayed as shattering the yoke and bursting the bonds of God's commandments in order to break away from God. This state of affairs resulted in the disgrace of depravity. However, in Jeremiah 30:8, using the same terminology, God promised to break the yoke off the neck of the people and to burst their bonds, so that strangers would "no more make a servant of the people." A similar rhetorical pattern is found in Psalm 107, in which, in terminology much like that of Is 42:7

whereby, they passionately appeal for freedom. A people who had an experience and memory of "the yoke" of exile themselves and who further, had felt that yoke broken by God in their release from captivity, they should have been the people committed to maintaining and extending the freedom of others, especially the freedom of their neighbours. Westermann agrees that, "There can be no doubt that this is to be understood as a direct repercussion of what the entire nation had experience of, bondage in exile."[73]

Verse 7 is linked to verse 6, where in both the cases starts with the negative interrogative הלוא, but where as 58:6 focuses on the actions that precede and eventuate in liberation (loosening, undoing, letting go, breaking), those who have been released. Liberating the oppressed without also providing their resources for life is an incomplete exercise likely to lead to a little long substantive change in the condition of the poor.[74]

Thus, Isaiah 58 in its context strongly suggests that, in such kind of conditions, it is in acts of solidarity such as breaking of bread with the oppressed, performing a sign of hope on the journey toward their freedom from hunger will establish a social cohesion. This is true in the words of Calvin who appropriately points out, "it is not enough to abstain from acts of injustice, if thou refuse thy assistance to the needy."[75] Whybray also echoes this view when he observes, "the rescue of the oppressed is to be followed by positive actions."[76] The health and well being of the community does not come from ignoring our social responsibilities towards the poor and the oppressed but is possible only when radically participate and interact with the well being of the society.

In Isaiah 58:8 the word for healing is *arukah*, ארוכה and refers to the repairing of a wound.[77] What is being restored here is the covenant relationship with God. The use of this word for healing indicates that those being addressed have been wounded by their own self-righteousness, which has allowed them to ignore the poor and oppressed. Their ignorance not only denied the poor the opportunity to receive a compassionate response but also denied themselves the opportunity for health that comes from the covenant relationship with God. Sawyer suggests that the healing talked about in Isaiah 58:8, literally referring "to the new skin that

---

and 61:1, the psalmist records that 'some sat in darkness and the deepest gloom, prisoners suffering in iron chains, for they had rebelled against the words of God" (vv. 10-11).

[73] Westermann, *Isaiah 40-66*, 337.

[74] Blenkinsopp, *Isaiah 56-66: A New Translation with Introduction and Commentary*, 179-180.

[75] H. John Calvin, *Commentary on the Book of the Prophet Isaiah*, trans. William Pringle, 4 vols. (Grand Rapids, Michigan: William B. Eerdmans Publishing Company, 1948), 233.

[76] R. N. Whybray, *Isaiah 40-66: New Century Bible Commentary* (Grand Rapids, Michigan: William B. Eerdmans Publishing Company, 1981), 215.

[77] Ibid., 216.

grows over the wound"[78] means restoring them into a new human being. This view is also supported by Claus Westermann[79] and Whybray.[80] Isaiah 58:8 articulates a form of proto-kenotic theology in which healing of 58:8 comes through standing in solidarity with and sharing the pain of the disadvantaged.[81]

The mandates of these verses are the condition for what follows; an implicit "if" is followed in verse 8-9 by a double, explicit "the" as condition to consequence. The first "then" of verse 8 anticipates immense well being, here identified as light, healing, protection and safety.[82] Therefore, the fullness of God's presence is linked with the practice of justice. Hanson observes that,

> Persons who have thus experienced the restoration of human community through the practice of justice urged in 6-7 find that they have simultaneously become reconciled with God. Healing encompasses all aspects of their existence...In contrast to those who complained bitterly amidst their fasting that God did not hear them, those who have directed their attention to the needs of their neighbours in need find that God is present with them (v.9).[83]

The obedience of both individual and community is required to receive the blessings offered in Isaiah 58; obedience to God's righteousness leads to health and well-being for all. This theme is repeated throughout the OT. When the people of Israel follow God's word and law, they experience health, and when their behaviour defies God's word and law, they experience illness (Exod. 15:26).[84] Within the community, it is those with power who are particularly singled out in Isaiah 58.[85]

6.2.5.1.1. 'Neighbourliness and Community Solidarity' leads to Complete Well Being

At the heart of this passage is a plea for neighbourliness[86] and community solidarity. According to Hanson, "The appeal is an impassioned one to the

[78] John F. A. Sawyer, *Isaiah*, 2 vols. (Philadelphia: Westminster John Knox Press, 1984), 173.

[79] Westermann, *Isaiah 40-66*, 338.

[80] Whybray, *Isaiah 40-66: New Century Bible Commentary*, 216.

[81] Matthew L. Lamb, *Solidarity with Victims: Toward a Theology of Social Transformation* (New York: Crossroad, 1982), ix-xv, 1-27.

[82] Brueggemann, *Isaiah 40-66*, 190.

[83] Paul D. Hanson, *Isaiah 40-66, Interpretation: A Bible Commentary for Teaching and Preaching* (Louisville: Westminster John Knox Press, 1995), 206.

[84] John Wilkinson, *The Bible and Healing: A Medical and Theological Commentary* (Edinburgh: The Handsel Press Ltd., 1998), 14.

[85] Kwesi Dickson, "He is God Because He Cares," *International Review of Missions* 77, no. 306 (1998): 229, 231.

[86] Brueggemann, *Isaiah 40-66*, 186.

heart of the community. It is a plea to reclaim authentic humanity replacing cold, calculating self-interest with acts of loving-kindness that restore genuine communal solidarity."[87] One example of the conflict between self-interest and community solidarity is demonstrated in the inconsistency of making oneself hungry through fasting, while ignoring the hunger of others.[88] The people of Israel are being challenged to put the interests of the other above the interests of self, and in so doing to reap God's fall blessings that will lead to complete well-being for both individuals and the community.

Walter Brueggemann suggests the following responses on the part of those in power to undo the hunger, homelessness, and nakedness addressed in Isaiah 58. According to him,

> Bread needs to be shared with the hungry, which means either getting more to share or eating less. The homeless need to be brought into your house, which means either getting a bigger house or sharing the available space. The naked need to be clothed, which means either getting more clothes or sharing some of your own. A true fast pleasing to God requires sacrifice, but it is not only about what one denies self but also about what one actually does for others.[89]

Here, the relationship between health and justice and righteousness is pointed out. According to Alistair Campbell, "Health is not to be found by a grasping for advantage over others in an effort to insulate oneself against life's maladies: on the contrary, it is those who risk their own security to protect the neediest and most vulnerable that may hope to find some ways of living with their own vulnerability and finitude."[90] Christopher R. Seitz also points out that righteousness *(sédâqâ)* and justice *(mispät)* are key words in Isa 58[91] and a logical consequence of a community built on neighbourliness and solidarity. The people of Israel are being called to replace their self-righteousness with God's righteousness. That involves reaching out through acts of compassionate justice

[87] Hanson, *Isaiah 40-66, Interpretation: A Bible Commentary for Teaching and Preaching,* 206.

[88] John Oswalt, *The Book of Isaiah* (Grand Rapids, Michigan: William B. Eerdmans Publishing Company, 1998), 506.

[89] Walter Brueggemann, *Using God's Resources Wisely: Isaiah and Urban Possibility* (Louisville: Westminster John Knox Press, 1993), 67. Sincere, genuine belief in God requires neighborliness demonstrated in an authentic faith leading one to care for the poor, the homeless, and the afflicted. To be in covenant relationship with God is to be in relationship with one's neighbor, and it is impossible to be in meaningful relationship with one's neighbor without being concerned about their well-being. Isaiah 58 makes it clear that love of God and love of neighbor are inseparable.

[90] Alastair Campbell, *Health as Liberation: Medicine, Theology and the Quest for Justice* (Cleveland: Pilgrim, 1995), 44.

[91] Christopher R. Seitz, "Isaiah 40-66," in *The New Interpreters Bible* (Nashville: Abingdon Press, 2001), 498.

to include those who are marginalized and excluded by society.[92] John Wilkinson identifies righteousness that is understood as right relationship with God, self, others, and creation. He considers this relationship as of the characteristics of health throughout the Old Testament.[93] In this particular text, right relationships with the poor, the oppressed, the afflicted, and God are highlighted.

6.2.5.1.2. 'Justice and Righteousness' as Health

God's sense of justice reflected in vv. 6-7 requires care for the individual as well as addressing the social structures that create injustice. A response is required that addresses the root causes of inequity and restores the justice and righteousness that God desires for all, which will ultimately strengthen the health of the community.[94]

Healing is the restoration of health; consequently, one way to gain an understanding of health in biblical texts is to look at what is being restored when healing is referenced.

In addition to the explicit promise of the restoration of health, well-being is further described in images of light, having strong bones, abundant water, and the care of God, which are all characteristics of health. Listening to these, promises and the vivid images provide and help us sensitize the experience of well-being. Acting towards the poor and the afflicted with compassion and justice restores harmony with others and with God and will lead to individual and communal health and healing. Thus, Hanson rightly states that, "Acts of compassionate justice build up community, and those who participate in such rebuilding find that they have been reconciled with God and that healing and wholeness has been restored to their lives."[95] The vivid image of repairer of the breach and restorer of streets from Isaiah 58 should be looked from the perspective of sickness and illness being healed and repaired.

Health and community well-being is illustrated in Isaiah 58. The text implies that it is a community experience rather than an individual one, motivated by neighbourly attentiveness and compassionate justice.[96] This is in tune with the biblical understanding of health, which demands that we be concerned about the health of all. Therefore, "The future of the city, Jerusalem hinges on a rigorous either/or: either redeployed resources according to God's large passion for the

---

[92] Hanson, *Isaiah 40-66, Interpretation: A Bible Commentary for Teaching and Preaching,* 204-205.

[93] Wilkinson, *The Bible and Healing: A Medical and Theological Commentary*, 13-14, 19-20.

[94] The route to well-being in Isa 58 is based on neighborliness and community solidarity that leads to the pursuit of righteousness and justice. Right relationship with others and God is central to the health and well-being of both the individual and the community as a whole. When relationships are right then health may be restored and well-being experienced.

[95] Hanson, *Isaiah 40-66. Interpretation: A Bible Commentary for Teaching and Preaching*, 206.

[96] Brueggemann, *Isaiah 40-66*, 191.

hungry, homeless and naked—or endless self-serving that yields no communion, no light, no vindication, no healing, no water, no feeding, no delight, no nothing."[97] People must have experienced considerable human distress deriving from exclusion from the temple cult and isolation from the community as well as the physical suffering itself. The traditional thought of illness as God's punishment for past sins most likely induced one into condemning the patients without considering divine purpose in their suffering. The attitude of the community toward the patient was certainly influenced for the most part by the dominant religious ideology with its law of behaviour-consequence throughout the entire history of ancient Israel and furthermore by the interests of the priestly class who controlled the assignment of the degrees of purity in Israelite society in the post-exilic period.

Summary

In many passages, there is an interplay between metaphors of punishment and healing, an interaction found in Isaiah 19:22 and also in Isaiah 57:14-21. In these it reflects the interplay between punishment and restoration, striking and healing, that are a part of Yahweh's efforts to redirect human behaviour. Yahweh's goal is to restore his people to those who repent and turn to him. That restoration is depicted in terms of healing as well as providing comfort and peace. Post-Exilic Isaiah's rendering of *rapha* in 19:22, as well as in chapter 57, indicates that forgiveness of sins could be seen as a divine healing act. None the less, it is useful to observe that the concept of forgiveness and restoration is combined in the prophetic usage of *rapha*.

Trito-Isaiah's message in 58:2-8, with the usage of *arukah* invites us to call that health and healing is possible only when we practice justice and righteousness. It is through the compassion of God seeking justice, including of God being and with the suffering, that the Israelites would be healed and transformed to be responsible subjects religiously, politically and socially. By realizing and implementing God's righteousness or justice, the painful experience of exile, including being condemned as consequence of their iniquities, would be healed. The experience of exile is considered as an experience of being in restlessness, movement, being constantly unsettled and unsettling others. This means that exile could be an opportunity of transformation both individually and socially to experience and realize God's righteousness, God's justice and God's healing.

---

[97] Brueggemann, *Using God's Resources Wisely: Isaiah and Urban Possibility* 75. In Isa 58 the impact described is not on the poor themselves but on those who care for the poor with compassion and justice. The same is true for us. Care about the health and well-being of the poor is not only for their benefit. Our own well-being is ultimately dependent on our compassionate and just response to the needs of the other. The route to well-being in Isa. 58 is based on neighborliness and community solidarity that leads to the pursuit of righteousness and justice. Right relationship with others and God is central to the health and well-being of both the individual and the community as a whole. When relationships are right then health may be restored and well-being experienced.

Chapter 7

Analysis of Health and Healing in the Light of the Prophetic Understanding of *Rapha, Arukah, Shalom* and *Marpe*

Introduction

The prophets like Hosea, Isaiah and Jeremiah raised their critiques for the purpose of helping the Israelites to find healing. They "sought to bring the people to realize that at the depth of the catastrophes which shook their lives and brought intense suffering, God was present, providing the impulse for the return from a road leading to ruin and offering a new life."[1]

The prophets show us a God angry not because the legalistic scales of justice have been unbalanced. Rather, God is angry because the interpersonal dynamics of just relationships have been violated by oppression and violence. "God's concern is the prerequisite and source of [God's] anger. It is because [God] cares for [humans] that [God's] anger may be kindled against [humans]." God's anger and God's mercy are not in conflict but are directly related, both stemming from God's will to heal the world.[2]

W. McKane is of the opinion that, 'the hope of the prophets of Israel is summed up in one word: restoration."[3] The prophets saw God strike, break, tear, and afflict his people. They longed for the day when he would bring healing

[1] Bernhard W. Anderson, *The Eighth-Century Prophets: Amos, Hosea, Isaiah, Micah* (Minneapolis: Fortress Press, 1978), 34.

[2] Ibid., 82.

[3] W. McKane, *Commentary on Jeremiah*, vol. 1: 1-XXV (Edingburgh: T & T Clark, 1985), 10-11.

to Israel's wounds.[4] Religious apostasy had carried sickness, death, immorality, injustice, military defeat, economic chaos, famine, exile in its wake. Repentance and turning back to the Lord would bring health, life, victory, security, plenty, and resettlement to a humbled and submissive people.

The prophetic dream was to restore and heal the land and the people. As H. M. Wolf notes:

> The most remarkable descriptions of curse reversals in the Hebrew Bible appear in those passages in the prophets that deal with the restoration and rebuilding of Israel after a long period of shame and disgrace in exile. The once-battered nations now achieve a level of prosperity and blessedness that more than compensates for her great suffering and degradation. The curses of famine, disease, and war give way to unprecedented blessings of health, fruitfulness and peace.[5]

The prophetic literature of the pre-exilic, exilic and post exilic times was a time for corrective subversive alternative to the pre-dominant idea that health and healing was something very physical, but prophetic understanding corrected the notion that health and healing is not just physical but also spiritual, emotional, relational, ecological. Therefore, the prophetic literature is not just important for the study in the context of that time but has a big relevance of this time where relationships are broken, ecological crisis is at high risk, injustice prevails, violence and fear grips the health of the individual and community. In such a context which is so similar to the context of the prophets, the prophetic oracles have a significant relevance for our times. The call is to understand health and healing from a wholistic point of view.

7.1. *Rapha, Arukah, Shalom* and *Marpe* and the Prophets

Central to the prophetic concept of restoration was the root *Rapha*, occurring twenty nine times in verbal forms and nine times in nominal forms in the prophetic literature. Clearly, this prophetic usage of *Rapha* was anything but spiritualizing, neither was it to be understood merely as a poetic figure of speech. In the prophetic mentality, the healing of a devastated and broken nation was no less real-and in that sense literal-than healing of a sick body, nor were the reversals

---

[4] According to W. Rudolph (as restated by McKane), "there is a temporal order of doom and then salvation: the prophet is instructed that he must first false ideas and corrupt institutions; lies must be exposed and wrongs rooted out. It is a time for demolition, or a time for drastic action to kill the weeds and clean the ground. Rebuilding can only be done from the foundations, or a time of barrenness must be endured before there can be a return to fruitfulness" (Jer. 11). Although, McKane finds this interpretation of Jeremiah 1:10 "too tidy to be true", but it is both exegetically as well as historically accurate.

[5] H. M. Wolf, "The Transcendent nature of the Covenant Curse Reversals," in *Israel's Apostasy and Restoration*, ed. A. Gileadi (Grand Rapids, Michigan: Baker, 1988), 321.

of divine judgment-seen as divine exploits of salvation and deliverance-conceived of as merely spiritual acts or poetic figures. One could no more convince an eight-century B.C. or a sixth century B.C. Judean that his promised of healing was to be understood figuratively than one could convince him that the wounds and injuries inflicted on him by the fierce Assyrian or Babylonian army were figurative. The literality of the promised restoration would have to be just as real as the literality of the threatened judgment.

Yet this fundamentality is often missed by the modern readers when we talk about health and healing. An artificial dichotomy between literal and figurative healing has been constructed, a dichotomy seen in major Theological Dictionaries and leading Biblical Commentaries. Thus, A. Oepke, in treating the LXX usage of *iaomai* in his article in TDNT, distinguishes between "God the healer (in the literal sense),"[6] grouping instances of physical healing in the Old Testament under the first division, while everything is cited under the figurative heading. In fact, Oepke is convinced of the Old Testament origin of this latter sense that he states,

> In some measure under Old Testament influence, the figurative use of the terms came into its own again. Actually with regard to biblical usage, the reverse is true. When *Rapha* and its synonyms occur in the Hebrew Scriptures, they primarily refer to the literal making whole of a broken, or sickly condition, be it a body, a city, an inanimate object, or people.[7]

All three of the prophetic books of Hosea, Isaiah and Jeremiah are structured so as to underscore God's over arching healing love. Each book directly presents God as seeking health and healing, but also-in its overall structure-makes clear that the portrayal of anger and wrath is serving a rhetorical strategy meant to foster trust in the people a loving, patient, and healing God.

In the course of this study, I have explored the social connotations of the metaphor of illness, health and healing in the context of socio-historical dynamics in the Pre-Exilic, exilic and Post-Exilic period. The key background assumptions about illness and healing in Hosea, Isaiah and Jeremiah were investigated in the broad context of Ancient West Asia such as Egypt and Mesopotamia and in the Old Testament. For this investigation, a few categories with respect to illness and healing, which commonly appear in the societies of comparison, were selected; the concept of illness and healing, healing treatment, social situation of patients and most importantly illness etiology. The etiology of illness is more important in that it is the primary basis for a healing treatment that patients and consultants

---

[6] A. Oepke, *"iaomai"* TDNT 3:201-202. With the exception of Ezek. 47-48, where the LXX renders *Rapha* with related forms of *hugiazō*, *Rapha* is elsewhere rendered with *iaomai* or its derivatives.

[7] Michael L. Brown, *Israel's Divine Healer* (Grand Rapids, Michigan: Zondervan, 1995), 185.

will follow. Illness was mainly considered caused by the invasion or attack of foreign agents like supernatural beings.

In this respect, it is argued that while on the surface level it indicates physical or mental malfunction, in the Ancient West Asia illness fundamentally implies disharmony with the transcendental realm regardless of whether sin is involved or not. Even the natural occurrence of illness was ultimately attributed to supernatural beings. Hence, for therapy the restoration of harmonious relationship with the supernatural beings was required. Such harmonious relationship could be achieved by expelling the harmful agents or removing their influence from the body.

In ancient Israel dominated by monotheistic ideology, illness fundamentally implied the disrupted relationship with Yahweh. Illness arose mainly from Yahweh's punishment for sins or occasionally from Yahweh's mysterious motives. For healing, that is, restoration of the harmonious relationship with Yahweh, there was no need to identify which supernatural agents struck the body. Yahweh was the only controller or source of illness and healing. Hence the value of the prophets, who were the only legitimate healing consultants, consisted primarily in their personal relationship with Yahweh, not on their own technical proficiency. In the monolatrous system, prayer was the safest therapeutic option, making it unnecessary to identify who is the controller of illness. Prayer to Yahweh through repentance removed the bad influence of Yahweh or the attack of other supernatural beings under his control. The notion of illness and healing in terms of the invasion of foreign agents and the restoration of an intimate relationship with Yahweh through their removal respectively served as the interpretation of the metaphor of illness and healing in the prophetic texts.

Health which is understood today in line with modern medicine as physical health should not be overlooked with how the prophets have tackled with the issue in terms of not only physical but also of the wholistic aspect. The term health is often used to carry an implied value, namely, that health is good and that lack of health is bad, or should be prevented. Even more significantly, the concepts and conditions of health and disease historically have reflected social values. The human life which is interrelated and intertwined cannot be but one effecting the health of an individual. Martin Luther king's statement, "whatever affects one directly, affects all indirectly. I can never be what I ought to be until you are what you ought to be. This is the interrelated structure of reality."[8] Such statement appears to be appropriate to the context of health and well-being.

The prophetic understanding of health and healing is defined in the way in which the different metaphors were used to reflect upon the grave social realities of the life of the people and how that can be healed or restored in people's response to God's repeated calls of warning and repentance.

[8] Martin Luther King, *Strength to Love* (Philadelphia: Fortress Press, 1963), 70.

In certain prophetic texts, רפא is used for healing of sin and apostasy, presupposing the figure of sin as a serious illness (Jer. 3:22, Hos. 14:3). Thus Israel's unfaithfulness, waywardness, backsliding is a dangerous condition that only God can cure. In this case, the translation of heal is to be retained although it is acceptable to speak of figurative usage here, since the specific object of רפא is abstract (viz., the people's sinful condition pictured as an illness rather than the people and nation pictured as ill.[9]

Frequently, the prophets used רפא in terms of divine restoration for the nation after a time of judgment and chastisement (Isa. 6:10; Jer. 30:17; Hos. 5:13; 6:11). The prophets especially used רפא 'to heal' in relation to wounds, ulcers, and injuries as usages for the critical status of the people (Hos. 5:13).[10] To speak of this usage as figurative or spiritual can also be misleading, since the reality of the promised restoration had to be just real as that of devastating judgments inflicted. That is to say, the literality of the healing had to correspond to the literality of smiting. While it is true that the prophets could describe Israel as a sin-sick people needing healing (Isa. 1:4-7) and while their emphasis was certainly on repentance and reconciliation, they knew that there were serious consequences to sin, including social upheaval, military defeat, economic collapse, famine, plague, the destruction of the temple, war, and even exile and captivity. For the prophets, the promised healing would have to be equally comprehensive and in this sense, hardly figurative.[11]

The metaphorical images used by Isaiah (ex., Isa. 30:26) were not just as a beautiful poetry but they offered a concrete promises for a people whose condition at times appeared terminal. The metaphorical imagery powerfully expresses through vivid figures such as Israel's new skin arising (Jer. 30:17, 33:6), a physician applying healing balm (Jer. 8:22; 46:11; 51:8; Is 1:6) must be seen as inclusive and not exclusive. Healing of physical disease was not excluded from the wider metaphor of national healing and restoration.[12] Therefore, to say that the prophetic usage of רפא was metaphorical is not to say that it was merely figurative or spiritual in nature. The hope of the prophets was nothing less than the whole human wholly healed.

7.2. *Rapha, Arukah, Shalom* and *Marpe* in the Pre-Exilic Times

As discussed in the previous chapters, that the pre-exilic period was the period of economic prosperity and social dependability. But it was also the time where the

---

[9] Alan Kam Yau Chan, Thomas B. Song, and Michael L. Brown, "*Rapha*," in *New International Dictionary of Old Testament Theology and Exegesis*, ed. Willem A. VanGemeren (Grand Rapids, Michigan: Zondervan Publishing House, 1997), 1165.

[10] H. J. Stoebe, "*Rapha*," in *Theological Lexicon of the Old Testament*, ed. Ernst Jenni and Claus Westermann (Peabody, Massachusetts: Hendrickson Publishers, 1997), 1257.

[11] Chan, Song, and Brown, "*Rapha,*" 1166.

[12] Ibid.

sick role played an important part especially for the poor peasants at the hands of their oppressive rulers.

In a context where the nation had access to wealth and prosperity had led them to deny God and their responsibilities towards the life of another. The socio-economic context was syncretized with the foreign nation as a result of which Israel no longer maintained the health of the people nor did they seek God. Rather, they have turned their allegiance to foreign nations and have established a nation that is inflicted by serious illness.

Hosea in such a time as this uses the image of metaphorical languages to denote sickness and health. Hosea uses pictures of sickness and sores to illustrate the effects of invading forces on the territories of Ephraim and Judah (5:8-15). Hosea depicts Israel as a body eaten by larvae and decay (5:12), about to be torn by a vicious lion (5:14). The prophet's message of God being the only healer is to be seen. Yahweh who is the one that has inflicted maladies needs to turn back to the nation's great physician. The stark reality of both Israel's affliction and its promised restoration cannot be over emphasized. Hence, according to Brown to translate these in graphic terms like, larvae, decay, disease, sores, tear, smite, heal, bind up and cure into mere poetic figures would be thoroughly unbiblical.[13] Because they do entail real suffering, hardship, deprivation, starvation, war, disease and exile, to be followed by relief, resettlement, and healing. While it is true that the prophetic usage of these terms is, to a great extent, metaphorical, it should be stressed again that it is extremely misleading to reduce them to a non-tangible, poetic figures.[14]

It might have been better to state that Hosea's understanding of "illness" and "sores" connotes miseries afflicted by an enemy, along with merely human illness. That is to say, the "metaphorical" prophetic usage of רפא is understood to be inclusive and not exclusive. While it may not focus on literal healing of corporeal ailments, it certainly does not exclude that. As expressed by H. K. Nielsen "The prophet certainly spoke symbolically regarding this verse; however, the words also have validity in the case of real sickness."[15]

Hosea also pictured restoration in terms of healing. The matching verbs 'heal' and 'bandage' in Hosea is used to refer to the eschatological reference. By citing this, Hosea refers explicitly to Yahweh's ability to punitively strike out or to heal. Such understanding is also used in other prophetic where passages of this pattern of punishment and restoration for God's people, is associated with "healing" as a primary metaphor of restoration. (Jer. 33:1-3; Hos. 6:4-7; 11:1-2:1), and so on.

[13] Brown, *Israel's Divine Healer*, 187.

[14] Ibid.

[15] H. K. Nielsen as quoted by, Ibid., 188.

The word Rapha is used in Hosea as to forgive, and in its creational dimensions as to practice justice and righteousness (14:5).[16] Here we see the interrelationship between *Shalom* and justice. Health which connotes more than a physical well-being is *Shalom,* the vision of harmony in social order as well as in the created order. Whatever establishes wholeness and harmony in the social order and political community works for health. For John Wilkinson justice and righteousness are considered as one of the characteristics of health throughout the Old Testament. He identifies righteousness as right relationships with God, self, others, and creation.[17] In this right relationships with the poor, the oppressed, the afflicted, and God are highlighted. The right relationship reflected in a true fast represents the paradox of what one must give up to pursue righteousness and justice. Righteousness in the sense of a right relationship to a right standard is basic to the Old Testament concept of health. Thus, the illness which heightens the broken relationship with God is forgiven through the healing of the corporate heart that produces the healing of the corporate body.

It has often been said that healing is not an event, but a journey. Healing is ultimately the repairing and developing of relationships with God, with others, with ourselves and with the world and society in which we live. Thus, healing is the ongoing resource which will enable us to walk this path where we will grow into wholeness. Moltmann points out that because humanity plays the key role in the ordering of God's world, human reconciliation and healing will lead ultimately to the restoration of creation just as human's broken relationship with God lead to creation's fall.[18] Thus, the image of the cure of sickness is applied metaphorically in Hosea to the nation which was ravaged by misfortunes, is capable of full restoration of health. The vocabulary and the particular expressions of this usage are from an examination of the context, properly interpreted of sickness and healing.

Analysis of the texts revealed that the prophet Hosea's disease is not considered psycho-physical reality. Moreover, it was for him a metaphor for some other difficulties and problems-religious, social-economic and political nature has violated a healthy relationship between God and His people Israel.

---

[16] U. Duchrow and Liedke, *Shalom: Biblical Perspectives on Creation, Justice, and Peace* (Geneva: WCC, 1987), 48-49.

[17] John Wilkinson, *The Bible and Healing: A Medical and Theological Commentary* (Edinburgh: The Handsel Press Ltd, 1998), 13-14, 19-20. The people of Israel are being called to replace their self-righteousness with God's righteousness. That involves reaching out through acts of compassionate justice to include those who are marginalized and excluded by society. God's sense of justice requires care for the individual as well as addressing the social structures that create injustice. A response is required that addresses the root causes of inequity and restores the justice and righteousness that God desires for all, which will ultimately strengthen the health of the community.

[18] Jürgen Moltmann, *God in Creation* (London: SCM Press, 1985), 68.

Prophet Isaiah begins with an oracle that uses the imagery of "wounds" and "bruises and open sore" to describe the effect of God's judgment on the nation Israel.

Isaiah describes Israel's apostasy as a disease-ridden body for whom only repentance could bring cure. The socio-historical contexts describes this time as a time in which the people were reeling from a penal disaster. Yahweh inflicts physical impairments on Judah, so that its people may not be healed. For Isaiah, it is Yahweh that is believed to be the cause of many kinds of impairment-both cognitive and physical for Judah. The reason that Judah is sick is because the people are incapable of understanding and unable to pursue their own healing. Sickness and healing are never approached in the Bible from the medical and scientific point of view, but always from the religious point of view, that is to say, from the viewpoint of the particular relationship which they create or make apparent between the sick person and God.[19] Thus, Isaiah is commissioned to a ministry of hardening his people, lest upon their seeing, hearing, and understanding, it repents and is made well.

This is also the case in Isaiah 1:6 which refers to the desperate state of society because of its sin and disobedience to God's commands, and also in Ezekiel 32:27 and 37:11 (the Valley of the Dry Bones). In all of these passages the nation or society as a whole had a responsibility to obey God and His commands. Moreover, these texts also indicate that Israel's disobedience as a nation not only severed the relationship between herself and God, but also brought about her downfall physically within the created order, as an inevitable result of disobedience to God's laws which reveal an orderly pattern for all aspects of life. Thus, it was not only the spiritual condition of the individual that could determine and affect health but also the spiritual condition of society corporately. The idea of corporate personality together with the idea of the responsibility of society as a whole for the individual and also the belief of collective suffering (the latter being a result of society's disobedience), is evident in our own contemporary world.[20]

Isaiah's idea of *Rapha* is sometimes found in proximity to or parallel with *Shalom* (Isa. 57:18-19, Jer. 6:14; 8:11; 14:19; 33:6). *Rapha* is considered as decidedly holistic where the range of meanings includes deliverance from sickness, demons, death, and sin. The renewing of the relationship with God is seen in healing the wounds. Most of these texts have to do with the restoration of the community and the possibility of an ongoing people of Israel living in covenant

---

[19] H. Roux, "Heal," in *Vocabulary of the Bible*, ed. J. J. Von Allmen (London: Lutterworth Press, 1958), 404.

[20] There are many more examples of society's negative spiritual condition as a whole -and/or the negative spiritual condition of those who represent society- which potentially can have an effect on the health of society. Society's neglect of God's pattern for life (which is revealed through the commandments) might result in disruption to the natural pattern of life that God has ordained for both the environment and members of society.

with God. In this Isaiah refers to the repairing of a wound to healing and to establishing a healthy community.

An attention to literary concept quickly reveal a prevalent assumption of the prophetic books that illustrates the conceptual universe into which metaphors of physical and cognitive impairment fit. For the prophets, Yahweh wields punishment, imposes discipline, or bestows blessing with the goal of shaping the behaviour of God's people. The ultimate aim of such shaping by Yahweh is the restoration of the divine-human relation.[21]

As discussed above, Yahweh is frequently depicted as one who restores a people, so that "God as restorer" could be considered as "root metaphor" in Ricoeur's sense.[22] God as restorer functions as a root metaphor or major conceptual metaphor in many prophetic passages, while the metaphor of "God as healer" can be seen as a subordinate metaphor that adds richness to a network of metaphors that conveys God's restorative power. The passages that speaks of God's restorative actions most often used in the form of return in order to communicate that God will restore the health of the people. These passages emphasize that God can restore and renew Israel, with figures of physical and cognitive impairment or illness serving to illustrate God's power to wound or heal.

7.3. *Rapha, Arukah, Shalom* and *Marpe* in Exilic Times

The exilic period put the prophets of this time to play in the difficult role of providing voice and articulation to the faith and experience of this community in a very odd circumstance. The governing metaphor for this literature is that exile. In this brief definitive period in the Old Testament faith, pastoral responsibility was to help people enter into exile, to be in exile, and depart out of exile.[23] This is the time where God's call and commissioning Jeremiah as "to pluck up and to pull down, to destroy and to overthrow, to build and to plant" (Jer. 1:10) is articulated as a passionate hope. This image is most clearly seen in the concept of *Shalom* in Jeremiah 8.4-15 and Isaiah 53.4.6

Both these verses translate the word *Shalom* as healing/healed (see Jeremiah 8.15 and Isaiah 53.5). In both instances the context shows that health is considered to be much wider that just being physically free of disease.

The curses threatening Israel with a return to the sufferings of Egypt in Deut. 28:59-61 also employ *holt,* "sickness," this time in connection with

[21] Sarah J. Melcher, "With Whom Do the Disabled Associate? Metaphorical Interplay in teh Later Prophets," in *This Abled Body: Rethinking Disabilities and Biblical Studies*, ed. Hector Avalos, Sarah J. Melcher, and Jeremy Schipper (Atlanta: SBL, 2007), 118.

[22] Paul Ricoeur, *Interpretation Theory: Discourse and Surplus of Meaning* (Texas: Christian University Press, 1976), 64.

[23] Walter Brueggemann, *Hopeful Imagination: Prophetic Voices in Exile* (Philadelphia: Fortress Press, 1986), 1.

"affliction," a term which recalls the description of the Servant in 53:4 as one "afflicted, stricken."

> The Lord will bring on you and your offspring extraordinary afflictions *[mak-kôt]*, afflictions severe and lasting, and sicknesses *[wohöläyim]* grievous and lasting. And he will bring upon you again all the diseases of Egypt *[kol-madwëh]* ... every sickness also, and every affliction *(gam kol-holî wëkol-makkâ)*.

Infidelity involves a reversal of the exodus and of the Abrahamic promise. The Song thus describes the Servant bearing in his own person the effect of these curses. He himself experiences the threatened repetition of the "sickness" *(holî)* and "affliction" *(makkâ)* of the Egyptian "exile." Like the Egyptian suffering, however, it serves also as a proximate preparation for a (new) exodus and return to the Promised Land. The text employs that Yahweh has restored the Servant to health; i. e., removed the "pains" and "disease." Also, he shall not be shunned anymore.

The idea of healing of physical diseases was certainly not excluded from the wider metaphor of national healing and restoration. The hope of the prophets was nothing less than the whole human wholly healed, classically expressed in Isaiah 53:4-5. The biblical understanding of health is what is sometimes called 'maximal', in other words it goes beyond the narrow idea of health being the absence of disease and instead sees it as 'complete well-being at all levels of life, physical, mental, social, environmental and spiritual.'

Given the strongly political contexts of Isaiah material in relation to the Assyrian deportation, the Babylonian exile, and the post-exilic period of reconstruction, it is no wonder that salvation language in Isaiah, rooted historically in the exodus, has to do heavily with the political salvation of a people. But that salvation is linked strongly to social righteousness and justice; i.e. without them there can be no political wholeness and health.

Like Deutero-Isaiah, Jeremiah's oracles of health and well-being are a reflective of and responsive to the historical crisis in of the last days of Judah, culminating in the destruction of Jerusalem and the temple in 587 B.C.E. This crisis is the dominant and shaping event of the entire Old Testament.[24] In such a context the metaphor of sickness and healing is one of the more powerful and more radical in the tradition of Jeremiah.[25] Israel like any other community has trusted in its social order, but that social order is jeopardized and disoriented in its heart. The two terms used by Jeremiah is "sickness" and "wounds" to state of the society that does not function in the well-being of a community (Jer. 7:8-10).

[24] Walter Brueggemann, *A Commentary on Jeremiah: Exile and Homecoming* (Grand Rapids, Michigan: William B. Eerdmans Publishing Company, 1998), 1.

[25] Walter Brueggemann, "The "Uncared For" Now Cared for (Jer. 30:12-17): A Methodological Consideration," *Journal of Biblical Literature* 104, no. 3 (September 1985): 420.

In Jeremiah 8:11-13, the concept of sickness to the opposite of health is pictured as a fact that denies reality. Jeremiah also depicts wounds and sickness that moves toward restoration, in here, it employs metaphors of divine healing.

In contrast to the examples above, metaphors of healing and health can also be used to convey on irredeemable situation- to represent an incurable condition, as in Jer. 30:15. Similarly, when Jeremiah 51:1-19 speaks of Yahweh's irreversible judgment against Babylon, it employs metaphors of healing to refer to that nation's incurable wounds (51:9).

Jeremiah uses pictures of disease and healing to describe the destruction and subsequent restoration of Jerusalem (10:19; 14:17; 15:18; 30:12). A brief section of the longer periscope, Jeremiah 30:1-24, also serves as an example of the frequent interplay of punishment and healing as the larger passage moves towards restoration.[26]

The graphic imagery of restoration and repair is found throughout the book of Jeremiah. Jeremiah was part of a tradition that viewed Yahweh as the only genuine רפא. For example, in Jer. 17:14, "Heal me, oh Yahweh, and I shall be healed." The statement is part of the meditation which contrasts trust in Yahweh with trusts in humans. Jeremiah 17:5 states: "Cursed is the man who trusts humans, while Jer. 17:7 says: "Blessed is the man who trusts in Yahweh." In this light one can see that the theology expressed in this implies that healing is one thing for which Yahweh and his rightful intermediaries, not other professions, should be consulted.[27] Consequently, Jer. 17:14 may be translated as: "treat me, Oh Yahweh, and I shall be healed."[28]

Jeremiah emphasizes elsewhere that it is Yahweh who will heal. For example, Jer. 30:17 says: "I shall restore your health, and I shall heal your wounds." Similarly, in Jer. 33:6 one finds: "Indeed, I shall bring restoration and healing." Although these texts refer to Israel, the socio-political entity, as the patient, it is clear that these references are part of a theology that regards Yahweh as the only רפא that should be trusted. In the light of this, references are being made in the light of human רפא that has been labeled as futile because Yahweh is the only genuine רפא.

Six times in Jeremiah referred to the imminent "great collapse" with reference to Judah in 4:6; 6:1; 14:17; 48:3; with reference to Babylon in 50:22; 51:54. This means that the promised restoration of Judah and Israel could be no less comprehensive in its overall healing effects than the tragic, devastating collapse. Jeremiah was clear in his understanding about God's restorative and healing

---

[26] Melcher, "With Whom Do the Disabled Associate? Metaphorical Interplay in the Later Prophets," 119.

[27] Hector Avalos, *Illness and Health Care in the Ancient Near East: The Role of the Temple in Greece, Mesopotamia, and Israel* (Atlanta, Georgia: Scholars Press, 1995), 287.

[28] Brown, *Israel's Divine Healer*, 287.

activity to the people. For him, what the Lord "broke/shattered/smashed" could only be "repaired/healed/restored" by his hand.

The book of Jeremiah intervenes in a national disaster and moves the nation toward healing. The drama of the God's broken family helps survivors by presenting their experience in the narrowed domain of a family broken apart by infidelity. It reflects victims experience back to them in a way that does not traumatize them. And in the chaos of disaster's aftermath, it provides an explanation of the calamity and defends God. Therefore, the theology of Jeremiah's broken family enables the people of Judah to survive as the people of God.[29]

Another important issue analysis that arose out of Jeremiah metaphorical images is the image of the land.

The exile is the defining signature event of ancient Israel. The reason that, the exile became the matrix in which the ancient promises of land were reiterated afresh. Thus the prophetic traditions of Isaiah 40-55 and Jeremiah 30:31, assures exilic Israel that God will once again give land to Israel as it was first given to the heirs of the ancestors (Isa. 49:19-20; 51:2-3; Jer. 31:12-14, 33:6-9).

From this ideology Jeremiah brings out certain images of the sickness metaphor in Judah:

1. Illness as embracing Canaanite fertility rites and establishing Baal as the ruler of the land
2. Illness as social injustice due to Judah's whoring after Baal.
3. Illness in terms of polluting the land by aligning with Judah's political alliances.

Jeremiah uses the adultery metaphor in Jer. 3:1-10 to describe about the wounds that the people of Israel had inflicted upon the land. The idea of defile and pollution is describe here as in terms of Israel as a faithless wife who has gone "whoring" after other lovers thereby polluting the land. Judah, by pursuing the fertility rites of Baalism, has polluted the land 'committing adultery with stone and tree" (3:9). Yahweh, the faithful husband, had already divorced the faithless bride Israel, for adultery. Therefore, Yahweh threatens to divorce the fickle sister Judah, who has only pretended to repent of apostasy (3:6-10). Is this context, can there be any hope? Judah has already polluted the land and so there appears be to no chance of ever returning. After all a divorced woman who returns to a man, according to Deuteronomic law, also pollutes the land (Deut. 24:1-4). Would not that land greatly polluted if God's people returned after Judah's adultery and divorce? (3:1). Judah has had several husbands, including Baal. For this sullied

[29] Kathleen M. O'Connor "A Family Comes Undone (Jeremiah 2:1-4:2)," *Review and Expositor* 105 (Spring 2008): 201.

wife to be again united with Yahweh, her first husband, it would mean profaning the land as never before.[30]

The ideology in this text shows the wounds and bruises that Judah had inflicted upon the land by Judah's obsession with fertility cults before, during, and after the Babylonian destruction. Robert Carroll rights points out that, "Yahweh who is the owner of the land and the source of fertility is rejected by Judah. A righteous God cannot tolerate a defile abode forever."[31]

The sickness metaphor seen is also due to the social injustice. Although, the language of defilement reflects the cultic pollution associated with Judah's whoring after Baal, cultic and social corruption are closely linked. The harlot Judah, who lusts after lovers, also has the lifeblood of the innocent poor. The innocent are the oppressed in the land to which Yahweh pays special attention. Judah's treatment of the poor, the widow, the orphan, and the alien is the touchstone of justice in the Book of Jeremiah. Condemnation of social injustice in the land reflects the prophetic tradition that is found in the books of other prophets of justice, such as Amos. Thus, health and well-being of Judah is deteriorated by causing illness to the oppressed, the widows, orphans and the aliens. Healing can only come if the poor are not exploited by the wealthy and defend the rights of the poor. Healing and prosperity in the ideology of Jeremiah are dependent on denouncing Baal, acknowledging Yahweh as the true source of fertility, and never gaining prosperity at the expense of the poor.

Illness is also linked with Judah's political alliances. By seeking political security through powers such as Egypt or Assyria Judah was effectively forsaking Yahweh as the pure fountain of living water (Jer. 2:13-19). The image of idolatry was used as a metaphor by Jeremiah to describe the illness of Judah. By becoming involved in seeking aid from foreign powers was tantamount to idolatry, whether or not the recognition of the specific deities was part of the deal. The result is that the land is laid waste, profaned by the path of foreign armies cross sacred soil. Judah flits from one impotent lover to another, from Egypt to Assyria, unaware that the consequence will be shame and insecurity, disgrace and not prosperity. The folly of this political policy was exposed with the fall of Jerusalem. By seeking other alliances, Judah's alliances with Yahweh was ventilated and the land violated. The land is wounded and sick because it is lying desolated (6:8), wasted (7:34) and lifeless wilderness (9:10). The land is the victim of Israel's pollution, Babylon's devastating armies, and Yahweh's anger. The suffering of the land ideology highlights the personal anguish of land-people-God relationship. This relationship model highlights the idea of the understanding of health in Old Testament, where when illness of one effects the whole community so also the

[30] Walter Brueggemann, "Land, Fertility and Justice," in *Theology of the Land*, ed. B. Evans and G. Cusack (Collegeville, Minn: Liturgical Press, 1987), 57.

[31] Robert Carroll, *Jeremiah: A Commentary* (Philadelphia: Westminster John Knox Press, 1986), 136.

health and well-being of one relates to all, that health is total and not confined to only one aspect of life.

The healing metaphor is portrayed by Jeremiah in terms of hope and restoration. In the political realities surrounding the fall of Jerusalem and the exile of the people from Judah to Babylon as outlined in the text of Jeremiah, the ideology of the prophet seemed to play into the hands of the enemy. According to this ideology, the land had to be purged and cleared of its defiling inhabitants.

The metaphor of healing seen by Jeremiah is a vision that is beyond pollution, beyond the purging, and beyond the exile where there will be redemption, a restoration of land-God-people relationship and healing. God's people will return home, and Yahweh will again plant the people in Yahweh's own land. According to Robert Carroll, this implies that "the land, once pristine, pure, and prepared for Yahweh's bride, must again be emptied, purified, and prepared for the return of Yahweh's transformed people. The empty vineyard will again be planted with choice vines."[32]

The land is a gift from God. The heart of Israel life was centered in assurance that the land is their very being of existence. But with the experience of exile, their land has been polluted and taken away. The health of the community was distorted because Judah had failed to keep the covenant with God. The breaking down of relationship between God and the people led them to be unhealthy in dealing with one another and also distorted their relationship with God. The only possibility to bring health and wellness in this distorted life is through restoration and redeeming the land through forgiveness and healing.

7.4. *Rapha, Arukah, Shalom* and *Marpe* in Post-Exilic Period

There is interplay between metaphors of punishment and *Rapha*, in most of the texts in the Post-Exilic period. One such example is seen in Isaiah 19:22 that Yahweh will strike Egypt, striking and healing: they will return to Yahweh, and he will hear their entreaties and heal them. Here, *Rapha* is perceived in terms of salvation.

The concept of salvation in the Old Testament is derived from the great event of Israel's deliverance from Egypt in the Exodus. Thus, the terms for 'salvation,' ישועה *(yeshua)* and ישע *(yasha)*, are derived from the verb root that means to deliver safely to a place of ease and peace. The flight from Egypt to the entry into Promised Land formed their core of the image of salvation. This image was communal, and envisioned the distress from which deliverance was needed as primarily external to the people of Israel. Each of these elements was modified in the course of history of the Hebrew people during the long period covered by the Old Testament and the Apocrypha.[33] Trito-isaiah's communal

[32] Robert Carroll, "The Myth of the Empty Land," *Semeia* 59 (1992): 79-93.

[33] James N. Lapsley, *Salvation and Health: The Interlocking Processes of Life* (Philadelphia: The Westminster Press, 1952), 31-32.

understanding of salvation was closely related to the basic understanding of human in corporate rather than individual terms. God's covenant was with the Israelites, not with individuals, and by participating in the life, clan, tribe, and nation did the individual find identity and meaning. This communal conception continued to dominate the Jewish thinking till the New Testament. Within this communal understanding developed an individual notion of health. Though the wisdom literature aims to get wisdom not salvation yet the Séptuagint translated חכמה (*chokmah)* with the word *soteria*, which is salvation in New Testament. This is sometimes translated as שלם, peace. Hence, there is a close connection between deliverance and peace. Salvation is thus a work on the whole personality and is to have its effects on the whole human. This idea is linked to the idea of health to that of salvation. The Biblical view of redemption is far from being a wholly solitary experience. According to J. A. T. Robinson, the Biblical word 'body' stresses the fact of human solidarity, never "the self-sufficiency, self-determination of isolation of each man [*sic*] from his neighbour."[34] This Hebraic conception of the body is supported by the modern science.

Abe describes the breadth of salvation,

> Salvation is used in the Old Testament to translate different Hebrew words among which are *ysw'h* and *ys'* from the stem which is niph'al and hiph'il. The niph'il has the sense of 'to deliver'. The root has the fundamental meaning of 'to be broad', 'to become spacious', carrying the sense of deliverance. The most significant proper name derived from this root is savior. 'Saviour' is the translation of the hiph'il participle (Judg. 3:9, 15. Isa. 19:20)....Thus in all the Judeo-Christian theology and the traditional religions of Africa, salvation of both the soul and the body is their ultimate goal pursued vigorously in every practical religious expression. Thus salvation in these religious contexts is total: deliverance from the clutches and consequences of sin (spiritual) and from eco-political and social injustices and agony (physical).[35]

Salvation as *Shalom* is found both in the Old Testament and New Testament. In Acts 7:26, "would have set them at one" is, literally, 'was reconciling them (conative imperfect tense, expressing an earnest effort) into peace.'[36]

However, throughout the period of Old Testament salvation and health remained essentially separate ideas, though occasionally linked. This linkage is rooted in the Hebrew assumption that the body and the spirit cannot be divorced.

---

[34] J. A. T. Robinson, *In the End God...* (New York: Harper & Row, Publishers, 1950), 100.

[35] G. Abe, "Redemption, Reconciliation, Propitiation," *Journal of Theology for Southern Africa*, no. 95 (1996): 3.

[36] W. E. Vine, *Vine's Expository Dictionary of Old and New Testament Words* (Grand Rapids: Flemming Revell, 1981).

There is no such thing as the salvation of the soul or even the spirit in the Old Testament apart from the body. The land of the dead שְׁאוֹל (*sheol*) is a shadowy place of half life, but not of salvation. This unity of the person made healing and health a choice metaphor for the prophets in speaking of the remedy for the tribulations of the nation of Israel, and led to a striking development.[37]

Wilkinson therefore opines,

> The nature of well-being is implied in the characteristics we have already discussed and derives its identity from the human constitution and the human relationship with God. This well-being is holistic for it affects the whole of human being. If the desire of well-being is confined to the body then the result is likely to be not health, but ill health resulting from a 'healthism' in which the health of the body is regarded as a desirable end in itself. On the other hand if the desire is confined to the soul or spirit this too will lead to ill-health from neglect of the body. Thus, the nature of well-being is that wholeness of being and uprightness of character which are related to Old Testament calls 'holiness.'[38]

Isaiah also portrays the relationship between *Shalom* and *Rapha,* which is sometimes found in proximity to or parallel with *Shalom* (Isa. 57:18-19, Jer. 6:14; 8:11; 14:19; 33:6). רפא (*Rapha*) is decidedly holistic where the range of meanings includes deliverance from sickness, demons, death, and sin. The renewing of the relationship with God is seen in healing the wounds. Most of these texts have to do with the restoration of the *community* and the possibility of an ongoing people of Israel living in covenant with God. Isaiah refers to the repairing of a wound and a healthy מרפא (*marpe*) community.[39] מרפא *marpe* sometimes written as מרפא means remedy, cure and healing. It is also used as רִפְאוּת (*riput*), as referred to healing. The root is also found in several personal names: *rapu* רפוא healed; *rephael* רְפָאֵל, God healed; *repha,* רפיה in nominative forms, as *marpe* מרפא.

Given the strongly political contexts of Isaiah material in relation to the Assyrian deportation, the Babylonian exile, and the post-exilic period of reconstruction, it is no wonder that salvation language in Isaiah has to do heavily with the political salvation of a people. Hammer's idea of salvation of Israel from political bondage also involves salvation for being a light of justice to the nations. God's concern for the health of all peoples and nations, also for Israel's ancient enemies, calls Israel to that prophetic task.[40] But that salvation is strongly linked

---

[37] Lapsley, *Salvation and Health: The Interlocking Processes of Life*, 34.

[38] Wilkinson, *The Bible and Healing: A Medical and Theological Commentary*, 17.

[39] R. N. Whybray, *Isaiah 40-66* (Greenwood: S.C.: Attic, 1975), 216.

[40] Paul L. Hammer, "God's Health for the World: Some Biblical Understandings of Salvation," *Ex Auditu* 5 (1989): 85.

to social righteousness and justice, i.e., without them there can be no political wholeness and health. Further, though Isaiah material is much concerned with the salvation of Israel from political bondage, it also involves salvation for being a light of justice to the nations. God's concern for the health of all peoples and nations, also for Israel's ancient enemies, calls Israel to that prophetic task. There is also concern for personal salvation, i.e., for a renewed relationship with God that can deal with the sins of idolatry and rebellion. The Old Testament understanding of health is about the right relationship with God, therefore, breaking the relationship entails unhealthy and unwell. This understanding of salvation is primarily this worldly and has to do with political health of both Israel and all other nations, as well as personal health of the individuals in their relatedness to God, to others, and to God's whole creation. Among other images, Isaiah wants salvation to sprout forth from the earth to bring God's health to all.

Isaiah also links health to justice and righteousness. For him, health without justice and righteousness is no health at all. H. C. White defines Justice:

> Justice is an interpersonal relationship implying both a claim and a responsibility. Justice bespeaks a situation that transcends the individual, demanding of everyone a certain abnegation of self, defiance of self-interest, disregard of self-respect. The necessity of submitting to a law is derived from the necessity of identifying oneself with what concerns other individuals or the whole community.[41]

Justice-righteousness also has a creational dimension.[42] The prophets univocally voiced out that when justice is not practiced, the fish, animals, water, and trees are adversely affected.[43] Such biblical witnesses declare the necessary connection made for us by God between the health of the environment and human health.

The extreme sociological problems of Israel and Judah resulted in a singular beam of light, focusing on the corporate life of the people of God. The prophet do provided a simple and a comprehensive description of health and wholeness.

---

[41] H. C. White, *Shalom in the Old Testament* (Philadelphia: United Church, 1973), 25.

[42] U. Duchrow and Liedke, *Shalom: Biblical Perspectives on Creation, Justice, and Peace* (Geneva: WCC, 1987), 48-49.

[43] An unjust people destroy the nonhuman creation. Animals, birds, and fish died because of unrighteousness (Hos. 4:1-3). God makes a covenant with the animals because the people had failed (Hos. 2:18). God spoke to the earth because the people were not listening (Jer. 22:29). They were warned that if they did not keep the covenant (including Sabbath rest for the land) the land would vomit them out (Deut. 20:19). God comforted the soil and animals concerning the invasion of the land because of the people's unrighteousness, saying, "Do not fear O soil; Do not fear, animals of the earth" (Joel 2:21-22). When Jeremiah and Ezekiel say, "You say peace, peace [health, health] but there is no peace [health]," it is because there is no justice-righteousness.

Hence, there are few conclusions that need proper attention in order to understand health and healing from these three prophetic texts:

- Health in the prophetic understanding has a broader meaning than only restoration to physical health. The basic concern of human in the prophetic literature is one of totality, that is, health is total. Their understanding incorporates both the physical and the corporeal. Health is not static to healing physical disease but it also implies to the community well-being in terms of their relatedness with one another.
- Health in the prophetic texts has also connotes a relationship with *Shalom*. The word *Shalom* does not only mean absence of war but it also means health and well-being. It means the vision of harmony in social order as well as in the created order. Whatever establishes wholeness and harmony in the social order and political community works for health. *Shalom* has to be understood not as a static condition but as dynamic reality immediately related to human beings' constant search for human dignity. It is not just an inner feeling but a dynamic reality that is expressed in concrete human relationships and actions. *Shalom* includes search and goal of full humanity for all. In other words, it is a struggle for human dignity and social justice. Thus, a healthy מרפא (*marpe*) community is possible only when one works for the wholeness of the whole community.

Therefore, after analyzing the above remarks the implications for health and healing for the prophets of the Old Testament stretch beyond the individual to the communal and beyond personal well-being to social, political and environmental conditions. It stresses both in physical and mental well-being, in forgiveness and in forthcoming deliverance.

It is true that the prophetic books often used the root רפא metaphorically based on the image of Israel as a sin sick body in need of healing. However, one cannot say that the prophetic books ignore or exclude physical healing. Following are few of our research findings:

- The use of רפא was not merely spiritualizing. The "healing" that the prophets longed for was just as literal as the divine smiting that the nation had experienced. The prophetic concept of healing did not center on the curing of physical sickness, but it most certainly included such concepts. In many instances the prophets used the healer metaphor that is conveyed by the Hebrew רפא with God as subjective, however there are several other verbs and nouns focusing on the healer metaphor which are to restore, make whole, medicine, balm, disease, wound, sickness, etc.

- God's healing was more than a medically verifiable physical process. Apart from the physical health and healing, the prophets focus more on the spiritual healing of Israel and Judah than on the physical healing of an individual.
- Unlike the former prophets that finds several references to prophets as agents of healing process, physicians and other healing agents are not prominent in the prophetic books. The prophetic books speak more about leaders that failed as agents of healing or false prophets that tried to cure the wounds of God's people.
- The healer metaphor does not merely refer to the healing of people. There are several prophetic texts discussing the healing of the land, city, temple and creation.
- God's healing was not restricted to his elected people alone; he even offered healing to Egypt (Isa. 19:22) and tried to heal Babylon (Jer. 51:8-9).
- The prophetic books depict God as the only real healer. There are no limits to God's performance as healer. God is healer in the present time, but will also be a healer in the future (Isa. 19:22; 30:26; 53:5; Je. 30:17; 33:6; Mal. 4:2).
- The healer metaphor is sometimes used with other metaphors for God in the immediate literary context. The metaphor is used in the way that God is proclaimed as a father and proclaims that He will heal and that He will also be like dew to Israel.
- Health is also associated with justice and righteousness in the prophetic texts. The health and well-being of the community depends on our actions towards the oppressed, poor, orphans, widows and the vulnerable.
- Health is connected with restoration of hope for the people. Most of the texts have to do with restoration of the community and the possibility of an ongoing people of Israel living in covenant with God. Words like this, delivered to people in exile, surely do speak to physical needs, but their overwhelming word of hope is about God's reconciliation with the people who might have thought God was through with them. The prophets also portrayed God as the one who caused them the illness. Even though God has inflicted the blow, it is his responsibility to renew the relationship and heal the wounds. Isaiah and Jeremiah give a hope to the people that the people will be healed and their life restored to health.
- The prophetic understanding of health is wholistic because no individual can relate to oneself without the other. Individual action alone will not bring about God's righteousness and justice that leads to

well-being. While individual behavior is indeed significant, but is not sufficient to ensure health.

- These thoughts are in line with the Old Testament understanding of life which does not have a dualistic nature but Life is a unity of body, mind, spirit and the senses. A soul is a living being, a biological and functional personality. A mind, incorporeal but mindful, is the seat of awareness. The breath of life is the vital force that animates the human being's essence. Health is more than the absence of disease. It is a dynamic equilibrium between the universe and the person. Disturbing this balance causes ill health. To be healthy, a person needs equilibrium of enzymes, proper function of body fluids, tissues, and metabolic substances, and happiness of spirit, mind, senses and body. So, also the understanding of life in the prophetic texts is wholistic.
- Health is restoration of relationship between God and humans. Seeking and aligning bond with other foreign god's would only bring wounds and disease to the people. But restoring of these relationships with God would entail health and well-being to the nation, socially, politically, religiously and economically.
- Healing not only is ascribed to physical healing but also of divine forgiveness.
- Healing also implies to restoration of the land. Healing the land involves healing the bitter experience of the people and asking for forgiveness for all in it, in order for the people to be healed and released to be a healing community.
- Healing is eschatological in the prophetic texts, where a person is not only healed of his/her physical illness but also wholly and fully restored.
- Health and healing is inclusive of all human beings despite their disabilities. Health and healing does not confine in the prophetic texts only to the able and fit personalities as it does in the Pentateuch, (especially in purity and pollution theories, that a person with disability is not fit to take part in the social life of the community). However, the prophetic understanding is wholistic and inclusive. For the prophets health and healing thus embraces all human, whether the lame, people with disabilities, the blind, the poor, the oppressed, and the neglected as wholly healed.

Conclusion

Challenges of Prophetic Understanding of Health and Healing to the Contemporary World

Concept like health, and the cluster of other concepts to which it is related, such as healing, disease, illness, and so on, are variously understood depending on the purposes to which we wish to put them. The term health is often used to carry an implied value, namely, that health is good and that a lack of health is bad, or should be prevented. Even more significant, the concepts and conditions of health and disease historically have reflected social values. For instance, health is defined in terms of individual functioning, reflecting individualistic social values.

Today more than ever the lack of well-being is evident in the many ways that the dignity of human life is threatened. Instead of efforts to create and sustain human wholeness and well-being, there are ongoing efforts to destroy human life. As we confront a wide variety of threats to human dignity and well-being, too often our moral vision reflects a division, a lack of integrity that prevents us from working together to create a more compassionate, hospitable, holistic, human society.

In our context, we are faced with the evil tentacles of corruption in every aspect of human life: physical, political, economical, spiritual, and environmental. People are 'sick' today to these grievous aspects, which have controlled our lives to such a point that one often hears the sign of resignation: "We can't live without being corrupt." It is in such a context the message of the Old Testament prophets offer us a renewed understanding of what it means to be human and whole.

The general tendency of Medicine in the last century has been to think of the individual as being essential unit of disease. The importance of treating a person as a whole was not recognized. It is also noted that staying healthy was a means to an end - to survive, earn a living, raise a family or accomplish a noble goal. Today the quest for health has become an end in itself-find the ideal diet or the ultimate exercise and create the perfect body. For many, our health and our body have become our modern gods.

Health as mentioned earlier cannot be understood individualistically but in a relational and global perspective. It is so because global health is not just a medical or social topic. Global health, human health and world peace are very much a basic political subject. Therefore, perception of health and healing, centered on the individual, needs to give way to a communitarian and wholistic perspective. Such result of change will affect not only the practice of medicine, but our very understanding of the relationship between fundamental matters such as life and death, sickness and healing, individual and community, part and whole and so on.

As noted earlier the concept of health has always been defined from individualistic perspective; but health in the prophetic understanding is far from individualistic. Health for them is always a social and relational phenomenon; it concerns individuals, and is intimately bound up with the nature and quality of their relationships with others. We are intimately intertwined in our humanity, and no one of us can flourish apart from others.

Health cannot be understood without seeing human in his/her integrity and in the wholeness of ones being and the nexus of his/her total relationship. The basic concern of human in the prophetic texts is one of totality, that is, health is total. Thus, health is more than a physical problem. The Christian revelation of the divine purpose is to make human "every small amount whole," and to build up the Kingdom of God within the lives of human beings, supplies the perfect answer to the ills of society, whether individual, communal, or national. This therefore, points to the need to interpret the nature of human afresh in terms of its purpose and wholeness. It is one of the vital indications reflecting the quality of life in the prophetic texts. It sees the health in terms of wholeness. It is not found in nostrums but rather in a holy and clean way of life, cleansing of body and spirit. Therefore, wholistic health is concerned with the integration of mind, body, and spirit. Its goal is positive "wellness" rather than the absence of symptoms of disease. It accents personal responsibility for good health and sees illness as an opportunity for growth. This sense of wholeness, of well-being, is not confined merely to the individual person, but extends beyond the individual to the community as well. Our well-being depends not only on our physical condition, but also on our inter-relationship with the community as well. The truths conveyed is that human being is a unified whole, rather than a loose fusion of separate and disparate entities. This means that a human person is a single integrated totality of psychophysical functions. If the totality is broken up, neither soul nor body nor person continues to function or exist. The Hebrew world view is anti-dualistic and actively 'holistic' or 'monistic.'

Harmony, balance, integration, unity and mutual interrelation of all things and events characterize the approach to health, healing and wholeness. Everything is part of the whole, and there is a basic flow and rhythm that maintains this unity and oneness. Ultimate reality is expressed and experienced in different manifestations of the Cosmic Whole. In this sense, health and spirituality are one and the same. Both are directed to wholeness,[1] fullness of life, purity and integration. Wholeness is holiness.

If the prophetic understanding is taken as a guide for defining the well-being of the heart-mind, the person in social relationship, and all its sources for vitality, then the so-called spiritual dimension cannot simply be pasted on like a poultice to a person's health. By definition and in every dimension of living, Yahweh is witnessed by the prophets as the source and goal of our individual and communal health. God as healer is not a major metaphor in the Hebrew Bible, but it plays a significant part in the prophetic books. The doctor or physician image occurs in the prophetic books at pivotal places, witnessing God's willingness to restore, rehabilitate, and repair all that has-been damaged or hurt.

God's chief concern for the created world is for its moral health, and rejects whatever disrupts this wholeness. Hence, the call is to promote moral wholeness as part of environmental and physical health. The idea of healing is a process in which separation and alienation gives way to fellow human and communion with God which brings it a state of *shalom* in the sense of total well-being.

1. Health and Healing in the Context of India

Wellness in the Indian context is the totality of the individual, family and the community; the concept of corporate responsibility in Indian health system, is the same as *shalom* in the Old Testament.

The understanding of health and healing as wholistic is the pre-requisite etiology in the context of India. Like in the western societies and in western medicine, the predominant notion of health is that it is the absence of physical and/or mental disturbances. So, also in our society, health is determined by the existence of an inner and outer balance (harmony), and disease is considered to be caused by a lack of such a balance. In the same manner healing is psychosomatic, involving the body and the soul and in consonance with one's community's expectation of health. A harmony of mind, soul and body, and of one's relationship with the environment and with other human beings plays an important part in

[1] Wholeness might be the best one-to-one synonym, but even that is terribly inadequate. The word has to do with the totality of things and the relationship of all things within that totality, with the harmony of all things, human and otherwise in God's creation, the harmony of relationships, the coming together in gentleness of that which shares participation in the creation of Yahweh. It has to do with well-being, not only of the nonphysical. The Hebrew did not tolerate the soul-body distinction, it included physical prosperity, material prosperity, and all that we are. Underneath this term is the assumption of a webbed inter-connectedness of all life, which resists any pulling out of some quarter such as the intellectual or the spiritual, and views us as wholes. *Shalom* has to do with the well-being and prosperity of the most fully-blossomed possibility for all that we are. The emphasis is on the relationship of the one with the other.

maintaining health. Disturbances to this harmony lead to disease, and the goal of treatment for disease is to restore harmony. In most traditional cultures, healing is part of a socio-religious system in which the power and meaning of life are to be found in the relationship one has with one‘s own self, with other people, with the physical environment, with the invisible world of spirits, and with God. Treatments, therefore, must deal not only with particular aspects of a sick person‘s body but also with issues related to God or the spirits, and the social context of a patient‘s life.

Such a comprehensive understanding of health challenges any understanding of health as something that is simply about having a strong and functional body, and enjoying mental well-being. Rather, it leads us to an understanding that people with chronic physical or mental sickness, and who cope with their ailments and live in harmonious relationships with their fellow human beings and with God, may be healthier than those who are physically and mentally healthy but have little awareness of, for example, the meaning of their lives. Thus, healing today is possible only through advocating and working for justice. A cursory of suggestions are made in the context of India for a renewed understanding of health and healing.

1.1. Economic Justice

Every woman, man and child has the right to the highest attainable standard of physical and mental health without discrimination of any kind. Still, in spite of health being a human right, the majority of people do not have access to that right.

The main cause of inadequate access to health, and therefore of disease in India, is economic poverty. Poverty is the result of oppression, exploitation and war. No amount of immunizations, medicines and health education can significantly ameliorate illness that is due to poverty.

Economic poverty is also closely linked to inequities in social structures, which are often feudal or oppressive, and tend to limit peoples' ability and opportunity to experience the economic benefits that poverty alleviation efforts may provide. Those interested in maintaining the status quo perpetuate inequitable social structures, and special efforts are needed to bring about change.

The churches are called to see poverty as a justice issue that must be raised in the centres of power at local, national, regional and global levels. Along with calling for justice, the churches must pressure those in power to commit themselves to a more just distribution of available resources for health both within and between nations.

The prophets of the Hebrew Scriptures (Old Testament) cried out against any oppression and exploitation of the poor. Therefore, it is a mandate for every human beings to be aware that working for the liberation of the economically poor contributes to healing. This includes advocacy, in the sense of speaking with and on behalf of the marginalized and underprivileged. Such advocacy must also include all efforts towards the transformation of structures that produce poverty, exploitation, harm and sickness. With special reference to access to health care.

1.2. Health in a Context of Establishment of Just Social Systems

Isaiah described ailing Israel using physical symptoms to describe the inward sinful state of the nation (Isaiah 1:5). The Old Testament prophets proclaimed social righteousness in the corporate political and economic order, prophesied against institutional sins, and warned of God's judgment. Corporate sin is as important to God as individual sin: Amos condemns legalized oppression of the poor in the same passage as adultery (Amos 2:6-7). Health development in the larger context of development should therefore take place with some understanding of the political/social milieu with an eye toward helping to health corporate sin and sickness. This is not to say that one should get involved in politics but it is to say that one should have some understanding of the cultural system and its barriers to development in order to creatively work within the system. For instance, as regards health, awareness of the existing health facilities, public health programs, and health insurance programs are important so that by knowing these things, we can serve and encourage individuals in the society to work toward change in their own society, ultimately helping to heal corporate sin and sickness.

1.3. Health and Healing in the Context of Community

The idea of community is implicit in development if we are to help establish the Kingdom. We need to establish new communities of believers where relationships in every area, including social, economic, and spiritual, are in the process of being redeemed. These counterculture communities become a witness to the community's neighbours as pockets of freedom in the midst of oppression. While involving in the community it aims to help not only to heal individual sickness, but also there is a need to consider the social realities of the culture and the underlying structural sicknesses. Hence, health relief and development should be performed in conjunction with other types of development and with some broader anthropological understanding of existing systems in order to work creatively within these systems to maximize development on an individual and corporate basis.

1.4. Health in the Context of Gender Issues

Healing is interpreted in the broadest sense of inclusiveness. Thus, it is not only limited to physical ailments but to illnesses of oppression, racial discrimination, tribalism, violence, gender discrimination and all sorts of conflicts in one's life. It is holistic healing which does not make any distinction between the body and soul in the Old Testament. Holistic healing in the context of India should treat suffering symptomatically and look at the causes of deterioration in their health services. Such healing does not focus on the health of an individual at the expense of the whole nation.

Gender injustice is one of the major determinants of ill health of the nation. Women, who are often regarded as being of less worth than are men, usually get fewer chances than do boys and men to access education and achieve economic independence. Lack of knowledge, information, and poverty are among the determinants of ill health. In particular, gender injustice increases both the risk and vulnerability of girls and women to HIV infection.

The Christian concept of dignity, which is based on the teaching that all human beings are created in the image of God, challenges every teaching that says women are subordinate to men. Thus, recognizing them and challenging any discrimination that hinders the growth of the individual and community will usher health and wholeness.

1.5. Health in the Context of Ecology

The prophets understood health in terms of ecological health. This understanding lays particular stress on the impact of social, political conditions on the environment that was around them. The prophet's social, economic, political and moral ecology shares the same thematic focus, being centrally concerned with the relation between nature and the social order. The prophets portrayed the ill health of the nation in terms of war and conquest that has left the country devastated: forests cut down, crops burnt, cities reduced to rubble. People were deported first to Assyria, and in later war, to Babylon. Not until the Persians had conquered Babylon were the exiles in that land allowed to return home and rebuild the Temple. The ideal set before human beings are the one that is of interdependence between the world of nature and the world of human. Justice and righteousness, for the prophets are not just ethical qualities, concerned exclusively with the relation between Yahweh and his people but they are a reflection of the fundamental world order established by Yahweh, which includes the health and well-being of the natural world.

Health is regarded as a robust function, an approach toward optimal conditions. In the context of India, there are similar views that are beginning to emerge regarding ecosystem health and a close link between human and ecosystem health is gaining increased recognition. However, to achieve health, ecological 'wounds' must be repaired, which is impossible until society 'sees' the wounds. The planet's ecological life-support systems sustainably, damage to them must be both prevented and repaired.

However, repair requires awareness of damage, which, in this case, mandates a high level of ecological literacy. Prevention of ecological damage will only be successful on a planetary scale if human society endorses precautionary practices that reduce the probability of ecosystem damage. The Church and the society must begin to endorse precautionary practices to protect human health, which is no longer regarded as merely absence of symptoms of disease and malfunction.

1.6. Healing through Reconciliation and Promoting Peace

Traditional concepts of health and sickness support the view that disharmony in relationships between individuals or within families leads to alienation, separation and brokenness, and may provoke the onset of mental and physical disease. In traditional societies, the family or a community mediator, such as a village elder, listens to both sides in order to foster reconciliation and help heal broken relationships.

Deaths due to armed conflicts and other forms of political violence continue to be a reality for many especially in the context of India particularly in North East India. State terrorism through low-intensity conflict, torture, rape, imprisonment and other forms of human rights violations has made the well-being of mind, body and spirit, i.e. wholeness, impossible. Thus, the urgent need for healing can be made possible through reconciliation for harmonious relationship and for the well-being of the community. Modern sciences, increasingly have acknowledged the importance of harmonious relationships with regard to physical and/or mental well-being. Research has indicated that living at peace with oneself, and having a social network and a harmonious relationship with God might protect people from physical and mental diseases, and may help people overcome disease or cope with chronic sickness. By contrast, broken relationships are often associated with unresolved guilt, anger, resentment and meaninglessness, and these conditions may well be potent suppressers of the body's powerful, health-controlling immune system, while many consider that living in harmonious relationships is one of the strongest things that can help improve immune systems.

Generally, healing can result from the reconciliation of relationships, and this is needed on all levels: On the personal level, healing means reconciliation with one's personal or family history (e.g. the healing of memories), or being able to cope with burdens. Healing in this context means the restoration of a person to his or her community and to God, and living in a way that takes responsibility for creation to which the prophets concern was. Therefore, Healing has to take place between families, wider groups of people, and nations. In particular, there is the challenge for the church to find ways of being a credible witness to the gospel by working at healing its own divisions.

1.7. Rediscovering the Church as a Healing Community

The Christian Church has a specific task in the field of healing which cannot be surrendered to other agencies because healing is an integral part of its witness to the Gospel and an expression of salvation. The Church and the Christian congregation explicitly is the corporate fellowship of the People of God wherever it manifests itself and is mandated by its Lord to exercise the healing ministry, which must be kept under constant review in each generation to see if it lives up to its task. The local congregations realizing that they belong to a body are called to bring about healing in one way or another through the ministry of the Word, the Sacraments and prayer, while other healing services, laying on of hands, and anointing may also play a part in it, provided that proper medical means are not discarded and that the patient is not exploited.

In many cases, social relationships and contacts are extremely beneficial for sick people. In this respect, both parishes and groups involved in other Church and church-run social work contexts can play a positive role. To be a reconciling and healing community is an essential expression of the mission of the church to create and renew relationships in the perspective of the kingdom of God. This means to proclaim Christ's grace and forgiveness, to heal bodies, minds, souls and to reconcile broken communities in the perspective of fullness of life.

It is in the way people are received, welcomed and treated in a local community that has a deep impact on its healing function. The way a network of mutual support, of listening and of mutual care is maintained and nurtured in a local congregation expresses the healing power of the church as a whole. The proclamation of the word of God as a message of hope and comfort, the celebration of the Eucharist as a sign of reconciliation and restoration. Each individual member in a local congregation has a unique gift to contribute to the overall healing ministry of the church.

The research is by no means exhaustive and can still be a working concept especially in the context of India where the health and well-being of an individual and the community at large is threatened and lost.

A closer look at the scripture reveals that God created everything good. But at a point in time disease crept into our world. In spite of this, God has the prerogative of health and healing.

Today we live in a broken world, a world that is shattered by war, ethnic violence, political upheaval, discrimination in terms of caste and gender. To quote K.C. Abraham, "today we are increasingly aware that healing is just not matter of correcting some maladjustment in the body. Rather it is to release the healing potential within the individual and the community. We know how many kinds of illness are caused by factors that impinge on our system. Internal conflict and tension, hatred and guilt affect our health."[2] All positive steps towards reconciliation and peace are, therefore, important and, in the long run, often effective contributions to the physical, emotional and social health of people.

We are spiritual beings created in the image of God; *shalom* concerns the body, mind and spirit. From a Christian perspective, every human being should be in a relationship with God, and this comes about through an individual having a spiritual attitude.

---

[2] K. C. Abraham, "*Healing - Some Biblical and Theological Perspectives,*" *Religion and Society* 48, no. 4. (December 2003): 103.

The message of liberation is an integral part of the life of the church. Participating with oppressed people in the building of a just social order is part of what leads to the reign of God, which is life in its fullness, i.e. *Shalom*.

Bibliography

Primary Sources

Books/Book Section

Achtemeier, Elizabeth. *The Community and Message of Isaiah 56-66*. Minneapolis: Augsburg Publishing House, 1982.

________. "Minor Prophets 1." In *New International Bible Commentary*. Peabody: Hendrickson Publishers, 1996.

Allen, Leslie C. *Jeremiah: A Commentary*. Louisville: Westminster John Knox Press, 2008.

Alt, Albrecht. *Hosea 5:8-6:6*. Munchen: Chr. Beck, 1964.

Andersen, Francis I. *Hosea: A New Translation with Introduction and Commentary*. New York: Doubleday & Company, 1980.

Andersen, Francis I., and David Noel Freedman. *Hosea. The Anchor Bible*. New York: Doubleday, 1998.

Anderson, Bernhard W. *The Eighth-Century Prophets: Amos, Hosea, Isaiah and Micah*. Minneapolis: Fortress Press, 1978.

Baumann, Gerlinde. *Love and Violence: Marriage as Metaphor for the Relationship Between YHWH and Israel in the Prophetic Books*. Translated by Linda M. Maloney. Collegeville, MN: Liturgical, 2003.

Blenkinsopp, Joseph. *A History of Prophecy in Israel*. Philadelphia: Westminster John Knox Press, 1983.

________. *Isaiah 1-39*. New York: Doubleday, 2000.

________. *Isaiah 56-66: A New Translation with Introduction and Commentary*. New York: Doubleday, 2003.

Box, G. H. *The Book of Isaiah*. London: Leipzig, 1905.

Bozak, B. *Life Anew: A Literary-Theological Study of Jeremiah 30-31*. Rome: Pontifical Biblical Institute, 1991.

Bracke, John M. *Jeremiah 1-29*. Louisville, Kentucky: Westminster John Knox Press, 2000.

________. *Jeremiah 30-52 and Lamentations.* Louisville: Westminster John Knox Press, 2000.

Bright, John. *Jeremiah. The Anchor Bible.* New York: Doubleday & Company, 1965.

________. *Jeremiah.* 2nd ed. New York: Doubleday, 1978.

Brueggemann, Walter. *A Commentary on Jeremiah: Exile and Homecoming.* Grand Rapids, Michigan: William B. Eerdmans Publishing Company, 1998.

________. *Isaiah 1-39.* Louisville, Kentucky: Westminster John Knox Press, 1998.

________. *Isaiah 40-66.* Louisville: Westminster John Knox Press, 1998.

________. *Like Fire in the Bones: Listening for the Prophetic Word in Jeremiah*, ed. Patrick D. Miller. Minneapolis: Fortress Press, 2006.

Calvin, H. John. *Commentary on the Book of the Prophet Isaiah.* Translated by William Pringle. 4 vols. Grand Rapids, Michigan: William B. Eerdmans Publishing Company, 1948.

Carrol, Robert P. *From Chaos to Covenant: Prophecy in the Book of Jeremiah.* New York: Crossroad, 1981.

________. *Jeremiah: A Commentary.* Philadelphia: Westminster John Knox Press, 1986.

________. "Blindsight and the Vision Thing: Blindness and Insight in the Book of Isaiah." In *Writing and Reading the Scroll of Isaiah in Studies of Interpretive Tradition*, ed. D. Craig, C. Broyles and Craig A. Evans, 79-94. New York: Brill, 1997.

Cheyne, T. K. *Introduction to the Book of Isaiah.* London: A & C Black, 1895.

Childs, Brevard S. *Isaiah and the Assyrian Crisis.* London: SCM Press Ltd., 1967.

________. *Isaiah.* Louisville: Westminster John Knox Press, 2001.

Clements, R. E. *Isaiah.* Grand Rapids, Michigan: William B. Eerdmans Publishing Company, 1980.

________. "Isaiah 53 and the Restoration of Israel." In *Jesus and the Suffering Servant: Isaiah 53 and Christian Origins*, ed. William H. Bellinger Jr. and William R. Farmer, 39-54. Harrisburg, Pennsylvania: Trinity Press International, 1998.

Conrad, Edgar W. *Reading Isaiah.* Minneapolis: Fortress Press, 1991.

________. "Reading Isaiah and the Twelve as Prophetic Books." In *Writing and Reading the Scroll of Isaiah: Studies of an Interpretive Tradition*, ed. Craig C. Broyles and Craig A. Evans, 1, 1-17. New York: Brill, 1997.

Couturier, Guy P. "Jeremiah." In *The Jerome Biblical Commentary.* Englewood Cliffs: Prentice-Hall, 1968.

Craigie, Peter C., Page H. Kelley, and Joel F. Jr. Drinkard. "Jeremiah." In *Word Bible Commentary*, ed. David A. Hubbard, 26. Dallas, Texas: Word Books, 1991.

Davies, G. I. *Hosea*. Grand Rapids, Michigan: William B. Eerdmans Publishing Company, 1992.

________. *Hosea*, ed. R. W. Whybray. Sheffield: JSOT, 1993.

Delitzsch, Franz. *Isaiah, Commentary on the Old Testament,* Vol. 2. Grand Rapids, Michigan: William B. Eerdmans Publishing Company, 1973.

Diamond, A. R. *The Confessions of Jeremiah in Context: Scenes of Prophetic Drama*. Sheffield: JSOT, 1987.

Fretheim, Terence E. *Jeremiah: Smith & Helwys Bible Commentary*. Macon, GA: Smith & Helwys, 2002.

Garrett, D. A. *The New American Commentary: Hosea, Joel.* Vol. 19a. London: Broadman & Holman Publishers, 1997.

Gitay, Y. *Isaiah and His Audience: The Structure and Meaning of Isaiah 1-12.* Assen: Van Gorcum, 1991.

Goldingay, John. *Isaiah*. Peabody: Hendrickson, 2001.

Gray, G. B. *A Critical and Exegetical Commentary on the Book of Isaiah*. Edinburgh: T & T Clark, 1912.

Hamlin, E. John. *A Guide to Isaiah 40-66*. London: ISPCK, 1979.

Hanson, Paul D. *Isaiah 40-66, Interpretation: A Bible Commentary for Teaching and Preaching*. Louisville: Westminster John Knox Press, 1995.

________. "The World of the Servant of the Lord in Isaiah 40-55." In *Jesus and the Suffering Servant: Isaiah 53 and Christian Origins*, ed. William H. Bellinger Jr. and William R. Farmer, 9-22. Harrisburg, Pennsylvania: Trinity Press International, 1998.

Haram, M. "The Literary Structure and Chronological Framework of the Prophecies in Isaiah XL-XLVIII." *Supplement to Vetus Testamentum* 9 (1963): 127-155.

Harrison, Roland K. *Jeremiah and Lamentations: An Introduction and Commentary.* The Tyndale Old Testament Commentaries. Downers Grove: InterVarsity Press, 1975.

Hayes, J. H., and S. A. Irvine. *Isaiah, the Eight Century Prophet: His Times and Preaching*. Nashville: Abingdon Press, 1987.

Herbert, A. S. *The Book of the Prophet Isaiah 1-39*. New York: Cambridge University Press, 1973.

Holladay, William L. *The Architecture of Jeremiah 1-20.* Lewisburg: Bucknell University, 1976.

________. *Jeremiah 1: A Commentary on the Book of the Prophet Jeremiah Chapters 1-25*. Translated by Paul D. Hanson. Philadelphia: Fortress Press, 1986.

Hong, Seong-Hyuk. *The Metaphor of Illness and Healing in Hosea and its Significance in the Socio-Economic Context of Eight-Century Israel and Judah.* New York: Peter Lang, 2006.

Hubbard, D. A. *Hosea: An Introduction and Commentary.* Downers Grove: InterVarsity Press, 1969.

Hyatt, J. P. *The Book of Jeremiah: Introduction and Exegesis.* Vol. V. The Interpreter's Bible. Nashville: Abingdon Press, 1956.

Kaiser, Otto. *Isaiah 1-39.* Philadelphia: Westminster John Knox Press, 1974.

Kay, W. "Isaiah." In *The Bible Commentary*, ed. F. G. Cook, 5, 266. Grand Rapids, Michigan: Baker Books, 1981.

Keil, C. F. *The Prophecies of Jeremiah.* Vol. 1. Grand Rapids: William B. Eerdmans Publishing Company, 1950.

Keown, Gerald L., Pamela J. Scalise, and Thomas G. Smothers. *Jeremiah 26-52.* Vol. 27. Dallas, Texas: Word Books, 1995.

Kissane, E. J. *The Book of Isaiah 1.* Dublin: Brown & Nolan, 1960.

Kizhakkeyil, Sebastian. *Isaiah: An Exegetical Commentary.* Bangalore: Asian Trading Corporation, 2006.

Lundblom, Jack R. *Jeremiah 1-20: A New Translation with Introduction and Commentary.* New York: Doubleday, 1999.

Mays, James. *"Hosea": The Old Testament Library.* Philadelphia: Westminster John Knox Press, 1969.

Mays, James Luther. *Hosea: A Commentary.* London: SCM Press Ltd., 1969.

McKane, William. *A Critical and Exegetical Commentary on Jeremiah: Introduction and Commentary on Jeremiah 1-XXV.* Vol. 1. Edinburgh: T & T Clark Limited, 1986.

McKenzie, J. L. *Second Isaiah.* New York: Doubleday, 1968.

Motyer, J. Alec. *Isaiah: An Introduction and Commentary.* Downers Grove: InterVarsity Press, 1999.

Muilenburg, James. *The Book of Isaiah: Chapters 40-66, The Interpreter's Bible.* Vol. 5, ed. George R. Buttrick. Nashville: Abingdon Press, 1956.

Oestreich, Bernhard. *Metaphors and Similes for Yahweh in Hosea 14:2-9 (1-8): A Study of Hoseanic Pictorial Language.* Frankfurt: Peter Lang, 1998.

Oswalt, John N. *The Book of Isaiah 1-12.* New International Commentary of the Old Testament, ed. R. K. Harrison and R. D. Patterson. Grand Rapids, Michigan: William B. Eerdmans Publishing Company, 1986.

________. *The Book of Isaiah: Chapters 1-39.* New International Commentary of the Old Testament. Grand Rapids, Michigan: William B. Eerdmans Publishing Company, 1986.

________. *The Book of Isaiah: Chapters 40-66.* Grand Rapids, Michigan: William B. Eerdmans Publishing Company, 1998.

Paterson, John. *Jeremiah: Peake's Commentary on the Bible*. London: Thomas Nelson and Sons, 1962.

Peake, Arthur S. *Jeremiah I: The Century Bible*. Edinburgh: T.C. & E.C. Jack, 1910.

Reventlow, Henning Graf. *Liturgie und Prophetisches Ich bei Jeremia*: Gutersloh, 1963.

Rudolph, W. "Jeremiah." In *Jesaja XV-XVI*, ed. D. W. Thomas and W. D. McHardy, 130-143. Gloucestershire: Clarendon Press, 1963.

________. *Jeremia*. Tubingen: Mohr, 1968.

Sawyer, John F. A. *Isaiah*. 2 vols. Philadelphia: Westminster John Knox Press, 1984.

Schuller, Eileen. *Post - Exilic Prophets*. Wilmington: Michael Glazier, 1988.

Scott, R. B. Y, G. G. D. Kilpatrick, and J. Muilenburg. *The Book of Isaiah*. Nashville: Abingdon Press, 1956.

Seitz, Christopher R. *Isaiah 1-39: Interpretation*. Louisville: Westminster John Knox Press, 1993.

________. "Isaiah 40-66." In *The New Interpreters Bible*. Nashville: Abingdon Press, 2001.

Skinner, John. *Prophecy and Religion, Studies in the Life of Jeremiah*. Cambridge: Cambridge University Press, 1922.

________. *The Book of the Prophet Isaiah: Chapters XL-LXVI*. Cambridge: University Press, 1951.

Smith, Gary V. *Isaiah 1-39*. Nashville: B & H Publishing Group, 2007.

Smith, P. A. *Rhetoric and Redaction in Trito-Isaiah: The Structure, Growth and Authorship of Isaiah 56-66*. New York: E. J. Brill, 1995.

Streane, A. W. *The Book of the Prophet Jeremiah, together with the Lamentations*. Cambridge: Cambridge University Press, 1882.

Stuart, Douglas. "Hosea." In *Word Biblical Commentary*, ed. David A. Hubbard and Glenn W. Barker, 31. Waco, Texas: Word Books Publishers, 1987.

Stulman, Louis. *Order Amid Chaos: Jeremiah as Symbolic Tapestry*. Sheffield: Sheffield Academic, 1998.

Sweeney, Marvin A. *Isaiah 1-4 and the Post-Exilic Understanding of the Isaianic Tradition*. Berlin, New York: Walter de Gruyter, 1988.

________. *Isaiah 1-39 with an Introduction to Prophetic Literature, Forms and Literature*. Grand Rapids, Michigan: William B. Eerdmans Publishing Company, 1996.

Thompson, J. A. *Jeremiah: New International Commentary on the Old Testament*. Grand Rapids, Michigan: William B. Eerdmans Publishing Company, 1980.

Torrey, C. C. *The Second Isaiah*. New York: Scribner's, 1928.

Volz, Paul. *Der Prophet Jeremía übersetzt und erklärt,10; 2nd edn.* Leipzig A. Deichen, 1928.

Walker, T. W. "The Metaphor of Healing and the Theology of the Book of Hosea." Princeton Theological Seminary, (Ph. D dissertation) 1997.

Ward, James M. "The Message of the Prophet Hosea." *Interpretation* 23, no. 4 (1969): 387-407.

Watts, John D. W. "Isaiah 34-66." In *Word Biblical Commentary*. Waco, Texas: Word Books. 1987.

Watts, John D. W. "Isaiah 1-33." In *WBC,* 4-7. Waco, Texas: Word, 1985.

Westermann, Claus. *Isaiah 40-66*. Philadelphia: Westminster John Knox Press, 1969.

Whybray, R. N. *Isaiah 40-66: New Century Bible Commentary*. Grand Rapids, Michigan: William B. Eerdmans Publishing Company, 1981.

Wildberger, Hans. *Isaiah 1-12: A Commentary*. Translated by Thomas H. Trapp. Minneapolis: Fortress Press, 1986.

________. *Jesaja 13-27*. Neukirchener Verlag: Auflage, 1989.

________. *Isaiah 1-12*. Translated by Thomas H. Trapp. Minneapolis: Fortress Press, 1991.

Williamson, Hugh Godfrey Maturin. *A Critical and Exegetical Commentary on Isaiah 1-27*. Vol. 1. New York: T & T Clark, 2006.

Wolff, Hans Walter. *A Commentary on the Book of Hosea.* Translated by G. Stansell Hermenia. Philadelphia: Fortress Press, 1974.

________. *Joel and Amos*. Philadelphia: Fortress Press, 1977.

Young, E. J. *The Book of Isaiah*. Grand Rapids, Michigan: William B. Eerdmans Publishing Company, 1965.

Zimmerli, W. *A Commentary on the Book of Isaiah*. Philadelphia: Fortress Press, 1979.

Zvi, Ehud Ben. *Hosea*. Grand Rapids, Michigan: William B. Eerdmans Publishing Company, 2005.

Journal Articles

Ackroyd, Peter. "Isaiah 1-XII: Presentation of a Prophet." *Vetus Testamentum Supplement* 29 (1978): 16-48.

Barre, M. L. "New light on the Interpretation of Hosea VI 2." *Vetus Testamentum*, no. 28 (1978): 129-141.

Bracke, John M. "Jeremiah 15:15-21." *Interpretation* 37, no. 2 (April 1983): 174-178.

Bright, John. "Prophet's lament and its answer, Jeremiah 15:10-21." *Interpretation* 28, no. 1 (January 1974): 59-74.

Brueggemann, Walter. “Jeremiah’s Use of Rhetorical Questions.” *Journal of Biblical Literature* 92, no. 3 (September 1973): 358-374.

________. “The "Uncared For” Now Cared for (Jer. 30:12-17): A Methodological Consideration.” *Journal of Biblical Literature* 104, no. 3 (September 1985): 419-428.

________. “A World Available for Peace: Images of Hope from Jeremiah and Isaiah.” *Sojourners* 17, no. 1 (1988): 22-26.

Ceresko, Anthony R. “The Rhetorical Strategy of the Fourth Servant Song (Isaiah 52:13-53:12): Poetry and the Exodus-New Exodus.” *Catholic Biblical Quarterly* 56, no. 1 (January 1994): 42-55.

Clements, R. E. “Beyond Tradition History: Deutero-Isaianic Development of First Isaiah’s Themes.” *Journal for the Study of Old Testament* 31 (1985): 95-113.

Diamond, A. R. Pete. “Jeremiah’s Confessions in the LXX and MT: A Witness to Developing Canonical Function?” *Vetus Testamentum* 40, no. 1 (January 1990): 33-50.

Evans, Craig A. “Isaiah 6:9-13 in the Context of Isaiah’s Theology.” *Journal of the Evangelical Theological Society* 29, no. 2 (June 1986): 139-146.

________. “To See and Not Perceive: Isaiah 6:9-10 in Early Jewish and Christian Interpretation.” *Journal for the Study of the Old Testament* 64, no. Supplementary Series (1989): 61-64.

Fideles, Paul S. “The Cross of Hosea Revisited: The Meaning of Suffering in the Book of Hosea.” *Review and Expositor* 90 (1993): 175-190.

Gench, Roger J. “Jeremiah 8:18-9:3.” *Interpretation* 62, no. 1 (January 2008): 74-76.

Jones, Douglas. “The Tradition of the Oracles of Isaiah of Jerusalem.” *ZAW* 67 (1955): 226-246.

Kelley, Page E. “The Holy One in the Midst of Israel: Redeeming Love (Hosea 11-14).” *Review and Expositor* 72 no. 4 (1975): 465-472.

Kruger, P. A. “Prophetic Imagery: On Metaphors and Similies in the Book of Hosea.” *Journal of Northwest Semitic Languages* 14 (1988): 143-151.

Marshal, R. J. “The Structure of Isaiah 1-12.” *Biblical Review* 7 (1962): 19-32.

Oswalt, John N. “Isaiah 52:13-53:12: Servant of All.” *Calvin Theological Journal* 40, no. 1 (April 2005): 85-94.

Secondary Sources

Books/Book Section

Ancient Near Eastern Texts Relating to the Old Testament. Translated by A. Leo Oppenheim, ed. James B. Pritchard. New Jersey: Princeton University Press, 1969.

Office of Research and Analysis of the American Lutheran Church, 'Health, Life, and Death: A Christian Perspective'. Minneapolis: The American Lutheran Church, 1977.

Aitken, K. T. "Hear." In *New International Dictionary of Old Testament Theology and Exegesis*, ed. Willem A. VanGemeren, 175-181. Carlisle, Cumbria: Paternoster Press, 1996.

Albright, W. F. *Archaeology and the Religion of Israel.* 5th ed. Baltimore: John's Hopkins University Press, 1968.

________. *Yahweh and the Gods of Canaan*. London: Althone Press, 1968.

Anderson, A. *Psalms (1-150)*. Vol. 1-2 The New Bible Commentary. London: Marshall, Morgan & Scott, 1972.

Atkinson, D. "Towards a Theology of Health." In *Health: The Strength to be Human*, ed. A. Fergusson, 5-38. London: InterVarsity Press, 1993.

Avalos, Hector. *Illness and Health Care in the Ancient Near East: The Role of the Temple in Greece, Mesopotamia, and Israel.* Atlanta, Georgia: Scholars Press, 1995.

Barr, James. *The Semantics of Biblical Language*. Oxford: Oxford University Press, 1961.

Barth, Karl. *Church Dogmatics*. Vol. 3. Edinburgh: T & T Clark, 1961.

Beach, K. *Preaching from the Types and Metaphors of the Bible.* Grand Rapids: Kregel, 1981.

Boorse, Christopher. "The Distinction between Disease and Illness." In *Concepts of Health and Disease: Interdisciplinary Perspectives*, ed. Arthur L. Caplan and H. Tristram, 551-552. Massachusetts: Addison Wesley, 1981.

Bradshaw, B. *Bridging the Gap: Evangelism, Development and Shalom*. Monrovia: MARC, 1993.

Bright, John. *Covenant and Promise*. London: SCM Press Ltd., 1977.

Brockington, L. H. *The Hebrew Text of the Old Testament: The Readings Adopted by the Translators of the New English Bible.* Oxford: Cambridge University Press, 1973.

Brown. "*Rapha*" In *Theological Dictionary of the Old Testament*, ed. G. Johannes Botterweck, Helmer Ringgren and Heinz-Josef Fabrey, XIII, 593-602. Grand Rapids, Michigan: William B. Eerdmans Publishing Company, 2004.

Brown, F., S. Driver, and C. Briggs. "*arûkâ*." In *The Brown-Driver-Briggs Hebrew and English Lexicon*, 74. Peabody, Massachusetts: Hendrickson Publishers, 2005.

________. "*Shalom*." In *The Brown-Driver-Briggs Hebrew and English Lexicon*, 1022-1023. Peabody, Massachusetts: Hendrickson Publishers, 2005.

Brown, Francis, S. R. Driver, and C.A. Briggs. "*Shalom*." In *A Hebrew and English Lexicon of the Old Testament*. Oxford: Clarendon, 1951.

Brown, Michael L. *I am the Lord Your Healer: A Philological Study of the Root Rapa in the Hebrew Bible and the Ancient Near East.* New York: New York University, 1985.

________. *Israel's Divine Healer.* Grand Rapids, Michigan: Zondervan, 1995.

Brown, Robert McAfee. *Making Peace in the Global Village.* Philadelphia: Westminster John Knox Press, 1981.

Brueggemann, Walter. *Living Toward a Vision: Biblical Reflections on Shalom.* New York: United Church, 1978.

________. *Hopeful Imagination: Prophetic Voices in Exile.* Philadelphia: Fortress Press, 1986.

________. "Land, Fertility and Justice." In *Theology of the Land*, ed. B. Evans and G. Cusack, 173-196. Collegeville: Liturgical Press, 1987.

________. *Using God's Resources Wisely: Isaiah and Urban Possibility.* Louisville: Westminster John Knox Press, 1993.

________. *Peace.* Missouri: Chalice Press, 2001.

Bullinger, E. W. *Figures of Speech in the Bible.* Grand Rapids, Michigan: Baker Books, 1968.

Campbell, Alastair. *Health as Liberation: Medicine, Theology and the Quest for Justice.* Cleveland: Pilgrim, 1995.

Chan, Alan Kam-Yau, Thomas B. Song, and Michael L. Brown. "*Rapha.*" In *New International Dictionary of Old Testament Theology and Exegesis*, ed. Willem A VanGemeren, 3, 1162-1173. Carlisle, Cumbria: Paternoster Press, 1996.

Childs, Brevard. *Introduction to the Old Testament as Scripture.* Philadelphia: Fortress Press, 1979.

Clines, D. J. A. *The Dictionary of Classical Hebrew.* Sheffield: Sheffield Academic Press, 1993.

Dahood, Mitchell. *Psalms II: 51-100.* Garden City, NY: Doubleday & Company, 1968.

Douglas, J. *New Bible Dictionary.* London: InterVarsity Press, 1982.

Duchrow, Ulrich, and Gerhard Liedke. *Shalom: Biblical Perspectives on Creation, Justice, and Peace.* Geneva: WCC, 1989.

Eidewall, G. *Grapes in the Desert: Metaphors, Models, and Themes in Hosea 4-14.* Stockholm: Almqvist & Wiksell, 1996.

Eissfeldt, O. *The Old Testament: An Introduction.* New York: Harper & Row, 1965.

________. *Old Testament: An Introduction.* Oxford: E. T. P. R. Ackroyd, 1996.

Elazah, and Cohen. *The Jewish Polity.* Indiana: Indiana University Press, 1985.

Erlandsson, S. *The Burden of Babylon: A Study of Isaiah 13:12-14:23.* Lund: C. W. K. Gleerup, 1970.

Exum, J. Cheryl. *Fragmented Women: Feminist (Sub) Versions of Biblical Narratives.* Valley Forge, PA: Trinity Press, 1993.

Farber, Walter. "Witchcraft, Magic, and Divination in Ancient Mesopotamia." In *Civilizations of the Ancient Near East,* ed. J. Sasson, 4 vols. New York, 1995.

Fishbane, Michael. *Biblical Interpretation in Ancient Israel.* Oxford: Clarendon, 1985.

Fohrer, G. *A History of Israelite Religion.* Translated by David E. Green. Nashville: Abingdon Press, 1972.

Freeman, David L., and Judith Z. Abrams, eds. *Illness and Health in the Jewish Tradition: Writings from the Bible to Today.* Philadelphia: The Jewish Publication Society, 1999.

George, K. M. "The Threat of HIV/AIDS: Some Theological Considerations." In *HIV/AIDS: A Challenge to Theological Education,* ed. Samson Prabhakar and George Mathew Nalunnakkal, 1-10. Bangalore: BTESSC/SATHRI, 2004.

Ghalioungui, Paul. *The House of Life; Magic and Medical Science in Ancient Egypt.* Amsterdam: B. M. Israel, 1973.

Glueck, N. *Hesed in the Bible.* Cincinnati: Hebrew Union College Press, 1967.

Gowan, Donald E. *Eschatology in the Old Testament.* Edinburgh: T & T Clark, 1986.

Grant, E., and H. H. Rowley. *Dictionary of the Bible.* Edinburgh: T&T Clark, 1963.

Gray, Mark. *Rhetoric and Social Justice in Isaiah.* New York: T & T Clark, 2006.

Hanegraaff, H. *Christianity in Crisis.* Eugene, Ore: Harvest House, 1993.

Hanson, Paul. *The Dawn of Apocalyptic.* Philadelphia: Fortress Press, 1975.

Harrison, R. K. "Healing." In *The Interpreter's Dictionary of the Bible,* ed. George R. Buttrick and Keith R. Crim, 2, 541-548. Nashville: Abingdon Press, 1976.

Harrison, R. K., and R. D. Pastterson. "Wound." In *New International Dictionary of Theology and Exegesis,* ed. Willem A.VanGemeren, 2, 4-5. Carlisle, Cumbria: Paternoster Press, 1996.

Hengstenberg, E. W. *Christology of the Old Testament and a Commentary on the Messianic Predictions.* Grand Rapids: Kregel Publications, 1970.

Herzog, Zeev. "Settlement and Fortification Planning in the Iron Age." In *The Architecture of Ancient Israel: From the Prehistoric to Persian Periods,* ed. A. Kempinski and R. Reich, 231-274. Jerusalem: Ahva Press, 1992.

Hill, John. *Friend or Foe? The Figure of Babylon in the Book of Jeremiah MT.* Vol. 40 Biblical Interpretation Series. Leiden: E. J. Brill, 1999.

Holt, E. K. *Prophesying the Past: The Use of Israel's History in the Book of Hosea.* Sheffield: Sheffield Academic Press, 1995.

Hulster, Izaak J. de. *Illuminating Images: An Iconographic Method of Old Testament Exegesis with Three Case Studies from Third Isaiah*. Utrecht: The British Museum, 2007.

Hvidberg, Flemming Friis. *Weeping and Laughter in the Old Testament*. Leiden: E. J. Brill, 1962.

Jamieson, Robert, A. R. Fausset, and David Brown. *Job-Isaiah: Critical, Experimental and Practical on the Old and New Testament*. Vol. 3. Grand Rapids, Michigan: William B. Eerdmans Publishing Company, 1945.

Jayne, Walter Addison. *The Healing Gods of Ancient Civilization*. New York: University Books, 1962.

Johnson, A. R. *The Cultic Prophet in Ancient Israel*. 2nd ed. Cardiff: University of Wales Press, 1962.

Jr., Martin Luther King. *Strength to Love*. Philadelphia: Fortress Press, 1963.

Kass, Leon. "The End of Medicine and the Pursuit of Health." In *Concepts of Health and Disease: Interdisciplinary Perspectives*, ed. Arthur L. Caplan, Jr. H. Tristram Engelhard and James J. McCartney, 10-19. Massachusetts: Addison Wesley, 1981.

Keefe, Alice A. *Woman's Body and the Social Body in Hosea*. London: Sheffield Academic Press, 2001.

Kelsey, Morton T. *Healing and Christianity in Ancient Thought and Modern Times*. London: Harper & Row Publishers, 1973.

Kittay, Eva. *Metaphor: Its Cognitive Force and Linguistic Structure*. Oxford: Clarendon, 1987.

Kleinman, A. *Patients and Healers in the Context of Culture*. Berkeley: University of California, 1980.

Koch, Klaus. *The Prophets I*. Philadelphia: Fortress Press, 1983.

Kohler, Ludwig. *The Hebrew Man*. SCM Press Ltd., London, 1956.

Kovar, Mary Grace. "Health Assessment." In *The Encyclopedia of Aging*, ed. George L. Maddox, 302-305. New York: Springer Publishing Company, 1983.

Krasovec, Joze. *Reward, Punishment, and Forgiveness: The Thinking and Beliefs of Ancient Israel in the Light of Greek and Modern Views*. Leiden: Brill, 1999.

Kropel, M. C. A. *A Rift in the Clouds: Ugaritic and Hebrew Descriptions of the Divine*. Munster: Ugarit-Verlag, 1990.

Kutscher, E. Y. *The Language and Linguistic Background of the Isaiah Scroll with an Obituary by H. B. Rosén (p. ix-xi)*. Leiden: E. J. Brill, 1974.

Lamb, Matthew L. *Solidarity with Victims: Toward a Theology of Social Transformation*. New York: Crossroad, 1982.

Lambert, W. G. *Babylonian Wisdom Literature*. Oxford: The Clarendon Press, 1960.

Lapsley, James N. *Salvation and Health: The Interlocking Processes of Life.* Philadelphia: The Westminster John Knox Press, 1952.

Leclerc, Thomas L. *Yahweh is Exalted in Justice: Solidarity and Conflict in Isaiah.* Minneapolis: Fortress Press, 1990.

Leupold, H. C. *Exposition of Isaiah,* 2 vols. Grand Rapids: Baker Book House, 1971.

Long, W. M. *Health, Healing and God's Kingdom: New Pathways to Christian Health Ministry in Africa.* Oxford: Regnum, 2000.

MacArthur, J. *Charismatic Chaos.* Grand Rapids, Michigan: Zondervan, 1992.

Maclennan, John. *Prophet, People, and the Word of Yahweh.* Zurich: EVZ-Verlag, 1970.

Maddocks, M. *Journey to Wholeness.* New Delhi: ISPCK, 1995.

Malul, M. *The Comparative Method in Ancient near Eastern and Biblical Legal Studies.* Kevelaer: Butzon & Bercker, 1990.

________. "Terror of the Night." In *Dictionary of Deities and Demons in the Bible,* ed. van der Toorn, B. Becking and P. W. van der Horst, 851-854: Leiden, 1999.

Mbiti, J. *Concepts of God in Africa.* New Delhi: ISPCK, 1975.

McDonald, J. I. H. "Synchronic Exegesis." In *The SCM Dictionary of Biblical Interpretation,* ed. R. J. Coggins and J. L. Houlden, 657-658. London: SCM Press Ltd, 1990.

Meier, S. A. "Angels and Demons." In *Dictionary of Deities and Demons in the Bible,* ed. K. van der Toorn, B. Becking and P. W. van der Horst, 54-55. Leiden: Brill, 1995.

Melcher, Sarah J. "With Whom Do the Disabled Associate? Metaphorical Interplay in the Later Prophets." In *This Abled Body: Rethinking Disabilities and Biblical Studies,* ed. Hector Avalos, Sarah J. Melcher and Jeremy Schipper, Society of Biblical Literature, 115-129. Atlanta, 2007.

Michaels, J. Ramsey. *1 Peter.* Vol. 49 Word Biblical Commentary. Dallas: Word, 1988.

Moltmann, Jürgen. *God in Creation.* London: SCM Press Ltd., 1985.

Moore, Michael S. "The Laments in Jeremiah and IQH: Mapping the Metaphorical Trajectories." In *Uprooting and Planting: Essays on Jeremiah for Leslie Allen,* ed. John Goldingay, 228-252. New York: T & T Clark, 2007.

Moughtin-Mumby, Sharon. *Sexual and Marital Metaphors in Hosea, Jeremiah, Isaiah and Ezekiel.* Oxford: Oxford University Press, 2008.

Mowinckel, Sigmund. *He that Cometh.* Oxford: Blackwell, 1956.

Mueller, U. B. *Sickness and Healing.* Translated by Douglas W. Stott. Nashville: Abingdon Press, 1981.

Muilenburg, James. "The Terminology of Adversity in Jeremiah." In *Translating and Understanding the Old Testament*, ed. H. T. Frank and W. L. Reed, 42-63. New York: Abingdon Press, 1970.

Muthunayagom, Daniel Jones. *The Relationship Between Election and Israel's Attitude Towards the Nations in the Book of Isaiah*. Delhi: ISPCK, 2000.

________. "Contemporary Approaches to Old Testament Interpretation." In *Interweaving Methodology and Praxis: Exploring Disciplinary Options in Today's World*, ed. Indukuri John Mohan Razu, 147-169. Bangalore: BTESSC/SATHRI, 2007.

Myers, Jacob M. *II Chronicles*. Garden City, New York: Doubleday, 1965.

Naude, Jackie A. "See." In *New International Dictionary of Theology and Exegesis*, ed. Willem A. VanGemeren, 1007-1015. Carlisle, Cumbria: Paternoster Press, 1996.

Nel, Philip J. "Shalom." In *Dictionary of Old Testament Theology and Exegesis*, ed. Willem A. VanGemeren, 4, 130-135. Grand Rapids, Michigan: Zondervan Publishing House, 1997.

Nelson, James B. *Embodiment: An Approach to Sexuality and Christian Theology*. Minneapolis: Augsburg Publishing House, 1979.

Nordenfelt, Lennart. "On Medicine and Other Means of Health Enhancement: Towards a Conceptual Framework." In *Goals of Medicine: The Forgotten Issues in Health Care Reform*, ed. Mark J. Hanson and Daniel Callahan. Washington DC: Georgetown University Press, 1999.

Nunn, John F. *Ancient Egyptian Medicine*. Oklahoma: University of Oklahoma Press, 1996.

O'Connell, H. Robert. *Concentricity and Continuity: The Literary Structure of Isaiah*. Vol. 188 Journal for the Study of Old Testament Supplementary. Sheffield: Sheffield Academic Press, 1994.

Oepke, A. "Iaomai." In *Theological Dictionary of New Testament*, ed. Gerhald Kittel, Geoffrey William Bromiley and Gerhard Friedrich, 201-202. Grand Rapids, Michigan: William B. Eerdmans Publishing Company, 1976.

Oswalt, John N. "Righteousness in Isaiah: A Study of the Function of Chapters 55-66 in the Present Structure of the Book." In *Writing and Reading the Scroll of Isaiah in Studies of an Interpretive Tradition*, ed. D. Craig, C. Broyles and Craig A. Evans, 177 191. New York: Brill, 1997.

Peggy, Day L., and C. Breytenbach. "Satan." In *Dictionary of Deities and Demons in the Bible*, ed. K. Van der Toorn, B. Becking and P. W. Van der Horst, 726-732. Grand Rapids, Michigan: William B. Eerdmans Publishing Company, 1995.

Pitt, T. Eric. *A Comparative Study of the Literature of Egypt, Palestine, and Mesopotamia*. London: Pedersen, 1931.

Powell, Marvin A. "Drugs and Pharmaceuticals in Ancient Mesopotamia." In *The Healing Part: Pharmaceuticals in the Biblical and Rabbinic World*, ed. Irene and Walter Jacob, 48-67. Leiden: E. J. Brill, 1993.

Rad, G. Von. *Studies in Deuteronomy*. Naperville: Allenson, 1953.

________. *Old Testament Theology*. Translated by D. M. G. Stalker. Vol. 1. New York: Harper & Row, 1962.

________. "Eirene." In *Theological Dictionary of the New Testament*, ed. G. Kittel, 400-417. Grand Rapids, Michigan: William B. Eerdmans Publication Company, 1964.

________. *The Message of the Prophets*. New York: Harper & Row Publishers, 1967.

________. *Old Testament Theology*. Translated by D. M. G. Stalker. Vol. 1. London: SCM Press Ltd., 1975.

Rakowski, William. "Health Beliefs." In *The Encyclopedia of Aging*, ed. George L. Maddox, 305-307. New York: Springer Publishing Company, 1987.

Ricoeur, Paul. *Interpretation Theory: Discourse and Surplus of Meaning*. Texas: Christian University Press, 1976.

Ringgren, H. *Israelite Religion*. Translated by John Sturdy. Philadelphia: Fortress Press, 1966.

Rinngren, H. "Understanding." In *Theological Dictionary of the Old Testament*, ed. G. Johannes Botterweck and Helmer Ringgren, 2, 99-107. Grand Rapids, Michigan: William B. Eerdmans Publishing Company, 1975.

Ritter, Edith K. "Magical-expert and Physician: Notes on Two Complimentary Profession in Babylonian Medicine." In *Studies in Honor of Benno Landsberger on His Seventy-fifth Birthday*, ed. Hans. G. Guterbock and Thorkild Jacobson. Chicago: The University of Chicago, 1965.

Robinson, H. Wheeler. *Corporate Personality in Ancient Israel*, ed. C. S. Rodd. Edinburgh: T & T Clark, 1981.

Robinson, J. A.T. *In the End God...* New York: Harper & Row, Publishers, 1950.

Robinson, Joseph R. *The Dead Sea Isaiah Scroll: A Literary Analysis*. Grand Rapids, Michigan: William B. Eerdmans Publishing Company, 1970.

Robinson, Th. *Die Zwolf Klienen Phopheten*. Tubingen: HAT, 1964.

Ross, Allen P. *Holiness to the Lord: A Guide to the Exposition of the Book of Leviticus*. Grand Rapids: Baker Academic, 2002.

Routledge, Robin. *Old Testament Theology: A Thematic Approach*. Downers Grove: InterVarsity Press, 2008.

Roux, H. "Heal." In *Vocabulary of the Bible*, ed. J. J. Von Allmen, 402-405. London: Lutterworth Press, 1958.

Rowley, H. H. *The Servant of the Lord and Other Essays on the Old Testament*. Oxford: Blackwell, 1965.

Schmid, H. H. *Shalom im Alten Testamentum*. Stuttgart: Katholisches Bibelwerk, 1971.

Schreiter, R. J. *The Ministry of Reconciliation*. Maryknoll, New York: Orbis Books, 1998.

Sebald, W. G. *On the Natural History of Destruction* New York: Random House, 2003.

Seybold, Klaus, and Ulrich B. Mueller. *Sickness and Healing*. Nashville: Abingdon Press, 1978.

Sigerist, Henry Ernest. *A History of Medicine: Primitive and Archaic Medicine*. Oxford: Oxford University Press, 1987.

Soskice, Janet. *Metaphor and Religious Language*. Oxford: Clarendon, 1985.

Stoebe, H. J. "*rapha*." In *Theological Lexicon of the Old Testament*, ed. Ernst Jenni, Claus Westermann, Mark E. Bidde and Peabody, 3, 1254-1259. Massachusetts: Hendrickson, 1997.

Stolz, Fritz. "*Hala* (*chalah*)" In *Theological Lexicon of the Old Testament*, ed. Ernst Jenni, Claus Westermann, Mark E. Bidde and Peabody, 3 vols. Massachusetts: Hendrickson, 1997.

Straub, Richard O. *Health Psychology*. Michigan: Word Publishers, 2002.

Supit, B. A. "Health, Healing and Wholeness." In *Towards Health-Care for All: CCA's Concern in Community Health, 1973-1983*. Singapore: Christian Conference of Asia, 1986.

Sweeney, Marvin A. *The Twelve Prophets*. Vol. 1. Brit Olam: Collegeville: Glazier/ Liturgical Press, 2000.

Toorn, K. Van Der. *Sin and Sanction in Israel and Mesopotamia: A Comparative Study*. Assen/Maastricht: Van Gorcum, 1985.

Vine, W. E. *Vine's Expository Dictionary of Old and New Testament Words*. Grand Rapids: Flemming Revell, 1981.

Vine, W. E., M. F. Unger, and W. White Jr. *An Expository Dictionary of the Biblical Words*. New York: Thomas Nelson, 1985.

White, H. C. *Shalom in the Old Testament*. Philadelphia: United Church, 1973.

Wilkinson, John. *Health and Healing: Studies in New Testament Principles and Practice*. Edinburgh: The Handel Press, 1980.

_________. *The Bible and Healing: A Medical and Theological Commentary*. Edinburgh: The Handsel Press Ltd, 1998.

Wilson, J. V. K. "Medicine in the Land and Times of the Old Testament." In *Studies in the Period of David and Solomon and Other Essays*, ed. T. Ishida, 337-365. Winona Lake: Eisenbrauns, 1982.

Wolf, H. M. "The Transcendent Nature of the Covenant Curse Reversals." In *Israel's Apostasy and Restoration*, ed. A. Gileadi. Grand Rapids: Baker, 1988.

Wolff, Hans Walter. *Anthropology of the Old Testament.* Philadelphia: Fortress, 1974.

World Health Organization: Basic Documents. Geneva: WHO, 1948.

Wright, David P., and Jacob Milgrom. "*atsar.*" In *Theological Wordbook of the Old Testament*, ed. G. Johannes Botterweck and Helmer Ringgren, 6, 336. Stuttgart: Kohlhammer, 1993.

Zvi, Ehud Ben. "The Prophetic Book: A Key Form of Prophetic Literature." In *The Changing Face of Form Criticism for the Twenty-First Century*, ed. Marvin A. Sweeney and Ehud Ben Zvi, 276-297. Grand Rapids, Michigan: William B. Eerdmans Publishing Company, 2003.

Journal Articles

Abe, Gabriel Oyedele. "Redemption, Reconciliation, Propitiation: Salvation terms in an African Milieu." *Journal of Theology for Southern Africa*, no. 95 (July 1996): 3-12.

Biggs, Robert D. "Medicine, Surgery, and Public Health in Ancient Mesopotamia." *Journal of Assyrian Academic Studies* 19, no. 1 (2005): 1-19.

Carroll, Robert. "The Myth of the Empty Land." *Semeia* 59 (1992): 79-93.

Carter, Karen S. "A Biblical Vision of Wholeness." *Brethern Life and Thought* 33, no. 1. Wint (1988): 60-67.

Dickson, Kwesi. "He is God Because He Cares." *International Review of Missions* 77, no. 306 (1998): 229-237.

DuToit, F. "Seeking to Establish Democratic values South Africa: Can truth help us?" *Journal of Theology for Southern Africa* 103 (1999): 49-63.

Ewert, David. "The Confessions of a Prophet." *Direction* 4, no. 4 (1975): 383-388.

Frick, Frank S. "Response: Reconstructing Israel's Ancient World." *Semeia* 87 (1999): 233-254.

Gordis, Robert. "Studies in Hebrew Roots of Contrasted Meanings." *Journal of Quarterly Review* 27 (1936): 55-56.

Gottwald, N. K. "Social Matrix and Canonical Shape." *Theology Today* 42 (1985): 307-321.

Hammer, Paul L. "God's Health for the World: Some Biblical Understandings of Salvation." *Ex Auditu* 5 (1989): 77-98.

Hanson, Mark J. "Defining Health and Health Related Concepts: Conceptual and Theological Considerations." *Word & World* 21, no. 1 (Winter 2001): 23-31.

Hasel, Gerard F. "Health and Healing in the Old Testament." *Andrews University Seminary Studies* 21 (1983): 191-202.

Huffmon, H. B. "The Covenant Lawsuit in the Prophets." *Journal of Biblical Literature* 78 (1959): 285-295.

Hummel, Horace D. "Enclitic Mem in Northwest Semitic, Especially Hebrew." *Journal for the Study of Old Testament* 76, no. 2 (1957): 85-104.

Judisch, Douglas MacCallum Lindsay. "Propitiation in the Language and Typology of the Old Testament." *Concordia Theological Quarterly* 48, no. 2-3 (April-July 1984): 221-243.

________. "Propitiation in Old Testament Prophecy." *Concordia Theological Quarterly* 49, no. 1 (January 1985): 1-17.

Kennedy, D. F. O'. "Healing as/or Forgiveness." *Old Testament Exegesis* 14 (2001): 463-465.

Lim, K. T. K. "Toward a Final Form Approach to Biblical Interpretation." *Stulos Theological Journal* 7, no. 1-2 (1999): 1-11.

Lindsey, F. Duane. "Isaiah's Songs of the Servant." *Bibliotheca Sacra* 139, no. 556 (October-December 1982): 312-329.

________. "The Career of the Servant in Isaiah 52:13-53:12" *Bibliotheca Sacra* 140, no. 557 (January-March 1983): 21-39.

Lohfink. "Ich bin Jawheh Dein Arzt." *Ich Will Euer Gott Werden, Biespiele Biblischen Redens Von Gott* 100 (1982): 46-47.

Mayhue, Richard L. "For What Did Christ Atone in Isa. 53:4-5." *Master's Seminary Journal* 6, no. 2 (Fall 1995): 121-141.

Menken, Martinus J. J. "The Source of the Quotation from Isaiah 53:4 in Matthew 8:17." *Novum Testamentum* 39, no. 4 (October 1997): 313-327.

Obaid, Thoraya Ahmed. "Religion and Reproductive Health and Rights." *Journal of the American Academy of Religion* 73, no. 4 (December 2005): 1155-1173.

O'Connor, Kathleen M. "Rekindling Life, Igniting Hope." *Journal for Preachers* 30, no. 2 (2007): 30-34.

________. "A Family Comes Undone (Jeremiah 2:1-4:2)." *Review and Expositor* 105 (Spring 2008): 201-212.

O'Kennedy, D. F. "Healing as/or Forgiveness? The Use of the term apr in the book of Hosea." *Old Testament Essays* 14, no. 3 (2001): 458-474.

Oller, Dale Dobin. "Jewish Genetic Diseases and Jewish Illness Behaviour: A Review of Selected Sociocultural Literature." *Jewish Social Studies* 6, no. 2 (1984): 177-187.

Premnath, D. N. "Amos and Hosea: Socio-historical Background and Prophetic Critique." *Word & World* 28, no. 2 (Spring 2008): 125-132.

Sisson, Jonathan Paige. "Jeremiah and the Jerusalem Conception of Peace." *Journal of Biblical Literature* 3, no. 105 (1986): 429-442.

Thiagarajah, Daniel S. "Shalom: A Central Vision for Holistic Healing of Humanity." *CSI Life: Magazine for the Church of South India* X, no. 2 (2011): 2-5.

Willis, John T. "Dialogue between prophet and audience as a rhetorical device in the book of Jeremiah." *Journal for the Study of the Old Testament* 33 (October 1985): 63-82.